XBRL® FOR DUMMI

D0863039

by Charles Hoffman, CPA, and Liv Apneseth Watson

with Marc van Hilvoorde; Christine Tan, PhD;
Raynier van Egmond; and Eiichi Watanabe

WILEY

Wiley Publishing, Inc.

XBRL® For Dummies®

Published by
Wiley Publishing, Inc.
111 River Street
Hoboken, NJ 07030-5774

www.wiley.com

WILEY

About the Authors and Contributors

Charles Hoffman: Charlie (Tacoma, Washington, United States), a certified public accountant (CPA), is credited as being the Father of XBRL. He was co-editor of the first ever XBRL taxonomy and played major roles in creating both the International Financial Reporting Standards (IFRS) and United States Generally Accepted Accounting Standards (US GAAP) XBRL taxonomies. He was a major contributor to the following: XBRL 2.1 specification, XBRL Dimensions specification, Financial Reporting Taxonomies Architecture (FRTA), and Financial Reporting Instance Standards (FRIS). Prior to his involvement with XBRL, Charlie served as an auditor for what was then Price Waterhouse, financial officer for a number of companies, and an accounting software implementation consultant. In 1997, Charlie was the recipient of the AICPA Innovative User of Technology award. He was named by *Accounting Technology* magazine as one of the 100 most influential people in the accounting profession. In 2006, Charlie received the AICPA Special Recognition Award for his pioneering role in the development of XBRL. Charlie is a graduate of Pacific Lutheran University (BA and MBA), and in 2007, he received the Distinguished Alumnus Award from PLU for his efforts in creating XBRL. Currently, Charlie is Director of Innovative Solutions for UBmatrix LLC. He maintains a blog about XBRL at `http://xbrl.squarespace.com`.

Liv Apneseth Watson: Liv (New York City, New York, United States) is one of the founders of XBRL International and serves on the XBRL International Steering Committee and as Vice Chairman of XBRL International. She has also played a number of leadership roles with XBRL US. Currently, Liv is a member of the Board of Director of IRIS India Business Services Private Limited. Prior to joining IRIS, Liv was the Vice President of Global Strategy at EDGAR Online Inc. [NADAQ: EDGR] where she was responsible for developing EDGAR Online's International business development strategy. Liv has presented XBRL to a wide range of audiences, from international standards bodies to Fortune 1000 companies, and speaks with authority about its benefits, potential applications, and broad adoption. Liv authored one of IMA's most successful CPE courses, "Accounting System Technology for the 21st Century." She has also authored several published articles on future trends of the profession for international publications and journals, including *Harvard Business Review* and *Strategic Finance* and writes a monthly column of financial and business reporting trends for *CPA2Biz*.

Marc van Hilvoorde: Marc (Oosteind, Netherlands) is a Chartered Accountant (CA) and a Certified Information Systems Auditor (CISA) in the Netherlands. He has performed duties in the fields of financial and IT auditing and consultancy work for PricewaterhouseCoopers and KPMG. His knowledge of XBRL and standards-based reporting has involved him in leading roles in some of the major XBRL implementations, including the Netherlands Taxonomy Project. As the technical project manager, Marc and his team were responsible for the development and delivery of the Dutch national taxonomy. Marc was involved in the development of XBRL as member of the

XBRL International Standards Board, member of the IASCF XBRL Advisory Council, and past chair of the Rendering and Domain working groups. He's an important contributor to the public debate on the future of the accounting industry, audit innovation, and XBRL assurance.

Christine Tan, PhD: Christine (New York City, New York, United States) is a university professor of accounting and has taught at the University of Melbourne, Baruch College; City University of New York, New York University; and the Melbourne Business School. Christine has consulted with governments and industry and business executives on matters pertaining to financial reporting and financial analyses. Her research has been published in leading accounting journals and presented at conferences around the world. She was also a key player in the creation of the US GAAP XBRL taxonomy. Christine is currently an Assistant Professor in Accounting at Fordham University and a Principal of Tag-IT Financial Tagging, LLC, a firm that provides XBRL consulting.

Raynier van Egmond: Raynier (Vashon, Washington, United States) is an IT professional with more than 25 years of ICT development and design expertise in financial and manufacturing industries and research. He has been involved in the XBRL community since its inception in 1999, and he's been an active participant in development of the XBRL standard. Raynier contributed to and coauthored several parts of the XBRL specification and best-practices definitions. He managed development and deployment of XBRL solutions worldwide for the private, public, and nonprofit sector and national governments. He was the architect of the final version of the Dutch government Netherlands 2008 taxonomy and consulted as technical manager for the project responsible for quality assurance and its deployment. Through his company XBRL Consulting Partners, Raynier now works on developing XBRL solutions for the corporate social responsibility auditing process, with special interest in Triple Bottom Line accounting, and for the public sector information-supply chain management.

Eiichi Watanabe: Ed (Tokyo, Japan) is a member of XBRL International Steering Committee representing XBRL Japan jurisdiction. Ed served various leadership positions at XBRL Japan since the inception of XBRL Japan in April 2001. He's the first Japanese person exposed to the XBRL world at the Technology Briefing for Federal Government held in Washington, D.C., in May 2000. Currently, he's a Technology Advisor at Tokyo Shoko Research, Ltd., Japan's oldest business credit information company. He's been engaged in Information Technology and Business Intelligence industries in various capacity for more than 40 years since 1966. He edited and coauthored several books, including *XML-based Business to Business Systems* (published by Ohmsha). He was a visiting professor at the Center for Research in Advanced Financial Technology of Tokyo Institute of Technology during 2001–2005, where he was a core member of the project team demonstrating the use of XBRL in building credit risk information infrastructure. He also served as a lecturer in computer science at Chiba University during 1991 through 1998. He graduated from Tokyo Metropolitan University with a BS in physics.

Dedication

Charlie would like to dedicate this book to his daughter, Sophia, and her dog, Lucy, because Sophia will get a big kick out of going to a bookstore, picking this book from the shelf, turning to this page, and seeing her and her dog's name here. (Hi, Sophia!)

Liv would like to thank the Watson twins, her daughters Ellen and Tess, which have put up with their mom traveling the world for the last ten years spreading the XBRL gospel.

Authors' Acknowledgments

The authors would like to thank Wiley's acquisitions editor Kyle Looper and project editor Kelly Ewing for guiding them through the creation of a *For Dummies* book. The authors would also like to thank all the great people of XBRL International and others who they have met over the past ten years as they endeavored to turn the idea of XBRL into a reality for the benefit of everyone around the globe. There are far too many names to mention — you know who you are!

Charlie would like to thank his coauthor and contributors; the book couldn't have been created without them. Charlie would also like to thank his company, UBmatrix, a leading provider of XBRL software, for its support in allowing him the time to create this book and to share what he has learned about XBRL over the past ten years while working with UBmatrix and participating in the XBRL International consortium. Last but certainly not least, Charlie would like to thank his ballroom dance teacher, Carina, who helped him periodically escape from the world of XBRL and hard work involved in writing this book into the world of Foxtrot, Cha Cha, Tango, and Rumba, which helped keep stress levels in check and to otherwise maintain a good state of mind during this sometimes arduous process. (And besides, now Charlie can Tango!)

Liv would like to thank Charlie for sharing his vision of what XBRL could be and the insights gained during the ten years he spent helping to create XBRL in this book. But most importantly, Liv would like to thank the Watson twins, Ellen and Tess, for standing by their mom while she travelled around the world planting the XBRL seeds that ultimately sprouted and helped get us to where we are today. I am so proud to be your mom.

Publisher's Acknowledgments

We're proud of this book; please send us your comments through our online registration form located at http://dummies.custhelp.com. For other comments, please contact our Customer Care Department within the U.S. at 877-762-2974, outside the U.S. at 317-572-3993, or fax 317-572-4002.

Some of the people who helped bring this book to market include the following:

Acquisitions, Editorial, and Media Development

Project Editor: Kelly Ewing

Acquisitions Editor: Kyle Looper

Technical Editor: Cliff Binstock

Editorial Manager: Jodi Jensen

Media Development Project Manager: Laura Moss-Hollister

Media Development Assistant Project Manager: Jenny Swisher

Media Development Associate Producer: Josh Frank

Editorial Assistant: Amanda Graham

Sr. Editorial Assistant: Cherie Case

Cartoons: Rich Tennant (www.the5thwave.com)

Composition Services

Project Coordinator: Patrick Redmond

Layout and Graphics: Samantha K. Cherolis, Melissa Jester, Christin Swinford

Proofreaders: Melanie Hoffman, Nancy L. Reinhardt

Indexer: Infodex Indexing Services

Special Help
Linda Morris

Publishing and Editorial for Technology Dummies

Richard Swadley, Vice President and Executive Group Publisher

Andy Cummings, Vice President and Publisher

Mary Bednarek, Executive Acquisitions Director

Mary C. Corder, Editorial Director

Publishing for Consumer Dummies

Diane Graves Steele, Vice President and Publisher

Composition Services

Debbie Stailey, Director of Composition Services

Contents at a Glance

Table of Contents

Introduction

*W*elcome to *XBRL For Dummies*! Whether you're a business person (such as a CEO, CFO, accountant, project manager, and so on) or a technical person (that is, a "geek," software architect, developer, or database administrator, and so on), you have done yourself a huge favor by picking up this book if you're trying to find out what this global XBRL phenomenon is all about.

Some of you may have heard about the Extensible Business Reporting Language, or XBRL, before, and you're perhaps somewhat curious about XBRL. You want to understand XBRL, but everything you've seen seems to be overly complex, technically oriented, and filled with jargon. Perhaps you can't really understand what XBRL is from the explanations you've previously encountered, and you have no idea where to even start.

And chances are, you really don't care about XBRL. The truth is, you shouldn't care about XBRL. What you do care about is what XBRL *provides* and how it will impact what you will likely have to do in the future. You're in luck, because we talk about that topic in this book. We're going to help you get started with XBRL.

About This Book

This book is a thorough introduction to the Extensible Business Reporting Language. This book isn't a programmer's reference book or an exhaustive cookbook of how to use XBRL. We wrote this book for smart, savvy, forward-thinking business people and technologists who want to see the complete picture and don't have a lot of time to muck around trying to pull all these pieces together themselves. We pull the important pieces together for you.

XBRL is a transformational technology that will have broad impact on every organization — its reach is global. This book covers important details as well as visionary and architectural aspects of XBRL. It provides the critical information you need to make business and technical decisions about how exactly to approach XBRL. This book explores both the business and technical impacts of XBRL.

Unfortunately, understanding XBRL means that you're going to run into technical terminology and perhaps even financial reporting and accounting minutiae. Trust us, if we could leave out this jargon, we would, but we can't. We explain all this important terminology so that both business people and technical people can understand it.

Conventions Used in This Book

To help important terms stand out in this book, we use an *italic* font. We also use **boldfaced** words to highlight key words in bulleted lists and numbered steps. Monofont indicates a Web address or a piece of code or XML/XBRL.

Some Web addresses may break across two lines of text. If that happens, rest assured that we haven't put in any extra characters (such as hyphens) to indicate the break. So, when you're accessing one of these Web sites, just type the address exactly as it appears in the book, pretending as if the line break doesn't exist. *Tip:* To avoid having to type these long links, go to www. dummies.com/go/xbrl. This takes you to a landing page where you can click the link you need.

Foolish Assumptions

You don't need to be a technical guru, an accounting guru, or any other guru to get the most out of this book. In fact, you don't need to know much about accounting or any of these other things at all.

This book does make some bold (and potentially foolish) assumptions about you, the reader. Here are our assumptions about you:

- ✔ We realize that you may be from any country, not just the United States. We've done our best to make this book globally applicable as XBRL is a global standard.

- ✔ We assume that you're a business person. Okay, well, you *might* actually be a technical person, but this book is primarily written for business people. Business people will be comfortable with it, and so will technical people. What we did not want to do is write a technical book business people would be forever lost in.

- ✔ We assume that you have some knowledge of business and financial reporting. Because business people generally understand business and financial reporting to at least some degree, many of our examples are financial reporting related. Technical people, don't worry: You will be fine. We don't get into debits and credits, which generally freak you out!

  ✔ We assume that you're no dummy. You may not be an expert on XBRL, but you're a smart, capable person within your area of expertise who is ready to see how XBRL can help you do things better, faster, and cheaper.

How to Use This Book

You can read *XBRL For Dummies* in either of two ways:

  ✔ Read each chapter in sequential order, from cover to cover. If this book is your first real exposure to XBRL terminology, concepts, and technology, this method is probably the way to go.
  ✔ Read selected chapters or sections of particular interest to you in any order you choose. The chapters have been written to stand on their own as much as possible.

A significant portion of this book explains the bigger picture about XBRL. The book is less about the angle brackets that make up XBRL and more about the *approach* you should take to working with XBRL. And remember, this book is about getting you started down the right path, not providing you with every aspect and detail of implementing a mongo XBRL system. (Although, hey, the book *is* very helpful to those of you implementing mongo XBRL systems.)

How This Book Is Organized

We have organized this book into five parts, each designed to serve a basic need:

Part 1: The Very Least You Need to Know about XBRL

This part provides you with the absolute minimum you need to know about XBRL. Chapter 1 provides a conceptual overview of XBRL to help you get your head around what XBRL is. Chapter 2 provides a solid grounding in the essential concepts that help you truly appreciate why XBRL is what it is and how it works. Chapter 3 provides important critical details of XBRL's parts and how those parts work together. Chapter 4 is an XBRL primer; you get a chance to look at the angle brackets should you care to. Chapter 5 finishes off this part. Here we explain how XBRL will impact various different types of people who interact with it.

Part II: Embracing XBRL for Classic Challenges and New Possibilities

The chapters in Part II focus on business information exchange as it exists today and an emerging alternative approach that views each of the links of your business information exchange process as part of a chain. Chapter 6 looks at what business information exchange is all about — how it's practiced today, its objectives, business and technical dynamics impacting it, and the possibility of a new model for business information exchange. Chapter 7 introduces the notion of business information exchange as being a chain, stepping back from the individual links introduced in the previous chapter. Chapter 8 takes a visionary look the future of business information exchange and XBRL's role in that future.

Part III: Successfully Pursuing and Executing an XBRL Project

Part III is about how to successfully use XBRL within your organization. It helps you avoid missteps before you make them. Chapter 9 helps you see how others are making use of XBRL. Chapter 10 helps you make a business case for XBRL. Chapter 11 helps you understand different approaches to implementing XBRL so that you can find the approach that is the best for you. Chapter 12 points out the things you need to consider when implementing a project which has an XBRL component by project phase. If you must comply with the U.S. SEC mandate, you'll appreciate Chapter 13.

Part IV: Working with XBRL Taxonomies and Instances

You can dig a hole with a hand shovel, but a backhoe is more efficient, depending on the size of the hole, of course. It's all about choosing the right tool. In this part, we help you understand the tools you need to work with XBRL taxonomies and XBRL instances. We also help you understand what to do with those tools.

Chapter 14 looks at what types of software applications you might use when working with XBRL and the purposes they serve. Chapter 15 is a step-by-step walk-through of things like creating, validating, and viewing XBRL taxonomies and XBRL instances. Chapter 16 reviews the modules of XBRL that make up the XBRL family of specifications in greater detail, pointing out where they can be helpful to you. Chapter 17 is XBRL taxonomy time! We focus on XBRL taxonomies, providing you with a boatload of useful information you will need. Chapter 18 is all about the XBRL instance, drilling into helpful details you need to know about. Chapter 19 is where we go out on a limb to help you plan your future. We take a peek at what may be coming in the short term and in the long term for XBRL.

Part V: The Part of Tens

Last, but certainly not least, the *For Dummies* institution: The Part of Tens. This part of the book has three chapters packed with XBRL tips, hints, and other advice. You may want to read this part first to get some instant gratification. Or, you may want to read it last to provide the icing on your XBRL cake.

Chapter 20 provides ten ways to find out more about XBRL sooner, flattening your learning curve, should you have a desire to do so. Chapter 21 describes important technical concepts in easy-to-understand business terms, terms needed to truly grasp how XBRL actually does what it does for those who care about that level of understanding. And finally, Chapter 22 ends your journey by providing explanations for a number of commonly confused odds and ends, which may be important to more technically inclined readers.

Icons Used in This Book

This icon denotes tips and tricks of the trade that make your projects go more smoothly and otherwise ease your foray into XBRL.

XBRL is all about computer technology used to solve a business problem. When you see this icon, the accompanying explanation digs into the underlying technology and processes, in case you want to get behind the scenes, under the hood, or beneath the covers. These paragraphs are eminently skippable by the less technically inclined.

Some things about XBRL are just so darned important that they bear keeping in mind. This icon lets you know of a fact that you need to file away for future reference.

This icon indicates pitfalls you need to be aware of. Disregarding these might come back to bite you.

Where to Go from Here

This is the easy part: You bought this book, you're wearing your "I ♥ XBRL" T-shirt, you have your favorite Starbucks coffee, and you have the desire to learn about XBRL. Now what?

Well, you open the book to Chapter 1 and settle in for a quiet afternoon of absorbing everything you can about XBRL, if that is your style. Or, for those who are more on the go, you can pick up this book for 15 minutes a day and flip through it looking for topics that are of interest to you. Or, you may have some other approach that works for you. That is the beauty of this type of book — all our chapters are meant to be read either as part of a whole book, or just on their own. You should never feel lost if you skip around or your pet eats Chapter 5.

The book has a companion Cheat Sheet online that is referenced at the front of this book. Check there for the Web address to access the online Cheat Sheet. Key concepts used throughout this book and a high level model of XBRL are described in the Cheat Sheet. It will be helpful to you no matter how you read the book.

If you want to do a bit more exploring right now, you may find these examples helpful. If you like reverse-engineering things to better understand them, these examples can help you down that path:

- ✔ **A "Hello World" example:** You can find a basic "Hello World"-type sample XBRL taxonomy and XBRL instance as well as a Microsoft Excel spreadsheet with macros that generate the XBRL on this Web page: `http://xbrl.squarespace.com/journal/2008/12/18/hello-world-xbrl-example.html`.

- ✔ **A comprehensive example:** You can see a more complex example of an XBRL taxonomy and XBRL instance at `www.xbrlsite.com/examples/comprehensiveexample/2008-04-18`.

- ✔ **A real financial statement example:** The U.S. Securities and Exchange Commission (SEC) has a great viewer with lots of big XBRL instances hooked to some big XBRL taxonomies — this is the real deal. Check it out at `http://viewerprototype1.com/viewer`.

- ✔ **Real XBRL taxonomies:** At `www.abra-search.com/ABRASearch.html`, you find a viewer that lets you explore a number of different XBRL taxonomies. ABRA-SEARCH.COM is Web site provided by ABZ Reporting GmbH, a provider of open-source software to the XBRL community.

So what are you waiting for? Go ahead and dive right into the phenomenal global world of XBRL. Ready? Set? Go!

Part I
The Very Least You Need to Know about XBRL

"Yes, I know how to analyze information in XBRL, but what if I just want to leak it instead?"

In this part . . .

This part provides you with the absolute minimum you need to know about XBRL. We start off by providing what amounts to a macro-level conceptual overview of XBRL to help you get your head around what XBRL is. Next, we look at why XBRL is what it is and how it works to bridge the gap between real world business systems. Jumping from the macro to the micro level, we then switch the focus to XBRL itself, explaining its working pieces from the big picture perspective. We then really move into the micro-level details, providing an XBRL primer focusing on the key components you need to understand. We wrap up this part by explaining how XBRL will impact you. We take a look at how different types of organizations might use XBRL and how it might impact specific roles within an organization, one of which might be your role.

Chapter 1

Wrapping Your Head Around XBRL

. . . .

. . . .

You may have heard about XBRL, but have no idea what it is — only that you need to start using it. If that's the case, you're in the right place. In this chapter, we journey into the world of XBRL by giving you all the things you need to get your head around XBRL in the form of a conceptual over-view. We explain what XBRL is, describe the environment that it fits into, give you some examples of who is using it and why, what benefits it provides, and what it might take for you to start using XBRL. Basically, in this chapter, we define a framework that you can use to get your head around XBRL and leave it to other chapters to drill into the details.

Answering the Question, "Why XBRL?"

Now that the United States Securities and Exchange Commission (SEC) man-dates the use of XBRL, stock exchanges around the world use it, and it's offi-cially supported by the European Parliament as well as the governments of the Netherlands, Australia, Singapore, Japan, India, and China. The Extensible Business Reporting Language (XBRL) is pretty much undeniably a global standard for business reporting. Obviously, XBRL is here to stay.

Your business operates on information, so you need to know the fundamen-tals of XBRL. This collection of information may be physically separated by artificial boundaries between the different business systems you use to oper-ate your business. This collection of information may not even be in your own business systems, but within the business systems of your suppliers, customers, and other business partners. If you can bridge this gap between different business systems, both those within your organization and other organizations within your supply chain, a more cohesive information set results, enabling you to see your business like you have never seen it before, and vastly improving your effectiveness in managing your business and the supply chains in which your business participates.

XBRL is, fundamentally, a language that helps businesses effectively and efficiently bridge the current gap between business systems by crossing these artificial boundaries.

Figure 1-1 shows the common relationships that most businesses have. Suppose that you work within the parent company. You'll likely have more than one business system, ranging from a big Enterprise Resource Planning (ERP) system and Corporate Performance Management (CPM) system to perhaps small but important spreadsheets that contain information. Those business systems are generally internal to your organization. You may need to exchange business information with subsidiaries, which also have business systems. The same is likely true of customers, suppliers, regulators, and a plethora of others with whom you interact and exchange all sorts of information. These systems are generally external to your organization. In the past, no standard for exchanging information between these internal or external systems existed, so you created homegrown, automated, one-to-one approaches or one-to-many approaches, or used approaches requiring a lot of human involvement that have been the norm to exchange information between business systems. With XBRL, more of these information exchanges can be efficiently automated by using one globally standard approach.

Don't be fooled into thinking that because XBRL is now used mostly for financial reporting or by regulators that you don't need to pay attention to XBRL. Assuming that XBRL is not applicable to you is like assuming that HTTP (Hypertext Transfer Protocol, one of the key ingredients of the Web) is not applicable to you. You may not care about the nitty-gritty details of XBRL or HTTP, but you care about using what they enable.

Managers at all levels of business need timely, complete, accurate business information that is relevant to their purposes. The vast amount of human capital that is currently expended to integrate this information manually, commonly using point solutions (such as entering data into spreadsheets), clearly demonstrates this need. (*Point solutions* solve a problem for a specific limited situation, but don't do anything to resolve related issues.)

Before the ubiquitous and now almost free (or certainly low cost) connectivity of the Web, integrating these various systems, using human capital and point solutions, such as spreadsheets, was the only real solution to this problem for most businesses. However, thanks to the Web and technologies such as XBRL, any organization now has at its disposal better, more effective, and more efficient methods to solve these types of problems. No longer do you have to be a gigantic multinational corporation to afford these types of integrated solutions.

It's not that business systems weren't interconnected before: Certain business systems that had to be interconnected *were* interconnected, regardless of the cost, because the benefits were so critical or the cost savings were so huge. For example, the ticketing systems of airlines are interconnected, allowing you to book flights from one location to another even if you're on different airlines for different legs of your journey. Today with XBRL and other enablers, however, the cost of bridging these types of gaps can be so low that the cost-benefit equation has shifted, meaning that more gaps can be bridged because the net benefit of doing so is so much larger. Smart businesses take advantage of these opportunities and become better, more competitive businesses.

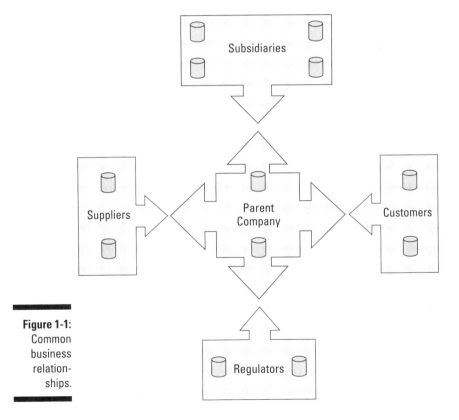

Figure 1-1:
Common
business
relation-
ships.

Looking at XBRL in Different Ways

One of the most confusing things about XBRL for those new to it is that it means so many different things to different people. Business reporting is a broad area. We want to cover all the bases in this book, so we want to be careful to include all the different views of what XBRL is. Depending on the situation, you can look at XBRL as

- ✔ A freely available, market-driven, open, global standard for exchanging business information
- ✔ An XML language
- ✔ A global consortium of more than 600 members
- ✔ A means of modeling the meaning of business information in a form comprehendible by computer applications
- ✔ A mandate from regulators from around the world
- ✔ A revolution for small investors, the most important shareholder initiative in a decade, and a leveler of the investment playing field
- ✔ A global agreement on business information concepts, relationships, and business rules
- ✔ One of the more successful Semantic Web metadata formats (we explain more about the Semantic Web in the upcoming section "Making life or easier")
- ✔ A better approach to exchanging business information
- ✔ A new way for companies to distribute their financial and other relevant business information

The fact is that all the preceding statements are true; they appeal to different audiences who have different focuses on different aspects of business information and the process of exchanging that information. The business community is generally concerned with making business information exchange the most effective that it can be at the minimum cost. Depending on your role in the business community, the term "effective" can have different meanings. Everyone understands what "minimum cost" means, however. (In Chapter 5, we look more at how XBRL affects different kinds of users.)

We do want to get one thing straightened out: When people look at XBRL, they think of business reporting because, well, business reporting puts the "BR" in XBRL. In reality though, XBRL is actually broader than what most people think of when you say "business reporting." From our perspective, XBRL is really more about *describing* business information and enhancing that information's *exchange* across internal or external business systems. One aspect of business information exchange is business reporting. For example, exchanging data or information between two business systems (computer to computer, no humans involved) isn't really seen as business reporting by many. However, that type of business information exchange is definitely within XBRL's scope. So basically, business information exchange includes what many know as business reporting. Business reporting is a subset of business information exchange. In this book, we use the term *business information exchange*, which includes but is not limited to business reporting.

Dispelling Common Misconceptions

One approach to understanding what something is, is to understand what it is not. Here are some common misconceptions and how they tend to get in the way of understanding XBRL:

- ✔ **XBRL is a standard chart of accounts.** In reality, XBRL is exactly the opposite. The first letter in the acronym XBRL stands for the word "extensible." *Extensibility,* or the ability to "tweak" an XBRL taxonomy is one of the primary values of XBRL. (An XBRL *taxonomy* is like a dictionary that specifies business concepts — we explain in the upcoming section, "Getting a Grip on XBRL Fundamentals.") If the data you're reporting is *fixed* (that is, a form that can't be changed), you may not need to use XBRL (although it can still provide significant benefit). Many of those adopting XBRL (such as the United States SEC) do so because of its capacity to be dynamic and to allow changes to the XBRL taxonomy. A standard chart of accounts is generally fixed, not allowing for changes of any kind.

  XBRL is a language for expressing concepts; creators of XBRL taxonomies decide which concepts they want in the XBRL taxonomy. It's not about data standardization (in other words, mandating one chart of accounts for everyone). In fact, XBRL itself doesn't define any concepts at all; users of XBRL do that.

- ✔ **XBRL requires companies to disclose additional financial information.** Nope, incorrect. What XBRL does is simply take what is being reported now and report it in a different format, in a format that is readable by automated computer processes. Remember, XBRL itself defines no taxonomies; the users of XBRL do.

- ✔ **XBRL is just about financial or regulatory reporting.** Oops . . . that's not right. XBRL is sometimes thought of as only for regulators or just for financial reporting because some of the early adopters were regulators who were using XBRL to collect financial information. Those industries were early users of XBRL, but they were only leading the pack. For example, XBRL Global Ledger is a canonical, or standardized, information exchange format for cross business system information exchange both internally and to external business partners. XBRL taxonomies also exist for exchanging nonfinancial information.

✔ **To learn XBRL, business users have to learn about angle brackets, XPath, XLink, and a lot of other complex scary technical stuff.** Whoa! Hold on there. Just because business users had to learn to use e-mail and a browser to be more effective doesn't mean they had to learn about all the technology standards underlying the Internet. Good software vendors hide the complexity of XBRL within their software, just as an Internet browser shields business users from HTML, HTTP, TCP/IP, and numerous other elements of technical infrastructure.

XBRL is still maturing, as is the software being developed to make use of XBRL. Software vendors are still exploring very clever and creative ways to get all the benefits without exposing the wiring under the hood. Much of the XBRL software that exists at the time of this writing is for technical users. The software, such as XBRL processors used by technical people, needs to be built first, and then the technical users create software for the business users. Be patient — business-user-friendly software is on the way.

✔ **Users of XBRL don't need to learn anything new.** Many people marketing XBRL say that business users don't have to learn anything new, which may not be fully accurate. Business users do have to think about things differently as XBRL enables process enhancements to current processes. Think of when the world moved from paper spreadsheets to electronic spreadsheets. Did business users have to learn new things? Certainly. Did it kill them? Certainly not.

✔ **XML is easier than XBRL, so I can just use XML.** XBRL is XML. You have the choice of using the freely available standard that is XBRL, or you can spend your resources to create your "own" version of XBRL, which does everything that XBRL already does in terms of additional functionality. That is exactly what the people who created XBRL already did . . . using XML. XML is a *syntax* (a set of technical rules governing the appropriate arrangement of symbols and words): XBRL provides additional business semantics (or business meaning) not provided by XML alone. With the XBRL standard, these semantics can be communicated to and used by others, effectively transferring business meaning.

If you did create your own version of XBRL, what you would have would be proprietary (as opposed to a global standard), so you would have no off-the-shelf software supporting it, and you would have spent a lot of time creating something that already exists. (Chapter 2 discusses XBRL and XML in more detail: Be sure to have a look at that discussion if you're trying to understand the relationship between XBRL and XML.)

✔ **You already have a global data warehouse, so you don't need XBRL.** Many companies believe that because they already have all their data in a data warehouse or data mart, they have no need for XBRL. If you are in this situation, consider two issues you have:

- Getting quality information in to the data warehouse

- Getting relevant and complete data out and into the hands of users

XBRL enables solutions to both of these concerns by providing a standardized method to solving such common issues, rather than requiring each global data warehouse to individually solve the same problem. This standard method opens up the possibility for business systems to communicate with one another, exchanging important information, such as data models, validation rules, analytical rules, reporting concepts, and so on between business systems such as global data warehouses. Just like other Web standards, XBRL transforms the current producer orientation into an information supply chain in which the providers and consumers of business information collaborate.

Compelling Reasons to Consider XBRL

You've probably already heard a lot of the hype and maybe even some of the compelling things that XBRL can do for you:

- Making business information exchange better, faster, and cheaper

- Making financial reporting more transparent and discoverable

- Explicitly articulating business meaning and thus enabling the exchange of that meaning between humans or between business systems

- Improving data integrity

- Integrating business systems

- Saving government agencies money and making them more efficient

But all those reasons may seem esoteric and perhaps even too far-fetched for most people to get their heads around. We want to provide you with some pragmatic, down-to-earth ways that XBRL can be good for you today. The following sections highlight what XBRL can do for you. (Better yet, the rest of the book fills in the details.)

Making life easier

Computers are great at handling routine, repetitive tasks for you. They do the hard, boring, complex work for you precisely as you tell them to do it. Here are some of the ways XBRL can make your life easier today:

- **Document domain knowledge:** People have a lot of knowledge about different business domains locked up in their heads. Documenting that knowledge within an XBRL taxonomy is quick and easy with XBRL. The semantic meaning will then be useful to others, not just you. You can see the value of documentation by examining the domain knowledge documented by other domains, such as financial reporting knowledge documented in the IFRS or US GAAP XBRL taxonomies.

✔ **Improve an information-supply chain:** Start with something simple and easy, but try to put together an information-supply chain making use of XBRL to solve a problem where you're using human intervention to make the connections between the links today.

✔ **Create and demand linked data:** *Linked data* is simply connecting one set of data with another set of data to make both data sets more useful. A new mantra of Sir Tim Berners-Lee (inventor of the Web) is "Linked data! Get out there and make it, be sure to demand it!" Create some linked data; if it makes sense, use XBRL. Or, use someone else's linked data. (See http://www.ted.com/index.php/talks/tim_berners_lee_on_the_next_web.html.) Contribute to the Semantic Web!

To avoid having to type these long links, go to www.dummies.com/go/xbrl. This takes you to a landing page where you can click the link you need.

✔ **Build an internal semantic Web:** Just as there is the Internet and intranets, there will be a Semantic Web and internal-use (that is, private, limited access) semantic Webs. A *semantic Web* is an approach to creating a web of information that is more like a computer-readable database (but still also usable by humans) than a bunch of human-readable pages of information, which a computer doesn't understand. Build an internal semantic Web, using XBRL because it's one of the more mature semantic Web technologies, and find out what the technologies can provide to your organization. Building an internal semantic Web can potentially give you an edge over your competition.

✔ **Work with business partners to create an extranet-type semantic Web:** This suggestions is the same idea as the building an internal semantic Web, but with business partners instead of within your organization.

Saving time and money

Say that you're one of those frugal folks. You really don't care about the Web or XBRL, but you do care about saving time, and saving time is saving money. Here are some of the ways you can employ XBRL to save money on tasks you probably already perform:

✔ **Improving integrity of information:** When you create a business report, try to leverage XBRL to improve the integrity of your business information by allowing XBRL to help you check computations and reportability rules to make sure that things add up and that you're properly providing all the correct information. Helping business information creators be sure their information "ticks and ties" is an often missed benefit of XBRL.

✔ **Collaborating with business partners:** If you're receiving information via fax, spreadsheets, or some other nonautomated means, try automating the process (no matter how small) by using XBRL.

✓ **Making business systems interoperable:** Rekeying information is an inefficient and error-prone process, but it's amazing how much rekeying still takes place. Prior to XBRL, the cost of automating some processes exceeded the potential benefits. XBRL flips that cost model on its ear. Today, you can achieve for pennies what would cost hundreds of dollars before XBRL existed.

✓ **Looking for good investments:** Scour the Web for companies that may have been overlooked in the past. Let search engines help you discover these investments. More and more companies are reporting their financial information by using XBRL, so take advantage of it!

✓ **Analyzing information:** Rather than gathering information into your analysis models by rekeying information, try to automate the process and grab the information you want to analyze from an XBRL instance.

✓ **Making your system more flexible:** XBRL makes your systems more flexible because XBRL was built to allow for changes to your information. XBRL isn't a fixed standard chart of accounts; XBRL is built to be dynamic, and flexibility is built into XBRL. You can leverage this flexibility within your system.

Helping you complete projects faster

At times, you might simply have a tactical need to improve a process or help a business project move along faster. XBRL vendors, and many companies using XBRL, are looking to make completing projects faster and easier by

✓ **Leveraging a global standard:** One of the major benefits XBRL provides is leverage. The global standard XBRL may not always provide everything you need to completely create an end-to-end solution to any specific problem in and of itself, but it does offer significant leverage. XBRL provides is the common components that you need in creating many different types of solutions. Building these common components by using the global standard XBRL provides significant leverage to these similar, common problems, therefore arriving at a solution faster, easier, and cheaper.

✓ **Empowering your workers:** Every employee today is a knowledge worker, powered by information. Workers depend on the information in your business systems. Much of this information has been stored in spreadsheets and other mediums that make reusing that information extremely challenging. XBRL changes all that. XBRL enables workers to collaborate on how they use, analyze, and relate to business information and related processes.

✓ **Standardizing information exchange between systems:** Many times, the information format doesn't really matter. When it doesn't matter what format you use to exchange information between business systems, use a standardized (often referred to as *canonical*) format like XBRL that offers a one-to-many type of exchange that works for many problems, rather than building one-to-one solutions for each specific information exchange between systems.

✔ **Building a system, not a point solution:** Rather than building one *point solution* after another (a solution that solves a specific problem but not related ones), build a system that allows for the easy of creation of a category of business information. Using a standardized information architecture can facilitate a wide range of process enhancements.

Getting a Grip on XBRL Fundamentals

Fundamentally, XBRL is a language that lets you effectively and efficiently bridge the perceived artificial boundaries between business systems, exchanging business information between those systems, be they internal or external to your organization. After all, there is only one Web, and we're all connected to it. Why should exchanging business information be so hard? How does XBRL make this information exchange process easier?

A simple example of exchanging information can help you understand how XBRL works. Chapter 4 dives deeper into the details, but for now, we keep this simple and focus on what's important in understanding the big picture. Figure 1-2 shows an example business report.

The figure shows a condensed set of financial highlights with which you should be comfortable. The information in the report is for Example Company. Two periods are shown, 2009 and 2008. Information is expressed in thousands of dollars. Two line items are shown: Net Income (Loss) and Sales, Net. Although this example is simple, it helps keep you focused on what is important.

Example Company
December 31,
(thousands of dollars)

	2009	2008
FINANCIAL HIGHLIGHTS:		
Net Income (Loss)	5,347	1,147
Sales, Net	244,508	366,375

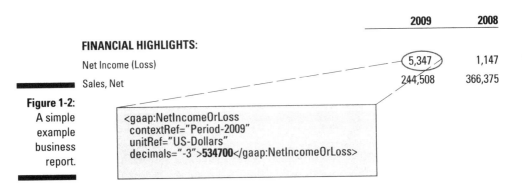

Figure 1-2: A simple example business report.

```
<gaap:NetIncomeOrLoss
  contextRef="Period-2009"
  unitRef="US-Dollars"
  decimals="-3">534700</gaap:NetIncomeOrLoss>
```

Simply put, XBRL is a language that lets you build what you probably typically think of as a *report*. This report is a physical document, just like other documents you're familiar with: a word-processing document, a spreadsheet, or maybe a PDF file. Like these reports, XBRL also has a document. The XBRL document, also called an XBRL *instance*, is built in the form of an electronic file and contains business information.

You may hear this type of XBRL document called an *XBRL instance, instance, instance document,* maybe *XBRL instance document,* or even *XBRL report.* In this book, we refer to it as an *XBRL instance.* Within this introductory section, we may use the more familiar term *report* at times.

An XBRL instance has four main parts:

- ✔ **Values:** The *values* are the text (individual values or entire narratives) and numbers in the report, the business information. Generally, the text and numbers come from some sort of business system, such as an ERP system or a spreadsheet. For example, a value would be a number like "5347" or text, such as "Inventory consists of finished goods and work-in-progress" or even a paragraph or so of narratives.

- ✔ **Context:** The *context* explains important information about the values. You need to understand what entity the value relates to, what period the values relate to, and if the values are actual, budgeted, and so on. For example, you want to be able to say that the information relates to your company and not some other company, and that the period is for 2009, not 2008.

- ✔ **Concepts:** By *concepts,* we mean technical representations of business terms. For example, "Net Income (Loss)" and "Sales, Net" from Figure 1-2 are business terms. These business terms are associated with the text or numbers contained on a business report, the values. You can represent these business terms as technical structures and give them unique names, such as "NetIncomeOrLoss" or "SalesNet." You don't want confuse one concept with another; the unique names help to differentiate concepts and the associated business term. The concepts are basically a controlled vocabulary of precisely defined business terms. These can be financial reporting terms, accounting terms, or even nonfinancial terms; they really can be any terms, but they'll likely be business terms of some sort. Values (like "5347" in the example) are reported for concepts and are reported within a specific context.

- ✔ **Dictionary:** Concepts are expressed within a *dictionary.* In XBRL, these dictionaries are referred to as taxonomies, but we want to use the more comfortable term, dictionary, for a moment. The dictionary doesn't necessarily define the concepts, but it does either define them or point to the definition or provide a definition in some manner. The important thing here is that the dictionary is the central location where concepts are pointed to information that defines that concept. The dictionary gives a precise definition about the meaning of each term *(semantics),* including references and examples. Other information helpful in making use of the concept is also provided, such as labels in any number of languages, relations of a concept to other concepts, and such. For example, a dictionary may contain the concept "NetIncomeOrLoss" or "SalesNet," express that the concepts have labels of "Net Income (Loss)" and "Sales, Net," respectively, and communicate the specific ways the concept relates to other concepts in the dictionary such as "SalesGross," "Taxes," and "Expenses."

You may hear what we have referred to as a "dictionary" above referred to as a "taxonomy" or "XBRL taxonomy" or maybe sometimes even "schema." For this initial explanation of XBRL, we will stick with "dictionary" a little longer allowing you can become comfortable with this new term. Throughout the rest of the book, we will use the term XBRL taxonomy.

Does this discussion sound familiar? Sure, you do work with these ideas every day, even though you may not think about it in this way. But all this XBRL stuff is not for the benefit of humans, at least not directly, but rather for the benefit of computers, to allow them to communicate with each other. What a computer needs to achieve effective communication is provided by the structure within the XBRL instance and XBRL taxonomy so that the computer can figure out what is a value, what is a concept, what is a context, and such. This structure is achieved by using the XML syntax, creating something many people refer to as a tag.

Tag — You're it: Tags add structure

Within the XBRL instance, the business information, or the value, is expressed in the form of what is often referred to as tags. *Tags* are the names of concepts defined in the dictionary, called an XBRL taxonomy. Each value has a specific tag, and that tag connects to the concept and its definition and all the other information contained within the dictionary. For example, one tag may be "Net Income (Loss)," while another tag may be "Assets."

Tags are used in many places. XBRL instances and XBRL taxonomies are collections of these tags. A tag's fundamental function is to add structure that enables computers to understand the pieces of an XBRL instance and XBRL taxonomy. People can still understand and work with this information. People don't work with the information at the tag level, but because of the tags, computers can work with the information and help people do all sorts of new, interesting, and helpful tasks.

Although you probably won't work at the level of the tags, understanding what tags are and how they work is helpful in understanding how the tags, and the structure they provide, enable computers to achieve this understanding. Tags look like this within the XBRL instance:

```
<gaap:NetIncomeOrLoss
 contextRef="Period-2009"
 unitRef="US-Dollars"
 decimals="INF">5347000</gaap:NetIncomeOrLoss>
```

The preceding code expresses the value `5347000` as being for the concept `gaap:NetIncomeOrLoss`. The other tags help explain the context of the information.

Concepts used within the XBRL instance are specified within the dictionary in the form of other tags, or *elements*, and look like this within the dictionary. (Keep in mind that the dictionary is referred to as an XBRL *taxonomy*.)

```
<xs:element
 name="NetIncomeOrLoss "
 type="xbrli:monetaryItemType"
 substitutionGroup="xbrli:item"
 xbrli:periodType="duration"
 xbrli:balance="credit">
```

The preceding code specifies a term as a tag within a XBRL taxonomy, which is then used within the XBRL instance to express a value. In our example, the term Net Income (Loss) is specified in the dictionary as the element "`NetIncomeOrLoss`. The definitions of terms specified come from accounting rules, regulations, laws, international standards, other written specifications, or from whatever governing body (a government, a regulator, a company, and so on) that wants to exchange information in this manner. Definitions may also come from your internal corporate data warehouse information models.

Dictionaries can be flexible

The dictionary, expressed as an XBRL taxonomy, isn't included within the business report; it's separate and referenced from the report (XBRL instance). This separation allows dictionaries to be shared by multiple reports. The dictionary may live on the Web, or it may live only within a company's intranet, but it has to be in a location where all the people and software that make use of the report can find it.

An XBRL instance is always connected with an XBRL taxonomy, the dictionary of what is contained within that XBRL instance. If your business information includes concepts not within the XBRL taxonomy, you can add your own concepts by using a formal process. Software can then use the custom information you add because the customization is *prescriptive,* meaning there is a prescribed, and therefore predictable, way these new concepts are added. Adding concepts to an XBRL taxonomy is called *extension*. You don't have to use this extension feature, but it's available if you need it.

XBRL doesn't itself define an XBRL taxonomy, which serves as the dictionary everyone must use; rather, different areas of business (called *domains*) usually create them. If a domain has created a dictionary that you like or that you're mandated to use, you can use that dictionary. You may even use multiple dictionaries. Or, if you don't find a dictionary that fits your needs, you can create your own dictionary. You can even modify the dictionaries of others, if the system you're using allows for these types of modifications.

If, say, the accountant (CFO, bookkeeper, controller) of a company has added new concepts to the dictionary, the accountant simply creates his own new dictionary and links it to the existing accepted dictionaries. This ability to extend the dictionary for each report and fit those new terms into the existing dictionary is one of the unique aspects of XBRL. For example, if your organization is in a specialized industry such as airlines or shipping, your company can add its unique subcategories of properties, plants, and equipment that may not exist within a general list of such assets.

You may wonder, "Well, if everyone adds their own unique stuff, then how do you understand others companies unique concepts?" The answer to this question is threefold:

- First, the concepts are defined in the extended dictionary provided so that you'll understand what the concepts are.

- Second, the extended concepts are clearly highlighted by the extension itself. Humans need to be involved in this part of the process, and this is where they should be involved, focusing on the unique aspects of a company, not rekeying all the information.

- Third, specialized industries and other groups will get together and agree on concepts specific to their industry or group. Over time, more and more concepts make their way to the public dictionaries and fewer and fewer extensions are needed. This continues to push human focus to the unique areas, allowing computers to help out with the agreed-upon, standardized areas of a business information exchange.

Dictionaries can enforce rules

The dictionary is actually more than an alphabetical list of terms. The dictionary can also specify rules and relations between concepts, and you can even include additional information about a concept. As we describe in Chapter 17, this is why a dictionary may not be a dictionary at all, but rather something called a taxonomy. You can go even further and create what is called an *ontology*. (See Chapter 17 for an explanation of the differences between dictionaries, taxonomies, and ontologies.)

The dictionary with a hierarchy, which is commonly referred to as a taxonomy, is commonly presented as a tree structure within software applications, looking much like the outline of a book. This setup helps dictionary creators categorize concepts. Categories can have subcategories that show relationships between concepts. Concepts can have many different relations, and the relations can be of many different types. For example, the category "Current Assets" may contain subcategories, such as "Cash," "Receivables," "Inventories," and so on.

An XBRL taxonomy can specify rules. For example, the XBRL taxonomy can specify that "Current Assets" is equal to the sum of "Cash," "Receivables," "Inventory," and all the other concepts defined as a component of "Current Assets." Other types of rules it can specify are if-then type rules. For example, if "Property, Plant, and Equipment" existed within the report, you'd expect that related concepts that express the depreciation method, asset life, categories of assets, and other policies and disclosures would likewise be in the report (if the report is a financial statement). Specifying rules not only helps to verify that the report is correct, but it also helps in the process of creating the report. Literally, the XBRL taxonomy can help guide you through the process of creating the report. It also helps those who specify what information the report creator must provide (such as regulators) in the report and do so with clarity. This formal process enables a computer to understand the report and dictionary and helps minimize errors, omissions, and miscommunications. This formal process allows for both people and computers to better work with these reports and the processes used to create the reports.

When predefined XBRL taxonomies are used, the tags in the reports are consistent. If the tags in the reports are consistent (as opposed to every organization creating their own XBRL taxonomy), the report's consistent structure greatly assists users in the process of comparing the information, if they choose to do so. Fundamentally, users can spend more time on the actual analysis and less time figuring out what data is comparable.

Users can change report organization

In XBRL, the creator of a report, such as a financial statement, tags it. These tags add structure, which helps computers understand and do things with the information within the report. The report includes all the numbers and narrative text, individual text, and any other values within the report. The creator uses an XBRL taxonomy, either one they pick or one they're required to use by a third party.

If someone using the report (or XBRL instance) doesn't like the way the creator organized the report, the user of the report can simply reorganize the report by creating his own relations and perhaps even his own concepts within an extension XBRL taxonomy. For example, you can compute EBITDA

(Earnings Before Interest, Taxes, Depreciation, and Amortization) in many different ways. Analysts, or even creators of the reports, can combine concepts that add up to totally new concepts the user may choose to create. Or, analysts can move numbers, policies, and detailed disclosures together to help with their analysis. Hiding information is a thing of the past. This ability to reorganize a report is achieved by using the structure provided by the tags.

In other words, if all companies in a given industry use the same XBRL taxonomy for creating their reports, these reports are basically a little database of reported information that anyone can easily use to perform comparisons or do other types of analysis. Users have more time available for doing the analysis because they don't need to spend as much time rekeying or mapping information. The tag structure provided by the report creator makes this time savings possible.

Further, the tags also provide efficiencies for the report creators. Report creators use those same tags to allow computers to check the report to ensure that everything adds up, the correct information is included, and so on. The XBRL taxonomy sets the verification rules, which are also available to the report users. These verification rules enable the automation of the information exchange process.

All these things working together — the tags, the dictionaries, the rules, the contexts, and so on — enable the automated exchange of business information across business systems. This arrangement sounds complex, and it is. Add to this complexity the flexibility that you have to add concepts and change relationships, and it becomes even more complex. The needs of business information exchange are why businesses use software to simplify the process.

XBRL processors "get" XBRL

You can create XBRL instances and XBRL taxonomies by hand or even by using rather simple macros. You can use an *XML parser* (application designed to work with XML documents) to read and create XBRL information. After all, XBRL is just XML.

Sometimes you may want to do all this creating by hand, but generally you won't. Enter a special piece of software called an *XBRL processor*. This handy tool understands the logical and the physical models of XBRL and how all the pieces fit together, and they can help you make sure that everything is correct, including the rules that make sure that the values in the XBRL instance (report) follow the rules specified in the XBRL taxonomy (dictionary).

And guess what? You can find many open source XBRL processors, free XBRL processors, and commercial XBRL processors. (Chapter 14 points you to these and other handy software.)

Computers can *read* (meaning import or export information) XBRL instances and XBRL taxonomies easily because all that they need to do so is contained in those files. If a human needs to read them, no problem: Apply a *style sheet* (information that helps a computer understand how to present the information for humans to read), use an XBRL viewer-type application, or simply import the information into your favorite brand of spreadsheet. You're not locked into any specific application or even any specific style sheet. Have it your way! The same computer-readable dataset makes the information flexible. And any viewer makes the entire dictionary available to you so that you can understand all the concepts, relations, rules, and so on from which the information in the report follows.

Many organizations can, and do, simply use Microsoft Excel spreadsheets to create their reports, cobbling together information from various business systems into some sort of business report. Others use specialized report writer software. Currently, these last-mile processes of financial reporting or other business reporting tend to be highly manual in most organizations. These processes will eventually leverage XBRL to streamline business report creation. XBRL will also make reusing reported information significantly easier.

Benefitting from Using XBRL

One of the early adopters of XBRL was the U.S. Federal Deposit Insurance Corporation (FDIC), which is a member of the U.S. Federal Financial Institutions Examination Council (FFIEC). The FDIC took the time to collect and communicate information about its implementation of XBRL to help others understand any benefits that existed. (This information is available on the Web at `http://xbrl.org/us/us/ffiec%20White%20Paper%20 31Jan06.pdf`.)

As an example of the benefits XBRL can provide, here is a summary of the advantages of using XBRL that the FDIC found:

- ✔ **Decreased total cost of ownership:** The FDIC reduced the total cost of ownership of their system from $65 million to $39 million, a savings of $26 million.

- ✔ **Greater timeliness of information:** The FDIC reduced the time it took to make information available from 45 days to 2 days. The FDIC achieved this time reduction by validating information as part of submission, using XBRL's ability to express business rules; providing those rules to software vendors so that those creating submissions could validate their own information; verifying information; and only letting valid information be accepted by the system.

✔ **Higher quality of information:** Contributing to the greater timeliness of information was the reduction of mathematical errors from 18,000 to 0 in the very first filing period XBRL was used. The FDIC reduced errors by, again, expressing the rules, making those rules available during creation of the information, and then not allowing information that violated the rules to come into the system. This higher quality of information also reduced the number of analysts needed to detect and correct mathematical errors by 33 percent because the analysts did not have to call banks and ask them to correct this type of error in their submissions. There are other types of errors than mathematical errors, so you still need analysts.

✔ **Greater reusability of information:** The FDIC makes the information it collects for banks available to the other five members of the FFIEC and to the public. Before XBRL, the information was converted to different formats for the different systems of the other members, and the information was made available in a format that was simple but not very usable to the general public. Today, XBRL is the format that everyone, including the FDIC and other FFIEC members, uses, and it's accessible to the general public. Anyone can obtain a standard, off-the-shelf XBRL viewer application and use the information, or computer applications can read the data feeds to reuse the information.

✔ **Greater flexibility of information collection:** Prior to using XBRL, the FDIC rarely dropped irrelevant information that it was collecting or adjusted the system for new information collected. When adjustments *were* made, it was a laborious and painful process to not only update the FDIC systems, but also to adjust the software vendor applications. The FDIC used various formats, including Microsoft Excel, Microsoft Word, PDF, and HTML, to communicate changes in information. When XBRL was implemented, changing the system became a breeze for the FDIC. The FDIC could communicate all changes in one format: XBRL. Software vendors could automate the process of reading the changes and change their software applications to support filing financial institutions. Because changing the collected information was so easy, the FDIC could adjust the information their systems collected more often, adjusting as frequently as their regulatory needs demanded.

Although the preceding benefits are specifically for the FDIC's implementation of XBRL, you can see that the types of benefits they discovered are quite general and relate to literally every system used to collect, manage, analyze, and share business information. Although some benefits may have more value for some systems than for others, we think that you can look at what the FDIC achieved and project from it what you may be able to achieve.

Chapter 10 helps you understand ways XBRL can improve your organization's effectiveness and efficiency and how to communicate that to your boss.

Discovering Other Ways to Use XBRL

By looking at other XBRL users and what they're using it for, you can get an idea of how you can use XBRL:

- ✔ **Wacoal is a company that has 36 subsidiaries operating in 23 countries, with 32 different proprietary business applications running on different platforms such as mainframes, microcomputers, UNIX, and PCs.** Wacoal wanted to integrate all these business systems. It didn't really matter what format Wacoal used to transfer the data; it just had to have one. Rather than create its own format, Wacoal used XBRL as the format.

- ✔ **CEBS (Committee of European Banking Supervisors) is a group of the central banks in Europe that regulates financial institutions.** The approximately 27 members collect solvency and liquidity information for the financial institutions they must monitor, and they use a standard information set called BASIL II, which is used globally. CEBS picked XBRL as the exchange medium for this standard data set so that the different regulators in the different countries could both collect information from the financial institutions they regulate and also exchange information between the 27 different countries, which would be harder if each country used a different format. CEBS's second option was to build and maintain its own standard for exchanging this information. Rather than create its own standard, CEBS leveraged XBRL.

- ✔ **The governments of the Netherlands, Australia, Singapore, and New Zealand think big!** These governments have already implemented or are in the process of implementing what they're calling SBR (Standard Business Reporting) throughout their entire governments! The goal of these efforts is to reduce the reporting burden on those who interact with the government, making the process better, faster, and cheaper for all parties involved. The governments made processes easier by both harmonizing the information between government agencies who use the information (that is, making it so that businesses don't have to report the same information multiple times to multiple different agencies), automating the exchange process by making the process electronic, and improving government outcomes (for example, harmonizing the definitions of the terms different agencies use). Projections by these governments predict that SBR will reduce company compliance costs by 25 percent annually — or more than $1 billion in combined savings per year!

If one regulator mandates XBRL, thousands, hundreds of thousands, or, in some cases, even millions of businesses will be required to use XBRL. In today's world, businesses commonly deal with more than one government agency and many times with government agencies in more than one country. XBRL may become the common language for communicating to government agencies and other regulators. Having that infrastructure allows businesses to experiment with XBRL and realize how useful it is, allowing them to use the same infrastructure for exchanging business information internally and with their business partners.

Chapter 9 provides more examples of how others are making use of XBRL to get you thinking about how you might be able to use it.

Making XBRL Work for You

No standard is perfect, and XBRL is no exception to this rule. If you do choose to make use of XBRL (and you likely will), you should realize the following:

- ✓ **XML is a syntax; XBRL expresses semantics.** XBRL goes further than many XML languages in providing the ability to express semantics or meaning. Understanding this difference is critical to understanding XBRL. (Chapter 2 covers this concept in more detail.) Just realize that comparing XML and XBRL isn't a good comparison.

- ✓ **XBRL is about creating information structured for meaning.** Currently, many business reports are unstructured, so reusing the information within the report in an automated fashion is impossible. It doesn't have to be that way. Providing information in a format structured for meaning has advantages. Chapter 21 explains the differences between unstructured information, information structured for presentation, and information structured for meaning. Understanding these differences is critical to understanding XBRL.

- ✓ **XBRL is a general-purpose specification.** Being general purpose, it has to serve many masters. No one system making use of XBRL will use 100 percent of its features. Rather, users will pick and choose the parts they need, ignoring the parts they don't need.

- ✓ **XBRL has no standard logical model.** As a result, you need to follow the physical model of XBRL, which leads to complexity, or create your own logical model, which makes working with XBRL much easier. However, if done incorrectly, this can lead to interoperability issues. You can solve this situation by creating a proper logical model and making use of a well articulated *application profile,* which is a constrained subset of the full general-purpose XBRL specification and specifies your logical model. (Chapter 12 discusses application profiles and logical models.)

- ✓ **Specific proprietary solutions are commonly better than standards; standards provide leverage.** Proprietary solutions to a specific problem are commonly better than standards because that is how businesses differentiate themselves — by creating a good solution to a very specific problem. But the thing about proprietary solutions is that they can be expensive, and they lead to the minimum amount of interoperability, which doesn't provide what you really need — a standardized way to describe, exchange, and analyze business information.

✔ **XBRL taxonomies are data models.** Many people understand the benefits of a well-designed database schema and the ramifications of a poorly designed database schema. A database schema is a data model. An XBRL taxonomy may express a data model and can, and many times should, be treated as such. Just as you can have good and bad data models, you can have good XBRL taxonomies and not-so-good XBRL taxonomies. A bad XBRL taxonomy model leads to poor interoperability. Poor interoperability leads to people needing to be involved in information exchanges. When you consider your XBRL taxonomy data model design, you need to consider the extensions others will be creating. All these issues are best dealt with by using an information modeling layer, which can help you create good data models and thus good XBRL taxonomies. (Chapters 12 and 17 discuss information models.)

✔ **XBRL taxonomies can have different architectures.** XBRL is a general-purpose specification. You can choose from several ways to model your XBRL taxonomies, which dictate what your XBRL instances will look like and how they act. Many times, different architectures aren't as compatible as you might hope. This incompatibility may result in interoperability issues between different XBRL taxonomies, which is important to realize because, in all likelihood, your organization will be dealing with many different XBRL taxonomies. For example, you can report to different regulators, which use different XBRL taxonomies. Further, you may choose to make use of XBRL internally within your organization. Managing the interoperability of your internal business systems and various XBRL taxonomies architected in different ways can be a challenge. One way to deal with these realities is to create an abstraction layer between your internal implementation of XBRL and other implementations of XBRL, which helps minimize the impact of the whims of others on your important internal business systems. (Chapter 12 discusses how to maintain control by using an abstraction layer.)

✔ **XBRL is not a complete solution.** XBRL is a technology that provides significant leverage, and you can use it within a system. You can string together all the pieces you need, or you can adopt an architecture, an application profile, and an information model created by others. What you can't do is simply pick up XBRL, plug it in, and expect all your problems to be solved.

✔ **An island of XBRL isn't an effective goal.** Creating an island of XBRL within an organization doesn't serve any real purpose. All that approach does is create additional work and additional cost with no true marginal benefit to the system as a whole.

At first glance, you may not have considered the preceding aspects, the realities, of working with XBRL. But eventually, you'll run up against these issues.

Chapter 2 helps you become well grounded in the realities of working with XBRL. Considering these realities as you figure out how to apply XBRL within your organization can help you minimize false starts, point out dead-end paths, and otherwise learn from the missteps of others so that you don't make the same mistakes.

Chapter 2

Taking to Heart the Essential Concepts of XBRL

*T*his chapter is about *why* XBRL is what it is, *how* XBRL actually does what it does, and how you can make XBRL work for you. If you're the type who doesn't really care how your car works and you're just happy that it gets you to your destination, then you can probably skip this chapter. But for the rest of you, this chapter contains a lot of good information that helps you understand the best ways to implement XBRL.

We apologize that his chapter does get a little technical. However, if you're technically inclined or you're a businessperson who works with technical people, you'll find the information useful. We do stay at the big-picture level, however, which makes the technical stuff as painless as possible.

The Problem That XBRL Solves

Sharing information between business systems today, even in the age of the Web's connectivity, is difficult. Sir Tim Berners-Lee, the guy who created the World Wide Web, laments,

> *"Most of the Web's content today is designed for humans to read, not for computer programs to manipulate meaningfully. Computers can adeptly parse Web pages for layout and routine processing — here a header, there a link to another page — but in general, computers have no reliable way to process the semantics."*

With the volume of information humans have to deal with increasing at an estimated 30 percent per year, something has got to give. Fortunately, XBRL helps solve that problem. Recall that Sir Tim Berners-Lee said, "Computers have no reliable way to process the semantics." The first part of processing the semantics is to *express* those semantics, which XBRL does. XBRL steps up to meet the challenges of sharing information so that it's truly portable.

Building on Top of XML

Many technical people have questions about the relationship between XBRL and XML. They look at XBRL from the perspective of other traditional applications for XML and immediately are confused by XBRL, thinking it's overly complex.

This section gets a little technical. It's intended for technical people who understand XML and want to know what XBRL brings to the table. If you don't know what XML is, you may want to skip this section.

XBRL isn't like other XML languages

Comparing and contrasting XBRL to other applications that use XML is a good way to understand it. Many people who are familiar with XML make two fundamental mistakes when they run across XBRL:

- **They think that XBRL is an XML language that's just like other XML languages.** That's not the case. XBRL is an XML language, but it goes way further than most XML languages in meeting the needs of its user domain.

- **They don't spend enough time digging into what XBRL is or why XBRL is what it is.** XBRL has a lot to it, and this information can be hard to find and rather voluminous. (Of course, one reason why we're writing this book is to make the information easier to find and more concise!)

XBRL is both an approach to making use of XML *and* a layer on top of XML that an *XML Schema* (which describes information structures, much like a data dictionary) alone doesn't provide. XML provides the syntax XBRL uses, so XBRL can use the entire family of W3C (World Wide Web Consortium) XML specifications, which you can see at see www.w3.org.

XBRL uses a specific approach to using XML. For example, XBRL consciously makes it easy for its users to avoid using the XML content model. XBRL also builds upon XML, providing things necessary to effectively automate the process of exchanging business information. For example, think of the times when even the smallest math error can create devastating problems when exchanging information. XBRL had to solve these types of data integrity problems in order to be useful within its environment. Every software application didn't need to solve this problem separately with its own proprietary solution, potentially causing inconsistent results.

XBRL versus XML

The following list compares XBRL and XML. (Thank you to UBmatrix who originally published a white paper on this topic and others who have contributed to this work, making the information available under a creative commons license that provides the basis for this useful comparison.)

- ✔ **XBRL is XML; XBRL uses the XML syntax.** XBRL also uses XML Schema, XLink, Namespaces in XML, and other global standards from the XML family of specifications.

- ✔ **XBRL expresses meaning; XML articulates only syntax.** XML Schema constrains syntax, but doesn't express semantics. XBRL's fundamental goal is to express business meaning, called *semantics.* To do so, XBRL had to use the XML syntax to and family of specifications to build additional features. To do what XBRL does with XML, you'd basically have to reinvent what XBRL has already created. Every software vendor reinventing what many business users of XBRL need makes little sense.

- ✔ **XBRL allows content validation against the expressed meaning.** Traditional XML languages, validated by XML Schemas alone, don't express enough meaning. If that meaning doesn't exist (or isn't expressed), you can't validate information sets against that meaning. XBRL does express meaning and therefore does enable you to validate by using that expressed meaning. In addition, XBRL enables the exchange of that meaning to those consuming your information because it's expressed in a standard way separate from business applications. With traditional XML approaches, validation isn't as rich, so the necessary rules are embedded within the applications that read or write the XML. These rules are written application by application and in different, proprietary ways that are impossible to exchange across business systems because no one standard approach exists to enable such an exchange. With XBRL, you can exchange both the information itself and the business rules that support creating accurate information, allowing you to effectively communicate business information.

- ✔ **XBRL separates concept definitions from the content model.** Typically with XML, the concept definitions and the content model are mixed together. Further, XML provides you with only one implicit set of relations (because it has only one content model) and the definition of those relations is mixed with the definition of elements and attributes. XBRL, on the other hand, uses an *atomic approach* (flat XML content model) in defining concepts and moves the expression of relations away from the XML schema. This separation of concept and relation definition leads to the next benefit of XBRL.

✔ **XBRL can express multiple hierarchies of explicit relations.** Because XBRL separates concept and relation definitions, you can define more than one hierarchy of such relations. Further, the hierarchies of relations defined can be explicit, unlike XML's implicit content model.

✔ **XBRL provides organized, prescriptive extensibility (the ability for users to make adjustments).** XML's greatest strength is also its greatest weakness: XML is extensible everywhere, in every direction. XBRL is extensible in a specific, prescriptive, and therefore predictable manner. As such, the extensibility is usable without modifying software for the extension. You can think of this difference as XBRL always having the same shape.

✔ **XBRL provides a multidimensional model.** Online analytical processing systems (OLAP)-type systems can use XBRL's multidimensional model to provide flexible information presentation and the ability to "slice and dice" information. Business intelligence systems in particular are big users of the multidimensional model. Although you can make XML fit into a multidimensional model, it can be a struggle in many cases. XBRL fits quite nicely into the existing applications that make use of the multi-dimensional models. Alternatively, you can use an existing architecture and application profile that's intended to fit into an application that uses the multidimensional model. Getting information into applications that use the multidimensional model is important because more and more applications, such as business intelligence applications, are leveraging the characteristics of the multidimensional model.

✔ **XBRL enables intelligent, metadata-driven connections to information.** With XBRL, business users can connect information by adjusting metadata rather than by requiring technical people to write code. As such, rather than building multiple point solutions, XBRL enables the creation of effective and efficient solutions that allow extensibility and that don't require programming modifications to connect to new information or new information models. These metadata-driven connections are possible because of the prescriptive manner of XBRL's extensibility; the "shape" of XBRL is always the same. With XML, a programmer has to enable pretty much every new connection when writing code because XML communicates only technical syntax and does so at the data level, not the meaning level, of information and because the shape of different XML implementations can be so varied.

XML replaces a multitude of different approaches to exchanging data with one standard Web-friendly approach. Can traditional XML approaches do all the things that XBRL can do? Absolutely. XBRL *is* a traditional XML language with an additional layer built on top of it. In order to have the functionality of XBRL, most traditional uses of XML require building all of XBRL's functionality for each XML language created. But XBRL provides all this "out of the box" because things like expressing meaning and validation against that meaning are so core to XBRL's reason for being. XBRL already includes these pieces because business users have said they needed these features.

The Essential Objectives Driving XBRL

The XBRL Specification outlines the requirements that drove the development of XBRL. Here's a summary of the drivers behind the development of XBRL:

- ✔ The business reporting product must improve over the long term.

- ✔ The needs of all categories of users participating in the process of business reporting (preparers of business information, intermediaries involved in the preparation and distribution process, users of business information, and vendors that supply software and services to those participating in this process) must be balanced.

- ✔ Business information exchange in general must be facilitated, without a focus on financial information exchange or accounting.

- ✔ Extensibility is important because business information exchange can be dynamic; it may not be a static form.

- ✔ The ability to drill down from summary information to detailed information is important.

- ✔ Preparing, exchanging, extracting, and comparing information is the focus; presenting information is *not* the focus of XBRL.

- ✔ Existing technologies and approaches, such as XML, XML Schema, XLink, and Namespaces, should be leveraged rather than new technologies or approaches created.

XBRL Is Powerful but Not a Complete Solution or System

Although XBRL provides a substantial foundation of functionality to build on, XBRL itself isn't a complete running system any more than XML is a complete solution. XBRL offers a basis for delivering a diverse and rich set of functionality to achieve a system's goals, but it isn't a complete business solution in and of itself. If you had to describe what XBRL provides in a word, that word would be *leverage*. You can build a broad range of specific systems by using XBRL in a fraction of the time that it would take if you were to start from scratch.

On the other hand, given that XBRL is general in nature, it meets the needs of a broad set of information exchange use cases, which means two things:

- ✔ XBRL isn't perfect for any specific application of XBRL because XBRL isn't trying to be perfect for any one thing.

- ✔ XBRL is perhaps more than you need for your specific application of XBRL within your system.

The last point isn't a problem: Just use the pieces you do need and ignore the rest. Keep these important points in the back of your mind:

- ✔ **XBRL isn't a complete solution or system.** XBRL is a standard that provides a tremendous amount of leverage, but it is not in and of itself a complete solution or system. XBRL is used within solutions or systems.

- ✔ **XBRL can come in many dialects.** XBRL is a general-purpose language. Business systems have many different goals, which you can achieve in many different ways. XBRL users do so in different ways, basically creating what amounts to different dialects of XBRL that don't necessarily all interoperate well with each other unless they're made to do so.

- ✔ **Software tools may not be interoperable.** A key to effective information exchange is software interoperability, which XBRL International works hard to enable. However, if two different software vendors support XBRL within their applications, those applications may not necessarily be 100 percent interoperable. For example, if one software tool supports a module of XBRL (such as XBRL Dimensions) that another software tool doesn't support, you may have interoperability problems. Software tool interoperability must be created; it's hard work but achievable.

- ✔ **Business systems may not be interoperable.** If two business systems implement XBRL within the systems, you have no guarantee that the two systems will be interoperable, unless they're specifically *designed* to be 100 percent interoperable. For example, one system may support a module of XBRL (such as XBRL Dimensions) that the other system doesn't support. Or, if one system implements proprietary features (such as the addition of a non-XBRL attribute to a concept, deviating slightly from the standard) and the other one doesn't, the two systems may not interoperate correctly. As with software-tool interoperability, business-system interoperability is achievable, but it does take work.

- ✔ **XBRL taxonomies may not necessarily be interoperable.** If two groups create two XBRL taxonomies that use different architectures, those XBRL taxonomies may not be interoperable. Creating different taxonomy architectures isn't a characteristic of XBRL; it's a characteristic of how much (or how little) the two different systems work to make their systems interoperable. Systems sometimes process completely different sets of information, and interoperability isn't necessary. Or, systems can process the same type of information but implement XBRL taxonomy characteristics in different ways, so the systems aren't interoperable. For example, the US GAAP XBRL taxonomy, the IFRS XBRL taxonomy, and the EDINET XBRL taxonomy are all used for financial reporting, but these XBRL taxonomies are significantly different. (You can see a comparison of these three XBRL taxonomies at `www.xbrl.org/TCF-PWD-2009-03-31.html`.)

✔ **Extensibility makes interoperability even harder.** If you create an XBRL taxonomy to meet the need of a static reporting problem (for example, an unmodifiable form), interoperability is easier to achieve than if you use XBRL's extensibility. If you're not using extensibility features, you don't have to deal with all the ways users may extend the XBRL taxonomy. If you use XBRL's extensibility, you have to ensure that those extending your XBRL taxonomy do so in consistent ways and in only the ways you intend them to extend the XBRL taxonomy. The XBRL specification doesn't cover how to extend an XBRL taxonomy and not break the information model, so you must build your system to handle these sorts of issues.

✔ **Application profiles reduce risk and make interoperability easier.** To make implementing an XBRL system easier, you can create an *application profile,* which articulates an XBRL architecture (meaning it's 100-percent compliant with some specific constrained subset of XBRL), and all the automated validation rules you need to effectively constrain XBRL taxonomies and XBRL instances within a system against that XBRL architecture. You can even use an existing application profile that works correctly.

A downside of using someone else's application profile is that you must live within its constraints. If you can, implementing XBRL is substantially easier because you have less work to do, and the risk of the system not working as expected is reduced. (Chapter 12 discusses application profiles.)

✔ **Extending XBRL with XML extensibility is a possibility.** In many areas, XBRL does allow XML-type extensibility, and you can find many good reasons to use it. For example, you can add attributes to an XBRL concept, if you need to. If you're working in a *closed system* (where you have complete control over all of that system's aspects), XML-type extensibility can be a good strategy. However, this approach can have serious drawbacks. For example, if you add an attribute to an XBRL concept, an XBRL processor may be able to read that attribute, but the application won't know what to do with it. XBRL created extensibility the way it did to avoid just this situation. You need to be conscious of these types of things when you consider how to use XBRL. Be aware of both positive and negative impacts.

Decisions, Decisions

Life is full of tradeoffs, and XBRL is no exception. We can sum up the tradeoffs made in the creation of XBRL in one simple mantra: "Easy stuff should be easy, and hard stuff should be possible."

Furthermore, XBRL was designed by a committee, which anyone could join. In addition, any member could participate and push for what he desired. As with any committee-based design, XBRL isn't perfect. Neither is any other standard. Finally, during the creation of XBRL, many other Web standards were still in development and were unavailable for use.

Because of the tradeoffs made in the development of XBRL, XBRL has issues that may need to be overcome in certain situations or use cases. The following sections discuss tradeoffs made in the development of XBRL and provide insight on how to overcome any negative impacts.

XBRL uses XML

It may seem like an obvious choice today, but XML was an upstart in 1998 when XBRL got started. Perhaps you've heard the phrase, "Standing on the shoulders of giants," which was another mantra of those deciding the architecture of XBRL. The World Wide Web Consortium (W3C), the giant in this case, was working on a lot of different specifications to support XML. For example, specifications for encrypting XML or digitally signing an XML document didn't exist at the time. But everyone anticipated that they would exist, so XBRL didn't address these issues, but instead planned to leverage what the W3C would eventually create. As a result, users of XBRL can make use of W3C standards for encrypting and digitally signing their XBRL.

Standing on the shoulders of giants

Because of the choice to use XML and as many of the W3C specifications as possible, some things are easier, and some things are harder. If different choices were made, different things would be harder, and different things would be easier. With this decision, the right things are easy. For example, XBRL routinely gets criticized for using XLink to express additional information (resources) and relations. XBRL could have re-created a linking mechanism (what XLink already provided), creating a solution that more closely met XBRL's need, but the linking approach would be proprietary to XBRL. However, the folks building XBRL would've had to expend resources to figure out all the nuances of linking things together, basically reinventing what the W3C had created with XLink.

At the time of XBRL 1.0's creation, how schemas would be expressed was unclear. XBRL 1.0 provided a document-type definition (DTD), but the XBRL creators knew that XML Schema, or something like it, would exist. As such, the creators of XBRL didn't want to re-create an approach to expressing business concepts, but rather leveraged XML Schema to express business concepts within XBRL. Likewise, rather than create an XBRL-specific approach to expressing relations, they used XLink (W3C XML language for creating and describe links) to express such relations.

XBRL is a general-purpose specification

Early in XBRL's life, before it was even called XBRL, its prototypes were mainly related to financial reporting. XBRL's early name was even focused on financial reporting, partially because those who started XBRL came from that background. But as they thought about it more and more, those early pioneers realized that what they were trying to create would have applications far beyond financial reporting. So, they made a choice to focus XBRL not just on financial reporting, but rather on business information exchange in general.

The world of business information exchange is extraordinarily complex. XBRL had to provide a common baseline for the many types of business information exchange. No one will ever use all the features or characteristics of XBRL at the same time. Most XBRL users won't have *all* the problems of business information exchange in their use cases for XBRL; they'll have a smaller set of problems. All that XBRL provides may seem excessive for these smaller use cases.

However, XBRL's users will use what they need and ignore the parts that aren't applicable to their situation. This choose-what-you-need approach is one reason XBRL is created in a modular manner.

One impact of this all-purpose nature of XBRL is that, at times, it can be too flexible and have too many options, so systems that make use of XBRL must constrain that flexibility and eliminate undesired options by using an application profile of XBRL (see Chapter 12.)

XBRL uses an atomic approach

One early and unanimous choice in the early development of XBRL was to use an atomic approach to expressing values as opposed to the more constraining content model or document model generally used by XML. The decision's primary driver was flexibility.

To understand this choice, you need to understand the two options:

- ✔ **Atomic approach:** This approach models information independently of other information to which it might relate. Separating the information from its relations to create atomic, stand-alone pieces of information is quite flexible. However, understanding information that relates to or is even dependent on other information is more challenging because information isn't bound together like more traditional XML languages, which bind information together using the XML content model.

- ✔ **Document approach:** In this approach, you can express information that depends on other information. However, this approach isn't as flexible and makes using information independently harder. This approach leverages the XML content model to bind things in order to keep them together. The content model creates one explicit hierarchical information model. The downside is that separating information for independent use is more challenging.

One of XML's greatest strengths is its hierarchical nature — its ability to express related information in the form of a content model. However, the constraint of a content model has two downsides:

- ✔ You can express only one content model, and that content model is implicit. By *implicit,* we mean that you really don't understand if the content model expresses, say, a document, a transaction, or something else. It's simply a content model and what it represents is implied.

- ✔ After you express the content model, you can't easily change it so that you can easily communicate those changes to software applications that use that information model. Basically, the document approach's content model was too constraining.

The constraining content model prevented extensibility, which was high on XBRL's priority list. For that reason, the atomic model was the obvious choice.

However, the atomic approach has some downsides. You must create relationships in order to provide human-readable renderings. For example, rendering XBRL into some human-readable formats involves another step, such as generating a usable content model, because most XML tools for rendering rely on the content model to generate the formatting.

If you feel you need to use the content model when you use XBRL, you can. However, at times, the XBRL's other pieces, which work quite well when you don't use a content model, are harder or impossible to use. For examples, XBRL Dimensions and *tuples,* or compound facts (see Chapter 22), don't work together well; think twice before you attempt to use XBRL Dimensions and tuples together. The impact of the choice to fine-tune XBRL for the atomic approach is that XBRL is quite flexible in specific areas, yet retains constraint in other needed areas.

Reuse is more important than presentation

XBRL separates the notion of expressing business information and the presentation of that business information. The XBRL creators had a hard enough time agreeing on how to *express* business information: Agreeing on every nuance of how to *present* that information would have been impossible.

This separation of the presentation and the information itself means that information users can easily make their own choices about how to present information. The information's creator doesn't dictate how to present that information.

As a result, information can be truly interactive, reformatted on the fly at the whim of the information's users. The downside is that the information's creators may not want users to have that much flexibility in terms of presentation. However, the creators can lock down the presentation. In addition, the separation of presentation and data makes presentation a little bit more difficult for creators and consumers of XBRL.

The Realities of Business Reporting . . . er . . . Information Exchange

XBRL isn't just about business reporting. Fundamentally, a business report's purpose is to exchange information, but you're not limited to using business reports for that exchange. The point is, you need to look at business information *exchange,* which business reporting is a *part* of.

The world that business operates in today is different than the world businesses operated in yesterday. Tomorrow's business environment will be different than today. The business-information-exchange environment is likewise different.

The creators of XBRL needed to make guesses about the future and give consideration to the past. The following sections discuss premises about the future that the XBRL creators were working under.

Paper has its advantages, as does digital

Paper is a convenient way to express many types of information. It's simple, it's flexible, and it's a blank slate. But paper also has its disadvantages:

✓ **Paper is physical.** Paper must be physically transferred from one place to another in order to be used by multiple parties. Copiers and fax machines made the process of multiple people using the same document simultaneously easier.

✓ **Paper is two dimensional.** Paper has only two dimensions, whereas business information can have more than two dimensions. Approaches to accommodating three dimensions — say, by repeating information and locking down specific dimensions — do work. However, as the number of dimensions increase, so do the challenges of expressing the information on this two-dimensional medium. For example, expressing sales by period, by business segment, by geographic area, by product, or by sales person is possible on paper. However, electronic pivot tables make working with the information much easier.

✓ **Paper is static.** After you get information on the paper, it's fixed, and you can't change it because the formatting of the information and the information itself are so tightly bound together.

✓ **Paper has limited richness.** You can put only certain things on paper. For example, you can't put video on paper.

Electronic "paper" formats (meaning HTML, PDF, word-processing documents, and many spreadsheets) are a little better than the "dead-tree" format of a physical piece of paper. You can create multiple copies using digital paper, and you can transfer it over the Web, but electronic paper is two-dimensional and static and has limited richness.

Why stick with paper (the dead-tree type *or* the electronic type) if other potentially better options are out there? What if we could have more than two dimensions to work with, and they were more dynamic and offered better richness?

New technologies help us visualize the vast quantities of information we have to work with today, quantities that will be even greater tomorrow. We have all heard the phrase "A picture is worth a thousand words." Visualizations can be worth a thousand pictures. For an example, check out the Moritz Stefaner Web site at `http://moritz.stefaner.eu/projects/relation-browser`. Moritz Stefaner calls itself an "information aesthetics" company. At its Web site, you can read about a radial browser the company has created to "display complex concept network structures in a snappy and intuitive manner." Moritz Stefaner has created a demo of this browser that illustrates countries and geographical features from the CIA's *The World Factbook* (see Figure 2-1).

We get into how electronic visualization tools, such as radial browsers and pivot tables, can provide more function than a piece of paper more in Chapter 6 when we discuss the notion of interactive information.

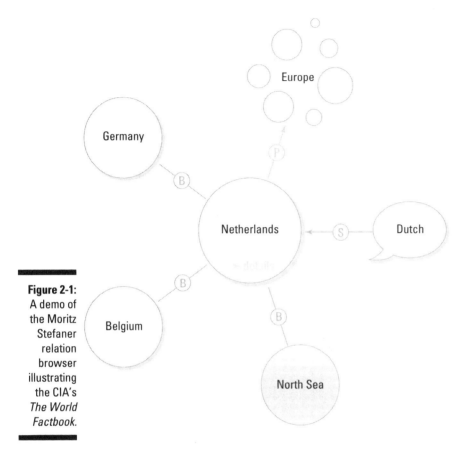

Information needs to be portable

To effectively reuse information, the information needs to have context. Simply exchanging data between business systems doesn't automate processes. Although the business system that generates the data understands the context of the generated information, if the receiving system doesn't understand that context, the data isn't reusable. To help drive home this point, a popular view of what is called the *knowledge continuum* can help you understand the differences between data, information, knowledge, and wisdom:

✔ **Data** is a piece or a set of measurable or observable value(s). Data is a set of raw facts, such as a list of names and associated addresses or the zip code 98406.

✔ **Information** is data in some context, and it's usually filtered from the complete set of all data. Information helps you understand; it informs. For example, all the customer names and addresses in your accounting system are information; the information has context because you realize that the addresses are for customers and not for suppliers.

✔ **Knowledge** is information that you can apply to solve a problem. For example, using the zip code of the customer addresses in your accounting system to find all the customers in a specific area provides you with knowledge.

✔ **Wisdom** is the application of knowledge to arrive at a decision, usually when you have multiple options. For example, using the zip code from your customer address list and knowledge of traffic patterns helps you plan where to open additional stores.

What constitutes data and what constitutes information may not seem that different, but they are. Information provides context that allows one data value to be understood in the context of other data values. In data exchanges, the contextual information is stripped from the data so that a receiving system doesn't have the required context to use the information in automated computer processes. Humans are required to reconstitute the information. Again, keep in mind that we're talking about dumb computers exchanging information, not smart humans who can look at the data and properly imply certain things. In most cases, computers simply aren't capable of correctly implying context; they do far better if given the proper context explicitly.

You can't realize the knowledge and wisdom until you correctly contend with data and information. More importantly, you can't just leap from data to knowledge. You have to grab hold of certain rungs as you try to climb to the higher levels. To exchange information effectively and make it portable between your business systems, you must exchange *information,* not data.

Syntax is not enough

Structured information has two parts: syntax and semantics. Both are important, but for different reasons:

✔ **Syntax:** The syntax of a language describes the valid form that information may take. For example, this valid fragment of XML

```
<Name>John Doe</Name>
```

doesn't give any indication of its significance or correct usage.

✔ **Semantics:** The semantics communicates the *meaning* of the information. For example, "the balance sheet must balance" or "Assets = Liabilities + Equity" is meaning.

Suppose that one business system sent another business system balance sheet information, and the balance sheet didn't balance. (Don't laugh: In Chapter 1, we discuss how financial institutions made 18,000 errors in their submissions to the FDIC.) For automated information exchanges to work, the meaning of the information must be correctly expressed during creation and correctly interpreted during receipt. This meaning, such as "the balance sheet must balance," is critical to creating reliable automated information exchange processes because it's the meaning that keeps garbage out of the information being exchanged.

When we talk about structured information, we mean information structured for *meaning* like XBRL, not information structured for *presentation* like what you'd see on an HTML Web page. There is a big difference between <bold>1000</bold> and <Sales>1000</Sales> (see Chapter 21).

You need to be explicit

Suppose that you received a piece of paper bearing the information in Figure 2-2. Could you understand that information well enough to effectively rekey that information into, say, a spreadsheet and compare the information with the same information received from ten other companies?

Example Company
As of December 31,
(Thousands of Dollars)

	2007	2006
Breakdown of Property, Plant and Equipment, Net:		
Land	5,347	1,147
Buildings, Net	244,508	366,375
Furniture and Fixtures, Net	34,457	34,457
Computer Equipment, Net	4,169	5,313
Other Property, Plant and Equipment, Net	6,702	6,149
Property, Plant and Equipment, Net, Total	**295,183**	**413,441**

Figure 2-2: Humans can understand the organization of information in this form.

Sure, you could. You'd realize that all the information relates to the company Example Company because it says so on the top of the page. You know that you need to take the numbers and multiply them by 1,000, because it says that the report is showing the information in "thousands of dollars." You know that the two columns of numbers add up because of the single underscore above and the double underscore below the total.

A computer, on the other hand, can't read that printout and imply what a human would be able to imply. All this information must be communicated explicitly.

Seems like a lot of work, being explicit and all, and it is. But it's more work to express the information implicitly and even more work to verify the implicit information is accurately articulated by manually adding up all the numbers printed on the piece of paper.

Why should humans do this? Besides, humans aren't very good at repetitive actions such as this task; they make mistakes. But computers are very good at doing the same repetitive thing over and over and over. They run into problems only when they run into something new that they don't know how to handle.

Being explicit makes information actionable. You can receive information without prior knowledge of the information, without human intervention, and without custom coding of software applications and get a computer system to do the right thing with that information.

Specialized business systems are growing

The number of specialized business systems we use is growing. Here are a few examples:

- ✔ Databases, data warehouses, data marts, and even spreadsheets
- ✔ Business-intelligence systems
- ✔ Content-management systems
- ✔ Knowledge-management systems
- ✔ Enterprise Resource Planning (ERP) systems
- ✔ Web services interfaces to these and other systems

Because of the ubiquitous, cheap connectivity offered by the Web, more and more systems, be they your internal systems or external systems of your business partners, can and will need to be integrated. Business users need simple approaches to achieve this integration. Each report is a business user exchanging information with another business user for some purpose.

Keep business rules separate

Metadata is information that describes or classifies other information. Business rules are a type of metadata: a way of expressing semantic meaning important to understanding and getting information exchanged correctly.

Another way of saying this is that business rules are a formal and implementable expression of some user requirement. Here are some examples of business rules:

- ✔ "Assets MUST equal total liabilities plus total equity."
- ✔ "If property, plant and equipment (PPE) exists on the balance sheet, then a PPE policy and a PPE disclosure MUST exist and they MUST contain. . . ."

Today, business rules are generally stored within each individual application that makes use of those business rules, which causes two problems. First, the approach to expressing the rules is different for each system expressing the business rules. The second, related, problem is that applications that use data can't exchange the business rules that support the data between applications because each system has its own format.

Because of this dilemma, the important business rules are stripped from information when that information is exchanged between applications. Typically, the business rules are re-created in the receiving system using some different proprietary form, which results in two versions of business rules that can wind up being different in many cases. But what if a global standard for expressing these business rules existed? You could express the rules once and then exchange them between applications along with the information being exchanged.

That's one of the things XBRL offers: a global standard for expressing business rules, separate from applications, that everyone — the creators of information, consumers of information, and all the parties in between — can use. That means users create the business rules just once, saving both the receiver and the sender time and improving the quality of the information exchange.

Business information exchange is a chain

Business information exchange is a chain. Most people look at business information exchange from their own perspective as one of the links in that chain. Never before has this fact been as evident as it is today with the ubiquitous connectivity offered for pennies to anyone else on the planet via the Internet. This same technology, the Web, which caused our information overload problem, will be the solution to our information overload problem.

Consider an example from the railroad industry. In the United States, during the evolution of the rail system, competing railroads used different gauges of rails as they spread all over the countryside. At first, it was done by accident because the railroads were usually so far apart and disconnected that they had no need to standardize the width of the tracks. As progress was made and tracks converged into the same cities and towns, a different reason emerged for keeping track widths different: It ensured the rail operators could force freight and passengers to shift one carrier to another.

For a while, when rail travel and transport was a novelty; people were willing to put up with the inconvenience. But as people became dependent on rails for travel and for the shipping of goods, they began to question why all this switching had to take place — especially the owners of the freight, who had to pay significant sums for the labor and time to get their goods from one carrier to the next. The desire for efficient commerce pushed the country toward a common gauge, a standard. In much the same way, commerce is pushing the need for a common approach and vocabulary for exchanging business information today.

After the standardization of the gauges, railroads still faced competition. Instead, railroads competed on the merits of their service rather than the gauge of their track. Many of the lessons from this experience remain relevant today.

Much like a materials-supply chain in manufacturing, an information-supply chain is a critical piece of logistical infrastructure enabling a far more capable organization. An information-supply chain extends upon a preexisting model in the physical world: material-supply chains. If you look at the life cycle of information across organizations, you start to see the information-supply chain.Information-supply chains are so important to understand that we devote all of Chapter 7 to explaining them in greater detail.

Chapter 3

Glancing at XBRL's Parts

*Y*ou may have heard the phrase, "Spare me the details; just give me the 50,000 foot perspective." That's what this chapter is all about: XBRL's big picture. We also introduce you to XBRL's sometimes-baffling terminology.

In this chapter, we give you a grounding in the new age of business information exchange that XBRL is ushering in. We emphasize the key ingredient that makes XBRL work, which is probably a lot simpler than you think: agreement.

Explaining XBRL in the Elevator, at the Water Cooler, or to Your Boss

Say that you were riding on an elevator, and someone said, "Hey, I just found out I have to do my reporting in some funny-named format called XBRL to such-and-such regulatory agency. But I don't even know what the heck it is. Do you know anything about XBRL?" You have about two minutes to answer before the doors ding, and you have to exit the elevator. Here's about as simple an explanation of XBRL that you can give:

> *"XBRL is an acronym for the Extensible Business Reporting Language. XBRL is a freely available, market-driven, open, global standard markup language, backed by a formal technical specification. You can use XBRL to define and model the meaning of business information so that computer applications can effectively exchange that information without any human intervention. Humans can still get everything they have today, and they still maintain control of these exchange processes. One of the primary benefits XBRL gives*

business users is the ability to cheaply and efficiently automate all sorts of business-information-exchange processes. Another is more flexibility for consumers of business information. Think of XBRL as enabling the creation of a pipeline to distribute oil or gasoline, rather than using individual tanker trucks."

Suppose that you later saw that person again at the water cooler, and he now wants more information. The following list provides you with ammunition for that discussion:

✔ **Freely available, market-driven, open, global standard:** XBRL is *global,* so it isn't the property of any one nation. *Open* means that it's freely licensed. You don't pay royalties or have to contend with restrictions to use the XBRL *standard* — standard in that it's not proprietary to any single software vendor, but rather a standard supported by many software vendors. *Market-driven* means that the business community is the group getting together to create the standard.

Standards are basically a set of commonly agreed-upon technical rules and guidelines that those implementing XBRL have agreed to follow. Standards lead to interoperability between different software applications and business systems, as opposed to non-interoperable, proprietary solutions.

✔ **Markup language:** By *markup language,* we mean a way to express information by using tags — in XBRL's case, the XML syntax. Basically, a markup language determines the structure of the tags in a file that contains business information.

✔ **Specification:** The XBRL *syntax* (the technical rules) is articulated within a technical specification called the XBRL specification. The XBRL specification defines the XBRL markup language's syntax and describes what is and isn't acceptable. XBRL uses the XML syntax and therefore follows the rules specified by the W3C's XML specification. A *specification* is a set of documents plus additional infrastructure, such as a conformance suite, which allows software vendors to test their software. XBRL is really a set of specifications.

✔ **Information:** Information is data plus context. (Chapter 2 goes into the distinction between data and information.) The biggest thing to understand is that XBRL is about information, not just data.

✔ **Meaning:** When we say *meaning,* we're talking about expressing an idea. In computer science, *semantics* refers to encoding meaning of information so that humans, as well as computers, can understand the significance of the information. Some examples of semantics are the definition of a concept, such as Cash, and rules, such as Cash is a current asset and adds up to Total Current Assets, or that you must disclose the components of cash if Cash is presented.

✓ **Computer application:** Basically, this term means software applications or business systems. Humans can do more than computers because humans are quite smart. Computers are dumb, really dumb. You have to give a computer explicit instructions to get it to do the right thing. The fact that computers are so dumb and need such explicit instructions is where the capability of defining clear rules becomes important.

✓ **Exchanged:** What *exchanged* means is that information in one place is moved (transported) to another place effectively. For example, exchange can take place from one organization to another, or from one business system to another business system.

✓ **Humans:** We humans still need to work with all this information. Information that is usable for humans isn't necessarily usable by computers. If a computer can use something, you can typically use that information for human presentation as well. If a human needs to get involved in an exchange process, it will take more time to execute, process costs will increase, and the potential for error increases.

TIP

If your boss asked you to do a presentation on why your organization might choose to use XBRL internally and you could use only one graphic, Figure 3-1 would be it. Think of each box in Figure 3-1 as a volume of resources expended. An effective exchange of business information requires a number of components, including

✓ Analysis, interpretation, and decision-making

✓ Distributing and transmitting reports

✓ Verifying, reconciling, and correcting information

✓ Rekeying and report generation

✓ Discovery and gathering information

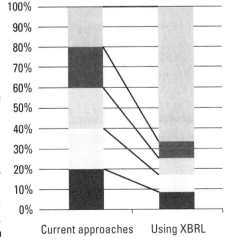

Figure 3-1:
Where XBRL saves you time and money when exchanging information.

What XBRL does is to decrease the time and money spent on nonvalue-added processes so that you can devote more attention and effort to work on the value-adding activities.

Getting the Big-Picture View of XBRL

These XBRL parts make up the whole — the organization, the specification, the taxonomies, best practices, and the software that makes everything work. You can divide the world of XBRL into the following main areas:

- **Standards bearer:** The *standards bearer* is the organization — in this case, XBRL International — that stands behind the XBRL standard. The standards bearer is a group of members that meets to collectively solve problems so that each member doesn't individually create his own solution to the same problem. In XBRL's case, the problem is the exchange of business information.

- **Specifications:** One thing that XBRL International created was a specification, or really a family of specifications. XBRL is, among other things, a specification for how to articulate business information so that computer applications can exchange that information. (See the upcoming section "The XBRL family of specifications.")

- **Taxonomies:** One of the things you can do with the XBRL specification is to create taxonomies that allow information to be exchanged in a way computers can understand. Taxonomies aren't *exactly* the same as dictionaries, but they're close enough for our purposes here. (Chapter 17 explains the differences.) XBRL is an open standard, so anyone can create XBRL taxonomies, but some XBRL taxonomies are so important that XBRL International members helped enable their creation. One example of a taxonomy created by XBRL International is the dictionary of terms that a company needs to report its financial information per International Financial Reporting Standards (IFRS). Another example is the taxonomy for financial reporting under US GAAP. Others now maintain these early XBRL taxonomies, but XBRL International started the process. (See the upcoming section "Key common taxonomies.")

- **Best practices:** If you wanted to, you could just pick up XBRL, read the specification, and then exchange information to your heart's content. However, if you do, you'd learn some things the hard way by making mistakes — things that others have probably already learned about using XBRL in the real world — and that doesn't make sense. Best practices provide valuable guidelines gleaned from real-world experiences by using XBRL in real-world situations. These best practices also provide necessary discipline to the process of using XBRL. Best practices come both from XBRL International and production systems built by others who share information about their experiences. (See the section "Gleaning Guidance from Best Practices," later in this chapter.)

✔ **Software:** XBRL truly comes to life when software makes everything work like a well-oiled machine. The complexities of the technical specifications and knowledge of best practices are built deep into software that is enabled to create or otherwise use XBRL. (See the upcoming section "Bringing XBRL to Life with Software.")

Agreeing to Agree

XBRL may be something that you have to use because some evil regulator sent you a letter nicely asking you to submit your information, using XBRL, but you may actually *want* to use XBRL. Why? Because it provides you with something useful and/or it saves you money.

Agreement is an important element that acts as the invisible glue to make XBRL really work. Agreement among the people trying to exchange information by using XBRL isn't magic, but it certainly makes moving the technology forward easier. Other invisible dynamics that have a significant and often hard-to-see impact on XBRL include *interoperability* (agreeing to make software work together) and *formalization* (agreeing to slightly more formal processes to make the automation process possible in order to reduce costs for everyone).

Agreement

Agreement does all sorts of powerful things. Many times, agreeing on complex issues is hard or even impossible. Although there are formal agreements, agreements don't necessarily need to be formal. For example, you probably know what LOL and :-) mean. We wish we could point you to the technical specification that indicates that if you want to tell someone that you're "laughing out loud" when you text them, that the global international standard is LOL, but we can't. Agreement solves all sorts of problems, and sometimes, it certainly causes some new problems. So what is the point? If people find XBRL useful, they'll use it. If they don't, they won't.

Interoperability

Tim Bray, one of the editors of the original XML specification, said it nicely:

> *"Any nontrivial language needs an automated validator if you're going to get software to interoperate."*

One software vendor can easily create software products that interoperate with its own products. Getting two different software vendors to create products that interoperate is more challenging. Imagine the challenges of getting *every* software vendor to have interoperable software. You can do it, however. It's been done for other things; it can be done for XBRL.

Validation — making sure that everything works correctly — is key to achieving interoperability. The more that software can validate the information integrity and other such interoperability issues, the less humans have to toil to achieve effective information exchange. For example, if a computer can help ensure that things that should add up do actually add up, then automation is possible. However, if information doesn't tick and tie, automation is impossible because the information isn't reliable. Getting things to interoperate isn't magic, just a lot of hard work. Specifications, although a start, aren't enough because people create specifications, and people make mistakes.

When we say validation, we don't mean a human pops in on every process to ensure that the process is working effectively. We want humans to appear for some cases. But the benefits of XBRL are realized when we can remove humans from the equation where appropriate, and let computers do the job better and for less cost.

Formalization

A typical goal of implementing XBRL within some business process is to facilitate reliable, automated business information exchange in a defined, consistent, and orderly fashion. Face it, computers aren't as smart as you. Unlike humans, computers have no capacity for judgment. Humans, using judgment, can overcome most problems. People do ingeniously figure out how they can make these dumb tools do useful things. The problem with humans, however, is that we make mistakes, we are expensive, and if we get involved, things take more time.

What we want XBRL to do is help automatically and reliably exchange business information. We're consciously using the term *business information exchange* and not *business report* because business reports are only a subset of all the different types of business information exchanges. (We won't bring you to tears of boredom with the details of business information exchange here; see Chapter 6 for that.)

An informal ad-hoc information exchange process and a formal, prescribed information exchange are different, however:

- ✔ **Informal (ad-hoc) exchange:** Many processes today are informal ad-hoc exchanges of information, typically involving spreadsheets or word-processing documents. In this scenario, organizations with some business purpose for exchanging information rely on their human resources to define, compile, format, disperse, interpret, clarify, correct, understand, and finally agree upon the information exchanged.

- ✔ **Formal (prescribed) exchange:** There are many formal processes for exchanging information. If you make a travel reservation, think of all the systems that need to exchange information to coordinate your airline travel, your rental car, your hotel, and all the associated payment information — quite a complex set of tasks to wire together. However, doing so vastly improves the user experience and saves fellow travelers boatloads of money. Well, computers can replace humans for thousands of less complex processes (but, of course, not every process).

An example of an informal exchange is the process of *rekeying,* which involves correctly putting information from a spreadsheet or other document into another spreadsheet or document. Guess who does this rekeying? That's right: humans. Using XBRL can reduce (but doesn't eliminate) the reliance on the human factor with its accompanying potential for error. The result is an information exchange that doesn't need the same level of interpretation, clarification, and correction that occurs in an informal ad-hoc exchange.

Computers need these formal prescribed processes to successfully meet your information exchange needs. Computers can't operate with informal processes. Just by adding discipline and formality, you can turn an informal process into a formal process, thus allowing computers to do more of the work. Some parts of the exchange may be harder, but if you look at all the aspects of the exchange together, the combined process will be significantly improved and easier. The result is an information exchange that doesn't need the same level of interpretation, clarification, and correction that takes place in an informal ad-hoc exchange. You can automate a reliable exchange process that offers a net benefit to you for expending this effort.

You still have control over deciding which processes should be formal and which ones can remain more informal; XBRL doesn't make that decision. XBRL merely enables process formalization in a standard way should you choose to automate an information exchange process.

Meeting the Standards Bearer

The standards bearer, XBRL International, is the champion and custodian of the XBRL standard. To ensure that the standard reflects business needs at a local level, the organization includes groups knows as *jurisdictions,* which focus on the progress of XBRL in their regions.

These local jurisdictions focus on the progress of XBRL in their regions and also contribute to XBRL International goals and objectives. Members of XBRL International join the consortium through their local jurisdictions, except in areas where no jurisdiction has been established.

Jurisdictions do things like

- ✔ Promote XBRL in their area
- ✔ Organize the creation of XBRL taxonomies needed for that jurisdiction
- ✔ Provide education
- ✔ Perform a marketing role, such as explaining the benefits of XBRL to governmental and private organizations in the area

The scoop on XBRL International

Established in 1999 by its members, XBRL International is a not-for-profit consortium that is the custodian of the XBRL specifications. At last count, XBRL International had about 600 members. Its members are companies and governmental agencies from around the world who worked together to create XBRL and who now work to help maintain, enhance, and promote XBRL for the benefit of both members and nonmembers.

XBRL International members decided that working together to create a standard, common solution was better than what they had been doing in the past, which was each creating different individual solutions to exactly the same problem: exchanging business information. Regular activities of XBRL International include

- ✔ **Conferences:** XBRL International sponsors conferences that are currently being held every six months. At the conferences, members and others interested in XBRL meet to conduct business, hold educational classes, discuss issues, figure out best practices, present case studies, and so on. All these things help make XBRL even better.

- ✔ **Ongoing support:** Some XBRL International members work between conference meetings to support the family of XBRL specifications. These members participate in working groups and other committees that conduct the day-to-day business of managing the XBRL standard to meet the needs of those who choose to use it.

For more information on XBRL International, see its Web site at www.xbrl.org. For a list of XBRL International members, see the members' Web page at www.xbrl.org/view members.aspx.

You can find a list of XBRL International jurisdictions on the XBRL International Web site at www.xbrl.org/jurisdictions.aspx.

The XBRL Family of Specifications

As well as being a community of practitioners and users, XBRL as a standard is literally a specification, or more correctly a family of specifications called *modules*. A *specification* is an explicit set of requirements that must be satisfied by any material or product that is to be of practical use (and thus of value) to the community that uses the standard in its own work. The family of XBRL specifications, well, specifies what the XBRL that business users exchange must look like. These technical specifications ensure that different software created by different people will work the same way in both software applications.

XBRL isn't just one specification: It's one base specification and additional modules, each of which adds specific functionality to XBRL. You start your XBRL work with the base specification and add on modules as you need that functionality. You can simply ignore the specification modules you don't need. The additional specification modules came about because people using XBRL in the real world discovered that the functionality was necessary. And rather than have each user of XBRL create the additional required functionality, the members of the consortium worked together to create modules that all users could use as needed.

Keep in mind that the rock upon which XBRL is built is the XBRL 2.1 specification, and the modules don't work with older versions of XBRL (2.0, 2.0a, or 1.0). Chapter 16 goes into more detail. Here are the modules and a bit about what they do:

- ✔ **XBRL Dimensions Specification:** The XBRL Dimensions Specification (XDT) allows XBRL taxonomy authors to define and restrict dimensional information that XBRL instance authors may then use.

- ✔ **XBRL Formula Specifications:** This collection of specifications allows XBRL taxonomy creators to express business rules within a taxonomy. These specifications also allow XBRL instance creators and users to validate XBRL instance information against those business rules. XBRL Formula enables users to programmatically generate XBRL instances based on a set of business rules.

- ✔ **XBRL Rendering Specifications:** These specifications provide standard mechanisms for rendering information contained within XBRL instances so that a human can use the information.

- ✔ **XBRL Versioning Specifications:** These specs communicate changes made to XBRL taxonomies, as well as concepts, resources, and relations contained within an XBRL taxonomy.

✔ **Generic Linkbase Specification:** The generic linkbase specification allows anyone to create new types of XBRL taxonomy resource or relations networks, which are stored in the form of a linkbase. XBRL International also uses the generic linkbase specification to define new XBRL modules.

Key Common Taxonomies

Although the XBRL taxonomies created to express certain common vocabularies are really not *directly* part of XBRL, they're an important *indirect* part of XBRL, and they certainly show what XBRL is for. XBRL International and its jurisdictions are key players in making available some of these globally used vocabularies. One example is the taxonomy that is used to report under IFRS.

A couple of important things about these XBRL taxonomies help you see what XBRL makes possible. Before XBRL, there really was no standard way to express the semantics of a domain in a form that a computer could understand. No standard language existed, which is one reason XBRL was created. But now, because XBRL exists and because XBRL is a global standard, agreeing on what syntax to use to express these semantics is possible.

Another thing is that creating the XBRL specification itself was relatively easy compared to creating, or even agreeing to create, some of the XBRL taxonomies that express business information for a domain. Two cases in point are the IFRS taxonomy and the U.S. Generally Accepted Accounting Principles taxonomy (US GAAP). The investment in person-hours that it took to create either the IFRS or the US GAAP taxonomies dwarfed the total hours needed to create XBRL itself.

Gleaning Guidance from Best Practices

Imagine that you have a good dictionary, you can speak and write the English language, you have a computer and a word processor, and you know how to type. So you can write a good mystery novel, right? Of course not. What you have are only raw materials. You need guidance or a template to turn the raw materials into a good mystery novel.

This same idea applies to XBRL. The XBRL specification explains the legal syntax that dictates how you must use XBRL. But you need more. You need a tried-and-true recipe for achieving a given result. Or, you need to spend a fair amount of time figuring out precisely the right way to write that page-turning mystery novel. This is where best practices come into play.

Best practices can provide you with a template for arriving at a desired result. Best practice guidance generally comes from people who use XBRL, figure out what does and doesn't work, and then share that insight. Using this guidance provides much-needed discipline to the process of using XBRL effectively, rather than just haphazardly coming up with a solution and hoping that it meets your needs.

Although not part of the XBRL specifications, these guidelines help bring the wisdom of experience by outlining known best practices for implementing XBRL. Some examples of these best practices that help with the creation of solid XBRL taxonomies and XBRL instances include

- ✔ **Formal best practices:** XBRL International itself created some best practices, such as Financial Reporting Taxonomy Architecture (FRTA) at `www.xbrl.org/technical/guidance/FRTA-RECOMMENDATION-2005-04-25.htm` and Financial Reporting Instance Standards (FRIS) at `www.xbrl.org/technical/guidance/FRIS-PWD-2004-11-14.htm`. FRTA and FRIS are an accumulation of good information learned over years of building financial reporting XBRL taxonomies and XBRL instances. The main purpose of FRTA and FRIS is to place additional constraints on XBRL taxonomies and XBRL instances used for financial reporting. The constraints are intended to enhance the comparability of financial information captured in XBRL. Many of these constraints are also appropriate for other nonfinancial-reporting-type XBRL taxonomies and XBRL instances.

- ✔ **Publically shared project information:** Some projects share information. For example, the U.S. Securities and Exchange Commission shared the architecture document for the US GAAP Taxonomies (UGT) with the public at `http://xbrl.us/Documents/SECOFM-USGAAPT-Architecture-20080428.pdf`. The SEC invested tens of thousands of dollars creating this architecture, which provides insight into what you need to consider when determining your XBRL architecture. Why reinvent the wheel?

- ✔ **Grassroots efforts:** Less formal, but just as useful, are grassroots efforts to determine the best ways to use XBRL. A grassroots effort by several individuals with significant XBRL expertise (Charlie was one) analyzed most of the existing high-quality, publicly available XBRL taxonomies and noticed many characteristics, both good and bad, of these XBRL taxonomies and the resulting XBRL instances. The analysis, published in a white paper, created an approach to creating XBRL taxonomies and XBRL instances that maintained all the good characteristics, but minimized the negative ones. The group even created an architecture called XBRL Simple Application Profile, which explains the approach and allows anyone to use it. At the very least, you can learn a lot about XBRL from this information, or you can use that architecture rather than inventing your own recipe. See `http://xbrl.squarespace.com/xbrls` for a summary of the problem, a specification that solves the problem, business cases and examples that show you how to use the application profile, and other information to help you discover whether this application profile might help you.

To avoid having to type these long links, go to `www.dummies.com/go/xbrl`. This takes you to a landing page where you can click the link you need.

Bringing XBRL to Life with Software

XBRL-enabled software solutions shield users from complexities of the XBRL specifications while delivering the rich functionality users need to complete their business tasks. All the complexity of business information exchange doesn't go away, but the software absorbs it, shielding the user from complexity.

Whether you realize it, you experience the same kind of shielding when you use a spreadsheet program, a Web browser, or even a word-processing program. Each program offers you an intuitive and simplified experience while you perform complex tasks. You never need to deal with the underlying technologies: The software does that for you, thanks to smart programmers.

XBRL truly comes to life within software. Actually, XBRL itself doesn't really come to life: It's more that your business information comes to life. As Christopher Cox, ex-chairman of the U.S. SEC, says, with XBRL, you get "interactive data." No longer is your information locked into a single format on a piece of paper, word-processing document, or spreadsheet.

But do a few applications that generate or consume XBRL, basically creating islands of XBRL, really have any value? Not really. To reach its full potential, XBRL must be supported by not only new applications, but also your existing business systems.

Two broad classifications of software can make use of XBRL:

 ✔ **Existing software applications:** These are all the existing applications in the world that you may need to input or export XBRL to or from. For example, if you have an ERP system, you want to get information out of that system and into XBRL, so the software vendor likely needs to modify the system.

 ✔ **XBRL-specific software:** These applications enable you to work with XBRL, including XBRL validators, XBRL taxonomy-creation tools, and XBRL instance-creation tools.

Having a few software applications that can generate and consume XBRL doesn't get you or anyone else where you want to be. The more software that supports XBRL, the more useful XBRL is to you and others. Going to the software superstore and buying one XBRL software application and then trying to understand how XBRL benefits you will leave you unsatisfied.

Features of XBRL in software and XBRL-specific software

In general, the types of features and functionality that XBRL-specific software performs or that are embedded with your business systems generally fall into these broad categories:

- **XBRL processors:** The principle piece of XBRL software is the *XBRL processor* (or *XBRL processing engine*, as some people call it). Pretty much every other software tool that uses XBRL likely has an XBRL processor underneath it, serving that software application. XBRL processors do the heavy lifting, such as reading, validating, and, when needed, working with all that XBRL.

- **Viewing:** You need a way to look at information expressed in XBRL, for example, to see whether that information is correct. You also want to look at XBRL taxonomies in order to understand them, even if you never create one. You use viewer-type software applications to view these taxonomies. XBRL instance viewers help you read those documents. Taxonomy viewers, well, they help you have a look at XBRL taxonomies. Keep in mind that if you're looking at an XBRL instance, you'll also likely to want to look at the underlying XBRL taxonomy.

- **Creation and editing:** Although viewing is helpful, you also need to *create* XBRL instances and XBRL taxonomies, which is where instance- and taxonomy-creation and editing software comes in. Again, if you're creating or editing an XBRL instance, you need, at a minimum, to view the XBRL taxonomy. You also may need to edit the taxonomy if you're allowed to add concepts and relations and so on. Further, you may need additional functionality, such as the ability to create business rules that you want to put into your taxonomy.

- **Analysis:** That "someone else" you give your information to may be analyzing it and will likely want to view that XBRL instance information. To do so, they need to view the XBRL taxonomy upon which the XBRL instance is based. To do comparisons across different periods or across different providers of information, they need combined XBRL instances. What you may not expect is that they may also want to create XBRL taxonomies so that they can change the view that they see of the information they receive, or they may want to add information, such as ratios, additional computed values, and so on, to an XBRL instance and therefore an XBRL taxonomy.

✔ **Other software:** Some examples of other functionality you may need include the ability to perform different levels and types of validation, storage of all that XBRL within some sort of database, versioning XBRL taxonomies and XBRL instances, cache copies of XBRL taxonomies locally on your computer, and mapping XBRL to other information formats or other formats to XBRL or even one XBRL taxonomy to another. Clever XBRL search applications may even be in the future. And then there are all those utility applications for doing different odds-and-ends and one-off tasks.

Be sure to check out Chapter 14, where we drill into software in more detail.

A word about the XBRL processor

The XBRL processor or XBRL processing engine is a key piece of software, and you need one to do anything serious with XBRL. If you look at XBRL outside the framework of an XBRL processor, it's tough to see why XBRL has *any* value. This perspective is the wrong one, and we mention it here because many have made that mistake, and we don't want you to fall into that category.

XBRL was built anticipating that an XBRL processor, not just an XML parser, would be used. An XBRL processor understands the semantics of XBRL, not just the syntax of XML. XML parsers don't understand XBRL semantics. In fact, XML parsers understand only syntax. Although XBRL processors do understand syntax, they're all about the semantics of information, which is why XBRL processors are so valuable in working with XBRL.

XBRL processors do provide services such as validation to be sure that you're following the XBRL specification and best practices, that your XBRL taxonomy information model (basically how the taxonomy is constructed) is properly and consistently constructed, and other boring stuff like that, which helps ensure interoperability between the software applications that use XBRL. Business users take all these services for granted because they're all done behind the scenes, and they don't have to bother with it (nor should they be bothered). What business users care about are whether everything ticks and ties and foots and cross-casts and that the integrity of their information is accurate per their business rules. Accurate business information boils down to ensuring that information integrity is correct and that they're complying with the rules that they're accountable for.

Being sure that the business information is right is why XBRL was created, and XBRL processors, behind the scenes, specialize in helping users achieve that goal. XML parsers aren't even in the ball park of doing what an XBRL processor can do. Can you make it so that your software can do all these things? Sure, you can. But you'd basically end up re-creating an XBRL processor, and why would you do that if you can simply go buy one? Sometimes, though, you have reasons to build your own. Just realize that you have options, and you have to make this decision for yourself.

Middleware software vendors offer several commercial versions of XBRL processors, and numerous groups have created open-source XBRL processors. Chapter 14 discusses software and even tells you where you can get one of these XBRL processors.

Looking at XBRL Logically

The XBRL specification articulates physically what XBRL must look like. But many times, looking at XBRL logically instead of physically makes understanding what you're looking at easier. Take, for example, the logical model of a spreadsheet, which goes something like this:

- An electronic spreadsheet is made up of workbooks.
- A workbook contains many sheets.
- A sheet contains rows and columns.
- Rows and columns intersect, and that intersection is called a *cell*.

Maybe you never think about the logical model of a spreadsheet, and that's good: It means that the logical model is being communicated so well that it disappears into the background.

Keep in mind the following as we discuss XBRL from a logical perspective:

- The creator of business information and the information consumer may speak different languages. But creators and consumers agree on one universal thing : They don't like "geeky" looking stuff.
- Information is text or numeric. Numeric information can perhaps be associated with one of a number of different currencies.
- Information is reported under different scenarios, such as budgeted or actual, audited or unaudited, and consolidated or unconsolidated.
- Information is provided in a set, such as the set of information for the end of the year for 2009, or the set of information for Company A versus the set of information for Company B.
- Information is aggregated in multiple ways. For example, trade accounts receivable may be aggregated by category, by current/noncurrent portions, or by its net/gross components. These three ways of looking at the details all add up to the exact same total.

Because situations like the preceding ones exist within business reporting, XBRL has to provide the capabilities to express information for such situations. XBRL needs to be able to handle many other types of situations; the preceding examples just provide a taste. When working with XBRL, it helps to fit such situations into a model that you understand.

Framing a Logical Perspective to Understand XBRL

Although XBRL doesn't have a formal logical model, a high-level model can be effectively implied. (Chapter 4 covers the gory details, and Chapter 1 provides an introduction to XBRL.) Figure 3-2 provides a graphical view of XBRL's logical model, kindly provided by Charlie, freely useable under a creative common license.

In the XBRL specification, XBRL is broken down into two broad components that establish the pinnacle of the logical model:

✔ **XBRL taxonomy:** An XBRL taxonomy is something similar to a dictionary used by an XBRL instance.

✔ **XBRL instance:** An XBRL instance is a business report built in a special way and published in a special format.

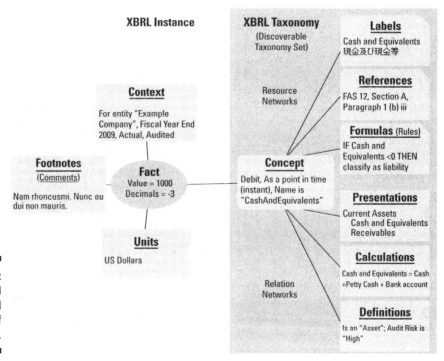

Figure 3-2:
A high-level
logical
model of
XBRL.

XBRL taxonomies express meaning

An XBRL taxonomy expresses meaning, a controlled vocabulary, used by an XBRL instance. This meaning is expressed in three forms:

- **Concepts:** XBRL taxonomies express technical representations of business terms. The XBRL taxonomy can define business terms itself, or it can point to definitions of business terms that exist outside the XBRL taxonomy. For example, NetIncomeOrLoss is the name of a concept that a taxonomy might express.

- **Relations:** XBRL taxonomies express relationships between concepts. For example, an XBRL taxonomy can express the relation between the concepts NetIncomeOrLoss and Sales and Expenses. XBRL provides three types of relations: presentation, calculation, and definition (see Chapter 4). You can also create your own types of relations, if you want.

- **Resources:** XBRL taxonomies add information to a concept. For example, the easier-to-read English label Net Income (Loss) is a resource associated with the concept NetIncomeOrLoss expressed within an XBRL taxonomy. You add a resource to express another label in another language. XBRL provides three types of resources: labels, references, and formulas (see Chapter 4). You can also create your own types of resources, if you want.

These three different mechanisms, within an XBRL taxonomy, for expressing meaning work together and provide what is necessary to express the business meaning needed to effectively communicate and exchange business information.

XBRL instances communicate and transport information

An XBRL instance provides a means to publish and transport business information. An XBRL instance is a physical document, just like other documents you're familiar with: a word-processing document, a spreadsheet, or maybe a PDF file. XBRL instances contain the following:

- **Reference to XBRL taxonomies:** XBRL instances always reference one or more XBRL taxonomies that establish the concepts, relations, and resources used by the XBRL instance.

✔ **Contextual information:** XBRL instances express contextual information needed to properly understand a fact value. For example, the period a fact value relates to is an example of context. Numeric information has a need for additional context information — for example, units. (Do the numbers refer to grams, dollars, degrees, or some other unit of measure?)

✔ **Facts:** XBRL instances report facts. A *fact* is information being reported. A fact is always associated with a concept from an XBRL taxonomy. A *fact value* is the value for a concept from the XBRL taxonomy within a specific context. Fact values can be text or numeric. For example, the value 1000 may be for the concept NetIncomeOrLoss and the period 2009 and expressed in EUROS.

✔ **Footnotes:** XBRL instances can also contain miscellaneous comments. In XBRL, comments are known as *footnotes* (not to be confused with what an accountant calls a footnote in a financial report).

An XBRL instance is always associated with one or more XBRL taxonomies. The XBRL taxonomies aren't physically within the XBRL instance, but are generally available via the Web or a private intranet or extranet. They always need to be available because the XBRL taxonomies are critical to understanding the fact values within an XBRL instance.

Networks provide options

Relations and resources exist within networks. A network provides you with options, more than one way of expressing a relation or resource. If you have, say, two ways to express a relation, there will be two relation networks. Networks simply provide the logical separation between the sets of relations or resources. You can have categories (or roles) of relation or resource networks. This setup simply allows for grouping similar things together.

Looking at networks from the opposite perspective and providing an example can help you understand what a network does: Imagine that you had two ways to express the components of concept Trade Receivables, Net:

✔ Trade Receivables, Net = Trade Receivables, Gross less Allowances for Doubtful Accounts

✔ Trade Receivables, Net = Trade Receivables, Net, Current plus Trade Receivables, Net, Noncurrent

How would you separate these two relations within an XBRL taxonomy? That is what a network does, creating physically and logically separate sets of relations or resources so that you can express more than one set of relations in a way a computer can understand. Otherwise, a computer can't keep the relations or resources straight.

XBRL taxonomies are flexible sets

XBRL taxonomies associated with an XBRL instance should be looked at as a *discoverable taxonomy set* (DTS). The set of XBRL taxonomies can include only one XBRL taxonomy, or it can include multiple XBRL taxonomies that work together to provide the meaning needed by the XBRL instance.

Creators of an XBRL instance can, but aren't required to, change the DTS. The process of adding your own XBRL taxonomy to modify another XBRL taxonomy is known as *extension*. Extensions can add new concepts, resources, or relations. They can also indicate that specific resources or relations aren't to be used by adding new pieces to the DTS. Basically, XBRL taxonomies are flexible.

Chapter 4

An XBRL Primer

*I*n this chapter, we take a look at the physical "stuff" of XBRL, and we have to tell you that there are some tags and angle brackets. We expose XBRL to you in layers or levels, with each level building on the previous. Not everyone needs to understand XBRL at each level. Business users interact with XBRL through software tools. Good business-user software tools should hide the technical aspects of XBRL from you. We don't teach you how to use software tools here; rather, we give you a solid grounding in XBRL so that when you pick up those tools, you'll know enough about XBRL to quickly become comfortable with *any* XBRL tool.

We don't try to cover every nuance of XBRL in this chapter: That would be overwhelming for most of you. Instead, we focus on the important details you really need to know. We provide a solid foundation of things you'll use all the time and provide a framework you can use to grow from, if you need to. We even point you to the appropriate resources that you can use to drill into any additional details, if your heart so desires.

Getting Ready for a Geek-Fest of XBRL

In this chapter, we show you XBRL fragments from a basic but complete XBRL taxonomy and XBRL instance that you can find here:

- ✔ **XBRL taxonomy:** `http://xbrl.squarespace.com/storage/examples/Example.xsd`

- ✔ **XBRL instance:** `http://xbrl.squarespace.com/storage/examples/Example-instance.xml`

Go to www.dummies.com/go/xbrl to avoid having to type these long links. This takes you to a landing page where you can click the link you need.

We want to keep the code fragments to a minimum and as simple as possible. This chapter's code fragments are focused to help you zoom in specifically on the current discussion. All this chapter's fragments come from these basic examples. The examples provide you with a perspective to see where the focused fragments we're discussing fit into an overall XBRL instance or XBRL taxonomy.

Grasping the XBRL Framework

The XBRL Specification doesn't actually provide a logical model. At XBRL's highest levels, we can, however, imply a logical model. As we dig deeper into XBRL, though, we rely on XBRL's physical model in order to explain it.

The core of XBRL is the XBRL 2.1 Specification (www.xbrl.org/Spec Recommendations). Modules build upon the base XBRL specification, providing additional functionality. You choose whether to use other XBRL modules based on your needs. In this chapter, we stick with the base XBRL Specification. (Chapter 16 gets into the other XBRL modules.)

The XBRL Specification provides a framework that divides XBRL into two main parts:

- ✓ **XBRL taxonomies**, which are XML schemas that define the concepts and articulate a controlled vocabulary used by XBRL instances, and XLink linkbases, which provide additional information about those concepts.

- ✓ **XBRL instances**, which contain the facts being reported, along with contextual information for those facts.

We break our explanation of XBRL into two parts: XBRL taxonomies and XBRL instances. An XBRL taxonomy has a lot more moving parts to it than an XBRL instance. But XBRL taxonomies and XBRL instances interact with each other. We put these two pieces of the XBRL framework together and explain how the two interact.

After we cover these key parts, we drill into the pieces that make up an XBRL taxonomy and an XBRL instance. We give you the level of understanding of the important details that you need without overwhelming you with areas of XBRL you'd likely never run across.

XBRL for XML geeks

If you happen to be knowledgeable about XML, you may find these tips useful:

✔ XBRL has an XML schema (see `www.xbrl.org/2003/xbrl-instance-2003-12-31.xsd`), which defines how you create XBRL taxonomies and XBRL instances.

✔ Another schema describes how to create XBRL Linkbases (see `www.xbrl.org/2003/xbrl-linkbase-2003-12-31.xsd`).

✔ If you're familiar with traditional approaches to creating XML languages, when you first look at XBRL, you may get confused. XBRL doesn't just build a traditional XML schema that explains how instances are to be created. What XBRL does is build a layer on *top* of what XML provides that is used to create a metalanguage, which is used to create in part something you may be familiar with, an XML Schema.

✔ In XBRL, a taxonomy schema (which is part of an XBRL taxonomy) serves the same function as an XML Schema. A taxonomy schema defines XML elements and attributes, just like XML languages normally do. But XBRL adds metadata needed for business reporting, such as period information

and whether a concept is a point in time, for a period of time, and so on. This additional metadata is common in business reporting, so XBRL adds it to the schema. The taxonomy schema is the XML Schema, which articulates how to create XML instances in XBRL.

✔ Another part of an XBRL taxonomy is the linkbase. You can add metadata to the XBRL taxonomy via the use of linkbases. While not required, linkbases provide useful information for understanding an XBRL taxonomy and using an XBRL instance. Linkbases enable the expression of many kinds of semantics.

✔ XML Schema elements with a specific `substitutionGroup` attribute value are XBRL concepts. All XBRL concepts are global because of the way XML Schema `substitutionGroup` attributes work. This makes the elements of a taxonomy schema a flat list. You can use linkbases to add any number of hierarchies to that flat schema.

✔ An XBRL user should work with the help of an XBRL processor, not just an XML parser. In most cases, you'll drive yourself mad if you try to use XBRL with only an XML parser.

A big part of the XBRL framework is the flexibility offered by XBRL's extensibility. We show you how XBRL's extension capabilities are provided by XBRL taxonomies and used by XBRL instances. After introducing the important key ideas, we drill into the key notions to expand your level of understanding in a few specific areas. We finally point you to other chapters that expand on the foundation we lay in this chapter.

Discovering Fundamentals of XML for XBRL Users

As XBRL is an XML language, we need to tell you a little about eXtensible Markup Language (XML). XML is a language for creating markup languages, which XBRL is. XBRL is an XML language. XBRL uses other pieces of the XML family, including namespaces, XML Schema, XML Base, XLink, XPath, and XPointer.

If you want to dig into the details of XML, we recommend Lucinda Dykes and Ed Tittel's *XML For Dummies* (Wiley).

Exploring XBRL Taxonomy Parts

XBRL taxonomies have various physical pieces and express concepts, resources, and relations (see Chapter 3). These pieces, described in the following sections, work together to provide the functionality you need to express the meaning of business information that is to be exchanged.

Taxonomy schemas and linkbases

XBRL taxonomies are comprised of two parts:

- ✔ **Taxonomy schemas** are the XML Schema part of the XBRL taxonomy. Taxonomy schemas contain concept definitions that take the form of XML Schema elements. For example, the business concept Cash may be an XML Schema element that has a name attribute value of `"Cash"` and other attributes.

- ✔ **Linkbases** are the XLink part of the XBRL taxonomy and are also XML documents. The term *linkbase* is an abbreviation for link database. Linkbases are physical things used to express a logical thing, networks. Networks come in two types: resource and relation. (We explain networks, resources, and relations in the upcoming section "Networks and extended links.") Resource and relation networks are expressed in the XLink syntax in the form of what is called an *extended link*.

Extended links are basically containers that hold the data contained within linkbases. We don't want to get into a big technical discussion of extended links here; if you want that, read the XLink specification at `www.w3.org/TR/xlink`. Chapter 22 provides more information on XLink and linkbases.

Discoverable taxonomy sets

A single XBRL taxonomy may be comprised of a set of multiple taxonomy schemas and linkbases. This set has a specific and important name in XBRL: *discoverable taxonomy set* (DTS).

A DTS is governed by discovery rules, specified by the XBRL Specification, that XBRL processors understand. A DTS can contain any number of taxonomy schemas and/or linkbases and can start from either a taxonomy schema, a linkbase, or an XBRL instance.

Networks and extended links

Networks are a logical aspect of XBRL expressed physically as a set of linkbases. Linkbases exist within the physical model and are collections of extended links. Extended links work slightly differently in XLink than they do in XBRL. In XLink, each extended link is physically separated. In XBRL, a role attribute is added to an extended link. A network is a collection of all the extended links of a specific type with the same *extended link role*. An extended link role is nothing more than a unique identifier expressed as a role attribute of an extended link.

You use networks to separate and organize resources and relations. Networks have different extended link roles and different unique identifiers, which creates the separation. Network roles and extended link roles are exactly the same thing. The creators of XBRL taxonomies define these roles within taxonomy schemas.

Resources and relations within networks

Physically, networks come in two types categorized by the type of extended links they use:

✔ *Resource networks* provide additional information about a concept. The additional information is in the form of an XLink resource. Of the five standard types of linkbases, label and reference are resource linkbases, and they express resource networks. Resources can have different resource roles to help further categorize resources. An example of additional information is an English label, Property, Plant and Equipment, with a standard role that is associated with the concept of the name `PropertyPlantAndEquipment` within a taxonomy schema. An example of a reference is a URL to a company's accounting manual or, say, some descriptive information about the chapter, section, subsection, or page of that manual.

✔ *Relation networks* express relations between concepts using XLink arcs. Of the five standard types of linkbases, presentation, calculation, and definition are relation linkbases, which they express as relation networks. Relations (expressed as an XLink arc) can have different arc roles to help further categorize relations. An example of a relation network is the presentation network with the network role Balance Sheet that indicates that the concept `PropertyPlantAndEquipment` is part of that Balance Sheet and related to Assets.

Identifying XBRL Instance Parts

Compared to XBRL taxonomies, XBRL instances are simple and straightforward. XBRL instances are single physical files that contain the following pieces: references to DTS information, facts, contexts, units, and footnotes. All these components help you use that business information on your terms.

We encourage you to refer Chapter 3. We drill into the explanations of each of these parts later in this chapter in the section "Drilling into XBRL Instances." We devote all of Chapter 18 to explaining XBRL instances in even more detail.

Achieving Flexible Business Information Exchange

XBRL taxonomies and XBRL instances provide for business information exchanges, the fundamental objective of XBRL. Key relationships between the components in this chapter are critical to understanding XBRL. This understanding can make the difference between making XBRL meet your needs and fighting XBRL at every step along the way. This section explains these key ideas both logically and how they're physically implemented.

Defining concepts and organizing with taxonomy schemas

Concepts are defined in taxonomy schemas, which are really XML schemas. The XBRL concepts are XML Schema elements. Basically, XBRL leverages XML Schema as the means of defining XBRL concepts. XBRL adds a few attributes to XML Schema elements.

Taxonomy schemas can point to other taxonomy schemas already defined. XBRL uses the XML Schema mechanisms (import and include) to combine sets of concepts defined in separate physical files. XBRL also provides mechanisms (schemaRef and linkbaseRef) for combining DTS components. All these taxonomy schemas become part of the DTS. These mechanisms allow you to build modular taxonomy schemas. Another discovery mechanism for taxonomy schemas is any reference from a linkbase to a taxonomy schema.

Taxonomy schemas can also point to resource or relation networks that likewise become part of the DTS.

Using networks to separate and organize sets of resources

Resource networks are physically contained in XLink linkbases in the form of extended links with a specific role. A resource defined within these networks allows you to add information to the XBRL concepts defined in the taxonomy schema. XBRL provides two types of resource networks in the XBRL specification: labels and references. (See the section "Drilling into Resource Networks," later in this chapter, for more information.) The XBRL modules add other types of resources, such as formulas and formatting information (see Chapter 16). You can add your own types of resources using the Generic Linkbase specification (see Chapter 16). Taxonomy schemas or XBRL instances can connect a resource network to the DTS.

Separating and organizing sets of relations by using networks

XLink linkbases physically contain relation networks in the form of extended links with a specific role. Relation networks allow you to associate one concept with another concept in various ways for many purposes. XBRL provides three types of relation networks in the XBRL specification: presentation, calculation, and definition. (See the section "Drilling into Relation Networks " later in this chapter, for more information.) You can add your own types of relations using the Generic Linkbase specification; refer to Chapter 16. Taxonomy schemas or XBRL instances can connect a relations network to the DTS.

Exchanging facts with XBRL instances

XBRL instances contain the information that is being exchanged. That information is expressed in the form of facts. Each fact is associated with a concept from an XBRL taxonomy, which expresses the concept and either defines it or points to a definition of the concept external to the XBRL taxonomy by using one or more XBRL references. Concepts are associated with an XBRL instance by being part of the DTS. Other information in networks connected to the XBRL instance provides additional information that helps you understand and use the facts within an XBRL instance. Contextual information is also associated with facts to help further explain things like which entity and which period a fact relates to. Numeric information has additional contextual information called units. You can use XBRL footnotes (not to be confused with what an accountant calls a footnote) to communicate additional information, such as comments.

Gaining flexibility through extension

The ability to express concepts, resources, and relations is well and good, but if the XBRL taxonomy isn't exactly what you want, guess what? You can change it. This characteristic is why XBRL is called the Extensible Business Reporting Language. One of the most powerful features of XBRL is that it's dynamic when it needs to be. Although this extensibility is there if you need it, you don't have to use it.

XBRL's need for extensibility makes the physical syntax level seem somewhat confusing. All these separate components provide the required flexibility needed to make XBRL's extensibility work as needed. The good news is that XBRL processors hide much of this physical syntax from you. The logical view of XBRL is much easier to work with.

We get into the details of how extensibility works later in the section "Gaining Flexibility Through Extension"; for now, just realize that it exists. You never change someone else's taxonomy schema or linkbases, but you can create your own taxonomy schemas or linkbases, which add to or change things others have defined by becoming part of the DTS. You can even nullify what exists in someone else's taxonomy, rendering it unusable. As such, you can change the overall DTS, effectively virtually changing what you should never change physically. Further, the users of the XBRL instance information can clearly see the changes you've made because you communicated those changes in the form of an XBRL taxonomy that is part of the DTS.

Achieving interoperability through validation

Does all this stuff seem complex? Business reporting *is* complex; sometimes incredibly complex. The good news is that computers, not you, deal with this complexity. Software guides you through the process, makes sure that you follow the rules of XBRL, and otherwise helps you achieve your goals. Software verifies that everything is okay by checking to be sure that your code doesn't have any errors, a process known as *validation*. You can make a mistake in lots of different ways and places, so you can check for errors in many different ways. (Chapter 12 covers validation in detail.)

Demystifying the DTS

XBRL requires everything in an XBRL instance to be explicitly defined. An XBRL instance must directly or indirectly physically reference all those XBRL taxonomies whose concepts, resources, and relations have bearing on the XBRL instance's contents. The first thing an XBRL processor does when it encounters an XBRL instance is attempt to discover all its related XBRL taxonomies; if it can't, it goes no further!

Many times, when people refer to an XBRL taxonomy, they really mean DTS.

Schema files in XML and XBRL taxonomies work differently. The XBRL taxonomies must exist and be discoverable. XML can provide hints about the schema or point to a schema, or it may not provide a schema at all. Not with XBRL. Those schemas that are XBRL taxonomies must exist because the XBRL taxonomies enable you to understand the information in the XBRL instance. Figure 4-1 shows how multiple taxonomy schemas and linkbases are brought together into a DTS.

In Figure 4-1, the XBRL instance is connected to a set of two XBRL taxonomies. Each XBRL taxonomy is comprised of one taxonomy schema and two linkbases. The DTS is the combined set of all taxonomy schemas and linkbases from both XBRL taxonomies.

Note that an XBRL instance is never part of the DTS, but it can contain references to taxonomy schemas, XML Schemas, and linkbases that are part of the DTS.

Grasping the functioning of networks

When we talk about networks in this book, we're not talking about computer networks, broadcasting networks, or any other form of communication. Although *network* is clearly not an accounting or business term, it's a way to describe something that does occur in business information.

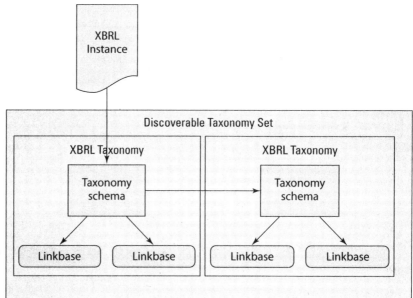

Figure 4-1:
A DTS.

Networks have two important states:

- ✔ **Unresolved or raw form:** In XBRL jargon, this state is called the *base set*. A base set is the actual physical relations in what can best be described as an unresolved or raw state. For example, if a relation is expressed between two concepts, and then another relation is created to prohibit that relation, in the base set, two relations exist. These two relations are more the physical form of the actual relations. To better understand what we mean, contrast it to the resolved form.

- ✔ **Resolved form:** In XBRL jargon, this state is called a network or a network of relations. A network is the resolved form of the set of relations. If you have two relations — one that defines a relation and a second that prohibits that relation — the resolved form of this set of relations is no relation. The resolved form of the set of relations is more the logical result of all the physical relations.

Here's an example of a network: Property, Plant and Equipment, Net is an accounting concept that would likely be designed in a calculation network in XBRL to denote their mathematical accounting relationship, shown in Figure 4-2.

Figure 4-2 shows that XBRL is saying that Property, Plant and Equipment, Net = Land + Buildings + Furniture and Fixtures + Other. To express relations in an XBRL taxonomy, you must have at least one network because all resources and relations exist within a network.

(=) Property, Plant and Equipment, Net
  (+) Land
  (+) Buildings
  (+) Furniture and Fixtures
  (+) Other

When to use networks

When you build an XBRL taxonomy, you express resources and relations within networks. Understanding why you'd use a network helps you understand what networks are. You separate relations into different networks for two general reasons:

- ✔ **Convenience:** The taxonomy creator may want to create several smaller networks rather than one big network. For example, in the US GAAP taxonomy, the information contained in the taxonomy is broken up into multiple networks. Another way that the taxonomy may have been created is by combining all those networks into one single network. Sometimes working with several smaller pieces rather than one big piece is easier. Networks allow you to create pieces, if you want.

- ✔ **Out of necessity:** Sometimes you *have* to create networks. Eliminating conflicts when one parent concept has two or more possible sets of child concepts is another reason to create a network. For example, it would be impossible to express these three different ways to arrive at the one value for Receivables, Net in one network:

  - Receivables, Net = Receivables, Gross minus Allowance for Bad Debts

  - Receivables, Net = Receivables, Net, Current plus Receivables, Net, Noncurrent

  - Receivables, Net = Trade Receivables, Net plus Financing Receivables, Net plus Other Receivables, Net, and so on

On the left side of Figure 4-3, nothing is physically separating the three ways to compute Receivables, Net. Humans can see this separation; we understand that they're distinct. But how would a computer know that they're separate? However, on the right side, see how networks physically separate the three different computations? Computers need to be told that the three computations are, in fact, separate. Otherwise, they'd collide. Networks provide that physical separation, communicating that separation to software applications.

Conflicts would exist	Networks separate conflicting computations
	Network (By Component)
Receivables, Net	**Receivables, Net**
Trade Receivables, Net	Trade Receivables, Net
Financing Receivables, Net	Financing Receivables, Net
Other Receivables, Net	Other Receivables, Net
	Network (By Net/Gross)
Receivables, Net	**Receivables, Net**
Receivables, Gross	Receivables, Gross
Allowance for Bad Debts	Allowance for Bad Debts
	Network (By Current/Noncurrent)
Receivables, Net	**Receivables, Net**
Receivables, Net, Current	Receivables, Net, Current
Receivables, Net, Noncurrent	Receivables, Net, Noncurrent

Figure 4-3:
Showing how networks help avoid conflicts.

Trying to express all three of these relations within one network would result in collisions in the relations. To get around this issue, you must use three different networks, one expressing each of the different calculation relations.

Other important aspects of networks

Here are some other important points about networks to keep in mind:

✔ You shouldn't physically change networks others created, but you can create your own networks, hide original relationships to effectively nullify them, and redefine new relations. Networks exist within a set of physical files. You may not change someone else's physical file. Instead, relations you create take precedence over the existing relations that existed, in effect creating new relations. You create new relations by prohibiting someone else's relations, creating new relations, or both. This process, in effect, creates a new set of relations and also documents exactly how you've changed what previously existed.

✔ Although you may not change someone else's taxonomy's set of physical files, you don't have to use the linkbase files that contain the relations. If you don't refer to the linkbase files, for all practical purposes, the relations don't exist in the context of the DTS because the file will never get discovered. (Chapters 17 and 18 discuss XBRL taxonomies and XBRL instance in more detail.)

✔ You can't order networks within XBRL. For example, say that you have three networks: Balance Sheet, Income Statement, and Cash Flow Statement. Users of an XBRL instance may use them in the order of Income Statement, Balance Sheet, and Cash Flow Statement. Although XBRL has no means for prescribing a specific order, you can use proprietary approaches to prescribe the specific order of networks — but keep in mind that they're proprietary and shouldn't be relied on outside of any specific piece of software that supports that proprietary approach.

✔ Users can fabricate a network to their liking without the creator of the XBRL instance being involved or otherwise consenting by using XBRL's extensibility. As a result, XBRL is sometimes called interactive data. Users can make use of the XBRL instance information as they see fit, without consideration for how the creator of the information may want it used. However, when information users do reorganize information, they take on the responsibility of getting the relations correct.

Drilling into Taxonomy Schemas

Taxonomy schemas are one of two parts of an XBRL taxonomy (linkbases being the other) for expressing the information model of XBRL instances. Taxonomy schemas have several pieces, each of which helps you express meaning relating to that information model. You don't have to use all the pieces, but you can, if you want.

The important pieces of a taxonomy schema are concepts and pointers to other concepts, resources, and relations. (We explain each piece of the taxonomy schema in the next sections.)

XML namespace prefixes add readability to XML markup. Although these prefixes aren't required, they can be anything you want (clearly within the bounds of proper XML syntax). We use these namespace prefixes when we show you XML markup:

✔ xs: XML Schema namespace

✔ xbrli: XBRL Instance namespace

✔ link: XBRL Linkbase namespace

✔ basic: Taxonomy schema of our example

Concepts

Essentially, taxonomy schemas are all about concepts, modeling the pertinent aspects of a collection of business concepts (controlled vocabulary) related to some exchange of business information. XBRL instances use concepts from a taxonomy schema to express fact values for the purpose of exchanging this information.

Concepts have the following characteristics expressed as attributes of XML Schema xs:element elements:

- ✔ **Name:** Every concept must have a name attribute. The name identifies the concept within a taxonomy schema.

- ✔ **ID:** Every concept may have an id attribute. If you're using linkbases, you need that id when you add resources or express relations because this id is how the resource or relation is connected to the concept. The id does two things. First, it uniquely identifies a concept across all taxonomy schemas. Second, relations and resources use id's (not names) as unique keys to create the connection between the relation or resource and the concept to which the relation or resource relates.

- ✔ **Type:** Every concept must have a type attribute. You may know the term as *data type* from other technologies. Data types constrain content, such as string, integer, or date. XBRL has similar primitive types, but it also has a number of more specialized types common to the business world, such as monetary or shares. You can also define your own types.

- ✔ **Substitution Group:** Every concept must have a substitutionGroup attribute, and the value of that attribute will most likely be xbrli:item, which means the element is an XBRL concept.

  Substitution groups can get pretty involved. Just realize that there is a lot to them and be careful how you use them. Ninety-nine percent of all the substitution groups you run across will be xbrli:item, which is straightforward.

- ✔ **Period Type:** Every concept must have an xbrli:periodType attribute. The xbrli:periodType provides information about the kind of period the concept relates to. Two values are most commonly used: instant and duration. An instant xbrli:periodType denotes a point in time. Conversely, a duration xbrli:periodType denotes a span of time between two instants. For example, a balance sheet reflects information as of a specific point in time, say December 31, 2008, and thus has a xbrli:periodType value of instant. An income statement reflects information for a span of time, such as "For the Year Ended December 31, 2008," or a duration from January 1, 2008 to December 31, 2008, and thus has a periodType value of duration.

Another possible value for periodType is xbrli:forever. Read the XBRL Specification for more information.

✔ **Balance:** Concepts may have a xbrli:balance attribute, but aren't required to. If it does have a value, the value must be either debit or credit. If you're an accountant, you get debits and credits. If not, you probably don't have to deal with debits and credits, or you have an accountant helping you, so go ask them about debits and credits.

Here's what a concept looks like within a taxonomy schema expressed as an XML Schema element:

```
<xs:element
 name="NetIncomeOrLoss"
 id="basic_NetIncomeOrLoss"
 type="xbrli:monetaryItemType"
 substitutionGroup="xbrli:item"
 xbrli:periodType="duration"
 xbrli:balance="credit"
 >
```

The preceding code fragment expresses the concept NetIncomeOrLoss in the form of an XML Schema xs:element element within a taxonomy schema. The element has a number of attributes. Many of these attributes are provided by XML Schema, including the name, id, type, and substitutionGroup. The xbrli:periodtype and xbrli:balance are attributes added to XML Schema by XBRL. The values for the attributes are rather straightforward; refer to the list before the code fragment.

Sometimes concepts are referred to as *elements* because they exist within the physical part of an XBRL taxonomy known as a taxonomy schema, which is an XML Schema. But not all XML Schema elements within a taxonomy are concepts. Single value XBRL facts always have a substitutionGroup value of xbrli:item, which is how you know they're XBRL concepts.

Pointers to other concepts, resources, or relations

Another piece of the taxonomy schema that you may find are references to other taxonomy schemas and linkbases. You can create references using the following elements:

✔ **Import:** You can use an XML Schema xs:import element within a taxonomy schema file to refer to another taxonomy schema or XML schema file. Each imported XML Schema has a different namespace identifier.

✔ **Include:** An XML Schema xs:include element does something similar to the xs:import element. The difference is that included files pull elements into the namespace of the file containing the include element, and included files don't contain a namespace identifier.

You will rarely use include. However, XBRL GL does make extensive use of the include element.

✔ **LinkbaseRef:** A link:linkbaseRef element or linkbase reference points to a linkbase, which contains networks of either resources or relations.

These pointers allow you to use taxonomy schemas, XML schemas, or linkbases others have created; let you modularize your taxonomy so that you or others can use some parts of your XBRL taxonomy without being forced to use other parts; and otherwise physically separate the files that make up your XBRL taxonomy.

Drilling into Resource Networks

Resource networks let you express additional information for concepts. Labels and references are two types of resource networks that the XBRL standard provides. The XBRL Formulas specification provides a third type of resource. This list explains these different types of resource networks:

✔ **Label:** Label resources, as the name suggests, allow the creator of an XBRL taxonomy to create labels for each concept in the taxonomy. Basically, they provide a more user-friendly label in place of the ugly XML element names. Another use for labels is to provide multilingual support and multidialect support. Labels also provide documentation for a concept, such as a human-readable definition of the concept.

✔ **Reference:** Reference resources allow the creator of an XBRL taxonomy to express references to external sources (such as a paragraph in a manual) that explain or further define a concept in human terms. References are pointers to a reference, not the references themselves.

✔ **Formula:** Not in the base XBRL Specification but added by the XBRL Formula Specification, formula resources allow the creator of an XBRL taxonomy to express various types of business rules. XBRL instances that make use of an XBRL taxonomy that contains these rules must comply with these rules. (See Chapter 16 for more information about XBRL Formula.)

You can express an infinite number of different types of resource networks. You can specify your own type of resource networks using the XBRL Generic Linkbase Specification (see Chapter 16).

Resources are connected to concepts in a taxonomy schema. Resources can have different resource roles, many of which XBRL predefines, but taxonomy creators can also define their own resource roles. These roles let taxonomy creators further categorize resources, if needed. (If you need to understand how to create resources, see Chapter 22.)

You can categorize resources by the preceding resource roles. This categorization helps when partitioning one type of resource from another. This resource role is different than the role of the network (extended link role), which contains the resources. Finally, remember that the resources are connected to the id element of a concept expressed within a taxonomy schema.

The documentation for each concept expressed in an XBRL taxonomy is commonly implemented as labels with a specific label role of www.xbrl.org/2003/role/documentation. XML Schema offers documentation in the form of an xs:appinfo element, but it's not standardized, not extensible, is generally ignored by most XBRL processors, can't be prohibited, and therefore is a bad idea to use.

Labels typically contain human-readable text, such as Assets. However, labels can contain XHTML markup that allow you to use labels to do all sorts of clever things. Whether these clever things are a good idea is another story. The best practices around the use of XHTML in labels have yet to be established. Be aware of this nifty feature, but be careful!

Drilling into Relation Networks

You can use the following types of standard relation networks to express relations between concepts:

- **Presentation:** Presentation relations allow you to express a simple parent-child type of relationship, basically a hierarchy. Presentation relations are primarily intended to help organize the XBRL taxonomy. You can also use presentation-type relations to help generate human-readable renderings of an XBRL instance.

- **Calculation:** Calculation relations allow you to express certain types of computations between concepts within an XBRL taxonomy. XBRL calculation relations handle only addition and subtraction, and concepts must be in the same XBRL context. This is many times helpful, but can also be somewhat limiting. Need more power in your computations? Then use XBRL Formulas (see Chapter 16).

- **Definition:** You can use definition relations for many purposes. Definition relations basically let you express any type of relation. You can define any arc role, which explains what type of relation you've created. For example, the XBRL Dimensions Specification uses definition relations to express multidimensional type relations.

You can express an infinite number of different types of relation networks. You can specify your own type of relation networks using the XBRL Generic Linkbase Specification (see Chapter 16).

Relations and the concept in a taxonomy schema to which the relation relates are connected. XBRL processors understand this connection. Relations can have different arc roles, many of which XBRL predefines, but taxonomy creators can also define their own arc roles. Arc roles differentiate or categorize relations, should you have that need.

We don't show you an example of the XML within a linkbase here because the physical XML is far too complex, and explaining these details would be more distracting than helpful. Chapter 22 has an example.

Drilling into XBRL Instances

XBRL instances are the physical documents that contain business information that is published, transferred, or otherwise exchanged. Here are the parts of an XBRL instance:

- ✔ Reference(s) to XBRL taxonomy(s)
- ✔ Contexts
- ✔ Units
- ✔ Facts
- ✔ XBRL Footnotes (that is, comments)
- ✔ Other technical odds and ends

Figure 4-4 shows the components of an XBRL instance and the relation to XBRL taxonomies that support the instance. The figure shows the components of an XBRL instance and the relations between the components on the left, the connection between the XBRL instance and the XBRL taxonomy, the relations between the XBRL instance and the XBRL taxonomy, and the relations within the XBRL taxonomy on the right.

References to XBRL taxonomies

XBRL instances always refer to an XBRL taxonomy or a set of XBRL taxonomies, collectively known as the DTS. Because the XBRL taxonomies make up the DTS that determines the controlled vocabulary and the other semantic meaning expressed by the XBRL taxonomies, you'll want to know where to get those all those XBRL taxonomy pieces. The references to these physical files tell you where to get the XBRL taxonomy pieces that explain the controlled vocabulary the XBRL instance uses and all the other meaning expressed for the information model by the DTS.

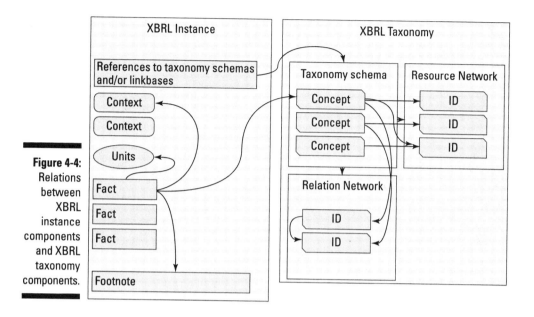

Figure 4-4:
Relations
between
XBRL
instance
components
and XBRL
taxonomy
components.

An XBRL instance can refer to pieces of the DTS in two ways:

- **SchemaRef:** A link:schemaRef element, or schema reference, points to a taxonomy schema file or an XML schema file. Those files can contain references to even more files. These physical files may be components others created or components created by you that express new concepts, relations, or resources used by your information model or that modify the information of other XBRL taxonomies you refer to. Your modifications are commonly referred to as an *extension*.

- **LinkbaseRef:** A link:linkbaseRef element, or linkbase reference, points to a linkbase that contains relations or resources. The linkbases themselves generally reference the taxonomy schemas that contain the concepts associated with that linkbase.

You can connect linkbases directly to XBRL instances with a `linkbaseRef`. Alternatively, you can use a `schemaRef` to connect linkbases to a taxonomy schema, which then references one or more linkbases.

An XBRL processor is responsible for grabbing all the referenced XBRL taxonomy pieces that make up the DTS, putting all the pieces together correctly, and communicating any issues relating to that process to the user of the XBRL instance.

Here is an example schemaRef:

```
<link:schemaRef xlink:type="simple" xlink:href="Example.xsd" />
```

The preceding code fragment shows a schema reference to the taxonomy schema with the name `Example.xsd`. A linkbase reference is similar, with the only difference being a different element name.

Software can add linkbases to a DTS dynamically by connecting the linkbase to the XBRL instance. For example, consider an XBRL instance that refers to an XBRL taxonomy that has only English labels in it. Suppose that someone else creates a linkbase that provides Spanish labels for that same XBRL taxonomy. Further, suppose that your native language is Spanish, and you'd prefer to use those Spanish labels, but the linkbase isn't physically connected to the XBRL instance. No problem! All you have to do is load the XBRL instance, which will automatically load the DTS that the XBRL instance points to. Then you use your software to point to the linkbase with the Spanish labels. Voilà! You can use the Spanish labels! Pretty slick, eh? That is why XBRL is sometimes referred to as interactive data.

You can use the same approach to reorganize the way you view XBRL instance information. If you don't like the way the creator of the XBRL instance or XBRL taxonomy organized the information, you can simply reorganize the instance information by creating your own XBRL taxonomy extension. You can then use your view, provided by your XBRL taxonomy, instead of the XBRL instance creator's view of the information it contains.

Giving facts context

Contextual information helps users of the information in the XBRL instance understand the context in which the information is being used. Context is provided using the xbrli:context element, which contains

- ✔ **ID:** Every context within an XBRL instance has an id that uniquely identifies the context so that one or more fact values can refer to it. A context id attribute can look something like X10B72009. These IDs have no meaning, other than to uniquely identify the context. They're like an identification number. The meaning is expressed within the elements and attributes of the context.

- ✔ **Entity:** The xbrli:entity element is part of the context and has two pieces; the first is required, and the second is optional. The required piece is the xbrli:identifier element. The scheme attribute of the xbrli:identifier element communicates which identification scheme is being used. The value of the xbrli:identifier is the actual identifier from that scheme. For example, the U.S. SEC has a numbering system called a CIK number. XBRL instances going to the SEC use a pointer to that scheme, which may be something like www.sec.gov/CIK. The identifier value is the actual CIK number, such as 0000066740.

The second and optional piece of information is the entity xbrli:segment element. You can put any information you desire into the xbrli:segment element in order to provide information that helps users gain needed contextual information to understand the fact value. Note that the XBRL Dimensions specification is a way to express this type of contextual information, and the use of XBRL Dimensions information in the xbrli:segment element is emerging as a best practice. However, any valid XML is allowable, other than XBRL. (We discuss XBRL Dimensions in Chapter 16.) You can express an infinite number of elements within a segment.

✔ **Period:** The xbrli:period element communicates contextual information about the period to which a fact value relates. The xbrli:periodType attribute is defined within a taxonomy schema. The xbrli:periodType on a concept within the taxonomy schema must match the period used within a context used on that concept. The two common xbrli:periodType values are

  - **Instant:** If the XBRL taxonomy concept defines the concept as an instant, the element used within the period will be xbrli:instant and will contain a single date — for example, <xbrli:instant>2009-12-31</xbrli:instant>.

  - **Duration:** If the taxonomy concept says duration, two elements will be within the xbrli:period, xbrli:startDate, and xbrli:endDate. Each one has a value to communicate the starting and ending dates of the duration (date range). The start date may look like <xbrli:startDate>2009-01-01</xbrli:startDate>, and the end date may look like <xbrli:endDate>2009-12-31</xbrli:endDate>.

There is one other possibility for period, but its usage is rare. The value xbrli:forever means no date is provided, and that context is always applicable.

✔ **Scenario:** The xbrli:scenario element works in a manner similar to the xbrli:segment element of the xbrli:entity context described earlier in this list. The xbrli:scenario element is optional. The xbrli:scenario element can contain any valid XML other than XBRL. One way of expressing this information is to use XBRL Dimensions, and it's becoming a best practice to use this approach. Literally, you can put any type of contextual information into the xbrli:scenario element, such as whether information is actual, budgeted, and so on. You can express an infinite number of elements within a scenario.

Putting these pieces together, here's an example of a xbrli:context element:

```
<xbrli:context id="D-2009">
 <xbrli:entity>
  <xbrli:identifier scheme="http://www.Sample.com">SAMP</identifier>
     <xbrli:segment>
       >>>>>segment information would go here<<<<<
     </xbrli:segment>
 </xbrli:entity>
 <xbrli:period>
  <xbrli:startDate>2009-01-01</xbrli:startDate>
  <xbrli:endDate>2009-12-31</xbrli:endDate>
 </xbrli:period>
  <xbrli:scenario>
    >>>>>scenario information would go here<<<<<
  </xbrli:scenario>
</xbrli:context>
```

The preceding code sample shows the components a xbrli:context element from an XBRL instance. The context has an id value of D-2009, which is the same value of the contextRef on one or more facts, which we discuss in the upcoming section "Expressing the values for facts." The entity xbrli:identifier element has a value of SAMP, which comes from the scheme http://www. Sample.com. The segment element in our example is empty (we just wanted to show you were it would be located) — see Chapter 22. The xbrli:period element has a duration (a period of time) value with a start date of 2009-01-01 and an end date of 2009-12-31. As with the xbrli:segment, the xbrli:scenario element values aren't shown, as we don't want to get into this topic at this time (see Chapter 22).

Units provide additional context for numeric facts

In order to provide the proper context for a numeric value, you need to know the units for the numeric values. For example, say that you have a value of 1,000. Is that some particular currency, and if so, is it U.S. dollars, euros, yen, or some other currency? Or, is it square feet, the number of employees, or something else?

An XBRL instance contains units whenever you have any numeric fact values. A xbrli:unit element contains the additional context:

- ✔ **ID:** Every xbrli:unit element has an id attribute that uniquely identifies the unit so that numeric fact values can point to it. The id on the units works exactly the same way that a context id attribute works.

✔ **Measure:** Units generally have one xbrli:measure element, but they can have any number of measures. The value of the xbrli:measure element is the actual units for the fact value — for example, iso4217:EUR, which is the ISO currency code for the euro. If the fact value has no units, such as a percentage, the measure would have a value of xbrli:pure, which indicates that it's a pure number with no real units.

Have a look at how you can express units within an XBRL instance:

```
<xbrli:unit id="U-Monetary">
  <xbrli:measure>iso4217:EUR</xbrli:measure>
</xbrli:unit>
```

The code sample of unit shows the unit element with an id attribute value of U-Monetary that would correspond to one or more fact unitRef attribute value, which ties the fact to this unit. The xbrli:unit element has a xbrli:measure element with the value of iso4217:EUR, which means that the ISO 4217 standard currency code value of EUR for euros is the unit of measure.

Expressing the values for facts

An XBRL instance's meat is the fact that the XBRL instance is communicating. What a fact looks like can be slightly different depending on whether it's numeric. Numeric facts need to indicate the units in which the numeric fact value is expressed and the decimal places of the numeric value.

These parts make up a fact in an XBRL instance:

✔ **Concept name:** Every fact is data for a concept defined by one of the taxonomy schemas within the DTS of the XBRL instance. For example, a concept name may be something like gaap:CashAndCashEquivalents. The concept name is actually not exactly the name from the taxonomy, but rather the qualified name (sometimes called the QName), which is the name plus what is called the namespace prefix of the taxonomy schema from which the concept came. A *namespace prefix* is basically shorthand for referring to a namespace identifier. The *namespace identifier* basically identifies the taxonomy schema. We know, boring technical stuff. But the technical people dig this sort of thing and make all these connections behind the scenes for you.

✔ **ID:** Facts can have an id attribute that uniquely identifies the fact, but it's optional. Generally, the id isn't really necessary on a fact.

✔ **Context reference:** Every fact has a contextRef or context reference attribute. The contextRef attribute refers to one of the id attributes of a context element defined in your XBRL instance. The context element contains information that's necessary to understanding the context in which the fact value is being used.

✔ **Unit reference:** Every fact with a numeric concept has a unitRef or unit reference attribute. The unitRef refers to one of the id attribute of one of the unit elements defined in your XBRL instance. Concepts like strings, dates, and a few other odds and ends don't need unit information, so you don't need to provide one for facts with those types. Your software can help you sort out whether units are needed on a fact.

✔ **Decimals:** Every fact with a numeric concept must have either a decimals or possibly a precision attribute. Both the decimals and precision attributes provide virtually the same functionality, explaining the number of decimal places to which the fact value is accurate. Decimals are preferred because most people to understand them more easily. You can specify, say, 2 as the decimals value to indicate that a fact value is accurate to 2 decimal places, or -3 to indicate that a number is accurate to thousands. Software applications generally guide you to the appropriate choice.

✔ **Fact value:** Facts have a value, which is referred to as the fact value. A fact value can be a number, such as 1000, a text, such as LIFO, or any other data type, including an entire narrative with several paragraphs of text. The taxonomy schema determines and enforces the data type.

Here is an example of a numeric fact:

```
<basic:NetIncomeOrLoss
  contextRef="D-2009"
  unitRef="U-Monetary"
  decimals="-3">5347000</basic:NetIncomeOrLoss>
```

The preceding XBRL instance fragment shows a fact with the value of 5347000. That fact expresses information for the concept basic:NetIncomeOrLoss. It points to a context with the contextRef of D-2009 and units information with the unitRef of U-Monetary. (Refer to the earlier sections "Giving facts context" and "Units provide additional context for numeric facts.") The numeric fact is accurate to −3 decimal places (in thousands), as you can see in the decimals attribute value of -3.

Commenting with XBRL footnotes

XBRL instances can also contain what are basically comments but are referred to in XBRL as *footnotes*. XBRL footnotes are used in the XBRL instance as comments or notations that refer to one or more fact values.

XBRL footnotes are effectively a resource network physically contained within an XBRL instance. The footnote network is expressed as a linkbase and operates just like any other resource type linkbase.

Footnotes are good to know about and useful if you have a special case where you need them, but in the grand scheme of things, they really aren't that important. (For more on footnotes, see Chapter 22.)

Many people confuse XBRL footnotes with the term *footnote* as it applies to a financial statement. They're not the same thing. What XBRL footnotes actually provide in terms of functionality, how people use them, and how software vendors implement them are rather inconsistent, and you should avoid using footnotes, if possible. When a specific regulator or someone *does* specify what they should be used for and how they operate, however, you should follow the guidance of that regulator.

Gaining Flexibility through Extension

Many businesses need XBRL-required information models to be dynamic (flexible), and XBRL was created to fulfill that need. XBRL lets you modify XBRL taxonomies, but you don't *have* to if you don't need to.

We use the term *modified* in a special way here. These modifications don't change other people's physical files, but rather those creating extensions add new XBRL taxonomy components that can *virtually* change what others have created. It also articulates how you changed it.

Here are two terms you need to know to understand how extension works:

- ✔ **Base XBRL taxonomy:** You can think of a *base* XBRL taxonomy as an XBRL taxonomy that another XBRL taxonomy is extending. Other terms sometimes used to refer to these taxonomies are *standard taxonomies* or *anchor taxonomies*. For example, a taxonomy mandated by a regulator may be a base taxonomy.

- ✔ **Extension XBRL taxonomy:** You can think of an *extension* XBRL taxonomy as an XBRL taxonomy that extends some base XBRL taxonomy. Other terms sometimes used to refer to these taxonomies are *custom taxonomy* or *company taxonomy*. Extension XBRL taxonomies are generally customizations created of some base XBRL taxonomy for someone's specific use. For example, a company that files with a regulator who allows extension may create a company extension taxonomy that extends the base taxonomy created by the regulator.

An XBRL taxonomy that is a base has no real physical difference from a taxonomy that is an extension. In fact, an XBRL taxonomy can be both a base and an extension. For example, an XBRL taxonomy may extend some other XBRL taxonomy, and then someone else can use those two XBRL taxonomies as the base for its extension XBRL taxonomy.

XBRL extensibility has two fundamental facets:

✔ **Extension:** Adding to or altering, through extension, an existing DTS. Extension entails creating a new extending XBRL taxonomy that references (but doesn't directly impact or replace) the original, which is often referred to as the *base* XBRL taxonomy. The extending XBRL taxonomy adds concepts, resources, relations, or resource/relation networks.

✔ **Prohibition:** Removing by nullifying relations or resources from an existing taxonomy, through extension XBRL taxonomy. The key point is that you're getting rid of something by adding something. Note that you can't prohibit concepts themselves. Prohibiting a relation or resource entails creating one or more new resources or relations in the new extending XBRL taxonomy that voids and nullifies a specific resource or relation in the referenced pre-existing base XBRL taxonomy.

Neither type of extension has any impact on the pre-existing base XBRL taxonomy. Many organizations can concurrently extend the same base XBRL taxonomy in entirely different ways with zero impact on each other or the base XBRL taxonomy. But, extensions can impact the overall DTS.

Understanding extension

Suppose that someone created an XBRL taxonomy that included concepts, resources, and relations. An extension can

✔ Add one or more new concepts.

✔ Prohibit the use of existing resources, effectively nullifying them.

✔ Prohibit the use of existing relations, effectively nullifying them.

✔ Add one or more new resources or relations.

✔ Add one or more new resource or relation network.

The user who wants to extend some base XBRL taxonomy creates a new XBRL taxonomy, pulls that base XBRL taxonomy into her extension XBRL taxonomy by referencing it, and thus modifies the DTS with the extension and/or prohibition information from the extension XBRL taxonomy she created. So basically what you're doing with either extension or prohibition is adding pieces (taxonomy schema or linkbase) to the set that comprises the DTS, thus modifying the overall DTS.

The exact opposite of an extension is a form. A form is static. The person completing the form can't change a form to meet his needs. (The creator, though, can update the form from year to year to add new things.) If your information is static like a form, the extensibility features of XBRL may not be that useful to you. But other XBRL features, such as the ability to express the semantics (meaning) of the form, might still be useful, such as form computations or other relations. The underlying point here is that forms are static and don't need extension, whereas many types of business information aren't forms; they are dynamic.

Here are two examples of static versus dynamic data:

- ✔ **Static:** Most tax forms
- ✔ **Dynamic:** Most financial statements of U.S. public companies

Reasons to extend

The three primary reasons why you may want to create an extension XBRL taxonomy are to

- ✔ **Tweak existing information models.** If need be, you can totally redefine relations or create your own XBRL taxonomies, which is fine. However, if another XBRL taxonomy exists and it's close to what you need, rather than creating a new XBRL taxonomy, simply extend the existing one to get what you desire. An example is a form that you might like to tweak a little. You like 90 percent of what exists in that form, but you don't like the other 10 percent and want to add another 5 percent, rather than starting from scratch. So instead you simply create an XBRL extension. You're extending the form to create a new, modified form based on another form.

- ✔ **Express information your way.** Often, organizations even in the same industry use different terminology — for example, different labels for the same concept or different ways to compute values. If need be, maybe you can tweak those models, if the system in which you operate allows it. Or, you may simply want to add labels in a different language than what someone else provided. How you tweaked the base XBRL taxonomy information model is articulated within your extension XBRL taxonomy information model, and those who use your XBRL instance information can see and understand the tweaks you made.

- ✔ **View information your way.** You can totally reorganize someone's taxonomy and not change the meaning of the information expressed by taxonomy. For example, the US GAAP XBRL taxonomy is a consensus-based taxonomy created by accountants. Analysts have a different view of exactly the same information. Analysts could reorganize portions of the US GAAP XBRL taxonomy or totally reorganize the entire taxonomy if they see fit and not change the meaning of the information model at all.

What *is* allowed with respect to XBRL taxonomy extension is typically based on the agreed practices of business partners or regulators for the system with which you interact.

One scenario in which extensibility is valuable is in the financial reporting of publically traded companies. Particularly in the United States, even companies in the same industry don't all report similar information in precisely the same way. In other words, financial statements aren't forms that must be filled in; they're more dynamic. Financial statements have a lot in common, but companies have flexibility in reporting their financial information, taking into consideration the unique aspects of their business. Flexibility, in this case, may mean including a concept that no other business uses, adding things up slightly differently, or putting things in one place rather than in another. XBRL was built to handle this flexibility.

Chapter 5

Pinning Down How XBRL Affects You

In This Chapter

▶ Figuring out what XBRL user group you belong to

▶ Understanding aspects of XBRL important to your viewpoint

▶ Viewing XBRL from other perspectives

*I*n this chapter, we examine XBRL from your perspective and how it may impact you and your organization. We can't discuss each individual person, so instead we categorize you according to patterns. This chapter helps you see specifics, such as how XBRL will impact you as a person and your organization.

Why XBRL Is Worth Your Time

XBRL is definitely not a fad, and it has a proven track record of providing significant benefits to those who have implemented it. In fact, Chapter 9 is packed with examples of all sorts of ways organizations are already putting XBRL to work for them. You may be introduced to XBRL because you're

✔ **Pushed in by a mandate:** You may be using XBRL not because you want to, but because someone else mandates that you supply them with regulatory reports in an XBRL format. Why would people force you to use XBRL? First, they want to take advantage of the benefits XBRL offers. Second, they have the power to require you to bend to their will. You guessed it — big government!

In the United States, good examples of mandates to file information to governmental agencies is the SEC mandate for public companies and the FDIC mandate requiring all FDIC-insured banks to use XBRL to submit their regulatory filings.

✔ **Drawn in to proactively seek its benefits:** XBRL isn't some useless government program dreamed up by politicians trying to help their constituents. XBRL was actually created by the market. Companies and individuals got together to create XBRL because of the significant benefits of global agreement and standardization as opposed to fracturing the business-reporting world into competing proprietary technology fiefdoms.

This same standard that helps companies exchange business information with those mean government regulators can also help you exchange business information within your own organization or with your business partners. You can exchange information from one department to another department; your company to a business partner; your company to your accountant; your company to your bank; or your government agency to another government agency or to your constituents.

XBRL is more than about the simple exchange of information (see Chapter 6). XBRL has other aspects that assist in improving the quality of information exchanged and decreasing the costs of information exchange. Many people decide to use XBRL even if they're not mandated to do so.

✔ **Not getting left behind:** XBRL also has a bit of a "Let's keep up with the Joneses" aspect to it. Why would you want to keep up with someone else who is making use of XBRL? Well, because they can derive economic benefits that make competing with you easier. XBRL is one of those cases where you don't want to be left behind because the benefits are that profound. The risk, of course, is that waiting too long to adopt XBRL can cause problems for you down the road.

Defining You

The type of organization and the individual role that XBRL will affect is broad. Pinpointing who XBRL affects is like asking, "Who will the Web impact?" XBRL's impact may not be as pervasive as the Web itself, but it will be rather pervasive. More than likely, you work within some type of organization, or you fulfill some sort of role within that organization.

All XBRL users have things in common. For example, each user exchanges information with someone else, whether it's up or down the information-supply chain. (See Chapter 7 for more on information-supply chains.) Everyone exchanges information, and we tend to have different roles in, and therefore different perspectives on, the process.

All organizations looking at XBRL will likely be in the following situations:

✔ **Change is challenging.** You may not have the time to change, but you realize that change is the only constant. If you've been around a while, you may have exchanged business reports on stone tablets, like Fred Flintstone. You then adopted a new technology: paper. Now, you use a lot of electronic spreadsheets. With the electronic spreadsheet, paper became obsolete for some things. In turn, electronic spreadsheets solved a lot of problems, but caused many others.

✔ **You're facing information overload.** You're now in the digital age. Some reports are no better than electronic pieces of paper. With the volume of information increasing at an estimated rate of 30 percent per year, you're becoming overwhelmed with all the information you need to consider when making decisions. Sorting through those zillions of results returned by your favorite search engine takes too much time.

✔ **You use information.** Everyone is a potential user of information, no matter where you work.

The transition to XBRL is not without its bumps and bruises. Naysayers try to hold onto the status quo, evangelists push for a brave new world, and everything eventually works out. This transition may take 5 or 25 years, but the future is pretty much inevitable.

Looking at business information exchange holistically (that is, looking at the chain, rather than focusing on a single link), Table 5-1 outlines the general categories of the types of functions performed by those in different roles

Table 5-1	Types of Functions
Function	*Possible Roles*
You define/specify information	Standards setter, a regulator, a corporate office, a boss
You create business information to submit to others	Company, an employee, a subsidiary
You receive information and store it somewhere	Information technology department, database administrator
You analyze information created by others	Investor, broker, business analyst
You're a third party, playing a supporting role	CPAs providing attestation, data aggregators making data usable, software vendors creating software

By organizational type

Unless you have a trust fund and XBRL is just a hobby of yours, you probably work somewhere. Your perspective on XBRL will be different based on the type of entity you work for. For example, if you're in government, you may specify that companies give you information in a certain format. On the other hand, if you're in the private sector, you provide the information specified by some evil governmental agency. Your perspectives are definitely different.

The following different types of entities use or may use XBRL:

- ✔ **Public or listed company:** If you work with a publicly traded or listed company on some stock exchange, you're probably at least aware of XBRL because some regulator has been knocking on your door asking for XBRL-based information. If you're a listed or public company, you'll probably be reporting to your regulator and/or stock exchange in an XBRL format soon, if not already. If you're a financial institution, the chances are even higher that you report to your regulator by using XBRL.

- ✔ **Private or unlisted company:** If you're a private or unlisted company, you may not be submitting information using XBRL yet, but then again, maybe you are. Many private/unlisted companies in Europe, Singapore, and other countries already have to use XBRL to submit information to government agencies.

Feel left out that you don't have to use XBRL? No need to worry; your time will come — probably sooner than you might think. Governments all around the world are understanding the benefits of XBRL. As they do, more government agencies are dropping their proprietary electronic filing formats in favor of XBRL or moving from paper-based filings to e-filing. Pretty soon, your banks will probably be using XBRL, requiring you to submit your initial financial information for obtaining a loan in XBRL. Heck, even those quarterly financials you probably have to provide will be in XBRL; you may even wind up doing these reports monthly because the job is so much easier.

- ✔ **Not-for-profit entity:** Not-for-profit entities also answer to someone: their contributors, foundations who provide grants, government agencies who provide grants, and so on. Yup, they're interested in XBRL, too.

- ✔ **Regulatory government agency:** If you're with a government agency that regulates others in some way, you're on the specifying side of the table, communicating what information others must provide to you. Sometimes this collected information is available to other governmental agencies or, if you're an elected official, your constituents, such as voters. Other times, the information isn't shared.

✔ **Nonregulatory government agency:** Even if you're a government agency that doesn't regulate others, guess what? There is no "get out of XBRL" card. Federal, state, regional, and local governmental agencies all answer to someone and exchange information with someone. For example, in the United States, approximately 88,000 state and local governmental entities report financial information to the U.S. Census Bureau. Similar types of arrangements exist in most countries. These agencies also exchange nonfinancial information.

✔ **Individual:** The final entity type is the individual. Yes, you'll be impacted, too. We're all pretty much in this category even if we fall into other categories as well. If you interact with some governmental agency (who doesn't?), chances are you'll likely be submitting information to them in XBRL someday.

Additionally, you'll likely use XBRL. XBRL levels the playing field, which makes getting information about, say, how your government is spending your money easier than ever. Also, all information submitted by organizations to regulators and stock exchanges will be available to you — helpful for making investment decisions!

By role within an organization

Within your organization, you perform some role. Your role interacts with those who perform other roles. The following sections describe the roles of others you may encounter.

A business executive's view

You're in the C-suite — you're the CEO, the COO, the CFO, the CIO. Or perhaps you're known as president, vice president, your majesty, or some other name. No matter what you're name, you all have one thing in common: The buck stops with you.

You're at the top, and it can be lonely up there. You have to make the tough calls. Will your strategy be that of a leader, or will your strategy be more of a follower? You may answer to shareholders if you're a public company or a bank if you're a private company. You may answer to contributors if you're a not-for-profit, your partners if you're a partnership, or taxpayers if you're in government. But one thing is for sure: You do answer to someone.

Just like everyone else, you have long-term strengths, weaknesses, opportunities, and threats to consider. But you also have short-term realities. Truth is, every one of these groups into which you may fit has a little CEO in them; we're all in charge of something. We may not steer the ship, but we are ultimately responsible for something.

As an executive, you probably think concretely and want only the big picture. So how will XBRL affect you?

- ✔ You'll realize that XBRL will be part of your future because someone will require you to submit information to them in the XBRL format. You can meet that challenge in several ways by analyzing your situation. Some approaches will save your organization a boatload of money over the long haul, but they're time consuming and expensive to implement. Over the longer term, however, they provide the most net benefits; they have the highest return on investment (ROI). On the other hand, maybe long-term ROI isn't the most effective solution, all things considered. You have some choices to make!

- ✔ You won't like XBRL if you've been trying to hide things in your financial statements or subscribe to the practice of earnings management. Information analysts will be able to reconfigure your financial information as they want to see it, rather than simply accepting it as *you* want them to see it.

- ✔ If your company is performing well, you'll really like XBRL, particularly if you're an under-analyzed company or a company outside the mainstream capital markets. Your company will get more attention, and investors may discover that your company is a good investment. In that event, the capital markets will likely reward you. XBRL makes getting noticed easier because analysts don't need to rekey data to perform analysis, which changes the cost benefit model of analysis by significantly reducing its costs.

- ✔ If your company is underperforming, you won't like XBRL so much. It will be easier for analysts to discover that your company is underperforming and also easier to find better investments. Don't blame XBRL for this issue, though; perform better.

- ✔ You probably won't like that lenders and investors are going to eventually start demanding financial information monthly rather than the current standard of quarterly.

An accountant's view

As an accountant, you're conservative (and should be). If change is too easy, mistakes get made; the wrong path is taken more times than necessary. You care about the bottom line.

You're most likely going to be the last group to adopt XBRL, particularly for financial reporting. You don't even want to move your financial reporting into business intelligence-type application because you don't think that it'll work. Eventually, you'll realize that using XBRL is a good thing, but adjusting will take time.

You're practical, think concretely, and can certainly relate to the big picture, but you really like details. You love electronic spreadsheets!

Here are some other things about you, the accountant:

- ✔ You'll like the business rules you can create with XBRL Formula. You'll realize that you can replace the manual disclosure checklist with an automated process for many, if not most, things.

- ✔ You'll enjoy the productivity increase you experience when you make the shift to XBRL. The quality will be incrementally better (your work is already high quality), but the effort to attain that level of quality will be reduced by an order of magnitude. You may not believe this good news, but it's true!

- ✔ You won't like all the efficiencies XBRL brings to the table because you worry you'll lose your job or, if you're a public accountant, you fear the hours you can bill will be reduced. However, you'll eventually realize that you're not going to lose your job, but simply change the tasks that you perform and the way you perform those tasks. You'll like that you'll do your external financial reporting monthly rather than quarterly. This increase in frequency means more work and more job security for you.

- ✔ You'll find XBRL somewhat frustrating in the short term. Making the transition to creating structured information, rather than unstructured information, will be a hard mental shift. Over time, you'll make this shift and see the benefits of structured information.

- ✔ You'll have a hard time understanding why XBRL is a good thing until you actually use good software that uses XBRL the right way. One day, you'll realize XBRL is a good thing.

- ✔ Eventually, you'll realize the possibilities and benefits of standardized audit schedules. For you, XBRL is a means to an end. Whatever the role you play, be it as an internal accountant, an internal auditor, or an external auditor, XBRL will stress your world like few other things have, but you will survive.

An analyst's view

As an analyst, you're at the end of the supply chain, an information consumer. You may not be at the very end; instead, you may summarize information for others, such as the CEO, who rely on your judgment but who don't do the detailed work you have to do.

You spend hours cleansing data or working with technical people to cleanse the data for you. A lot of garbage comes into your system, which makes your job harder. You also spend a lot of time rekeying information. You're beginning to like business-intelligence software more and more. You don't particularly care for relying on others to build your data models in business-intelligence applications. You're pretty good with both the big picture and details and tend to be a fairly concrete thinker.

Here are other things about you and your likely relationship to XBRL:

✔ You'll thoroughly enjoy business rules, particularly after the software used to create the business rules matures.

✔ You'll likely be frustrated by XBRL's extensibility in the short term because of the way taxonomies use this extensibility. Over the long term, you'll like the extensibility more as the modelers of taxonomies learn to use the extensibility correctly.

✔ You'll like XBRL's ability to help you model data. You'll likely become frustrated in the short term with how complex XBRL is, but over the long term, you'll discover ways to make this process easier.

A project manager's view

As a project manager, you spend much of your time in meetings or talking to people about what they've done or when something will be done. Your focus is narrow. You care about timetables, milestones, deliverables, and accomplishments.

You're probably a generalist, a jack of all trades and master of none. You manage the specialists, but you have to understand the specialists to make sure that they're serving your needs effectively and efficiently. You have deadlines. You have legacy systems that you wish you could throw out, but can't. The systems have to keep running.

You have to deal with consultants, or so-called hired guns, who may not have your best interests at heart. You have to deal with software vendors who seem to always believe that the software they sell is the best software. You're a practical and concrete thinker:

✔ You'll like the leverage you can get from XBRL, but you'll realize that XBRL won't be able to provide you with a 100-percent solution out of the box.

✔ You'll find that software vendors tell you that they can provide a 100-percent solution, but you'll find out that they're misrepresenting their software. This mistake will likely cost you.

✔ Others on your project team will likely try to convince you that they can do things with XML or SQL that instead should be done with XBRL.

A consultant's view

As a consultant, you're a hired gun. You're an expert in your area. You spend most of your time at work consulting on and championing for the application of emerging practices and technologies to make improvements. You spend much of your time attending meetings, reviewing research reports, and preparing briefs for stakeholders of your projects.

You have a toolkit that you try to keep current, but sometimes find keeping it updated difficult because you have to keep your billable hours up. You move from one process re-engineering project to another. Or you move from building one solution to building another. You move, move, move:

- People rely on you. You have to make the right choices. You realize that XBRL is about making yourself and software integrators like you more dispensable by lowering maintenance and total cost of IT ownership for your clients. But you realize that you can apply your skills in more interesting ways, particularly now that you have XBRL in your toolset.

- You'll eventually discover that XBRL can provide you with a lot to leverage. Chapter 2 discusses how you can leverage XBRL (particularly the part about how XBRL builds on XML). You may resist taking full advantage of this leverage because you bill by the hour and leveraging cuts your hours. Do your customers a favor and don't make this mistake.

- You may make the mistake early on of trying to use SQL or Schematron to validate XBRL. If you do, you'll wind up wasting a lot of time and then realize that an XBRL processor can do the same type of work in a fraction of the time.

A technical architect's view

As a technical architect, you're most comfortable using cutting-edge technology, and all the legacy systems you have to deal with drive you nuts. You can create a mean whiteboard model and enjoy debating concepts, the more theoretical and abstract the better. You're big on theory and hate the fact that you have legacy systems built with outdated technology.

You think abstractly and are effective at communicating abstract concepts to concrete thinkers. You concern yourself with exploiting patterns, using industry best practices, and creating an efficient and agile organization:

- You'll see and like the leverage XBRL offers.

- You'll like the discipline best practices XBRL provides.

- The flexibility of XBRL is a concern for you. However, you'll understand that open standards are good things, and you can find ways around many of the challenges XBRL poses.

✔ You'll like the stability of XBRL. However, you'll soon wish that you could adjust certain things, and you could use some direction in certain areas. You'd settle for a detailed roadmap from XBRL International so that you can do a better job of planning your architectural strategies.

✔ You'll like the separation of business rules from programming logic that XBRL Formula provides. You'll change your perspective on how you can perform common tasks. (Separation of business rules from programming logic is a little similar to the separation that has occurred between business applications and the databases those applications use.)

A developer's view

As a developer, you're a geek. You're incredibly smart, think abstractly, and don't understand why others can't do the same. You have a toolset you're used to, and you don't particularly care to deviate from that toolset. You either love Microsoft, or you hate Microsoft. You have to love Java and Linux, whether you like it or not. You spend a lot of time writing and debugging code, which you like and you find challenging and satisfying. You tend to do things the quickest way you can, sometimes not considering long-term ramifications:

✔ You may not take the time to learn about XBRL. You look at it and see it as nothing more than a complex XML language for those guys who like debits and credits.

✔ You'll like the intellectual challenge of trying to understand XBRL, but you'll probably make (or have already made) a bunch of mistakes figuring out how to best use the technology.

✔ You probably think you understand XBRL if you understand XML, but you'll most likely be incorrect. (Be sure to read Chapter 2.)

✔ You may want to build your own XBRL processor. If you go down that path, you'll regret that choice in about six months to a year.

✔ After some missteps, you'll eventually get on track and take advantages of XBRL and create software helpful in enabling business users to make use of XBRL.

A database administrator's view

As a database administrator, you hold the keys to the castle's data. Users and developers depend on you. Users drive you nuts with all the different ways that data is modeled. XML is also driving you nuts; you're trying to get that XML data into your data warehouse and then subsequently off to your OLAP applications and business-intelligence applications. The different data models make things more and more complex. Writing all that SQL to get some of the funky data models into the data warehouse is challenging, to say the least:

- ✔ You'll like the ease of getting XBRL taxonomies and XBRL instance data into and out of a relational database.

- ✔ If you like the multidimensional model for storing data, you'll really like XBRL.

- ✔ You'll be frustrated by the slow pace at which software vendors implement XBRL ETL (extract, transform, load) functionality within their products, but you'll be happy when they do.

- ✔ You'll be frustrated by the lack of a clear logical model for XBRL, which makes some information challenging to store.

A bureaucrat's view

You work in government, be it federal, state, regional, or local. You answer to taxpayers, and you're a public servant. You specify data that others submit to you, either directly or via some legislative process. You may make this data available to others inside government or to the public. You interact with other government agencies, and you sometimes have turf wars with these other agencies. The legacy systems you have to deal with are the oldest in existence. Your budgets are the tightest around, in many cases.

Everything you do seems to be scrutinized. You have an exaggerated need to be transparent, so all your actions need to be out in the open.

- ✔ You'll like that when you talk to other agencies about exchanging information, you don't have to start from a clean slate. Instead, rather than discussing their proprietary solution or your proprietary solution, you can start with XBRL and examine why it will or won't meet your data-exchange needs.

- ✔ You'll like that you don't have to try to figure out whether you should provide information in Excel, Word, PDF, or HTML; you can just provide everything in XBRL.

- ✔ You'll like the information-modeling capabilities of XBRL, particularly if you're familiar with the multidimensional model.

An individual's view

Think about how blogs have changed news reporting dramatically. Anyone can be a reporter. In the same way, XBRL will change investing. Anyone can be an analyst. Anyone can be a regulator.

Many believe that the market is the best regulator. XBRL helps make every investor a regulator, keeping tabs on companies. In addition, every taxpayer can keep better tabs on how their government spends their money, every contributor can better see how a not-for-profit utilizes their contributions, and so on.

How can individuals become better analysts and regulators and therefore better investors?

- ✔ Access to information will never be easier. Whether you access the information yourself or whether you use third-party software application, it will be easier.

- ✔ Transparency will dramatically increase. You'll have better visibility into what is going on within the companies you invest in, the governments you pay taxes to, and the non-for-profit organizations you contribute to.

Part II
Embracing XBRL for Classic Challenges and New Possibilities

The 5th Wave   By Rich Tennant

"I started running what-if scenarios in XBRL, like 'What if I were sick of this job and funneled some of the company's money into an offshore account?'"

In this part . . .

We start off this part by drilling into what business information exchange is all about. We look into how business information exchange is practiced today, its objectives, dynamics impacting it, and how all these things work together and impact business information exchange. We begin to realize that business information is a chain, and we introduce you to the notion of a business information-supply chain, looking at the chain itself rather than the individual links in that chain. We conclude this part by pointing out that XBRL will enable a transformation in business information exchange similar to the transformations that have occurred or are occurring in other industries.

Chapter 6

Exchanging Business Information

*W*ondering what business information exchange really is? Answering that question is the topic of this chapter. Business reports and reporting are a subset of the bigger area of business information exchange. Don't limit yourself by thinking of business information exchange only as the exchange of reports.

In this chapter, we look at what business information exchange is all about, how it's practiced today, what its objectives are, dynamics impacting business information exchange from a business and technical perspective, and how all these things work together to impact business information exchange. We end the chapter by painting a picture of a new model of business information exchange.

Streamlining Cross-System Exchanges

Businesses have been doing cross-system information exchanges for years. If you've ever been on a business trip or vacation in a foreign country and wanted to get cash from an automated teller machine and wondered how that happens, you're experiencing the results of years of effort and billions of dollars to make these types of transactions possible with just a few button pushes or clicks of a mouse by you. After all, as Arthur C. Clarke's third law of prediction states, "A sufficiently advanced technology is indistinguishable from magic."

But due to the complexity and expense, using such cross-system information exchanges have been out of reach for most companies. No more. Today, more and more businesses can benefit from the magic offered by the technologies that make transactions possible.

This chapter shows you that what many consider a business report is really a *business information exchange.* With the volume of information exchanged being so large, many people face increasing pressure to perform these exchanges more efficiently and effectively. The ubiquitous connectivity of the Web helps us see how inefficient many information-exchange processes really are. Before we were connected via the Web, we never really needed to consider whether there might be a better way. But because of the Web, the inefficiencies are now easy to see. Fortunately, the same technologies that are exposing the problem can also be a solution to the problem.

These changes can represent an opportunity because they provide a competitive advantage for you (if you use them and your competitors don't). On the other hand, these changes can represent a threat because they create a competitive advantage for others who use them if you don't.

Business Information Exchange Is More Than Just a Report

Just to be clear, when we discuss exchanging business information, we're including business reporting. A business report is a type of business information exchange, but other types also are business information exchanges, such as when accounting information of one business system is exported from that system and imported into another system. We're talking about the broader category business information exchange, not just business reporting or a report. Reports are only one way of achieving the objective of exchanging information.

Three distinctive traits make something a business information exchange:

✔ Information exists within one business system of some sort, and that information needs to exist within another business system.

✔ The business system providing the information understands the context of the information, but the receiving system doesn't understand how the providing business system manages this context (and vice versa).

✔ A lossless transfer or relocation of the information from the providing business system to the receiving business system occurs. (In other words, the original context isn't lost — it's guaranteed to be interpreted correctly and validated in the receiving system, or the meaning is otherwise correctly understood.)

Humans are good at relocating, so to speak, this data, plus the data's context from one business system to another business system, because humans can figure out how each system stores the context of the data. However, when humans are involved, transfers are expensive and error-prone, and they take too much time.

What we're *not* talking about here is what most people think about when you mention exchanging information, which is a business-to-business transaction. The most successful business-to-business transaction protocol is Electronic Data Interchange (EDI). The two primary EDI formats, X12, which is used in the United States, and EDIFACT, which is used in Europe, handle billions of dollars worth of transactions between banks, retail establishments, shipping companies, and more to enable everyone to do business. EDI is how business gets done. Although these transaction-based systems provide an example of the possibilities, we're not talking about that type of business information exchange; we're talking about the ones that XBRL enables. Business reports fall into that category, but XBRL isn't limited to just business reports.

One significant difference between transactions and what XBRL is meant to do is the flexibility of what is being transferred. Transactions tend to be smaller and change less often (if ever). Other types of business information exchanges may be larger and tend to change more often. One of XBRL's sweet spots is its flexibility in the right areas, thanks to its powerful extendibility mechanism. Another is its ability to handle large information sets.

Business reports, such as external and internal financial statements, are a good example of business information exchanges, but the category also includes the following:

- Internal and external audit schedules that support the financial statements

- Spreadsheets that contain information used to process and track all sorts of financial and nonfinancial information

- Reports submitted to regulators, governmental entities, and so on

- Tax filings and their supporting information

- Trial balances of subsidiaries used to create consolidated reports

- All the different "layers" of the preceding types of information, which is used to aggregate layers on top or drill down into supporting layers of information

- Employee lists and other information provided to an insurance company in support of your group medical insurance policy

- Combined information from multiple business systems after a business acquisition, such as a merger

✔ A holding company or parent company that provides autonomy to its subsidiaries in terms of operating their business segments (different financial-reporting systems), but that still needs to consolidate the financial information from the many systems to create a financial report

✔ Statistical indicators, such as gross domestic product per capita, unemployment levels, competitiveness indicators for manufacturing, and other labor-related indicators, particularly if the information is a mixture of numeric and alpha-numeric (or textual) information

Business reports have been done on paper for most of our lives. To think about business reports always in terms of what can be done on paper limits your thinking. Try to think outside the box. What if you could exchange business information using a better way than paper? And we don't mean spreadsheets, word-processing documents, PDF, or HTML, which are all simply electronic versions of the same paper reports. What if we got rid of the notion of a document altogether? Impossible? Well, maybe not.

Examining the Characteristics of Business Information Exchange Today

In the past, people have exchanged information verbally or by using mediums such as stone tablets, papyrus, parchment, vellum, and eventually paper. Sometimes seeing the possibility of change is hard.

Times have changed, and the following list looks at the characteristics of business information exchange today:

✔ **Proprietary and fixed formats that inhibit reuse:** Business information is generally locked into proprietary formats of one software application, such as Microsoft Excel, Microsoft Word, or other proprietary formats or locked into HTML and PDF. These formats make reusing information within another software application difficult. Although these formats often have functionality that lets you import or export information from one application to another, these processes typically don't meet information-exchange needs. Further, these formats tend to be fixed. After the information is in one of these formats, getting information into a different presentation format is challenging and generally results in expensive, time-consuming, human-intensive, and therefore error-prone processes.

✔ **Application-specific reporting concepts and contexts:** Many concepts and contexts are common to businesses. However, each business system implements these concepts and contexts in different ways. A business system understands the context and concepts used within that system. It doesn't understand the concepts and contexts of other business systems. Thus, moving information across business systems is a problem, particularly if the information that provides the context is stripped away during the exchange process. This lack of standard approaches to implementing and exchanging information makes the exchange process more difficult.

✔ **Physical location used to define information:** Analytical formulas articulated in spreadsheets and other proprietary software are described based upon the physical location of the data (for example, the cell at the intersection of column A and row 12). Managing connections that are physically defined can be challenging and costly, particularly if someone changes the spreadsheet by adding a row or column. Just because you can move information from one place to another doesn't necessarily mean that the system receiving the information understands what to do with that information. Remember, computers aren't that smart.

✔ **Application-specific business rules:** Similar to the limitations of physically defined information, business rules and controls are embedded within applications that can't exchange them because the business rules and controls are expressed in different proprietary formats, making it impossible or, at best, complex to exchange this information with another software application. (*Business rules* are things like formulas and computations that explain how one concept relates to other concepts. *Controls* are processing and workflow rules.)

Enterprise environments contain different business applications that hold operational and reporting data. These different applications require duplicate sets of rules for these different systems because no one standard rule set is centrally maintained and then shared between these different applications. This duplication and the resulting inevitable errors cause inconsistencies between the multiple rule sets.

✔ **Implicit relationships:** Relationships between reporting concepts and the relevant reporting standards, auditing standards, instructions, regulation, company policies, and so on are all implicit. Further, these relationships evolve over time as new standards are written to replace old standards. For example, experienced CPAs have developed their understanding of which GAAP standards, regulations, and Generally Accepted Auditing Standards (GAAS) requirements relate to specific reporting concepts based on years of experience. Inexperienced CPAs, investors, creditors, and other users with limited knowledge may be confused by their personal lack of knowledge of these implicit relationships, or they may imply relationships incorrectly.

✔ **Documents, forms, and presentation focus:** Documents are used to communicate data and therefore the data tends to be locked inside a document. Forms also lock data within the documents. All these physical characteristics, which are appropriate for paper-based communication, get in the way of reusing the data contained within the physical form or the physical document.

✔ **Spreadsheet hell:** The electronic spreadsheet solved many problems. If you ever had to construct a paper spreadsheet, you can really appreciate the benefits of the electronic spreadsheet. But electronic spreadsheets also caused many problems. Because of electronic spreadsheets, we can do more analysis, which results in a higher volume of spreadsheets — no way we could have the volume we have today if we were still using paper spreadsheets. Spreadsheets are difficult to check for mistakes. Linked-together spreadsheets can best be described as brittle; links are easily broken. Hundreds of spreadsheets are wired together into a process that has all the characteristics described earlier in this list. Spreadsheet users refer to this as *spreadsheet hell.*

✔ **Multiple versions of "the truth:"** Because there are multiple copies of information, particularly with spreadsheets, multiple versions of the same information exist. Keeping the different versions synchronized is challenging. This duplication leads to errors, which leads to work trying to figure out why the differences exist and which version of the truth is correct.

Clarifying the Objectives of Exchanging Business Information

To make decisions, we need information. We exchange information because someone knows something that someone else either wants to know or needs to know to make decisions. A manager needs to know the financial health of the department he manages. His boss needs to understand the financial health of the department because it's one of the many departments he is responsible for. The CEO wants to know because he's responsible for everything in the company. The bank wants to know because the company has borrowed money and it prefers to be repaid, so it keeps tabs on how the company is doing. Company investors need to know because they want to monitor how their investment is performing. Each of these people uses different information, but each person has similar needs for the business information they use.

Information exchanges need to meet the following fairly basic objectives in order to be effective. Inaccurate, untimely, or irrelevant information misses the mark:

✔ **Accuracy, quality, and data integrity:** How accurate is the information? You can generally only reduce errors, not totally eliminate them. What is the error rate of your information: 1 percent, 2 percent, or maybe 5 percent? What is the marginal value of dropping the error rate from 2 percent to 1 percent?

✔ **Timeliness:** How important is timeliness of the information? How much more valuable is data received in 1 day versus 30 days or 90 days?

✔ **Relevance:** How relevant is the information to the decisions you need to make? Do you have to sift through too much information to find those pieces of relevant information?

✔ **Completeness:** How complete is the information or data set you have for the decisions you need to make? Are you missing pieces of information that, if considered, may lead to a different decision?

✔ **Third-party verification:** At times, verification by an independent third party is important. Is the transaction that generated the information a real, valid, transaction, or is it fraudulent or manipulated in some way? Is the transaction that generated the information *arms-length* in that no one party can control both sides of the transaction, or could someone possibly manipulate the transaction by controlling both sides? Has the information been verified by an independent third party, such as a CPA providing an independent opinion on financial or nonfinancial information? Has the information been tampered with or altered in some way? Are controls, processes, and procedures in place to eliminate tampering with information?

✔ **Comparability:** How comparable is information created by two different companies? How comparable is one company's information across time periods? How much effort does comparing the information take?

✔ **Flexibility:** How flexible is your system in terms of change to your information models? If you want to collect additional data points or if you want to drop some data points currently being collected, how easily can you do it within your systems? Can you reconfigure prior information easily for comparability purposes? How easily can the user of your system reconfigure information to see it how they want to see it, rather than how you decided to present it? In other words, is the information, as Christopher Cox of the U.S. SEC says, "interactive"?

✔ **Simple presentation:** Is the information communicated in understandable language, as opposed to jargon and legalese? Is the information available in languages the users understand? Are the formats of the information helpful in ensuring a clear understanding, or is it confusing?

✔ **Usable format:** If an information user is blind, presentation of that information isn't useable to that person. Computers need different formats than humans.

✔ **Minimize total cost:** Another goal is to minimize total cost during the entire life cycle of the information. You need to consider many factors when determining total cost, including training, maintenance, software, and so on. For creators of information, total cost of creation is the issue. For information consumers, total cost of capture, validation, reuse, and analysis are the concerns.

Recognizing Business Environment Changes

The only constant in business is that things change. These changes require you to adapt. The process is a lot like the survival of the fittest: Fail to adapt, and you may not be able to survive. Understanding these dynamics help us adapt to the changes. Business information exchange is changing.

Take a look at the drivers impacting business information exchange:

✔ **Globalization:** Goods, services, capital, and people move across borders more easily than in the past. Companies operate in multiple countries with different compliance and reporting rules. The global economy is also tied together more than ever before. The global impact of the financial institution crisis that materialized in 2008 is an example of how interconnected we all are.

✔ **Increase in information volume:** The volume of information that we have to deal with is increasing at an overwhelming rate. Some estimates put the increase at a rate of 30 percent per year!

✔ **Shift from the industrial age to the information age:** We're moving from the Industrial Age, where manufacturing was king, to the Information Age, where your ability to process information is king. The largest retailer in the world, Wal-Mart, doesn't make one product. Wal-Mart is a conduit through which other people's products flow via an incredibly efficient physical-supply chain and information-supply chain. Many products these days aren't even physical, but rather digital. For example, CDs are no longer required to physically distribute music.

✔ **Moving to IFRS:** Eighty different sets of accounting standards exist around the world. Many of these financial-reporting standards are country-specific. Imagine doing business across countries and having to report to, say, the 27 different countries in Europe in 27 different languages. IFRS is trying to change all that. What if every country in the world used the same robust set of financial-reporting standards? This trend is blanketing the globe. Already more than 100 countries have adopted or will converge with IFRS.

✔ **A need for differentiation, not normalization:** Many people try to deal with a lack of comparability in information by creating standard slots to in which they try to fit the information into to normalize it. In many cases, this approach is typically the exact opposite of what needs to occur. For example, companies spend vast amounts trying to differentiate their companies for investors, only to have data aggregators normalize their data, removing key differentiators. Much of the normalization occurs because the cost of parsing and rekeying data is high. And with increasing amounts of information and the desire for more timely information, rekeying information simply is no longer economically viable.

✔ **Non-analyzed and underanalyzed information:** So much information exists that much of it isn't even analyzed or is underanalyzed. For example, of all the public companies in the United States, only about 20 percent of these companies have consistent coverage by sell-side analyst firms. Why? It's because of the high cost of parsing data from company reports, rekeying data into analytical models, and managing these concepts across companies.

✔ **Market reaction to lack of transparency:** With the crisis of investor confidence comes the need to rebuild and regain trust in capital markets. In a digital global economy, information — or more importantly, electronically exchanged information — is the lifeblood of business. Flexible, dynamic, timely, accurate, interactive data is more transparent because it's easier for users to use. "Sunlight is said to be the best disinfectant," wrote Louis Brandeis in 1913 before he became a U.S. Supreme Court Justice. When information is relevant, standardized, and publically available, it fosters intelligent decision-making. The markets are demanding more transparency from businesses these days.

✔ **Market's demand for customization for differing users:** End-users of information have differing definitions of what is relevant to them. Users should be able to easily obtain relevant information without laboriously sifting through irrelevant information. In an era of mass customization, one-size-fits-all products are hard to justify. Information technology has made customization easy and expected.

✔ **Stresses resulting in system failures:** There are no better examples of the stresses on information systems these days than a few highly publicized failures. Individual company scandals and failures that rocked high-profile American companies Enron and WorldCom and Satyam Computer Services (India) and Parmalat (Italy) are raising questions about current financial reporting and auditing models. The global mortgage crisis and related financial failures raise questions about how well current practices are meeting investor's needs for information.

✔ **Increased complexity:** New financial products are created using *financial engineering*. Derivatives, collateralized debt obligations, and mortgage-backed securities are good examples of this financial engineering. The mortgage crisis of 2008 was a good example of the problems these hard-to-understand securities cause. Computers are helping to create these new, hard-to-understand financial products. These types of products put even more pressure on the already hard-to-understand financial reporting standards.

✔ **Increased options through use of technology:** More and more options exist to those who need to exchange business information. New techniques, such as pivot tables and graphs, are overcoming the limitations of reporting on physical paper. Just as paper replaced stone tablets, other approaches to exchanging business information will likely replace paper.

✔ **New social structures:** New social structures are replacing old social structures, and one example is how blogging has impacted news reporting. Today, everyone is a reporter, or can be, if they want to. The successful Barack Obama campaign during the 2008 U.S. presidential election demonstrates the power of networking. The rise of social networking models on the Internet has driven the shift to a new development model — one that relies on open-source models along with mass collaboration or peer production to solve problems, analyze information, examine impact, make recommendations, and explore alternatives.

Enabling Technologies to Impact Business Information Exchanges

Technical drivers impact business information exchange, and new technologies are allowing new approaches. Some technologies have a small impact, while others, such as the Web, have a larger impact. The following technical drivers will have a big impact on business information exchange:

✔ **Ubiquitous connectivity:** The ubiquity and affordability of the Web has enabled management to use the Web to achieve its business strategies and execute tactics. Whether or not you make use of the Web, it has impacted our lives. The push for online bill paying, online banking, and online reporting will become stronger because of the massive amount of cost reductions that result. The Web of today will seem like a black-and-white TV compared to the big color screen and surround sound of Web 2.0 and Web 3.0 or the Semantic Web that is to come. Take what you can imagine and quadruple it. It's bigger than that.

✔ **Standardized structured syntax:** When everyone is connected via the Web, one of the first things you may think about is exchanging things between all those connected people. *Structured* is the key word. Hypertext Markup Language (HTML) was one of the things that made the Web take off. Although HTML was a way of presenting information, it wasn't the best way to exchange information. XML filled that gap, making information easier to exchange. XBRL is the XML language for exchanging business information.

✔ **Standardized semantics:** A great example of standardized semantics is the financial-reporting community's move from 80 different sets of financial-reporting standards to one set, the IFRS. Think about standardized semantics from the perspective of an investor who wants to find a good investment or a global conglomerate who has to report multiple regulators. Or, look at it from the perspective of a regulator who has to monitor the global banking system. More standardized semantics, or standardized metadata, are being created to make our lives easier. After this meaning is widely agreed upon, XBRL and other technologies offer ways to express the metadata in a form understandable not only to humans, but also to computers.

XBRL's Role in the Semantic Web

The Web is a tremendously useful technology for business. The first incarnation of the Web, Web 1.0, provided the key ingredient: the cheap, ubiquitous connectivity that anyone can leverage. Web 1.0's HTML pages and the HTTP protocols for viewing the pages in browsers helped the Web take off. We're not really sure when Web 1.0 got upgraded to Web 2.0, but Web 2.0 is generally considered to be when highly interactive sites, such as blogs and YouTube, allowed anyone to break a major news story, scooping the big networks and newspapers.

You know what people say about version 3 of software: That's when the software vendor's generally really get things right. Well, Web 3.0 — what is hailed as the Semantic Web — is what people are calling the third major version of the Web. The truth is, however, that Tim Berners-Lee, the inventor of the Web, says that Web 3.0 is more aligned with his original vision of what the Web should be.

We can't go into a detailed explanation of the Semantic Web here — that would take a whole book. In fact, Jeffery T. Pollock has already written *Semantic Web For Dummies* (Wiley). But because some people are calling XBRL the Semantic Web's most successful metadata format, know that XBRL and the Semantic Web are connected.

The Semantic Web can be thought of as all the stuff necessary to make the Web a big database in the sky. The Semantic Web provides a superset of metadata that ties specific metadata to the Semantic Web. It's not that everything will change and be different. It's more that something that doesn't exist today will exist in the future: one way of accessing all the data on the Web together as if it were one big database. Today, the data is there, but it takes many different formats, and much of the data isn't in a form that computer applications can easily reuse. The Semantic Web bridges these gaps and makes using all these databases as one big database in the sky possible.

We explain the Semantic Web and XBRL's role by walking you through a tangible example. The example we want to use is what has become one of the most valuable databases of information made publically available by the United States federal government: the EDGAR database of public company financial filings. EDGAR was made available during the rise of Web 1.0, and the U.S. SEC is now replacing it with the Next-Generation EDGAR system. (For more on the Next-Generation EDGAR, see Chapter 13.) Explaining what XBRL provides and explaining the differences between EDGAR and Next-Generation EDGAR can help you get a good grasp of why the Semantic Web is such a dramatic change and how XBRL helps enable this change:

✔ **XBRL is a database or structured publishing format.** Although EDGAR is considered a database, it really isn't a database; it's more of a big electronic file cabinet in the sense that you can't get information out of those documents contained in the database using any automated process. Just ask EDGAR Online, Inc., which has spent millions of dollars and has still been only somewhat successful in parsing the data to extract useful information from financial documents files and placed into the EDGAR system. Mostly, people who use this information simply rekey information to reuse it. Truth is, if EDGAR Online was successful in parsing the information to reuse it, we wouldn't need XBRL. In fact, we wouldn't need XML either; we could just keep doing what we've been doing, and automated parsing processes could automatically generate the structured information needed to turn the documents into a database.

Fact is, successfully parsing and reusing all the information from the EDGAR database is impossible, which is why XBRL does exist. Contrast EDGAR to the SEC's replacement for EDGAR: the new Next-Generation EDGAR system. The Next-Generation EDGAR system was designed and built to be a database, allowing easy access to the information within filings so that anyone can reuse that information easily and inexpensively. So, unlike the electronic filing cabinets of EDGAR, the Semantic Web will be more like the database provided by Next-Generation EDGAR. XBRL will be the structured format of the data inside Next-Generation EDGAR. Information will be retrieved out of Next-Generation EDGAR using queries, much like you query a database. The query results will be reliable, and therefore the query results will be useable in other processes.

✔ **XBRL is metadata.** Even if you have a standard database, if you don't have standard metadata, retrieving information is somewhat pointless because you can't compare the information with other information. This is where metadata comes in. XBRL, in the form of the US GAAP Taxonomy, and articulates common metadata that allows enhanced cross-company and cross-period comparisons. XBRL contributes to the Semantic Web by providing both a standardized approach to creating this metadata (the XBRL Specification for creating taxonomies) and the metadata itself (things like the US GAAP and IFRS financial reporting taxonomies). For example, if you wanted to do a cross-company query and find the Total Assets of all public companies as of a certain period, you can easily execute this query by using the Next-Generation EDGAR database, the common US GAAP Taxonomy term Assets, and the other common metadata.

✔ **XBRL is a transfer protocol.** The Semantic Web is more about reading information across databases. But you need to enable the other parts of CRUD (Create, Read, Update, Delete) to keep the data current. Although not directly a Semantic Web technology in this way, XBRL indirectly enables the information to exist in the form of a database. By being a transfer protocol, XBRL allows the information to be moved from, in this case, a regulated company to the regulator and from the regulator to analysts and investors like you. So, you can look at XBRL as the transaction protocol for business-reporting transactions. These transactions are complex, not like a general ledger entry, and require the flexibility offered by XBRL. The transactions need to be correct; they need to be sure the integrity of the information is there in order to automate processes. XBRL provides the ability to both express semantic information and validate the transactions against that semantic information, which allows XBRL to effectively enable automated information exchanges.

There will be only one Semantic Web just like there is only one Web, but internal-use-only semantic Webs will exist within an organization, just like internal-use-only Webs called *intranets* exist. Business partners will likewise share semantic Webs similar to what is known as an extranet.

Chapter 8 explains what all this means for you. Fundamentally, think transformational technology. The Semantic Web allows you to do old things in new ways and achieve new things that were once impossible. Missing this boat can put you at a competitive disadvantage.

Envisioning New Possibilities in Business Information Exchange

Throughout this chapter, we talk about what a business information exchange is. We show you the objectives required by business information exchanges, and we outline changes that have occurred within the business environment in which you operate. We even discuss enabling technologies that are being brought to bear in the task of exchanging information these days. And we give you insight relating to the Semantic Web and XBRL's role in the Semantic Web. But what does all this information mean? How will all these moving pieces impact business information exchange? What new possibilities do you have to work with? What characteristics might business information exchange have? Well, you're in luck. We have a list:

- New business information exchange model
- Format as a choice, rather than as a limitation
- Transparency and visibility
- Information that is self-validating
- Interactive information
- System flexibility
- Metadata-driven system changes
- Information portability
- One version of the truth
- Semantic Web of information
- Plug-and-play information exchange

We drill into each of these topics in more detail in the following sections.

New business information exchange model

Enabling technologies, which includes XBRL, offer new possibilities, a new model for meeting the changing needs of business information exchange of today's world. What will this new business-information-exchange model look like? It's hard to say exactly, but you can accurately predict characteristics based on the developments over the past 50 years of using computers:

- **Digital:** It'll be digital, not physical (not paper). But, the information can be turned into something physical when needed or preferred.

- **Global electronic distribution** (enabled by the Web): It will be transmitted over the Web (not via the postal service), connecting everyone in the world across the manmade political boundaries that act as a constraint.

- **Structured, accessible information** (enabled by XML syntax and XBRL semantics): The information won't appear as an unstructured document, but rather structured information that a computer application can get into and understand.

> ✔ **Interactive, flexible** (enabled by a multidimensional model): Information can be cast by creators of the information or recast by any user. The information will likely follow the flexible multidimensional model, which provides for interactivity.

> ✔ **Open standard metadata** (enabled by XBRL and domains expressing metadata using XBRL): Business applications will be able to exchange shared, rather than proprietary, metadata.

Format as a choice, not a limitation

For yesterday's business report, the report creator determined the report's format when the report was created, with limited thought to how others in the business and financial reporting-supply chain would consume and use the data. This approach is a significant limitation to users of information contained in that report.

Business information in XBRL will be able to be formatted in any number of formats as chosen by both the creator and the consumer of the information. The creator of the business information can make the report available in a format they prefer, but the users of the information can take advantage and control of that or use their own formatting to achieve their desired goals. Business-report formatting will be more like getting ice cream from Baskin-Robbins, with your choice of 31 flavors! You can change from one presentation format to another with just a click or two of your mouse.

Transparency and visibility

Sunlight will shine on information like never before for a wide variety of reasons. For example, flexible formatting by users of the XBRL information makes the information easier to use on the user's terms, as opposed to how the creator may have desired. For example, if information is provided to you in an inflexible format and you have to search for the nugget of information you want within a mountain of other information, the information can be hard to understand.

But if the information format is flexible, you can organize it to your liking. You don't have to search through the report because you can simply tell the software application what you want to see and how you want to see it. Crowd sourcing occurs. *Crowd sourcing* is harnessing the power of the masses, much like blogs harness the masses, making everyone a news reporter who can post information to the Web about what they know or something they may have observed. Many believe that the market is the best regulator. The *market* is you, part of the crowd. If the information is there to be used, someone in the market or crowd will find it and can use that information to make a point they want others to see. The Web, XBRL, and lots of people like you looking at all this information make it harder for unscrupulous people to get away with nefarious deeds that they've been able to get away with in the past.

Just like blogs turned everyone into an investigative reporter, XBRL helps turn everyone into a regulator. This transparency is similar to the transparency created by standardizing the underlying technology that allows blogs. The development of blogs has had a huge effect on the way people obtain their news.

Information that is self-validating

You can use business rules to verify exchanged information (see Chapter 16). XBRL won't necessarily detect fraudulent information: That's impossible. You can classify business rules into two general categories:

- ✔ **Computations:** Rules that check computations — for example Assets = Liabilities + Equity.
- ✔ **Reportability rules:** Rules that check information based on other information — for example, if a specific line item exists on a balance sheet, certain policies and disclosures must also exist.

Today, you can do many of these types of validation and verification using paper-based disclosure checklists and manual processes. Imagine being able to automate the process of verifying all the computations and reportability rules within a financial statement! XBRL can achieve this goal.

Further, with XBRL you can exchange rules because they're separated from the applications that generate the information. The rules are within the XBRL taxonomy, part of the metadata needed to effectively exchange the information just like the name of a concept, its definition, and so on. As a result, the creator and consumer of the information can share the same business rules, which makes the structure of the information more clear.

Interactive information

The best example of interactive information is a Microsoft Excel pivot table. The data isn't locked into a specific spot within a document; rather, the user of the information can pivot the information, slicing and dicing it as they see fit. If more information were structured for meaning as opposed to being locked within documents, you could make more information interactive.

And if information uses the same or similar XBRL taxonomies, comparing information is a cakewalk. Drag information from multiple companies into an interactive information pivot table, and it's automatically lined up for comparison. You can do this task by using metadata from the XBRL taxonomy and XBRL instance.

Another metaphor to help you understand interactive information is a Rubik's Cube. Consider a financial statement as an example. Think of the slicing and dicing of a pivot table. Rather than being in one fixed format like the financial statements you see today, imagine having a financial statement that you can easily reorganize just as you would the colored squares of a Rubik's Cube. Give the financial Rubik's Cube a twist, and you can see the numbers that you want, where you want to see them, formatted as you desire. You can put numbers, accounting policies, and detailed disclosures of the financial statement notes together just by a metaphoric flick of your wrist! You can do this reorganization because you're not constrained by the one fixed format previously provided by the creators of financial reports.

System flexibility

In Chapter 1, we discuss some XBRL benefits and point out that one of the primary benefits the U.S. FDIC sought was the flexibility to verify and adjust information that must be reported by filing banks. The FDIC wanted the ability to add concepts for additional disclosures and drop unneeded information easily.

Prior to the implementation of XBRL, these types of system changes were challenging. One example of a challenge was the communication of the metadata to software vendors who created software for filing banks. The FDIC provided the metadata in a variety of different formats, including Microsoft Word, Microsoft Excel, HTML, and PDF. Importing this metadata into systems wasn't reliable. With the FDIC's change to XBRL, the changes are now a breeze because all metadata is communicated using one format: XBRL. The systems are updated, rules are checked to ensure that they work correctly, metadata is generated, and software vendors can reliably read all the metadata. All these characteristics make changing the information model against which financial institutions report to the FDIC effortless.

Metadata-driven system changes

Another area of flexibility relates to extensibility. Suppose that someone creates an information definition (that is, an XBRL taxonomy) that is 80 percent or even 99 percent of what you need to create your business reports. Today, that form is useless to you because, of course, you want 100 percent of what you need. XBRL allows for additional information, the tweaking of relationships, and other modifications. XBRL taxonomy models are extensible: Users can add concepts, change relationships, and, in many other ways, tweak the XBRL taxonomy or otherwise adapt it without breaking it or having to create a totally new XBRL taxonomy.

XBRL's extensibility isn't the same as XML's extensibility (see Chapter 2). XBRL's extendibility is predictable. XBRL software is written expecting these changes, and it understands where the changes will occur and what to do with new concepts or new relations. Programmers don't need to write code in order to handle new concepts or relations because XBRL information is always in the same predictable shape. As such, adjusting a system is as simple as adjusting the systems metadata; you don't need to write new code. All you do is adjust the XBRL taxonomy.

The need to write code or adjust computer programs to adjust for changes causes many problems. First, it creates a situation where business users don't have control over their processes; they need to rely on programmers in the IT departments to make adjustments and prepare reports. The rise of the personal computer and the electronic spreadsheet are evidence that business users don't like having to go to programmers in order to change something. Additionally, if you must go to the IT people to make a change, the system is less adaptable and less flexible because it takes longer to make any change to the system.

XBRL changes the dynamics of business system modifications, keeping business users in charge of their processes without needing to resort to spreadsheets, which cause other problems. So, the IT department gets what they need (robust rather than brittle systems), and the business users get what they need (flexibility and control).

Information portability

If all we needed to do was exchange data, CSV (comma-separated values) or XML would work just fine. Exchanging data today isn't rocket science. But data portability isn't what we need; *information* portability is what is needed. A business system understands its data model; it doesn't understand the data model of every other business system.

But what if every business system understood one format, and systems could exchange that information because every system understood that model? That is exactly what XBRL is: that common denominator. XBRL is standard, and it keeps information in context, enabling reliable automated exchange of information between different business systems that understand XBRL.

One version of the truth

The more copies of information you have, the more versions of the truth exist, and the harder it is to keep multiple versions of the truth in sync. Spreadsheets are the epitome of multiple versions of the truth.

Spreadsheets are great tools when used appropriately. Used the wrong way, they can cause significant problems. (See the section "Examining the Characteristics of Business Information Exchange Today," earlier in this chapter.) Imagine having hundreds of copies of the same database. That is exactly what exists with spreadsheets. Auditing spreadsheets has major challenges. One benefit of paper-based spreadsheets as compared to electronic was that creating paper-based spreadsheets was such a time-consuming process that not as many copies of information existed. But going back to paper isn't really the best way to solve this problem!

Semantic Web of information

We talk about the difference between the U.S. SEC's EDGAR system and its new Next-Generation EDGAR system earlier in the section "Semantic Web." Contrasting these two systems fundamentally shows the difference between the functionality of a digital filing cabinet (EDGAR) and an intelligent database (Next-Generation EDGAR).

The SEC EDGAR system is a document repository, but you can't get information out of the documents reliably or inexpensively unless you read the document or cut and paste information manually (that is, rekey). The new SEC Next-Generation EDGAR system is a database. You can get to the documents, and you can get inside the documents and get information out of the documents, automatically and reliably.

Next-Generation EDGAR fits nicely into the vision of the Semantic Web. EDGAR was a fantastic system in its era, but it's more like Web 1.0 than Web 3.0, the Semantic Web. Future repositories of information will have the characteristics not of EDGAR, but rather of Next-Generation EDGAR.

Plug-and-play information exchange

The ultimate goal, which may or may not be achievable in all cases, can be described as plug-and-play business information exchange, similar to how the Universal Serial Bus (USB) standard allows for plug-and-play hardware. Imagine the ability to integrate one application with another application by dragging and dropping icons using your mouse.

An absurd goal? Maybe for some things, but very possible for others. And this vision isn't some science-fiction fantasy. For many business information exchanges, this goal is quite achievable today.

We're not saying that all systems that exchange business information will be, or should be, plug-and-play data exchanges. A transaction system used to process automated teller machine transactions may not be a good use case for XBRL. XBRL is designed more for business information exchanges, such as financial reporting. It's also designed to handle the hundreds of little information exchanges, such as financial reports, that you participate in creating each day during your normal part of doing business. Reducing the net cost of implementing an information exchange and making information exchanges easier makes it more economical to automate more and more of these types of large and small business information exchanges.

When EDGAR got a facelift

See for yourself: Go to the EDGAR systems (www.sec.gov/edgar/searchedgar/webusers.htm) and then to the new Next-Generation EDGAR systems (www.sec.gov/idea/searchidea/webusers.htm). Doing a simple comparison of information for different time periods of one company or comparing information across company shows the difference between the two systems. EDGAR and Next-Generation EDGAR are both publically available systems that anyone on the Web can access. To get the full flavor of the difference between Web 1.0 (EDGAR) and Web 3.0 (Next-Generation EDGAR), we encourage you to experiment using both approaches. (To avoid having to type these long links, go to www.dummies.com/go/xbrl. This takes you to a landing page where you can click the link you need.)

Chapter 7

Feeding the Business Information-Supply Chain

*I*n this chapter, we take a closer look at the information-supply chain. We begin by contrasting an information-supply chain with a physical-supply chain, which helps you see the fundamental idea of what an information-supply chain is. We then walk you through the steps of creating an information-supply chain. Finally, we show you how creating information-supply chains for yourself eventually could be as easy as writing a blog or setting up a social network.

The Different Types of Supply Chains

You may be familiar with a *business-supply chain,* which is an interconnected network of businesses that moves products or services from the point of origin to the consumer and all the points in between. The *physical-supply chain* spans many different organizations that are involved in all aspects, from obtaining and processing the raw materials to distributing the finished goods, perhaps to a store, where they're sold to a consumer. Retail models of supply chains, wholesale models, and many other business-supply chain models exist. These kinds of supply chains and the management processes that make these supply chains operate effectively and efficiently have been around for some time. Each organization and each stakeholder are like a link in the chain that helps the participants achieve some business objective.

These days, digital-supply chains are challenging some physical-supply chains. Consider how music was distributed when it was on a physical CD as compared to the improvements of music technologies that allowed iTunes and its competitors to distribute music and other media over the Web. The physical part of the music (the CD) is becoming a thing of the past because it is more of a constraint now that other nonphysical options of distributing music exist. These digital-supply chains are challenging physical-supply chains. The MP3 standard music format suddenly changed something physical to a digital distribution model.

Information distribution also operates like a supply chain. Before the computer, business information was in the form of paper, a physical media. Today, more and more information, just like music, is exchanged electronically as digital files. Many times, however, the business information is created digitally, transferred digitally, and then printed so that it becomes a physical medium again. But the new medium doesn't require physical distribution.

An *information-supply chain* is all the components, including people, processes, and technologies, required to collect information from the distinct processes that generate that information and then efficiently and effectively distribute it accurately and in a timely manner to the appropriate consumers of that information. The consumers turn that information into knowledge for one purpose or another.

To fully understand the notion of a supply chain, be it physical or digital, think of the entire supply chain rather than the links. For example, Wal-Mart's key competitive advantage is its supply chain. In his book *The World Is Flat* (Farrar, Straus & Giroux), Thomas Friedman writes,

> *"To appreciate how important supply-chaining has become as a source of competitive advantage and profit in a flat world, think about this one fact: Wal-Mart today is the biggest retail company in the world, and it does not make a single thing. All it makes is a hyper-efficient supply chain."*

A friction-free and zero-latency information-supply chain, straight-through reporting, is a new way of thinking about the flow of information that you need to understand. Although a totally friction-free and zero-latency business information-supply chain is a theoretical target that you can never really achieve, if you understand the idea, you can understand the existing friction and reduce it.

What do we mean by *friction-free* and *zero latency*? *Friction* generally slows things down. *Latency* is the time you have to wait to have something you want. We're using the metaphor friction-free and zero latency to conjure up an image in your mind. Another way to refer to this is *straight-through reporting,* which is all about maximizing the objectives you're trying to achieve while minimizing the costs.

The Information-Supply Chain

An *information-supply chain* is a set of components (organizations, people, and applications) that collects information and efficiently distributes that information to its consumers. The information-supply chain must meet all the objectives of exchanging business information. Enabling technologies let you achieve these objectives and offer characteristics that hadn't existed (see Chapter 6).

To understand the information-supply chain, we describe a specific, tangible example of one: external financial reporting. The processes and participants of the external financial-reporting-supply chain look something like Figure 7-1.

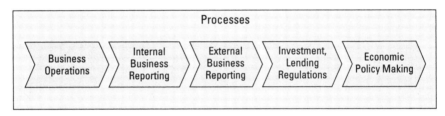

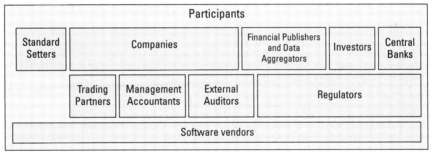

Figure 7-1:
The external financial-reporting-supply chain.

Source: XBRL International.

The typical large organization uses about 800 spreadsheets and word-processing documents to summarize the information that eventually becomes its external financial report. Figure 7-1 shows the processes and the participants in the external financial-reporting-supply chain. They work together to make external financial reporting work. Those that operate within the external financial reporting information-supply chain include

> ✔ **Standards setters**, such as the International Accounting Standards Board (IASB) and Financial Accounting Standards Board (FASB), set external financial reporting standards that others in the process use. The standards express semantics, such as concepts and the relations between concepts and rules, and otherwise define financial-reporting standards.

- ✔ **Companies** use the standards to create and submit their financial reports to central regulatory repositories, such as the U.S. SEC EDGAR database. (See Chapter 6 for more on EDGAR.)

- ✔ **Investors and other analysts** look at the financial information provided by the companies using the standards for external financial reporting. This group includes regulators, lenders, suppliers, customers, potential investors, and so on. Central banks are a type of analyst and use this financial information in the process of establishing economic policies.

- ✔ **Third-party accountants and auditors** play a role in verifying that everything is on the up and up. Transactions have to be arm's-length. These auditors do their best to prevent the use of fraudulent information, and they generally verify that the standards are correctly followed.

- ✔ **Regulators** make sure that the process operates fairly, smoothly, and in the best interest of the markets. Regulators, which include stock exchanges in some countries, may play the role of standards setters, or they may use standards set by others, such as IFRS, so that they don't have to create their own standards. Many times, regulators operate centralized repositories to store information.

- ✔ **Financial publishers** publish financial statements in a variety of formats for filing with regulators, mailing to stockholders, and otherwise disseminating the financial information.

- ✔ **Data aggregators** operate in this supply chain to take the information companies prepare, put it together to make it comparable in their own proprietary way, and then sell the information to analysts and investors. Data aggregators help the process because each analyst or investor doesn't have to rekey financial information themselves; it's a value-added service.

- ✔ **Software vendors** create software that assists their clients in their different roles within these processes. Different participants use different software in order to meet their specific needs.

Take note: In this model, data aggregators are rekeying data or developing costly sophisticated semi-automated parsing and mapping technologies. Do you really need data aggregators to provide these kinds of costly value-added services? Well, under the current model, it's certainly a necessary value-added activity.

The costly rekeying, mapping and parsing may sound like an obvious inefficiency, but other, not-as-obvious inefficiencies also result from this rekeying:

- ✔ **Timeliness** is decreased because of the time spent rekeying.

- ✔ **Errors** go up because humans, who make mistakes, do the rekeying.

✔ **Total cost** of the system goes up.

✔ **Systemic risk** of the system goes up.

Table 7-1 takes a closer look at how the roles look under the current historical supply-chain model and how it looks based on an emerging model that some systems are moving to.

Table 7-1	Comparing Old and New Models	
Aspect of Model	*Historical Model*	*Emerging Model*
Sets standards	Each country's own standard setter, such as FASB	One standard setter, IASB
Articulates standards in	Books (can sometimes be somewhat vague and hard to understand)	Books (will still be used), Web pages, XBRL
Creates financial information using	Spreadsheets, word processors	XBRL
Distributes information	Postal service on paper, HTML, or PDF on Web	XBRL and RSS feed
Aggregates, normalizes information	Manually rekeying by data aggregator, data is generally normalized	Substantially less rekeying, less normalization
Publishes information	Unstructured or structured for presentation; paper, PDF, HTML	XBRL structured for meaning; one version can be rendered as PDF, HTML, other formats, or printed on paper
Reconfigures financial report	Inflexible; you get one format	Flexible, interactive, users can adjust the format as they see fit
Regulates the market	Regulator	Regulator, the market itself (crowd-sourcing)
Analyzes information	Regulators, analysts and investors	Regulators, analysts, and investors (less rekeying)

We use external financial reporting as an example because information is available and external financial reporting has been through this change process to a degree in several countries around the world. As such, you can find clues as to how this process can work for other areas of business information exchange.

No new model will be perfect. Different mediums have different characteristics. New things are possible, but some old approaches and techniques should continue. Each different supply chain decides for itself what is and isn't appropriate.

Business strategy transformed by the new economics of information

The transformations caused by the Web and other technologies aren't unique to business, and no business is exempt from change, no matter how much it wants to be. In fact, the only constant in any supply chain is that things will change. Consider for a moment what is happening in other industries:

- **Everyone is in the news business.** More and more newspapers are struggling because of new economics of information. Blogs are making everyone a reporter who chooses to be a one. Professional journalists aren't always the first to provide information. Everybody with a decent cell phone can take pictures or video. Video's rich media is cutting into how much people want or need to read.

- **Digital photography is overtaking film.** Digital photography wreaked havoc on those businesses set up to process film. Not only that, but the removal from the physical film, converting the physical film into something a computer can understand, totally changed distribution channels.

- **Digital movies abound.** Digital movies (rather than film-based ones) are in the process of revolutionizing the movie business.

A business information exchange platform

Think about the bigger picture of business information exchange for a moment. We consider the platform or framework in which business information exchange takes place by focusing on one specific area of business information exchange: external financial reporting.

You can view external financial reporting as part of a platform. The platform's purpose is to enable businesses to obtain the necessary capital they need to operate, and part of this process is the exchange of financial information from the organizations who make use of capital to the investors and lenders who provide the capital. This process of exchanging external financial information has many participants (refer to Figure 7-1).

How is this important information created and communicated in today's global environment? We highlight a few characteristics to show that external financial reporting is a platform and that platform organization can create dramatic efficiencies:

- ✔ **One global set of financial reporting standards:** IFRS is getting more and more traction, replacing the approximately 80 different sets of financial reporting standards that did exist around the world, which made exchanging financial information more challenging. For example, imagine that you had to regulate banks that operate in 27 European countries, and they each had different financial reporting standards.

- ✔ **One global financial publishing format:** XBRL is becoming the publishing format for financial information. Working with IFRS, which is the metadata of the financial information, XBRL and IFRS together allow for a standard, flexible, reusable financial publishing format. Contrast that one format to the multiple formats generally used today to publish financial information.

- ✔ **One global capital market:** Because of IFRS and XBRL, analysis of financial information can be vastly easier because you use one standard set of metadata (IFRS) and one publishing format (XBRL) globally. Business analysts can more easily analyze and compare companies from any country in their search for good investments.

Is this the way external financial reporting works today? No, not yet. Maybe it never will. Political or business agendas could preclude the creation of one global capital market. The point here is to show that external financial reporting works within a platform and to demonstrate how efficiently a system can work. It's up to the participants of the external financial-reporting-supply chain, or other supply chains, to leverage the available tools to maximize the effectiveness and efficiencies of their supply chains. Some regulators, such as the U.S. SEC, are already doing so. Others will likely follow.

General business information exchange, much of which is business reports, also operates within a platform. You control that platform, at least for business information exchange in your organization. Your current platform for the distribution of business information, such as business reports, was designed and developed in the age of paper, long before the creation of the Web and other technologies. The tools and technologies your platform can leverage have changed — consider the Web — but the fundamental infrastructure components of that platform haven't yet changed much. Chapter 6 discusses these existing fundamental infrastructure's characteristics: paper-based, proprietary, inflexible document formats, and so on. These characteristics result in a lot of rekeying as information gets moved around within the current platform for exchanging business information.

Like the Web, XBRL is very much part of a new infrastructure that will allow new models for achieving the objectives within the platform for exchanging business information.

Large business systems, such as ERP and CPM, house much of this business information, while smaller, but important, spreadsheets house other information, and still more systems smaller than ERP systems, but larger than simple spreadsheets, contain other information. New types of specialty systems have been developed in order to meet specific objectives and to work together to create a way to supplement core systems, including

- **Business intelligence applications:** Business intelligence (BI) is the ability of a business to convert its data into relevant, timely, accurate information that generates competitive advantage and stakeholder value. Today, data from the workhorse of transactional systems, the relational database, is generated by Online Transaction Processing (OLTP) and put into data warehouses, which are also known as data marts or Online Analytical Processing (OLAP) systems. These data marts are accessed by flexible proprietary BI applications, which make use of the flexible multidimensional model.

- **Content-management systems:** Content management (CM) is the practice of supporting the life cycle of digital information of all sorts. This digital information, many times referred to as *content,* may take the form of word-processing documents, spreadsheets, text files, HTML, PDF, XML, audio, video, images, or other types of digital resources, all which require management.

- **Knowledge-management systems:** Knowledge management (KM) is the practice of consciously and comprehensively identifying, gathering, organizing, expressing, and distributing an organization's information and other resources, such as the skills of its people.

- **Flexible micro-applications:** Software commonly used today is generally too inflexible. New software-building tools, such as XSLT, AJAX, FLEX, WPF/XAML, and microformats, allow for the creation of much smaller and more flexible applications, adjustable not by technical people via programming, but rather by business people who edit domain metadata.

  These applications are small — we refer to them as micro- or nano-applications, and sometimes they're called *widgets.* These highly flexible applications make use of information across many different business software systems typically accessible via the Web. *Mashups,* which use data from a number of sources mashed up into one interface, are a good example of these flexible micro-applications.

- **Internal semantic webs**: The Semantic Web (capital letters, think Internet) is Web 3.0. It's the external system that everyone is connected to. In addition, every company will, or likely should, have its own internal semantic web (lowercase, think intranet or extranet) that provides the organization with one database in the sky for all their internal information. Companies can look at all their information as if it were one single database, using one set of metadata. That database will weave all information together into, well, a web of meaning that a company can leverage for competitive advantage.

These core and supplemental business systems make up your business information platform. XBRL will help weave core systems and supplemental systems together to create more robust yet flexible connectivity between systems for substantially less cost and effort.

Software is some of the most complex equipment ever created by humans. What is even more complex are the processes humans invent to undertake the business that the software was built for. XBRL and other technologies will help weave these systems together into hyper-efficient and effective information-supply chains that help you do business and that are flexible enough to evolve as your business adapts to the ever-changing environment in which you operate.

The new model of business information exchange is not *Star Trek* or *Star Wars*-types of notions, but rather the realities of living in the digital-integrated information age. The same technologies that are causing information overload can help solve the problems associated with information overload. Living in today's world with yesterday's technologies will be painful. (Chapter 8 explores these new possibilities.)

An information-supply chain in action

Every business is a member of numerous information-supply chains. Some are simple and straightforward, while others are more complex. In this, section, we walk you through the tasks you need to perform to create a simple information-supply chain. These steps better help you get a sense for what an information-supply chain is and what you need to do in order to set one up. These steps include references to specific chapters that can help you perform each step:

1. **Identify a process where information is exchanged (see Chapter 9).**

2. **Examine the existing process and see whether it has room for improvement and what the ROI may be (see Chapter 10).**

3. **Understand the information that is to be exchanged and express that information's definition in the form of an XBRL taxonomy (see Chapter 17).**

   4. **Create an instance of information that will be exchanged in the form of an XBRL instance (see Chapter 18).**

   5. **Transfer the information from its creator to its consumer.**

      This transfer can take a lot of different forms and is really dependent on a bunch of factors. Is the recipient within your organization or external to it? Is the recipient a human or a business system? Is the information confidential? How much security infrastructure is needed? Chapter 14 can help you find software to help transfer information.

   6. **(Optional) Store the information in something other than the final destination of the information.**

      For example, many systems desire to keep a copy of every XBRL instance received (document of record) as opposed to simply taking the information, extracting it, and feeding it to the application that will ultimately consume the information. Chapter 14 can help you find software for storing XBRL.

   7. **Consume the information within some process.**

      The consumption process may be consuming one XBRL instance at a time, simply feeding it as an input to some other process (see Step 8), or it may be analyzing a number of XBRL instances received.

   8. **Output information that is possibly the input for some other process.**

      Go back to Step 1 and repeat this list of steps.

Those are the basic steps. How often you repeat Steps 5 through 8 really depends on the process. You can exchange information hourly, daily, monthly, quarterly, annually, or some other period of time.

The preceding steps are the pieces of the process. The process is general. You can input the output of this process into another process. Conversely, your input may be from the output of some other process. (Chapters 11 and 12 can also help you with the details of implementing your information-supply chain.)

A Business Information-Supply Chain

You can understand what a business information-supply chain is by looking at one in detail. The state government of Nevada and IRIS Business Systems published a white paper that explains the vision of the state for creating a Nevada Business Portal (NBP). We use that white paper as a basis for explaining the NBP.

The NBP will be a complete end-to-end system, enveloping the state's individual agencies, constituencies that the state serves, and all the business systems within those entities:

- ✔ **Business systems within one state agency:** Many times, one state agency has many different business systems that it uses to transact its business.

- ✔ **Other state agencies:** One state agency interacts with other state agencies.

- ✔ **Constituencies:** State agencies also interact with their constituents, such as a business or an individual.

- ✔ **County and other local government agencies:** At times, interaction with other local governmental agencies occurs.

- ✔ **Other states:** In some cases, interactions with other states occur, such as when an insurance company operates in Nevada and also within another state.

- ✔ **Federal government:** In some cases, interactions with the federal government occur, such as in FBI background checks or submission of CAFR reports (financial statements of government agencies) to the U.S. Census Bureau.

The NBP system is based on other standardized business reporting systems created in the Netherlands and Australia (see Chapter 9).

Key aspects of the NBP include the following:

- ✔ Laws and regulations are created. The actual rules, policies, and procedures come from legislation, administrative rulings and other state agency decisions, and so on.

- ✔ These legislative and administrative decisions are articulated as platform-independent policies and procedures (and aren't locked into any one agency's proprietary business-system format) in a form readable and clearly understandable by both humans and computers (an XBRL taxonomy), enabling seamless cross-system interactions among the various state agencies and with constituents. This setup minimizes misunderstandings, misinterpretations, and illegal acts, such as an agency collecting information it's not legally entitled to collect.

- ✔ The NBP has a workflow-intensive framework, based on rules, policies, and procedures, that both drives and controls the system. The electronic and human-readable rules drive this workflow. Transactions are platform-independent and easily transferable using the same Web technologies to transfer information between state agencies, and between state agencies and constituents.

✔ The NBP stores and centrally controls the rules, polices, and procedures XBRL taxonomy accessed by all systems. Individual systems store transactions and must comply with the centralized set of rules, policies, and procedures.

Hence, when a business entity registered with the system initiates a transaction, the system looks at various criteria defined in the rules, policies, and procedures and automatically guides the business user through each step of the process and all transactions required for each step. The objectives that system is trying to achieve include

✔ **Reduced redundancy:** No multiple submissions to different agencies by constituents — information is submitted to the system once via one interface, and the system then distributes the information to the state agencies authorized to have the information.

✔ **Greater agency autonomy:** Agencies are free to use whatever systems they like; the only thing they must do is integrate with the NBP.

✔ **Clarity:** The rules, policies, and procedures are clearly communicated in a form both computers and humans can understand.

Here's a quick example to show you how this business information-supply chain works. Say that Mr. Walker, a citizen of Nevada, is planning to set up a trucking company called Business A. For this new company, he needs to obtain the appropriate licenses and clearances from a set of state agencies. Because it's a new business that currently has no systems in place, Mr. Walker can go to a Web site and complete forms to submit information. (Later, when he has business systems in place, he can build interfaces to the NBP's Web services interface.)

Mr. Walker goes to the Setting Up a Business section of the NBP. All the needed encryption, security, credentials, logins, and so on are taken care of. He fills in his information, the information is validated before he can submit it to the state, and then the process is integrated with other processes.

For example, Mr. Walker's registration needs to be approved by the Department of Motor Vehicles (because he has to have a commercial truck driver's license) and by certain County offices. Mr. Walker can view the status of his application throughout the process, receive updates via e-mail alerts, and view comment letters from state and county agencies until he either receives an approval or a rejection letter for starting his business.

You get the idea of how this business information-supply chain might operate and how you have similar types of transactions, only for different purposes and between different parties. But the idea of exchanging business information is fairly universal.

Building Your Own Information-Supply Chain in the Future

As little as 15 years ago, setting up a supply chain would have cost millions of dollars. Today, it costs substantially less. Granted, creating a bullet-proof, highly secure, robust system similar to what the FDIC or the SEC has will cost way more, but these systems are still less expensive than they once were and are significantly higher in functionality.

Think about what else has happened with Web 2.0. Before systems for creating things like blogs and wikis existed, you had to be a programmer to create them. However, today, because systems exist that enable you to create such systems, you can simply use the systems to add another instance of the type of system you desire to create.

Also, all these different systems (blogs, social networks, and so on) focus on one type of information. But where is the system for uploading business information to the Web and making that information available for others to use? In the future, creating a supply chain will likely be as easy as setting up some other things with which you may be familiar:

- **Blog** (www.blogger.com): If you want to become a news reporter, go here, and you can set up your own blog in a matter of minutes.

- **Wiki** (www.wikispaces.com): "Want to set up a wiki?" the site asks. You can have your own wiki up and running in moments.

- **Discussion group** (http://groups.yahoo.com): Discussion groups have been around for years; this site is one of the most popular.

- **Social network** (www.ning.com): Love Facebook.com or MySpace.com? Build your own social network.

- **Video channel** (www.youtube.com/members): How about your own on-demand TV channel?

- **Photo gallery** (http://picasaweb.google.com): Create your own photo gallery here.

- **Information-supply chain**: Well, sorry we're not quite there yet. . . . Maybe such a system will be the next billion dollar IPO!

Yup. Simple as that. Use a wizard, plug in the ability to receive information, validate, render, analyze, store — all the things you'd do with any information-supply chain. Just as enterprising people have created Web sites to facilitate the sharing of videos, photos, blogs, and wikis, it's just a matter of time before someone will create a Web site that allows you to set up your own information-supply chain, upload information, share it with others, and allow others to access the information.

Chapter 8

Seeing the Transformation of Business Information Exchange

In This Chapter

▶ Looking at transformational technologies

▶ Predicting impact from clues offered by other transformations

▶ Gaining insight from regulatory reporting and financial reporting changes

▶ Creating your own transformation

*T*his chapter is about peering into the future as best we can, based the past. The purpose is to help you plan your future. Predictions are never perfect, but they can be useful in understanding what something is, what it isn't, and how it may impact you. Looking at changes that have occurred in other industries can also provide clues to changes in your own industry. This process reveals clues as to what the future might hold and help you plan for that future by helping you see opportunities and fend off potential threats.

This chapter is also a visionary look into the future of business reporting and XBRL. We look at changes that are already occurring in regulatory reporting and financial reporting and extrapolate from those clues to help you see the broader changes that are likely to occur in business information exchange in general.

A Transformation Will Occur

The global consultancy firm Gartner classified XBRL as a transformational technology. Gartner defines *transformational* as something that "enables new ways of doing business across industries that will result in major shifts in industry dynamics." Major shifts mean lots of change and some winners and some losers.

Accounting Today, in its September 4–24, 2000, issue, said, "XBRL is perhaps the most revolutionary change in financial reporting since the first general ledger." Many other similar types of statements have been made, but these types of statements don't really help you understand *why* some sort of transformation will occur, what the transformation might look like and mean to you, or what you should be doing. For that, you need details. So how do you get details about something that hasn't yet occurred?

Well, getting details is actually not quite as hard as it may seem. One way to predict something is to look at similar types of things to learn from them. Then, you do your best to project what you have learned from the other things on to what you're trying to predict.

Two specific areas can help you understand the transformation that XBRL is being hailed for bringing:

✔ Transformations from other industries

✔ Transformations from areas of business reporting that adopted XBRL early

Gleaning clues from other transformations

Various industries have experienced transformations, and their experiences can give you a sense of the magnitude of the changes that are likely to be in store for business information exchange, which includes business reporting. In this section, we discuss big changes that relatively small-looking ideas caused.

Product codes

The UPC is a simple enough idea. In 1974, UPC codes began appearing on products you buy to relieve the congestion occurring in supermarket check-out lines. Consider these facts:

✔ PricewaterhouseCoopers projects that the UPC saves $17 billion annually in the domestic retail industry alone.

✔ Businesses such as Home Depot have more than 75,000 inventory items in their mammoth stores. These big-box stores, which displaced many smaller stores, couldn't have existed if the UPC wasn't around to help these stores keep track of their large inventories.

✔ The people who created the UPC code are now going through the process of expanding the code to collect additional information. For example, they want to be able to identify which batch a product came from to help with things such as product recalls, merchandizing, and so on. This UPC code expansions means not only do they find the UPC useful, but that its creators and users realize its potential.

Metal boxes

The standard shipping container perhaps doesn't seem that ingenious. The first idea it represents is to put items into batches or containers rather than shipping them in bulk — kind of like using a shopping bag when you go to the store. The second innovation behind the shipping container is that you take some steel and, rather than creating boxes of whatever size you want, use standard-size boxes that fit nicely onto ships, trucks, trains, and so on.

A simple enough invention, a 40-by-20-by-20 steel box. And yet, the standardized shipping container caused changes to how ships are loaded and unloaded. It also impacted ship, train, and truck construction and port and manufacturing facilities locations.

Busy ports in New York City and San Francisco ignored the shipping container and shrank as a consequence; new ports that adapted to containers, such as New Jersey and Oakland, built container cranes and grabbed the business. Today, the ports of New York City and San Francisco are tourist attractions. Rotterdam anticipated the impact of the standard shipping container and was the biggest harbor in the world for years, although now Asian harbors are the biggest in the world. Why are the Asian harbors the biggest? Well, because that location is where a great deal of the manufacturing moved because the efficiencies of the logistics made it irrelevant as to where the manufacturing facilities needed to be.

With the advent of the shipping container, the number of longshoremen performing manual loading and unloading in New York City plunged by 90 percent, and the time to unload and unload a ship went from 14 days to 14 hours. Achieving the levels of trade we have today without the shipping container and the efficiencies it enabled would be inconceivable.

Music

The MP3 is turning the music industry on its ear! Think about your music collection. Depending on when you were born, how did you store your collection of music? Before LPs became standard, you may have stored songs on a pre-LP (long-playing) format. You may have stored them on LP records, 45s, 76s, or even 8-track tapes. Then maybe you went to cassette tapes, reel-to-reel tapes, CDs, or maybe DVDs.

Then suddenly, the MP3 comes along. MP3 changes the format from physical to something digital that is portable on small, cool gadgets. Now you can use the format to create and store your own media, and what you're storing doesn't even have to be songs: It can be podcasts or audio books. You can play this media on your computer, in your car, on your phone, or on your iPod. Consider these facts:

✔ iTunes has a catalog of approximately 6 million songs. It costs iTunes virtually nothing to add songs to its catalog, and, once added, a song can be distributed globally via the Web for pennies. A music store would be lucky to have space for 10,000 CDs and, to sell the CDs, you have to get them to the store.

✔ Apple, a computer company, going into the music business? That thought is as absurd as someone trying to get into the book-selling business on the Web, errrr . . . like Amazon.com. Anyone can produce and distribute a song or other audio for pennies on his personal computer to anyone else in the world.

✔ Podcasts made it so that you can listen to your favorite radio shows anytime you want, not when the radio network airs the broadcast. Video podcasting is having a similar impact on the television shows we watch.

Digital photography

Photographs came in many different standard physical mediums, one of the most popular being 35mm film. Remember the little drive-up photo booths where you could drop off your pictures for processing? No? Well, at least in its day, it was a great idea, but you don't see many of these booths around these days. Consider this:

✔ Today, you can take a picture, get it onto your computer, and distribute it globally via the Web in less time that it takes to develop a Polaroid photo.

✔ Taking pictures no longer has a cost associated with it. (Well, maybe a little cost for memory to store the photos.)

✔ Processing photos requires only your personal computer.

Reading the clues provided by early XBRL adopters

Some areas of business information exchange are already seeing a significant amount of adoption of XBRL. Early adopters of XBRL fell in two primary categories: regulatory compliance reporting and financial reporting.

Some of the earliest adopters of XBRL were those who regulate you. All around the world, regulators are adopting XBRL. Around the world, each country has something of a common set of regulators. Here's a list of types of regulators that are already adopting XBRL in countries around the world:

✔ Capital market regulators (that is, regulators of stock markets)

✔ Tax offices

✔ Banking regulators

✔ National statistics offices

✔ Corporate registrars

Two things are worth pointing out: First, these regulators aren't the only categories that use XBRL. They're simply the common types of categories that different regulators have already expressed interest in, are currently undergoing implementation and have moved, or are currently moving to XBRL to help them collect information from those they regulate.

The second point we want to make is that just one regulator using XBRL can mean that XBRL will impact hundreds of thousands, or even millions, of users. Add up the number of users, and this number is quite big. Businesses required to use XBRL eventually realize that they can use XBRL for purposes other than simply providing information to those that regulate them. Further, each of these businesses, because of the regulatory use of XBRL, already have in place at least some of the infrastructure for using XBRL, which they can now leverage for uses other than reporting to regulators.

Why are these regulators making these changes? Chapter 9 discusses the benefits from changing to XBRL. You can also read about the specific benefits that one regulator, the U.S. FDIC, realized from its XBRL conversion in Chapter 1.

Clues from financial reporting leadership in changing financial reporting

One of the most pervasive and significant types of business reporting is external financial reporting. (For more on external financial reporting, see Chapter 6.) Financial reporting is another area that is making considerable use of XBRL, which isn't surprising because accountants started the XBRL snowball rolling in 1998. Since that time, the accounting profession has accumulated a lot of support for XBRL in the area of financial reporting. Much of this financial reporting is to regulators. The accountants realized early that XBRL had more applicability to reporting than just financial reporting. But financial reporting was what was used to drive XBRL's adoption globally, commonly by regulators collecting this financial information.

Calls for changes to financial reporting

Two significant industry transformational initiatives are worth pointing out, and XBRL plays a role in both initiatives. The American Institute of Certified Public Accountants (AICPA, the professional association for CPAs in the United States) calls for the first initiative. In a white paper issued by the AICPA Assurance Services Executive Committee called "The Shifting Paradigm in Business Reporting and Assurance," the AICPA explains the transformation that is occurring. You can get that white paper at `www.aicpa. org/Professional+Resources/ Accounting+and+Auditing/ BRAAS/downloads/AICPA_ASEC_ Whitepaper_Final_20082008 April_2008.pdf`. (*Tip:* To avoid having to

type these long links, go to `www.dummies. com/go/xbrl`. This takes you to a landing page where you can click the link you need.)

The second initiative, a combined effort of the six leading global audit networks, focuses on how to improve global capital markets. The Global Public Policy Symposium brought together many of the key players concerned with ensuring the quality and reliability of financial reporting that is so essential for the success and stability of global capital markets and to investor confidence. This group documents its vision in the white paper "Global Capital Markets and the Global Economy: A Vision from the CEOs of the International Audit Network" (see `www.globalpublicpolicy symposium.com/CEO_Vision.pdf`.)

Even before XBRL existed and before the Web took off, those who worked with financial information were already getting into position to get the maximum benefit from XBRL, and they didn't even know it. They were standardizing their metadata, even though most accountants didn't understand what the term metadata meant. (For more on metadata, see Chapter 21.)

Rather than each country creating and maintaining its own set of financial reporting standards, which resulted in about 80 different sets of financial reporting standards around the world, the idea was to create one high-quality set of financial reporting standards that everyone could use. This goal gave birth in about 1973 to IFRS. This process went on for a number of years with a lot of work and limited adoption, but as the world became more and more of a global community — and particularly when the Web took off — it seemed to get a bit of a kick in the pants. IFRS really took off when the members of the European Union (EU) agreed to use IFRS as the financial reporting standard for public companies (called *listed companies*) that were regulated by some member of the EU. Another thing that helped IFRS get going was XBRL. And XBRL helped IFRS! It was a symbiotic match made in heaven. IFRS was the metadata, and XBRL was the format used to express the metadata and exchange IFRS-based financial reports.

The transformation of financial reporting

Enabling technologies, changes in dynamics, and the mood caused by scandals and financial crisis are impacting one another and are creating a perfect storm for the initiation of transformation of the world of financial reporting.

XBRL is only part of these dynamics; it's simply an enabling technology that contributes to meeting the objectives of financial reporting in the 21st century. Sarbanes Oxley (SOX), IFRS, the Web, and increased transparency in general are other parts.

Chapter 9 is packed with examples on XBRL projects that are already changing financial reporting. Chapter 13 is dedicated to one major project, the U.S. SEC's mandate of XBRL for financial reporting by all U.S. public companies. All these financial reporting-related projects are just the beginning of a bigger trend.

Understanding the Transformation of Business Information Exchange

Business information exchange is a broad category. The uses of XBRL for external financial reporting and statutory reporting by listed or public companies are substantial by any measure. Regulators require much of this reporting. But a lot of financial reporting has nothing to do with government regulators, and a lot of business information exchange has nothing to do with financial information.

The internal use of XBRL will likely dwarf external use and reporting to regulators and investors. Further, the use of XBRL for nonfinancial reporting will likely dwarf its use for financial reporting.

Organizations will discover the benefits of XBRL from reporting to regulators, mandated by these regulators in many cases. Every organization will be able to realize the same benefits internally that regulators today are already realizing.

You may have heard the saying that there are three kinds of people: Those who make things happen, those who watch things happen, and those who wonder what happened. The question now is, "Which category will you put yourself in for this historical period of transformation of business information exchange?"

We mention financial reporting by publically listed companies, which are usually regulated by a stock exchange or some government agency, such as the SEC in the United States. Consider other types of external financial reporting: private companies; not-for-profit organizations; and federal, state, and local governmental agencies. Chapter 13 discusses how the SEC's mandate of XBRL will likely indirectly impact these types of financial reporting.

A plethora of nonfinancial information exchanges also exists: corporate-sustainability reporting, environmental or green reporting, carbon-footprint reporting, and triple bottom line. We could go on and on, but we think you can see our point: XBRL for regulatory reporting and external financial reporting is only a start.

Exposure to XBRL from a company's use in one area of business reporting gives them the infrastructure to use XBRL in-house for one specific use, which leads to the experimentation and use of XBRL in other areas. The internal use of XBRL will eventually dwarf the use of XBRL for reporting to external parties. Thousands of small (even tiny) information-supply chains (see Chapter 7) will be glued together because it's inexpensive to do so and the resulting benefits are so profound. The infrastructure offered by the Web and other technologies for things such as distribution of this information would have been cost prohibitive for smaller companies to implement — until now, that is.

Envisioning XBRL Killer Applications

We wish we could tell you about the XBRL killer app or apps that are changing the world, but at this stage of XBRL's evolution, we're not aware of such applications. Those killer applications haven't been built yet, as far as we know. XBRL is still maturing, so we have to wait for software vendors to make these applications available.

What we *can* do is describe to you the characteristics that such killer applications may possess and the types of things those applications might do:

- ✓ **Business-person-to-business-person information exchange:** The application would allow one business person to exchange information with another business person with no assistance required from the IT department. For example, you could maintain information in something that would look like a spreadsheet, and that information would automatically flow into some process for which one of your coworkers is responsible. The two of you negotiate the information exchange: You don't need to get your IT department involved, and you don't have to rekey to exchange this information (you know, like you're doing today with those spreadsheets).

✔ **Dynamic information:** The application would allow for dynamic information exchange, not just static forms: The business user can change the information set being exchanged. Again, no need to get the IT department involved to change your form.

✔ **Collaboration:** The applications let you do your job, and others in the information-supply chain do theirs in a collaborative way, so well that you may think that you're using integrated applications (you're not!). The connecting link between the applications is XBRL. The XBRL standard helps enable this collaboration.

✔ **Operating environment:** The application isn't just one application, but a collaboration of applications within a robust, business-user-friendly operating environment. An entire operating environment is built around the application, which is hopefully an open system. Think along the lines of how something like Apple's iPods integrate with iTunes, how users can order iTunes music, and how album covers are automatically downloaded for your music.

✔ **Agility:** The application is agile. The application enables proactive assessments and real-time processing of transactions. For example, for cost, logistical, or tax optimization, the system communicates with other systems within the information-supply chain by using — you guessed it — XBRL as the means of communications. Other standards, such as RSS, are also involved and assist in this process.

✔ **Radically tailorable tool, but within a rigid environment:** Preformatted templates may get you started, or you can build your own templates. All the templates are adjustable, configurable, and dynamic — not static forms. Highly skilled domain experts create these templates, lesser skilled experts adjust them within bounds, and even lesser skilled workers use the templates and the application infrastructure to do their job. You have flexibility where you need it, but not where you don't.

✔ **Building blocks:** Business users won't interact with XBRL at all. Rather, they interact with a logical model that is made up of several building blocks. These building blocks are constructed to work together, hiding the complexity of the XBRL syntax. There is a fairly small number of building blocks, but users can add more, if necessary. These building blocks are similar to Microsoft Visio shapes. Incredibly smart programmers engineer these building blocks, while highly skilled programmers that are XBRL experts construct them. These experts can build new building blocks, but they may not break the logical model.

✔ **Business-rules driven:** Business rules allow the user to interact with the business information and never make certain categories of mistakes. The application simply won't allow a business user to, say, create a balance sheet that doesn't balance or a movement analysis that doesn't properly foot. It's as though a little accountant lives in the application, in the form of rules, which always makes sure that all the *i*'s are dotted and the *t*'s are crossed.

✔ **Integrated internal audit process:** Thanks to a built-in internal audit process, all information is there to see, and the internal audit process is part of the building blocks. Creating information without the ability to audit the information yourself to be sure that you're doing things correctly is impossible.

✔ **Smart transactions:** Many business reporting transactions are more science than art. In an accounting system, for example, you can't post all transactions to any account. Ninety-nine percent of transactions are quite predictable and follow specific patterns.

Starting Your Own Transformation

This chapter looks at ways others are making use of XBRL. But what about a little closer to home? What about you and your company? What kind of transformation will occur there? Well, that's up to you.

If you're anxious to get the transformation process started in your organization, your department, or your group, but don't quite know where to start, flip to Chapter 7, which walks you through creating an information-supply chain. If that general guidance doesn't suit your needs, Chapter 9 walks you through how others are building information-supply chains and may provide inspiration for a way to create your own little (or big) transformation.

That is really all there is to it! Creating your own transformation may not cut your costs by millions of dollars or improve your efficiency or effectiveness on a large scale, but it will help you see what's involved with actually making use of XBRL. We encourage you to experiment. Remember that even Rome wasn't built in a day! Lots of small improvements can create quite an impact.

If you want more detailed guidance on how to get your project going, see Part III, which gets you started successfully pursuing and executing an XBRL project.

Part III
Successfully Pursuing and Executing an XBRL Project

The 5th Wave   By Rich Tennant

"I hate when you bring XBRL with you on camping trips."

In this part . . .

You have to understand how you can put XBRL to use for you, which is what this part is all about. We show you how others are making use of XBRL, discuss how you can make your own business case for its use, cover different approaches to making use of XBRL, and raise implementation considerations you need to keep in mind. And for those of you who must comply with the U.S. SEC mandate to report using XBRL, we have a special chapter just for you!

Chapter 9

Exploring the Common Uses of XBRL

XBRL is a powerful tool that businesses can use in many ways, but it's not an end unto itself. Not all organizations need all the characteristics XBRL has to offer; more to the point, some organizations may target only a subset of XBRL's characteristics.

One good way to understand the use cases for XBRL is to look at how others are using it. Many different organizations make use of XBRL. We can't cover all the possible uses in this chapter, but you can use this information to uncover your specific use cases for XBRL.

Gaining Knowledge from XBRL Projects Around the World

Online, you can find three particularly good lists of projects around the world that are making use of XBRL. These lists don't include every XBRL project, but rather all the projects for which public information exists, many of which are government projects:

✔ **XBRL Planet** (http://xbrlplanet.org): This site lists information for more than 100 worldwide projects. Many projects are from government organizations that provide detailed information. Regretfully, you don't find as much information about commercial organizations implementing XBRL, but some information, such as case studies, is available.

✔ **XBRL Info Wiki** (www.xbrlwiki.info/index.php?title=XBRL_PROJECTS): Maintained by XBRL Spain, this wiki has a great deal of information about all things XBRL, one of which is a list of projects from around the world. Again, many are projects of various government agencies.

✔ **XBRL Around the World Spreadsheet** (http://xbrl.org/BestPractices/WorldWideXBRLProjectsListing-2009-07-15.xls): XBRL International created a spreadsheet that contains a listing of XBRL projects around the world.

To avoid having to type these long links, go to www.dummies.com/go/xbrl. This takes you to a landing page where you can click the link you need.

In this section, we take a look at how some companies and other organizations are using XBRL.

Wacoal

Wacoal is a Japanese conglomerate that manufactures and sells women's intimate apparel with revenues of about $1.6 billion annually. The company needed to aggregate operational information from its 36 subsidiaries that operate in 23 different countries using 32 different proprietary business applications. The applications operated on multiple platforms, such as mainframes, minicomputers, UNIX, PCs, and so on, which provided data to the company's accounting subsystems.

The multiple disparate systems resulted in a significant amount of rekeying of data, which led to inefficient accounting and reporting processes and additional time needed to close the books. Wacoal wanted to improve these processes and reduce the high costs of developing and maintaining interfaces between these disparate systems.

Wacoal used XBRL to integrate these systems, creating a fully automated process with no manual rekeying. Wacoal used a canonical-based approach to achieve its results. The system is flexible for future integration changes without the need to modify applications. The monthly closing process is two days faster, and real-time processing and reporting of financial data is available daily.

Wacoal accomplished these goals with an estimated savings of two-thirds over the traditional approach (implementing an ERP system). Wacoal also estimated that it took one-sixth of the time to implement the system over the next best alternative.

For more information about this use case, see www.xbrl.org/business/
companies/breathing-new-life-into-old-systems.pdf.

U.S. FDIC

The FDIC currently captures data for about 9,000 banks. The FDIC moved
from an electronic system that used an internally developed proprietary
information-exchange format to an electronic system that uses XBRL as the
information-exchange format. The FDIC wasn't moving from a paper-based
system or a PDF or nontagged electronic system; the FDIC already had structured, tagged data.

The FDIC moved from a proprietary electronic data-exchange format that it
internally developed and maintained to a global open-standard format, XBRL.
This change helped the FDIC move from proprietary internally developed
software to more off-the-shelf software. Not all internally developed software
went away; in fact, the FDIC still has a significant amount of internally developed software. However, the amount is less than it would have had to create
had the FDIC not used XBRL.

The more software users, the lower the cost per user will be. As a result,
moving from proprietary internally developed software to off-the-shelf software can give you a significant savings, if off-the-shelf software meets your
needs. For example, Microsoft Word is an off-the-shelf software product; you
can go to any computer store and purchase it. The cost of developing
Microsoft Word was substantial because the number of supported features is
high, but because the number of users is large, the cost per user is low.
Imagine if every company had to create its own word-processing application.
The cost would be high, and the number of features would likely be lower in
order to reduce costs. If off-the-shelf software can meet your needs, the savings can be significant. Open-source software allows users to modify the
source code, allowing them to take something that may not quite be what they
need and tweak it as needed.

Now banks can submit information once to the Federal Financial Institutions
Examination Council (FFIEC) XBRL system, which in turn shares it with FFIEC
member agencies, such as the FDIC, Federal Reserve System (FRS), and Office
of the Comptroller of the Currency (OCC).

We point out the benefits the FDIC realized from XBRL in Chapter 1. Every
national bank in the United States, about 9,000 of them, file today with the
FDIC using XBRL. This number will grow to 65,000 financial institutions as
the FDIC rolls out the next phases of its project to credit unions, thrifts, and
other financial institutions.

Committee of European Banking Supervisors (CEBS)

The Committee of European Banking Supervisors (CEBS) is made up of about 27 regulators from the different European Union countries. The members collect solvency and liquidity information for the financial institutions that they monitor. The members are using IFRS for financial reporting by all financial institutions in Europe (rather than the 27 different sets of financial reporting standards used previously) to collect liquidity information. The members use Basel II for financial institution solvency reporting. CEBS suggests XBRL as the exchange medium for these standard liquidity and solvency data sets. In addition to each country collecting financial institution information within the country, the members of CEBS (the countries) also exchange information among themselves using XBRL. CEBS considered other standards and thought about creating its own standard, but decided to go with the global standard XBRL.

Belgium was first, going live with XBRL in 2006. Spain, France, Germany, Poland, Denmark, Greece, Ireland, Italy, and Luxembourg followed. Other European countries will likely follow suit. XBRL currently has no other alternative, unless each supervisor creates its own solution for exchanging this information.

For more information, see `www.eurofiling.info`.

Dutch Association of Water Boards

The 27 Dutch Water Boards (Waterschappen) are responsible for local water management in The Netherlands. Their objectives are to protect the land from flooding and drought and ensure proper waste-water treatment. The Water Boards maintain the predetermined water level, dikes, and water ways, monitor water quality, and treat both residential and industrial waste-water. Their reporting requirements are subject to both national and European legislation.

Starting in 2004, the EU, as well as the European Central Bank, require quarterly financial reports, called *Economic and Monetary Union (EMU) reporting*. Statistics Netherlands (CBS) is chartered to receive and process these reports, as well as for other decentralized government entities (provinces and municipalities). EMU is just one of the 50 reporting duties for the Water Boards. EMU reporting is required from tens of thousands of institutions in Europe; CBS has hundreds of thousands reporting relationships.

The Water Boards needed to implement a new reporting requirement for more transparency on their capital and exact financial status. And even if the reporting was both more frequent and in more detail, the Water Boards wanted a reduction in the reporting burden.

In July 2003, the implementation of XBRL reporting began, using off-the-shelf software that supported XBRL. The project reached out to the main suppliers of financial software in the industry. In April 2004, the first XBRL instances began arriving from reporting entities. The Water Boards' implementation costs were minimal. The total investment for development, software, training, and mapping were calculated as 10 extra man days and €8.000 Euros (about $12,000). Research in 2006 showed that reporting time decreased by 25 percent for the Water Boards that participated.

It was the first time XBRL was implemented in the public domain and on the receiving side as well as the preparing side of the reporting chain. This implementation is a full-cycle implementation that uses the public Internet as the communication channel for reports.

You can find more information about this project at `www.semansys.com/PDF/XBRL_Case_Water_Boards.pdf`.

Dutch SBR Project

The success of the small Dutch Water Boards project (see preceding section) ignited the Dutch government's interest in using XBRL for, well, everything! The Dutch government expressed the ambition to reduce its total administrative and reporting burden by 25 percent. Many of the major administrative burdens originate from gathering, manipulating, registering, retaining, and providing information.

In spring 2004, under assignment from the Ministries of Justice and Finance, the Dutch Taxonomy Project (NTP) started with the construction of a dictionary of elements (XBRL taxonomy) for the compilation and exchange of annual accounts, tax declarations, and economic statistics on the basis of the open standard XBRL. This financial report domain covers 70 to 80 percent of the entire information exchanged between the government agencies and companies. In the Netherlands, organizations must provide annual accounts to the Chambers of Commerce, the tax filings to the Netherlands Tax and Customs Administration, and the statistics to Statistics Netherlands. So the project focus is on a national (and thus multiagency) taxonomy to report in XBRL.

During the standardization process, analysis of existing legislation resulted in changes resulting in decreases in the amount of elements that companies needed to report. Smaller companies can now use the fiscal elements to create both the fiscal profit filing and the annual accounts because they now use the same definitions.

NTP is now rebranded into SBR. The Dutch SBR collaborates with both the Australian and New Zealand SBR programs. Australian SBR developed a business case in 2007. As a result, the government has provided support and funding for the SBR program. Thirteen Australian, state, and territory government agencies are involved in the delivery of SBR.

In 2009, the SBR program in New Zealand was still in the initial planning stages. The focus is on finalizing the business case, as requested by Cabinet. If the business case receives approval, the goal is to have full implementation by 2012.

For more information, see www.xbrl-ntp.nl/English.

U.S. SEC

Although not the first, one of the key XBRL implementations in the world is the U.S. SEC's use of XBRL for financial reporting by public companies regulated by that agency. The SEC closely watched the FDIC's XBRL project (see the earlier "U.S. FDIC" section) and started experimenting with XBRL in 2005 when it instituted a voluntary filing program whereby public companies and the SEC could test XBRL. Eventually, almost 100 companies participated in that voluntary filing program.

The SEC invested $5 million to assist in the creation of the XBRL taxonomy required for a production system, and that taxonomy was built between 2006 and 2008. It also spent $50 million to update systems to make use of XBRL.

Ultimately, the SEC mandated that all public companies it regulates must provide information to the agency in an XBRL format. About 500 of the largest U.S. public companies began reporting by using XBRL in June 2009. Other organizations are being phased in over a three-year period based on a company's public float.

A *public float* is a way many regulators determine company listing requirements. It's similar to *market capitalization,* which is the stock price times the total number of outstanding shares of stock. Public float removes the shares held by directors and executives, leaving only public investors.

Initially, the XBRL filings are supplemental to the current SGML or HTML filing formats. The SEC has stated that it will eventually drop the legacy formats and require only XBRL filings after it's sure that its XBRL system works with satisfactory results. Chapter 13 provides more information about the SEC's XBRL project.

Australian SBR Project

The Australian government has been watching the FDIC and Dutch SBR projects. In 2007, in its SBR Project, the Australian government funded the first phase of a massive project to use XBRL as the standard way to communicate between government and business, between government and consumers, and between governmental entities. The first phase of the project will be for the Australian Tax Office to implement XBRL. The cost savings of this project is projected to be $780 million in Australian dollars (about $650 million U.S.) per year!

The early efforts of the Dutch project, Australia, New Zealand, and Singapore have resulted in these countries working together to create one SBR approach usable by any country.

National Tax Agency of Japan

One of the earliest adopters of XBRL, the National Tax Agency of Japan (NTA) introduced an e-Tax filing system using XBRL 2.0 as the filing format in 2004, using the system for the electronic filing of corporate taxes by businesses in 2005. NTA announced that it would accept XBRL 2.1 filings in September 2008.

Tokyo Stock Exchange

In 2003, the Tokyo Stock Exchange (TSE) began to receive XBRL-based financial statements. TSE provides a database called TDnet that allows its users to browse a database of information via the Web for companies listed on that stock exchange. Over time, more and more data will become available in the XBRL format.

While the TSE was one of the first stock exchanges to make use of XBRL, other stock exchanges are already following suit or plan to do so. The Korean Stock Exchange, the Shenzhen Stock Exchange (China), and the Shanghai Stock Exchange (China) already put systems that make use of XBRL into production. The U.S. NASDAQ has built some prototypes to test XBRL.

Japan Financial Services Agency

Japan's Financial Services Agency (Japan FSA) launched a system called Electronic Disclosure for Investors' NETwork (EDINET). The system's users can browse information using the XBRL format for those companies that it regulates. Japan FSA regulates approximately 4,700 listed companies and 3,200 investment funds.

The MIX MARKET

Microfinance is the practice of providing financial services (credit, insurance, and banking facilities) in small amounts to poorer people, usually in developing countries. In particular, microfinance involves loaning small amounts to entrepreneurs who have no access to credit so that they can establish, operate, or expand a business.

The MIX (Microfinance Information Exchange) is a nonprofit organization created to increase the financial transparency, and therefore accountability, of microfinance organizations. The MIX MARKET is its Web-based information platform that collects information from more than 1,000 such institutions, including their financial data, audited results, and data relating to their social impact (such as the percentage of women borrowers). Microfinance institutions that join make information about their activities public and can compare their performance with that of similar organizations.

The MIX has basically created an SEC EDGAR-type system for the microfinance industry by using XBRL and a lot of off-the-shelf software. The MIX did create some proprietary aspects of its system, but using XBRL helped it to significantly reduce the costs of what it was trying to achieve.

Nevada's state controller's office

The State of Nevada's state controller's office operates a centralized debt-collection system for agencies of the state. That system uses 71 Microsoft Excel workbooks with about 18 sheets each that contain various categories of debt to capture information from the agencies.

The process of using Excel for this function results in data validation issues, internal control issues, issues relating to cutting and pasting information from the 71 individual spreadsheets into a consolidated spreadsheet, and so on. You probably know the drill and may use Excel-similar things for a different type of information.

The state built a prototype that included a centralized data repository in XBRL, a centralized debt collection XBRL taxonomy. The state of Nevada wanted to integrate the XBRL repository with vendors' payment systems so that one agency isn't trying to collect on debts when another agency is paying that company for payables owed by the state.

The state is also looking into using XBRL for grant reporting and sub-grant reporting, audit reporting, and other situations where spreadsheets are used. See `www.govtech.com/gt/653427` for more information.

Nevada Department of Agriculture

Not every XBRL project has to be huge, or even large. To test the utility of XBRL, the Nevada Department of Agriculture used XBRL to try to reduce costs and improve the processes and procedures relating to about 60 grants that it administers. Prior to using XBRL, the process was labor-intensive and therefore time-consuming and expensive. The department had a proliferation of spreadsheets and word-processing documents designed to gather, maintain, and analyze information.

The interrelationship between the grants management goals and XBRL's benefits were the driving factors for looking at XBRL as a solution. The department's goals for the project were timely and accurate data, stronger internal controls, reduced costs, standardized systems, seamless data exchange between business processes, and a common understanding of the elements between processes. XBRL met all these goals. Additional benefits were that the system created is scalable and adaptable and saves time.

As a result of the project, the grant program manager, a business person, can add or modify the grants in a database using an XForm that is tied to an XBRL instance. This approach facilitates automating and improving source data capture, audit trail, and data integrity.

A key piece of this solution is the XBRL GL adaptor, which draws data from the State data warehouse and transforms that data into XBRL GL instance documents. The department developed a grant and XBRL GL taxonomy that resulted in standardized reporting.

United Technologies Corporation

United Technologies Corporation (UTC) was one of the early participants in the U.S. SEC voluntary filing program that the SEC used to test XBRL. (See the section earlier in this chapter.) UTC wanted to get a grasp on XBRL proactively, before the SEC might mandate its use. As part of the process of creating its voluntary SEC filings in XBRL, UTC learned a great deal about XBRL. UTC found that it can implement XBRL for a reasonable price and without significant knowledge of the underlying technology. But UTC also realized that beyond the potential SEC mandate, it could find other internal uses for XBRL within its processes, resulting in saved time and money, as well as increased quality.

John Stantial, CPA and director of financial reporting for UTC, wrote an article called "ROI on XBRL," which was published by the *Journal of Accountancy*. You can read about the specifics of what UTC learned at `www.journalof accountancy.com/Issues/2007/Jun/RoiOnXbrl.htm`.

Deloitte Australia

The clients of Deloitte, an accounting firm in Australia, delivered financial information in different formats, including spreadsheets and output formats from the various accounting packages. For each format received, Deloitte created a process to transfer data from the clients' systems to the Deloitte systems so that Deloitte could do the write-up or other work. This tedious, time-consuming, and error-prone process provided little value. The lack of interoperability drove costs up and introduced other inefficiencies.

Deloitte Australia used XBRL as a standard data format for obtaining write-up work data from their clients. The net savings was 70 percent of what it had cost the company in the past. For more information, see `www.ubmatrix. com/downloads/Deloitte_UBmatrix_business_brief.pdf`.

U.S. Department of Housing and Urban Development (HUD)

The Federal Housing Administration (FHA) replaced a data warehouse used to translate a commercial chart of accounts into an USSGL, a federal chart of accounts, for an asset-servicing and accounting system. The data warehouse was expensive to manage and resulted in inefficiencies. Using XBRL, the FHA was able to integrate a family of disparate financial systems, including accounts receivable (loan servicing) and accounts payable (property accounting, contract management).

With the project fully implemented, the FHA is able to leave its legacy commercially based accounting systems in place but receive daily input in accordance with USSGL requirements. The FHA is now using a single source for multiple reporting requirements, eliminating duplicate data entry, duplicate data processing, and extensive reconciliation processes. With daily data transmissions and reconciliation, the FHA has better control over its cash and can close its books with less effort. The FHA removed a data warehouse, saving time and money and reducing complexity. Reporting is simplified through repurposed data, eliminating manual steps.

Accounting and ERP Software

Perhaps one of the most significant uses of XBRL as a canonical format is within software applications, such as accounting and ERP software. Prior to XBRL, it was impossible for this type of software to use one standard format to export information to because software vendors had no one standard established to agree on. Today, with XBRL, a format is finally available.

Various accounting and ERP software vendors already support XBRL within their systems. Generally, these software packages support the ability to export and sometimes import XBRL. These vendors include

- ✔ SAP
- ✔ Navision
- ✔ FRx
- ✔ Creative Solutions
- ✔ Hyperion (Oracle)

A survey of accounting software vendors done by XBRL-US and the American Institute of CPAs indicated that two-thirds of all accounting system vendors supported XBRL or planned to do so soon. (To read more about the survey, go to www.webcpa.com/article.cfm?articleid=3578.) Frankly, we've observed that the current support for XBRL in accounting software is somewhat overstated. We do believe, however, that accounting software will move in this direction as more users demand support for XBRL.

State of Oregon CAFR Pilot Project

The Oregon state controller's office created a pilot program that explored the steps necessary to build an XBRL taxonomy for government accounting standards used by state and local governments for financial reporting and then express the state's Comprehensive Annual Financial Report (CAFR) using XBRL. Approximately 88,000 state and local governmental entities create and submit CAFR reports annually.

The Association of Government Accountants XBRL pilot project is documented in a white paper called "XBRL and Public Sector Financial Reporting: Standardized Business Reporting: The Oregon CAFR Project" (see `www.agacgfm.org/research/downloads/CPAGNo16.pdf`).

At a fundamental level, the use case for CAFR reporting is quite similar to public companies reporting to the SEC or banks reporting to the FDIC. What is unique about this pilot is that it tries to understand the benefits to the creators of this information. Although the data collected by this study isn't great enough to be conclusive in terms of savings, the study does refer to similar projects, such as the Dutch SBR Project described earlier in this chapter, which realized a 75-percent time savings in the creation of financial reports.

Morgan Stanley

Morgan Stanley is a global financial-services firm. Morgan Stanley created a framework for doing its financial analysis using XBRL. Originally starting with XML, Morgan Stanley switched to XBRL when it realized that it needed features that it would have to recreate if the company stuck with XML. The new system replaced an older system based on Microsoft Excel spreadsheets. The older system suffered from inconsistencies between the many spreadsheets used, an inability to make global adjustments to all analysis spreadsheets, inconsistencies and errors in these spreadsheets, and maintenance issues.

Within the new system, Morgan Stanley created an XBRL taxonomy that defined financial-reporting concepts reported by organizations but also analytical concepts, such as return on equity and working capital. A central database shared by all analysts housed financial and analytical data so that when, for example, Morgan Stanley changed its economic forecast, all models impacted by this adjustment were updated in real time. The new system resulted in discipline and consistency in the analysts' workflow, which resulted in greater comparability across data for individual companies and across companies being analyzed.

Prior to the SEC requiring public companies to supply their financial information to the SEC using XBRL, Morgan Stanley was required to either key each companies' information into its models or purchase data from one or more data aggregators. Because of the time and effort involved, Morgan Stanley couldn't tag or analyze all information. As more and more companies provide their information in an XBRL format to the SEC, less information will need to be keyed into Morgan Stanley's system or purchased from data aggregators, and the more companies Morgan Stanley can follow via its analysis.

PricewaterhouseCoopers iDP

PricewaterhouseCoopers (PWC) developed an internal-use Web services platform called iDataPlatform, or iDP, that enables the distribution of information to *portlets* (think of them as individual workspaces) along with an XBRL-enabled Microsoft Excel spreadsheet and includes features that provide information visualization, consumption, and other such reporting tools. PWC employees use this information for various types of analysis.

PWC obtains information from a number of third-party data providers that feed the iDP system. That information is parsed from general ledger and financial regulatory reporting information from a number of available sources. PWC maps the information to both the IFRS and US GAAP XBRL taxonomies.

You can use iDP to structure data for reporting and analysis at the general ledger or financial-reporting level and perform analysis internally or for using peer company reporting. Leveraging the XBRL abstraction layer (of information taxonomies, presentation concepts, rules, and so on), iDP also enables consumers to collaborate in the customization of their own personal analytical presentations and concepts.

Identifying the Common Characteristics of XBRL Projects

Patterns of common characteristics exist within the XBRL implementations described in this chapter and elsewhere. We see the following characteristics:

- ✔ In the case of government-related projects, each country has common functions that make use of XBRL within that country. These common functions are regulators of stock exchanges and securities, banking regulators, business registrars, revenue reporting and tax-filing agencies, and national statistical agencies.

- ✔ One regulator mandating XBRL can require thousands, tens of thousands, hundreds of thousands, or even millions of businesses to report using XBRL.

- ✔ The areas of the world where XBRL are taking off the fastest are Japan, Europe, China, and Australia.

- ✔ At least one nonprofit (the MIX) has implemented XBRL.

- ✔ The implementation to date that will exercise XBRL's extendibility features the most is the U.S. SEC.

- ✔ SBR implemented by the Netherlands, Australia, New Zealand, and Singapore (and being watched by the United Kingdom with interest) is becoming a standardized approach for a government to make use of XBRL. You can consider SBR an application profile; see Chapter 12.

- ✔ We are not aware of any significant failed XBRL implementations.

- ✔ Stock exchanges and banking regulators are the two biggest groups to have implemented XBRL.

- ✔ The European Parliament is the largest governmental body that has expressed interest in XBRL.

Chapter 10

Making Your Own Business Case for XBRL

*T*his chapter helps you determine whether XBRL is right for you. Can you make a case for XBRL? After all, you need to see some value, or your life needs to improve in some way in order for you to make a good case for this technology. In this chapter, we help you do just that.

Evaluating Business Use Cases

Business use cases are about justifying why you do something. What value does some new thing add to a business, or how does it solve a problem more effectively or efficiently? If you see economic value, you make a change, which is basic decision-making. Make things more effective and more efficient where you can. You do these things daily so that you can survive as a business. So what exactly does XBRL make more effective? What does XBRL make more efficient? You have to articulate these reasons because they are your business use case — the reason for making use of XBRL.

If you're in business, you know the many theoretical measurements to evaluate the business case: ROI, present value of future cash flows, net benefit, and more. Fundamentally, all these different approaches measure what is being gained.

Evaluating a business case to determine the gain can be harder than you think because other factors come into play. You have to keep your operational systems running. You may see a positive ROI, but you may not have the cash needed to start a project. Or, perhaps other projects are higher priorities than your project.

Chapter 6 points out the business-information-exchange objectives that we're generally trying to achieve, a way of measuring the effectiveness of a business information exchange. If you don't know the objectives, refer to Chapter 6 because you need to keep them in mind when you're trying to make a business case for XBRL's use.

Solving a Business Problem with XBRL

XBRL solves the problem of taking information out of one business system and reusing that information within another business system. In many cases, XBRL enables the automation of such exchanges, but XBRL isn't appropriate for all business-information-exchange situations. In this section, we cover the specific characteristics that XBRL was engineered to provide — XBRL's sweet spot.

XBRL is a useful tool, but it's only a tool. You may have heard the saying, "If the only tool you have is a hammer, every problem looks like a nail." XBRL is a useful collection of open-source technologies, but you definitely shouldn't use it for every type of problem on the planet!

The creation of XBRL didn't change the actual business problem XBRL is trying to solve. The problem itself is the same before and after XBRL's creation. However, XBRL changed the cost/benefit model significantly. Implementations of business systems providing for automated information exchange that were expensive in the past will now cost significantly less. Benefits that were impossible to realize are now not only possible but practical.

XBRL has a sweet spot. Understanding how to access and map XBRL's capabilities to the business problems you're trying to solve helps you understand where XBRL can assist you and your organization. If XBRL's offerings don't match the desired business outcomes, drive new value in a project, or lower costs, XBRL may not be a good match for your project.

The following list highlights the key areas where XBRL can provide unique value to a business problem. We don't include things that other technologies, such as XML, provide with the same or similar value. This list reflects what XBRL uniquely brings to the table:

✔ **Flexibility within rigid systems:** This statement seems like an oxymoron. Extensibility is probably one of the primary values offered by XBRL. We discuss extensibility throughout this book, pointing out that XBRL isn't a standard chart of accounts; instead, it's a dynamic but *controlled* vocabulary. XBRL isn't flexible in every direction; it's flexible in *specific* needed directions. You can think of this flexibility as XBRL having a specific shape to it. You can't extend it everywhere, and where you can extend it is known. Yet the notion of a rigid standard of accounts is appealing because it provides something else that's needed: comparability. XBRL tries to balance these two dynamics: flexibility and rigidity. How you implement XBRL determines where within the spectrum of flexibility and rigidity you choose to be.

✔ **Reconfigurable information:** The U.S. SEC coined the phrase "interactive data," trying to explain XBRL in simpler language for the business community. We think *interactive information* is an even better term. Interactive information means that consumers of information are free to reconfigure information; they're not constrained by the creator of the information and how that person chooses to present the information. XBRL allows for easy reconfiguration of information.

✔ **Rules engine-based validation:** Business information is rich with important relationships that are fundamental to create, understand, or otherwise make use of this information. Verification of these relations is key to both the creation and use of the information. XBRL offers an opportunity to use a rules engine-based validation approach that allows for validation of these types of relations. An important characteristic of validation is that you get the capability to check important relations, such as numeric computations ("the total assets must equal the total liabilities plus equity of a balance sheet") and reportability rules ("if you have inventory on your balance sheet, you need to also have an inventory policy and a specific set of inventory disclosures").

Another characteristic of rules engine-based validation is that it's more robust and interoperable than validation implemented programmatically within each individual business system. Further, a rules engine-based approach is much easier for business people to make use of because the complexity is dealt with at the level of the rules engine that extremely highly skilled technical people create. As a result, less technically skilled business people can write good rules without having programming knowledge. Software applications guide business users through the process of creating business rules correctly. The rules engines also allow for better interoperability of applications and therefore even more value because they can exchange, and therefore repurpose, the rules between business software applications.

✔ **Clear communication and sharing of rich business-level semantics:** Because XBRL does such a good job of providing for the expression of business meaning needed within XBRL taxonomies, communications between those who write, say, regulations and those who have to understand the regulations can be more clear. Further, those involved in the process, such as software vendors who have to build software, can automate the process of reading the taxonomy metadata to easily update their systems. Finally, both humans and computers can read this standard metadata format. You can use a simple style sheet to change the funny-looking computer readable angle brackets into information readable by humans, just like a Web page or PDF, but computer applications can still read it.

✔ **Metadata-driven configuration, no IT involvement required:** Business people can easily configure the rich set of metadata, changing business systems dynamically, if necessary. Just as with rules, highly skilled, specialized technical people hide this task's complexity and build it into business systems. The complexity doesn't go away; rather, it exists deep within the infrastructure of the system, but hidden from business users. This well-thought-out balance between flexibility and rigidity empowers business users, making them far less reliant on IT help to adjust their systems. So rather than having to write code to reconfigure a system, a business user can simply use a software tool to edit an XBRL taxonomy.

✔ **Zero tolerance for errors:** Imagine having a math error in a financial statement. That mistake simply can't happen. Some systems have zero or low tolerance for errors of any kind. You can create robust rules-based system to keep out errors thanks to XBRL's rigidity (its consistent shape), the rich set of metadata available, and a rules engine that can verify the metadata. Another way to say this same thing is that you can build systems that allow business users to do *only* the right thing; they simply aren't allowed to make mistakes.

Don't read too much into what we're saying about a computer's ability to detect errors, though. Computers have limitations as to the types of errors they can detect. A computer can keep out errors only to the extent that a computer system can be told what is an error — basically, to the extent that you can write rules. Also, don't confuse those mathematical errors with the accuracy of the reported number. Finally, XBRL can't keep the bad guys from deliberately cooking the books. So don't conjure up unrealistic expectations in your mind.

✔ **Achieving agreement with exterior parties:** XBRL is an easy way to agree with external parties (or even internal parties, for that matter) on two things: a syntax and a metadata set. From a syntax perspective, the advantages of a canonical (standard) approach to, say, integrating business information systems is well understood. XBRL, and in particular, XBRL Global Ledger, is easy for software vendors trying to integrate their systems to have something to agree on. Frankly, many times the syntax makes little or no difference.

A step higher than agreeing on the syntax is agreeing on the metadata set. It's highly unlikely that two versions of something like the U.S. GAAP XBRL taxonomy will be created. Lots of data aggregators, financial analysts, accountants, and others are already using the U.S. GAAP, including the U.S. SEC. Historically, no one has synchronized these metadata sets, they haven't been that rich with meaning, and you couldn't use one standard way to express the metadata. Therefore, everyone created their own set of metadata, and the sets weren't really that robust because their use was limited. XBRL changes all those things. Creating an XBRL taxonomy, such as the one for U.S. GAAP, is extremely complex and takes thousands of hours for highly skilled accountants and technologists to create. Others will leverage this freely usable intellectual property, creating even more metadata and more synchronization between different business systems. The result is that mashing up data using the XBRL metadata will be trivial.

These specific differentiators help you understand the unique value proposition of XBRL. In Chapter 12, we explain how to achieve these objectives using XBRL. In the next section, we get even more specific and practical regarding who benefits and exactly how.

Gleaning XBRL's Practical Benefits

In Chapter 3, we explain the general ways XBRL saves you time and money. But you may be wondering about specifics. What's in XBRL for you? Well, that depends on who *you* are. The best way to make a case for something is to show, as specifically as possible, the benefits provided. The following groups all benefit from XBRL:

- ✔ **Everyone:** Everyone derives these benefits.

- ✔ **Those who specify metadata:** Meaning standards setters, legislators, regulators — or anybody else who is articulating some metadata set that others have to report against.

- ✔ **Consumers of information:** Those who consume or use information that others have created.

- ✔ **Creators of information:** Those who create information that is consumed by others.

It's rare for someone to be in only *one* of these categories. Business information exchange is a chain. In some parts of the chain, you may be the creator of information; in others, the consumer; and in others, the one who specifies the metadata.

Benefits to all

Here are the key benefits that everyone derives from using XBRL:

✔ **No need to create an individual approach to automated business information exchange:** If you're going to exchange any sort of information, you need to come up with an approach to do so. Each approach has its pros and cons. Some approaches are automatable; others aren't. XBRL offers an approach that you can use to create an automated information exchange.

✔ **Lower cost software:** One disadvantage of ad hoc approaches to business information exchange is that you pretty much have to create your own software for the approach you come up with. The more people use a specific approach, generally the more software that exists to support that approach. And the more users, the cheaper the software.

✔ **Higher function software:** This benefit follows along the same lines as the lower cost of software application. Because XBRL has more users, you generally see more features created for the software because a broader user base funds the creation of the software.

✔ **Less errors in information and easier-to-find errors:** Because information is structured, automating the process of using the information is easier. The easier it is to automate using the information, the more software can do to help users detect errors in that information. And the more the computer can help you, the less you have to do, such as find and correct errors.

✔ **Information communicated with clarity:** Because of the formal, standard approach XBRL uses to articulate meaning, understanding the information is easier, which helps everyone involved in a business information exchange stay on the same page.

✔ **Readable by both humans and computers:** Both humans and computers will be able to read and understand the information, which then allows automated information exchanges and enables computers to use their understanding of the information to provide even more ways humans can use the information. For example, rather than the one fixed format provided today, computers can render information using several different formats. Perhaps the greatest benefits of all may be that after computers universally understand this information, they can crunch the numbers and look for abnormalities in ways that they've never been able to in the past. XBRL may not be able to stop people from cooking the books, but it can certainly help find those who do.

Benefits to those who specify metadata

Those who specify metadata can expect to see these types of benefits:

✔ **No need to lock users into an inflexible standard vocabulary:** Many times, business users articulate an information set using inflexible standard vocabularies, such as forms, because allowing deviations from the standard vocabulary is just too complicated. With globally standard XBRL, providing flexibility is easier, so those specifying metadata can allow for more flexibility within their systems, if they need it.

✔ **Built-in multilanguage support:** XBRL offers a global standard way to provide for the many different languages humans speak around the world. This multilanguage support in itself can be a business case for adopting XBRL. You can author a document in your local language and, with just a click of your mouse, communicate that business information in any language the XBRL taxonomy is translated into.

✔ **Leverages standard vocabularies or metadata of others:** Because the XBRL standard exists, standard vocabularies or metadata can exist. Before XBRL, there really was no way to agree on one standard way to express a vocabulary. But with XBRL, there is a way: XBRL! Because of XBRL, you can create and use more standard vocabularies, and individual groups don't have to create their own and usually different (and therefore generally incompatible) vocabularies. You can leverage these standard vocabularies for all sorts of uses.

Benefits to consumers of information

Commonly, it's thought that consumers of information get the most benefit from XBRL. Creators of information do the hard work of tagging; consumers get the benefit of easily consuming and using the information, or so the perception goes. The examples in the next section clearly dispel this notion, but information consumers still receive significant benefits:

✔ **Aggregation:** If you've ever received information from two or more different people expressing information within a spreadsheet, you'll understand the problems of aggregating information using spreadsheets. The differently formatted spreadsheets can make extracting information from the spreadsheets challenging. Even if you have a standard spreadsheet format, unintentional errors or misunderstandings in communication always seem to creep up and cause problems with automating information exchanges of this sort. To make spreadsheet-based information exchange work correctly, you have to write a detailed specification for the spreadsheet format.

However, XBRL changes your information exchange options. The specification needed to exchange this information is explicitly documented by XBRL. That is what XBRL is: a specification of how to express this information so that automated processes can be effectively created enabling information exchange. Information exchange includes the process of taking detailed data and aggregating it effectively into summary information without the struggles caused by inconsistently formatted spreadsheets.

✔ **Drill down:** We mention in the next section that information can be brittle when linking that information is based on the physical location of the information in a spreadsheet cell. *Drill down* of information is also generally based on location. Drill down is basically the opposite of aggregation. Drill down is the ability to move from the summary numbers down into the detailed numbers that were used to calculate the aggregated total. XBRL solves this issue for drill down exactly the same way that it solves it for aggregation: by specifying a global standard format for the detailed information you're drilling into.

✔ **Flexible information format/set:** When you get a set of information from someone, how many times have you wished that you could see the information in some other form? The popularity of spreadsheets and business-intelligence software demonstrates this desire. With XBRL, reformatting information can be as easy dragging and dropping the information contained in an XBRL taxonomy or importing the XBRL instance information into an application of your choice. The presentation information doesn't hinder this process because it's separated from the information itself. This flexibility comes from the separation of information and the information's presentation format.

✔ **Not locked into one presentation format:** This benefit goes hand in hand with the previous one — you're not locked into one specific presentation format. If you want, you can export the information easily into PDF, HTML, or a spreadsheet or dump it into relational databases like you've never been able to.

✔ **Possible to automate comparisons:** Because the information is structured and flexible, you can take multiple information sets and easily create comparisons. Because one standard global information format is used, you have to compare lots of information. One reason the comparisons are so easy is because of the standard metadata used by different creators of information. The more standard the metadata, the easier the comparisons will be. Perhaps you want to do a cross-organizational comparison of some sort or a time series of information for one company's information.

✔ **Information is available faster:** Information becomes timely because many things are easier and users can automate many processes. Why have the world's leading stock exchanges and central banks become frontrunners in the area of XBRL? Because by decoupling the information from applications that XBRL provides from their infrastructure, they gain all the benefits of enabling dynamic provisioning with policy-based command and control to deliver available information faster. In other words, they can save millions in IT costs, while gaining millions of new revenues on the business side through gaining insight faster, which results in better risk management.

Benefits to creators of information

Most people see the benefits of XBRL to the information consumers (see preceding section) more clearly than the benefits to information creators. However, creators of information derive significant benefits, too. Along with the general benefits that everybody is privy to, creators of information also get these benefits:

- **Rules-based creation of information:** One of the more significant and exciting benefits of XBRL is the ability to have rules-based information creation. Rules-based information creation means far fewer errors within information and a greater ability to understand what information you're supposed to report. For example, if rules say that a number in one area needs to be the same value as a number in a different area, a computer process can easily tell you when the two numbers don't match. Automated validation enables rules-based information creation, guiding you through the process of creating the information as you create it.

  Another example is if you create a rule to say that if a value is provided, then you must also include some other set of information as well. These different types of rules make it easier for both those who need to report information to understand exactly what to report and those who consume that information to understand the information they're using. If you make the information so simple that a computer, which isn't smart, can understand it, humans will certainly be able to understand the information. Both error detection and interaction or workflow enhancements benefit from these rules.

- **Aggregation of information:** Many times, information comes from many other sources that are aggregated. The aggregated information set is then used to populate a form or a report. You can create sets of spreadsheets that hook the detailed and summary information together, but they tend to be rather brittle as the aggregation is based on the physical location of a number. If a row or column is added, the link breaks. Hooking this information together more solidly by using meaning, which doesn't change, rather than the physical location, which can change, makes systems that aggregate information far less brittle.

- **Not locked into a standard controlled vocabulary:** Because XBRL is flexible in nature, the need to lock a creator of information into a standard controlled vocabulary (such as a standard chart of accounts) becomes less necessary. As a result, creators of information can better articulate information that might deviate from the norm. This flexibility can make the information more meaningful to those with whom the creators are sharing it.

Increasing Both Reach and Richness

In their book *Blown to Bits* (Harvard Business School Press), authors Philip Evans and Thomas Wurster point out that the ubiquitous connectivity of the Web and standards such as XBRL are eliminating the tradeoffs between reach and richness of information and redefining the information channels that link businesses with their customers, suppliers, employees, and other business partners:

✔ *Reach* refers to the number of people who participate in the sharing of that information. Reach has to do with the quantity of people that you can get to.

✔ *Richness* refers to the quality of information, as defined by its user and reflected in characteristics of the information such as accuracy, timeliness, flexibility, interactivity, and so on.

Eliminating the historical tradeoffs between reach and richness means that your competitive advantage is up for grabs as your existing competitors and new competitors leverage these new information channels. Complacency on your part can be dangerous and can have disastrous outcomes.

To help give you a better idea of reach and richness, compare the reach and richness offered by a number of mediums. Figure 10-1 shows graphically the relations between the reach and richness of various mediums that were used to distribute information, comparing the reach and richness of each medium.

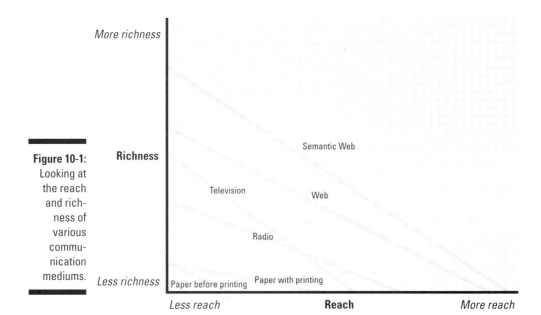

Figure 10-1: Looking at the reach and richness of various communication mediums.

The graph in Figure 10-1 shows richness on the vertical axis and reach on the horizontal axis. The line on the graph shows the general relationship between the amount of reach and the amount of richness offered by different mediums for exchanging information. Look more closely at these examples of information distribution systems and how richness and reach were impacted:

- **Paper before printing:** Consider a piece of paper with writing, say created by a monk in the Middle Ages, as the baseline of richness and reach. The monks can write information on paper and distribute the paper. Creating additional copies involves recopying manuscripts by hand. Others can take the paper and distribute it to someone else. To use this mechanism, people had to be able to read, and paper was heavy and therefore limited in reach because it was hard to distribute.

- **Paper with printing:** When the printing press was invented, the richness (what was published) remained about the same; however, printing had a significant impact on reach because now rather than someone having to hand-copy each printed page, they could create more pages. But the cost of a typesetting and printing machine was significant, so few people could afford to produce information in this manner. The photocopy machine reduced the cost of printing, making publishing easier for individuals, which increased reach even more.

- **Radio:** When the radio was invented, information no longer had to be printed at all; it could be transmitted easily to anyone who had an inexpensive radio receiver. Also, targeted information recipients didn't need to know how to read. However, publishing or broadcasting the radio signal was, and still is, quite expensive.

- **Television:** With the invention of the television, you could now receive not only audio, but also video. This method increased the richness over radio. Still, publishing (broadcasting the audio and video signal) was expensive.

- **Web:** With the invention of the Web, those who wished to publish had seemingly no limitation on either richness or reach. But computer applications couldn't play in the game because they couldn't read the information published as most information was published as Web pages for human consumption. As a result, the published information wasn't very reusable: an example is the mashup, which takes information from various sources, combining it onto one Web page or within one software application.

- **Semantic Web:** With the use of the Semantic Web, reach takes another gigantic leap forward. Now computer systems are also targeted as information consumers. Also, because information is structured for meaning and reusable, it becomes even more useful. Now one information creator can use information others have created with ease.

Today, anyone with Internet access can host a blog and provide any medium and potentially reach everyone on the planet who is connected to the Web for pennies. The point here is that the cost/benefit model has radically changed because both broad reach and deeply rich and reusable information is there to be leveraged. You have a new medium, a new tool, at your disposal. So do your competitors.

XBRL as a New Communication Medium

In 1964, Marshall McLuhan explained the phrase, "The medium is the message," which he coined to explain how a medium influences how a message is perceived. XBRL is an entirely new medium for communicating a message.

In Chapter 7, we outline many of the different characteristics between paper, electronic paper (such as HTML or PDF) or an electronic spreadsheet, and XBRL. These new characteristics mean new possibilities. Exactly who will leverage these possibilities and how isn't exactly known today. But we can walk you through one specific, focused example of how you might look at XBRL.

An XBRL taxonomy is a body of knowledge for some domain. The XBRL taxonomy contains the experience, insights, rules, conventions, and other insights and understandings of professionals who have an expertise within that domain. This knowledge is expressed in a form that is readable by both humans and computer software applications.

Because this professional domain knowledge can be effectively articulated in a form understandable by humans and computers, two interesting things can happen. Humans can more easily exchange this professional knowledge. If you look at an XBRL taxonomy, such as the US GAAP or IFRS taxonomies, you quickly realize how much information they really contain. That information will continue to grow as more people understand what they can do with XBRL and add even more domain knowledge to these XBRL taxonomies. For example, the XBRL taxonomy will grow to become an even more powerful ontology. (Chapter 17 explains the difference between a taxonomy and an ontology and why we believe that the taxonomies of today will look more like an ontology in the future.)

What makes this new communications medium even more powerful is that computers can help users of this information because software applications can also be made to understand this information. You can simply do more things with the information because the information is in XBRL.

Think about how books changed the world. A book can document information that one individual had in his head and transfer that knowledge to another individual. XBRL does the same thing. XBRL enables deep domain knowledge to be transferred to other humans and to computers, which further help humans make use of the information.

Fitting into the Extended Enterprise

How business intelligence is practiced has gone through an evolution, but what business intelligence is supposed to achieve has always been the same. Business intelligence is the ability of a business to understand the interrelationships between information and convert this understanding into competitive advantage and stakeholder value. Business intelligence has existed as long as there have been businesses because businesses are always looking for ways to obtain a competitive advantage.

In the earlier ages of business, getting information between continents or across continents could take months. In our modern age of computer information systems, we can exchange information from any point on Earth to any other point in a matter of seconds. Anyone can provide or consume information that can be in pretty much any format, including audio and video.

Business intelligence in the age of the computer has gone through an evolution. At first, reports were generated from isolated systems because computers were disconnected. Obtaining external information was difficult, and it was even more difficult to use the information even if it was collected because the format was generally not reusable without a lot of work and money, making it out of reach for most.

Eventually, systems evolved until separate systems gathered information into data warehouses or data marts, which made reusing the information easier but still costly. There was a trend toward getting all data into one homogeneous enterprise system. Generally, all this information still came from within an enterprise. But businesses still needed a lot of information from customers, suppliers, and other business partners to operate effectively and efficiently. More and more information was beyond the physical boundaries that an enterprise could make use of. Although the Web created the possibility of making use of this information efficiently, it also showed that because of the many different formats the information takes, reusing this information could be quite challenging.

As the connectivity of the Web became ubiquitous and inexpensive, businesses realized that they could use standards to minimize the problems of heterogeneous systems, making them operate more like a homogeneous system. Besides, getting businesses to agree on one common homogenous system is something that will never be achieved and is, in many cases, an unrealistic approach to integrating systems.

The term *extended enterprise* represents the idea that an organization is made up of not just its employees, but also its agents, suppliers, customers, and other partners on which a business relies to conduct business. You knowing the inventory of a supplier in real time, for example, or a customer knowing what you physically have on hand in your inventory is the information that greases the economic engine of commerce. The understanding that we're truly part of an extended enterprise is a realization that we're all interconnected in a global network and that the network runs on information. As we discuss in Chapter 7, we are, after all, part of an information-supply chain. The cost of interconnecting the extended enterprise has never been lower.

Maximizing Economics of Information

The purpose of information is to serve decision-makers, allowing them to arrive at better decisions. What is the value of better decisions? What is the value of spending five minutes instead of two hours to reach a conclusion? What is the value of having information now rather than in two days? Clearly, this answer depends on the impact of the decision, but you get the idea.

Organizations generally have a significant asset in the form of knowledge and insight. Unfortunately, at the present time, the vast majority of organizations have this information scattered among disparate systems and sub-organizations within the larger organization, which makes the knowledge and insight challenging to discover. And discovering knowledge and insight are even more challenging if you consider the extended enterprise (see the previous section).

An information-supply chain helps reduce the friction within this process of exchanging and then using business information (see Chapter 7). It's possible today to coalesce and harness knowledge of information to a versatile platform-agnostic format that you can leverage vertically and horizontally, across an organization and externally with business partners.

Walmart's key competitive advantage is its global information-supply chain. Walmart manufactures no products (see Chapter 7). With the cost of establishing an information-supply chain so low, and the benefits of having one so high, you can easily see why XBRL is considered transformational. Industry dynamics will change — they're changing now. How can you participate in these changing dynamics? Chapter 11 helps you see the different approaches to participating in the transformation XBRL has delivered. Chapter 12 shows you how to leverage XBRL's power in a practical manner.

Chapter 11

Evaluating Different Approaches to Implementing XBRL

*Y*ou already know what XBRL is. (If you don't, see Chapter 1.) You know you want to do something, but you're not sure what. You could use some clarification on your options for making use of XBRL. Guess what: You're in the right place.

This chapter covers the different approaches to implementing XBRL so that you can look at your specific environment and pick the approach that is right for you. We inventory the various approaches, breaking them into categories. We explain each approach and tell you their pros and cons. We don't tell you which approach is best for you: That decision is your job.

There is no right or wrong answer to implementing, or not implementing, XBRL. There are only mismatches between your desired result and the path you take. In this chapter, we help you understand the different paths and what is at the end of these paths. That way, you can decide what's right for you and your organization.

The Many Ways to Implement XBRL

We take all the different approaches to implementing XBRL and group them into categories. Here are the fundamental approaches that you can generally employ to implement XBRL:

✔ Do nothing. Taking no action is, of course, an action.

✔ Outsource the task of generating XBRL to an XBRL service provider.

✔ Bolt on the ability to generate or receive XBRL to an existing process.

✔ Purchase XBRL-supporting software that you can use with an existing or new process.

✔ Integrate XBRL into your existing business systems.

✔ Create entirely new systems to fully leverage what XBRL has to offer, unconstrained by legacy systems.

You most likely have a lot of different systems, and you'll therefore probably be taking a lot of different approaches. Using only a one-size-fits-all general approach is unlikely to be right for every department, business system, and process of an organization. Each unique situation typically calls for a different approach. (We don't talk about software applications here. Chapter 14 has information on vendors who can help fulfill your needs from a software or services perspective.)

Do nothing

Doing nothing is always a potential option. If you're mandated by someone else to provide them with XBRL-formatted information, it's hard to get around that. In that case, doing nothing may not be a viable option. But if someone else isn't requiring you to implement XBRL, you may be able to just do nothing. Of course, doing nothing is easy, but you may miss the boat and be left in the wake by your competitors who are leveraging what XBRL has to offer.

Doing nothing does have its costs. If you took Economics 101, you may remember the concept of opportunity losses. If your competition gains efficiencies from XBRL and you don't, it may have an impact on you.

Outsource

Another approach to meeting a requirement to provide XBRL is to outsource the whole deal. This approach is similar to the bolt-on approach (see the next section) in that the approach supplements an existing process. But unlike the bolt-on approach, which is internal, this process is external to your organization.

The only pro of this approach is that it causes the least disruption. You don't have to learn about XBRL; you don't have to do anything differently.

The cons, however, are many:

- ✔ You have the least amount of control over how your information is tagged, but you'll likely be involved to some extent.

- ✔ You'll experience a marginal cost increase with little or no marginal benefit because you're not leveraging the characteristics that XBRL offers within your organization. Also, it's time consuming because effort, and therefore additional time, is tacked onto the end of an existing process. Fundamentally, all you're doing is adding more work to the end of an existing process rather than using XBRL to improve the process.

- ✔ Outsourcing is likely to be more costly than other approaches to implementing XBRL over the long term. (The fact that this approach yields a net increase in cost will become clearer when we discuss your other alternatives.)

- ✔ You can't really leverage XBRL internally for other things or use it to improve internal processes.

All in all, you can really look at outsourcing XBRL work just like other work that your organization outsources. Typically, the same or similar pros and cons exist.

An example of this approach is a company that outsources the creation of XBRL U.S. SEC filings to its existing financial printer who already creates its SEC filings. In addition to providing the current services of rendering the filing in the required SEC format, the financial printer also provides the company with the XBRL format that it needs to fulfill the SEC's requirement for providing them with XBRL. Creating the XBRL format requires more of an understanding of the financial information contained in the filing because rather than simply reformatting information, you need to make decisions regarding tags, contexts, and other information required to prepare the XBRL submission.

Bolt on

Perhaps you don't want to outsource, but you want to minimize disruption. You may consider the option that's often described as a *bolt-on solution.* With this type of an approach, you bolt on a new process to, most likely, the end of some existing processes. The result of the bolted-on process is your XBRL-formatted output. Using this approach may mean buying software or creating software that, say, takes a spreadsheet or word-processing document, creates a mapping, and then generates XBRL using the input document and the mapping.

Alternatively, you can create internal systems that output the XBRL formatted information. You have to consider how the existing system is integrated with the new process and whether that new process uses off-the-shelf software or internally developed software of some sort. Table 11-1 outlines the pros and cons of the bolt-on approach.

Table 11-1	The Pros and Cons of the Bolt-on Approach
Pros	**Cons**
Causes minimal disruption.	Likely less costly than outsourcing, but more costly than other solutions over the long term because you're adding something to the end of a process.
Offers better control of the XBRL output because you understand XBRL better.	Can't really leverage XBRL internally for other things or improve internal processes.
Provides people inside your company with XBRL expertise, unless consultants do *every* aspect of the project	

If you use consultants to achieve everything, the bolt-on approach can look much like an outsourced approach (see preceding section). If you do take the bolt-on route, consultants can be quite useful in showing you the correct approaches to use XBRL.

Use consultants wisely and in the right roles. For example, hire consultants with XBRL experience to bring XBRL expertise into your organization. If you don't know any more about XBRL after the project than you did when you started, you miss an opportunity to internalize what you'll eventually realize are important skills your organization needs to have internally.

Examples of the bolt-on approach are the many new software products (see Chapter 16) created to work with XBRL. Many products try to serve specific niches, and some may meet your needs.

Purchase software

What if you didn't have to do anything to use XBRL other than install an upgrade to a new version of your current vendor's software product? Another less attractive alternative along these same lines is to buy a different off-the-shelf software product because your current vendor won't upgrade its product. A third alternative in this category is to purchase what would amount to an add-on product specifically designed to be integrated with a software product you already have via, perhaps, an import/export process. Perhaps it's semi-integrated into your other systems, having a relatively low marginal cost. Table 11-2 outlines the pros and cons of purchasing software.

Table 11-2	Pros and Cons of Purchasing Software
Pros	*Cons*
Tends to be a lower cost option, with potentially little or no marginal cost.	Can be frustrating because you don't have control over your software vendors' implementation schedules.
Usually a good long-term solution.	May be interoperability issues relating differing implementations of XBRL in different software applications.
Lets you focus more on things like workflow and making use of XBRL to solve problems and less on implementing IT solutions.	Less control as compared to integrating XBRL into your business systems yourself.
Will likely have lots of software that supports XBRL out of the box.	

You can mitigate lack of control over your vendor's implementation schedule if your vendor communicates when XBRL features will be implemented and if your vendor is good at meeting its commitments.

The difference between the software purchase option and the integrated approach, described in the next section, is really who is doing the integrating — you or your software vendor. Probably the biggest difference between the two relates to control and cost. Purchased software will likely cost significantly less; however, you have little control as to when (or if) XBRL features are implemented and what features appear.

Examples of this type of an approach are customers of SAP. SAP, an ERP vendor, has announced XBRL support. Customers of SAP will eventually get many XBRL benefits out of the box.

Integrate

One way of getting an integrated solution that fully leverages the characteristics of XBRL is to purchase or upgrade your off-the-shelf software. If you've internally developed systems, you can either switch to purchased software (unlikely) or integrate XBRL into your internal business systems. Another integrated option is all those subsystems that exist for various specialized purposes. A big category of this type of system is spreadsheets and other ad hoc-type systems.

To obtain the most benefit from XBRL, deeply integrate XBRL into your systems, leveraging its characteristics within your existing workflow or even using XBRL to dramatically improve your workflow. Use XBRL to reduce the friction within your information-supply chain (see Chapter 7). Table 11-3 covers the pros and cons of this approach.

Table 11-3	Pros and Cons of Integration
Pros	**Cons**
Tends to be the option with a high potential for upside benefit.	Tends to be the option with a high upfront cost. (Control comes with a hefty price tag.)
Offers the greatest control. Gives you the highest probability that you'll get exactly the XBRL features you want and need because you control all decisions about what features are implemented and when.	Tends to be risky and potentially more disruptive.
Has the lowest probability of interoperability issues between software.	

The best way to summarize this alternative is to talk about risk. The question isn't how to get rid of risk because you can never get rid of risk. You can pick the type of risk you deal with, but you can't reduce risk to zero for all categories of risk. Also, internally developed legacy systems are a reality. Many times, you wish you could throw them out and start over, which is the approach we discuss in the next section. However, most of the time, throwing out legacy systems and starting over simply isn't an option.

The great example of an integrated approach to implementing XBRL was used by FRS Financial Reporting Solutions Pty Ltd (FRS). FRS created an accounting engine called Virtual Chartered Accountant using a single, global, IFRS-compliant accounting language. The accounting engine basically enforced rules that guided system users through the process of creating all accounting entries entered into the system. The system, mapped to the XBRL taxonomy, needed to generate reports as an XBRL instance. The Virtual Chartered Accountant accounting engine was applied to reporting of retirement fund information. For more information, see the case study at www.xbrl.org/Business/Regulators/SA%20XBRL%20Case%20 Study%20-%20Success%20Story.pdf.

To avoid having to type these long links, go to www.dummies.com/go/xbrl. This takes you to a landing page where you can click the link you need.

Create

Imagine if you could use XBRL from scratch. This option isn't realistic for many, but it is an option for some. If you're starting a new business or if you've been thinking of scrapping what you have because it's at the end of its usefulness, starting over may be a viable option. If it is, when you re-architect your system, be sure to take a look at what leverage XBRL can provide.

Another alternative in this category is building a *super system*, or layer above your existing systems, kind of like an internal semantic Web. You can even build a super-system layer above the one or more business-information supply chains you participate in to operate your business effectively and efficiently, to stay on the edge of the competitive envelope.

You know if you fit into this category because you think of processes in different ways than most other people do. You really think outside the box. Your business systems tend to be state of the art and viewed as strategic weapons you use to compete in the marketplace.

Idealistic, maybe. These ideals are more something to strive for and attempt to achieve, but because technology is such a moving target, almost no one ever gets to business system nirvana. Table 11-4 lists the pros and cons of this approach.

Table 11-4	Pros and Cons of Creating Your Own System
Pros	*Cons*
Offers the most potential for upside benefit.	Tends to be the option with the highest upfront cost.
Most future-proof and flexible system.	Tends to be the most risky and potentially the most disruptive.
Offers the highest probability you'll get what you want and need. If you go this route, you're establishing the state of the art. Others have to try to emulate what you've achieved.	

The risks can be huge if planning is poor, but if you have the capabilities to pull this off, the rewards can be great. What is the value of Wal-Mart's information-supply chain? If you don't understand this question, you definitely don't want to take this approach. (See Chapter 7 for a discussion of the value of Wal-Mart's information-supply chain.)

An example of this type of approach is the NBP — see Chapter 7. The NBP's vision is to significantly reduce system friction between state agencies and the constituents they serve. Legacy systems are integrated with a state-of-the-art information-supply chain.

How Vendors and Regulators Fit into These Approaches

You may think we've overlooked two additional categories of approaches to implementing XBRL: software vendors implementing XBRL in their products and regulators mandating XBRL. However, these two use cases really do fit into one of the implementation approaches we cover in the preceding sections.

✔ **Software vendors implementing XBRL in their product:** If you're a software vendor, you have some choices to make about when, or even if, you'll support XBRL within your software application. Either you support XBRL within your product, or you don't.

If a software vendor chooses to implement XBRL within its product, the vendor needs to pick how it will implement it from the list of options we cover in this chapter. One thing the vendor looks at is whether it wants to purchase components, such as an XBRL processor, or if it builds its own XBRL processor. Perhaps the vendor needs additional infrastructure. The software vendor may even outsource, using a service that does any necessary XBRL processing and simply returns the XBRL output back to the software application.

The bottom line here is that software vendors that provide the applications most people use actually do fit into the previous categories.

✔ **Regulators mandating XBRL:** Another small group of XBRL implementers is regulators. "Now wait a minute," you ask. "Didn't you say earlier that regulators are one of the primary users of XBRL?" Well, yes and no.

Regulators will implement XBRL. However, for every one regulator implementing XBRL, hundreds, thousands, or even millions of businesses will use XBRL as a *result* of some regulatory mandate. So, compared in terms of volume of implementations, regulators will eventually be a small number of total XBRL implementations.

However, those implementations tend to be quite large. These regulators have to choose from the aforementioned variety of different implementation strategies and probably use different approaches to different aspects of the systems they'll be building.

Choosing Your Approach

Certain realities of life will likely directly impact your choice of an approach and should be in the forefront of your mind as you select your approach:

✔ **Net benefit over the long-term:** The net benefit of a solution over the long term should be the main driver of most decisions. You can take that further and look at the present value of future cash flows, a standard approach to measuring the value of a project. Another term used to describe this concept is ROI. We could go into an entire dissertation here about how the ROI needs to be considered relative to other potential uses of resources, but any good businessperson already knows this information. Suffice it to say that you need to factor these things when choosing your approach.

✔ **Short-term realities:** Although the best long-term option is the best theoretical driver, short-term realities also come into play. For example, you simply may not have the cash to pursue some approaches. Further, you have to keep your systems up and running 24-7 because you have a business to run. You need to factor these short-term realities into the equation.

✔ **Total cost:** A solution's total cost is always a consideration. Cash flow may be even more important. If you don't have the cash, your options may simply be limited.

✔ **Big picture:** In Chapter 7, we talk about the information-supply chain. Don't lose sight of the forest by looking at only one of the trees. Keep the entire chain in mind, not only one or two of the links.

✔ **Change-management capabilities:** Your capabilities to manage change in your organization are a consideration. With change comes the potential for disruption, risks, resource utilization issues, and so on. Can your organization handle a revolution, or do you need to evolve?

✔ **Submission of XBRL to multiple regulators:** If you are, say, a financial institution in the United States, you'll probably be submitting XBRL to two different regulators in the near future: the FDIC and the SEC. These two regulators use two different XBRL taxonomy architectures that aren't really interoperable, but the data you submit to both systems is the same data.

✔ **Differing implementations between software vendors (interoperability):** One software vendor will implement XBRL differently than another one does. For example, some may implement all the XBRL modules (XBRL Dimensions, XBRL Formula, and so on), but other vendors may implement only the base XBRL specification, not any modules. Others may be somewhere in between. These different software applications may not be interoperable. Some software applications may never need to interoperate, but some will.

✔ **Differing dialects of XBRL:** XBRL is a general-purpose specification (see Chapter 2). Certain XBRL taxonomies will likely use some XBRL features, and while other XBRL taxonomies will use other features. In other words, taxonomy architectures will vary. System architectures will also vary. This situation creates what can best be described as different dialects of XBRL. Many of these different dialects may never have to interoperate, but some will.

Chapter 12

Considering How to Implement Your XBRL Solution

. . . .

. . . .

*W*hat do you do when you're finally ready to implement XRBL? This chapter helps you get where you want to be with the fewest hiccups. It provides key information to help you understand snarls that others have encountered and how to avoid them. We also cover how to identify good consultants and determine the consulting expertise your project may need. Don't expect this chapter to show you everything you need to know about implementing XBRL. This book just helps you get started down the right path.

Discovering Your Vision

If you really don't care about where you're going, just start doing something, and you'll definitely end up somewhere! Now, we don't subscribe to that approach because most of us *do* care about where we end up.

The first part of creating a plan is having a vision of where you want to be when you're done implementing that plan. (See Part II of this book as well as Chapter 9 to help hone in your vision.) When you decide on a vision, be sure to live within your capabilities. Don't go overboard right away — we suggest you start with a prototype or proof of concept to get a feel for the waters.

The following starting points can prepare you for creating that grander vision:

- ✔ Try building a small internal information-supply chain, maybe automating some simple task that currently has some humans gluing the links of the information-supply chain together.

- ✔ Work with a trusted business partner within your extended enterprise and try automating a small external information-supply chain.

- ✔ Build an internal semantic Web of business information for your organization or maybe start even smaller and try out the technologies within your department.

If you tackle a small project prior to taking on a larger project, you'll begin to appreciate what's involved in an XBRL project.

Planning for Success

Establishing the right requirements and planning, two important keys to success, help ensure that you're solving the right problems. You may be familiar with things such as relational database technologies; lots of experience has been gained implementing such systems over the past 30 or so years. Although it's much newer, XBRL is certainly beyond its incubation period when no guidance, best practices, or other helpful information was available. On the other hand, XBRL hasn't crossed the chasm between early stages and mainstream adoption either. There's absolutely nothing wrong with exercising caution at this stage of XBRL's evolution, particularly if you're new to XBRL.

The following list offers useful, practical advice to help you make good choices that reduce your risk and remove barriers to a successful project:

- ✔ **Stick to best practices.** Best practices are a good way to protect your XBRL project from pitfalls that others have already fallen into. You don't need to reinvent the wheel if you don't have to. We cover a lot of these best practices in this book.

  Best practices drive discipline. XBRL International provides some information with regard to best practices (see Chapter 3), but a lot of other information is out there from other successful projects. (Chapters 17 and 18 are additional sources for finding best practices.)

- ✔ **Keep it simple.** You've probably heard the saying, "Keep it simple, stupid" — KISS, for short. You don't need unnecessarily complex approaches to get the results you want.

Ruthlessly and liberally apply KISS principles in your project to ensure that you can meet milestones and deadlines, pursue focused outcomes, and achieve success. Unnecessary complexity is the enemy of any implementation!

✔ **Start with a prototype or proof of concept.** Before you go too far, create a prototype or proof of concept to be sure that your requirements will be met. This step is particularly important if you're venturing down a new path.

An alternative to creating a prototype or proof of concept is to copy what others have done (see the next section). For now, remember that if someone else had similar requirements to yours and succeeded with a certain approach, what worked for them will most likely work for you.

Be sure that you do, in fact, have the same requirements as that other project. Sometimes, visiting and researching others who have implemented XBRL can supplement or perhaps sometimes be an alternative to creating a prototype or proof of concept. You need to provide hard, tangible evidence that what you want to do will work. You have to convince at least yourself that your path will lead you to success. You may even need to convince others. A good, well-thought-out prototype or proof of concept can help you provide this proof.

✔ **Borrow other good ideas.** Pablo Picasso said, "Good artists copy. Great artists steal." Reinventing the wheel is okay sometimes, but it's not always the best approach. Borrowing the proven ideas of others — with their permission, of course — is the ultimate form of best practices. How can you fail if you imitate something that is known to work? As long as your requirements are the same or similar to another successfully implemented project, borrowing someone else's idea only makes sense. You may not be able to copy exactly, but you can certainly find a lot of things worth leveraging from other successful projects.

The "If it wasn't invented here, we don't want it" attitude is an expensive mistake many people make. Besides, imitation is the sincerest and noblest form of flattery!

Architecting Your XBRL Solution

Say that you understand how XBRL provides an additional layer of help in areas where you need it above the XML syntax layer, so you're sold on using XBRL. But how exactly should you use XBRL? XBRL is a standard: It's not perfect. It's a general-purpose specification, but you need to solve a specific problem. How, exactly, should you be using XBRL?

The answer to this question is different for different use cases of XBRL. After all, XBRL is a general-purpose specification, which is generally a strength of XBRL. But sometimes something's strength can also be its weakness. Using XBRL incorrectly is like trying to fit a square peg into a round hole.

This section is important to both technical architects who have to make decisions but also for business users who provide important information to these architects. Having an appropriate list of what is important is critical to establishing system requirements. A correct understanding of requirements is key to deciding on an appropriate architecture.

As you start to digging into the details of XBRL, you'll start asking yourself these types of questions:

✔ XBRL is simply too complex for business users, so how do I make it easier while still complying with the standard?

✔ Different regulators who require us to provide data to them seem to be using different XBRL taxonomy architectures — do I have to implement each of these different architectures internally?

✔ How do I keep garbage out of my systems?

✔ How do I control the information model expressed in my XBRL taxonomy?

✔ XBRL doesn't seem to have many rules around controlling taxonomy extensibility — it seems too flexible, so how do I communicate to those extending my XBRL taxonomy how to do it as I intended?

We're not understating the case when we say this list of specific tactics for architecting your XBRL solution are keys to reducing implementation costs, maximizing your project's success, and maximizing the effectiveness and efficiency of your implementation. Applying the following techniques when appropriate provide significant advantages:

✔ **Simplify your life by using an application profile.** XBRL is a general-purpose specification. Few implementations need all of it. Reducing what you use cuts down on your costs and reduces user options, which makes XBRL easier to use. An application profile is in essence a specific subset of the full XBRL specification.

✔ **Maximize consistency, comparability, and usability via an information model.** Consistency makes many magical things happen. You don't get consistency unless you explicitly attempt to create it. An information model can help you achieve this consistency, resulting in the maximum possible comparability and business user usability. An information model is essentially formal documentation that explains how an XBRL taxonomy implements specific business requirements and how taxonomy components relate to one another.

✔ **Increase usability using a logical model.** Trying to work with XBRL's physical model is an exercise in futility. Don't do it. In fact, most business users can't do it even if they want to — it's simply too complicated. Usability is vastly easier by working with XBRL at the logical level. A logical model is simply an expression of the business problem in logical and easy-to-understand terms, which is then followed by your information model.

✔ **Reduce effort by using someone else's taxonomy.** Why create an XBRL taxonomy when you don't have to? You can many times benefit from leveraging XBRL taxonomies created by others. On the other hand, using someone else's taxonomy also has its drawbacks, such as forcing you to give up a certain amount of control over the taxonomy and selecting the architecture you'll use.

✔ **Maintain control with an abstraction layer.** Do you really want to give up control of your internal architecture to an external regulator or multiple external regulators who implement XBRL differently and can potentially change their architecture without your input? An abstraction layer can mitigate this risk. Think of an abstraction layer as a buffer between your implementation and the implementations of others.

Note that the preceding tactics aren't mutually exclusive. If you combine a solid application profile (architecture), an information model, and express a logical model interface to these, your life really can be a whole lot easier. You may choose to take this approach, but others may not be so enlightened. No problem: Just hide behind an abstraction layer, and you'll not be beholden to the whims of the XBRL taxonomy creation approaches used by others.

The following sections look at the preceding tactics in more detail.

Use an application profile to simplify

Application profiles are commonly used within computer science. An *application profile* is a set of technical characteristics and guidelines, or a profile that an application stays within. Application profiles can make things easier by establishing boundaries. For example, XML is an application profile, a fully compliant subset of SGML (Standard Generalized Markup Language). Building an XML parser is easier than building a fully compliant SGML parser due to SGML's complexity. XML took the parts of SGML that it needed and ignored the rest, therefore reducing complexity. XML is taking off, whereas SGML has a specific niche but never received broad adoption.

An application profile of XBRL is, in essence, a subset of the complete XBRL Specification that you use for a specific implementation. Application profiles are 100-percent XBRL-compliant. Application profiles are specific architectures or approaches to implementing XBRL. Rather than supporting all the features XBRL offers, unnecessary features and duplicate functionality are eliminated from your architecture. An architecture document generally communicates the aspects of XBRL that are used and those that aren't allowed. The architecture document is enforced by a *conformance suite,* which is a set of tests that allows you to be sure a software application properly supports that application profile.

If you create application profiles correctly, you can substantially reduce the amount of programming needed to support XBRL, your system can work better, and the system can be easier to use. Here are good examples of application profiles:

- **COREP XBRL Project:** This application profile (`www.eurofiling.info/corepTaxonomy/taxonomy.html`) is sound, consistent, and proven, but it's rather technical in nature. Documentation is sparse, but it does have many good examples.

- **US GAAP Taxonomy Architecture:** This XBRL taxonomy (`http://xbrl.us/Documents/SECOFM-USGAAPT-Architecture-20080428.pdf`) is well documented, and its architecture and application profile is fairly clear.

- **XBRL Simplified Application Profile:** Also known as XBRLS, this application profile (`http://xbrl.squarespace.com/xbrls`) was built specifically to make XBRL easier to use by business users. It uses many of the best ideas of the US GAAP XBRL taxonomy and the COREP XBRL taxonomy.

- **XBRL Global Ledger:** XBRL Global Ledger (see Chapter 17) is basically an XBRL application profile for specific types of transactions.

To avoid having to type these long links, go to `www.dummies.com/go/xbrl`. This takes you to a landing page where you can click the link you need.

Application profiles do have their downsides. One downside is that an implementation of one application profile of XBRL may not work with another application profile of XBRL. Every true application profile of XBRL will always work with software applications that support the full XBRL specification, but those general-software applications won't provide the ease of use or leverage of a software application tuned for one specific application profile. This drawback is okay if you work only with specific and known application profiles in your business-information-exchange supply chain. It can be an issue, however, if you must work with many different approaches to implementing XBRL.

Application profiles are basically a tradeoff. You give up flexibility, but they can make implementations easier to use and more robust, as well as reduce costs, complexity, the potential for errors, and so on. In many situations, some application profiles can be better than others. However, a general implementation of XBRL is unlikely to be better than a specific application profile, tuned for a specific purpose.

You're basically always using an application profile of XBRL. The application profile may be for general XBRL itself: Everything XBRL offers is allowed. Another profile may only allow certain XBRL modules. Every XBRL taxonomy has its own architecture and therefore its own application profile.

Use an information model to be consistent

Similar to an application profile that constrains the pieces of XBRL that you'll use in your architecture, an *information model* has to do with how your XBRL taxonomy is structured — in essence, constraining that structure. An information model helps you keep your XBRL taxonomy consistent, and it can also make working with XBRL easier. An information model also articulates how you should extend your XBRL taxonomy. Because an information model describes how your XBRL taxonomy is structured and how to use it, understanding that model is also helpful for anyone who may end up using that taxonomy.

XBRL taxonomies aren't simply random. Most, if not all, taxonomies use some sort of information model to create the taxonomy. That information model may or may not be formally documented, but it does exist. Formally documenting the information model makes consistently following the information model easier for both creators and users of that taxonomy.

You can take this one step further than formal documentation and talk about testing the information model to be sure that it's being followed correctly. The best way to test an information model is by using automated computer processes. Manually eyeballing a taxonomy for consistency and adherence to an information model, particularly a large one, simply isn't effective.

Something worth mentioning is the notion of a generated approach to creating an XBRL taxonomy. A *generated approach* means generating the actual XBRL taxonomy using software as opposed to keying every concept, relation, and resource into an XBRL taxonomy-creation tool. Many times, people create taxonomies by adding concepts and relations into a taxonomy via the use of a commercial taxonomy-creation tool. But another approach is to collect information in some other form, such as a spreadsheet, and then generate the XBRL taxonomy itself from that information by using a macro or other program. A computer-generated taxonomy can be significantly more consistent than one where humans add concepts one by one. It's incredibly difficult for humans to do things consistently without computers to help them.

Here are some information models that others have created:

- ✔ **XBRL Simplified Application Profile:** A simple-to-use and highly functional information model (`http://xbrl.squarespace.com/xbrls`) that works together with an application profile.

- ✔ **XBRL US GAAP Taxonomies Architecture:** Although it's undocumented, the US GAAP Taxonomy (`http://taxonomies.xbrl.us/us-gaap/1.0/doc/SECOFM-USGAAPT-Architecture-20080428.pdf`) does follow a specific information model.

The advantage of these out-of-the-box information models is that the documentation is made available in the form of a formal specification, the rules are documented and enforceable by XBRL-compliant software, and some XBRL software vendors support validation against these rules and even offer Web services to validate the adherence to the information model rules.

Increase usability using a logical model

The physical model of XBRL is quite complex. Most business users would have a hard time working with XBRL at the physical model level, nor should they really have to. When you implement XBRL using a logical model to which business users can better relate, it makes it significantly easier for the users to use XBRL within the system.

The logical model of SQL (structured query language) is an excellent example of how a logical model provides benefits. The logical model of a database (tables, fields, and rows) is almost universal. Another great example is the logical model of an electronic spreadsheet (workbooks, sheets, columns, and rows).

The XBRL Specification provides a logical model of XBRL at its highest levels, but this high-level model falls significantly short of meeting your real needs. Because the XBRL Specification focuses on the physical syntax of XBRL, many software vendors now use that physical model to implement XBRL within their software applications. Technical people are fine with working with XBRL at this level, for the most part. The typical business user is far less comfortable with XBRL's physical model. A logical model hides the physical model of XBRL from the business user.

You can work at a logical level instead of the physical model of XBRL in two ways:

- ✔ **Create your own logical model.** Although time-consuming, you can get exactly what you need. It takes a lot of specialized skill to build a sound logical model, however. It also takes a good understanding of XBRL to create such a model. Business people and technical people collaborate to create logical models.

✔ **Use someone else's logical model.** Others have defined logical models for XBRL implementations, so use their model. Rather than creating a logical model yourself, take a look at the logical models of others, pick one that fits your needs, and use that logical model.

Both the XBRL Simple Application Profile (XBRLS) and the US GAAP XBRL Taxonomies Architecture in the prior section have defined logical models.

A good, sound logical model pays significant dividends in terms of usability, design soundness, maintenance, and costs.

Use someone else's taxonomy

You may be required to use someone else's XBRL taxonomy, which means you may have certain architectural decisions imposed upon you. Or, you can choose to use someone else's taxonomy; therefore, you may impose certain architectural decisions upon yourself. Consider these situations:

✔ **Use a mandated taxonomy.** Some regulator may thrust a specific XBRL taxonomy upon you. For example, if you're a public company and you have to file with the U.S. SEC, you'll be mandated to use the XBRL taxonomy that it specifies.

✔ **Leverage a taxonomy.** You may need to implement some capability or system for which you could leverage an existing XBRL taxonomy. For example, if you're a bank and you want to collect financial information using XBRL from your borrowers, you could use the US GAAP taxonomy to do so because its financial reporting is so similar to your use case. With only a few adjustments, you can easily extend it to meet your needs.

✔ **Create a new taxonomy.** You may not have a taxonomy that's thrust upon you, nor is there a public taxonomy you can leverage. Not to worry — you can create your own XBRL taxonomy.

Life is a tradeoff. Using someone else's XBRL taxonomy is also a tradeoff. On the one hand, if you use an existing XBRL taxonomy, you can significantly reduce your maintenance costs and other efforts. If you can live with an existing taxonomy as it is, your taxonomy maintenance costs may be zero. If you need to make modifications, you have to maintain only the extension. If you create an entirely new taxonomy, on the other hand, you have to maintain and document the taxonomy throughout its life cycle.

If you leverage someone else's taxonomy, you're beholden to their whims to some degree. You'll have to use the architecture they've chosen. You have to live with their maintenance schedule. You have to live with their quality level and so on — you get the idea.

When you evaluate your options, consider who is responsible for maintaining the taxonomy you're considering leveraging. The ultimate question is, "How much do you want things that you don't have control over impacting your internal systems?" Also, keep in mind that you may be dealing with multiple XBRL taxonomies that have different architectures, different information models, and different logical models.

Use an abstraction layer for control

Think about the ramifications on your business systems if you have to work with multiple XBRL taxonomies, each with a different architecture or application profile of XBRL, different approaches to modeling their information, different logical models, and different ideas about how a taxonomy should be maintained over its life.

Building an abstraction layer between your internal implementation of XBRL and the outside world's implementations of XBRL can make a lot of sense in the right situations. Company size can be a major driver. The larger the organization, the higher the probability that you'll be interacting with more than one party using more than one flavor of XBRL-implemented models in more than one different way, both within and outside your organization.

An *abstraction layer* can protect you from these realities of using XBRL. Abstraction layers are common in computer science and are a way of hiding software implementation details. A good example of an abstraction layer is the Open Systems Interconnection Reference Model (OSI Model). An OSI Model separates the complex task of networking computers together into seven discrete and independent layers that you can implement independently of each other, but they work together in a formal manner. Technical people use this approach all the time.

Although it can be a big investment, an abstraction layer can eliminate many headaches that you'll run into if you don't have a plan for dealing with multiple XBRL architectures, information models, and logical models.

Executing Your XBRL Project

Say that you've identified the problem you want to solve and have determined that using XBRL could provide some good leverage. You've expressed your requirements, and you've chosen your approach to architecting your systems and proven that architecture by creating a prototype or a proof of concept. As such, you've tested the XBRL taxonomy information model and

XBRL application profile to be sure that your ideas will yield a system that will meet your requirements. Your project should now be on the road to becoming a stellar success.

You likely know how to execute a project, so we don't go into every aspect of executing projects successfully here. But what we do have for you in the following sections are specific considerations relating to XBRL.

Test your resulting XBRL instances

XBRL instances are where the rubber meets the road in your XBRL project. Probably the biggest mistake made in XBRL projects today is not creating XBRL instances that properly exercise systems that make use of XBRL. Yet, creating these XBRL instances is the key to building your XBRL taxonomy correctly. This is particularly true if users are allowed to extend your XBRL taxonomy. Testing makes sure that your system will correctly handle the XBRL instances coming into it and that your system rules keep XBRL instances with errors out of your system.

We go into the details related to creating XBRL taxonomies in Chapter 17 and creating XBRL instances in Chapter 18. What we go over here is the bigger picture of how to use XBRL instances to test your implementation, including the critical XBRL taxonomy, which, if not created correctly, can yield some unexpected results. You have several possible options relating to XBRL instances as they relate to your project:

- ✔ You may need to create XBRL instances as part of your project deliverables.

- ✔ You may not need to deliver any XBRL instances as part of your project, but you need to create them to be sure that your XBRL taxonomy is created correctly.

- ✔ You may have existing data that you can use to generate XBRL instances to test your XBRL taxonomy.

- ✔ You may not have existing data that's useful for creating XBRL instances to test your XBRL taxonomy, therefore you have to figure out some other approach to creating your test bed of XBRL instances.

You can use the following tactics to create XBRL instances to test your XBRL taxonomy. The primary objective of creating these XBRL instances is to help you understand the rules you need to get good information into your system and to keep garbage out of your system:

✔ **Monster instance:** The term *monster instance* describes an XBRL instance that includes every concept in an XBRL taxonomy. The benefit of creating this monster XBRL instance is that it can help you detect certain types of errors within your taxonomy relations. One common error detected using a monster XBRL instance is a cycle problem within your XBRL taxonomy. For example, one class of cycle problem you can easily detect by packing every concept into one XBRL instance is calculation relations that are expressed inconsistently.

Another type of common cycle error found with a monster XBRL instance are two calculations that could never work correctly within the same XBRL instance. Typically, all these cycle issues relate to taxonomy-modeling errors. You can use synthesized data to auto-generate a monster instance. Some software applications even offer a feature to generate these XBRL instances.

✔ **Fragment instances:** Another tactic you can use to test XBRL instances is to create fragments of specific areas of your taxonomy. Whereas the monster instance tests the interrelationships between areas of the taxonomy, creating fragments allows you to test specific, usually complex, areas or areas where the risk of error in the taxonomy is high. This helps you see whether those specific areas are working as expected.

✔ **Comparison instances:** You'll want to test how comparisons between XBRL instances work. You can test for two types of comparisons. One comparison instance is information for one submitting entity but for multiple submission periods. Another comparison is submissions of different entities for the same period.

✔ **Conglomerate instance:** Entities submitting information to you likely use specific combinations of relations networks together. In many cases, the permutations and combinations of these different networks can get rather complex. These specific combinations of relations networks are generally less than the entire taxonomy. The best way to describe this test is that it tests the key permutations and expected combinations to see whether they work together correctly.

✔ **Extension instances:** If your system allows extensions, you need to test them, too. You should create extension scenarios for all the non-extension instance testing scenarios discussed previously in this list.

✔ **Versioning instances:** Plan ahead for when the taxonomy changes. Build a new version of the taxonomy and test your versioning strategy to be sure that it works correctly. Build instances against both versions of the taxonomy and test your ability to perform comparisons across taxonomy versions.

Keep in mind that the fundamental goal of your testing is to be sure that your XBRL instances are working as you expect them to work. A well-constructed XBRL taxonomy is the key to an XBRL instance working correctly.

XBRL taxonomies are basically data models, so you should treat them as such. Many of those creating taxonomies aren't data modelers but are business-domain experts instead. You have to be sure that the business-domain experts who understand their domain are modeling the data using sound data modeling practices. Automated testing of adherence to your specified application profile and specified information model helps domain experts build high-quality XBRL taxonomies.

Building an XBRL taxonomy correctly without building XBRL instances is impossible; correctly documented XBRL instances is the only way you can assure yourself that the XBRL taxonomy works the way you desire.

If you don't have any tests, you won't see errors. Seeing no errors doesn't mean that you don't have any, though. What have you done to prove everything is okay? When you can prove to yourself that everything is right, most likely everything will be fine. But, you know how that goes: Every now and then, something unforeseen slips in. You certainly want to test known potential problem areas.

Store XBRL

You're going to receive XBRL instances, and you're going to have to store those XBRL instances or the information they contain somewhere. Many people think of XBRL taxonomies and instances as physical files, but they don't necessarily have to be physical files in all stages of their life cycle. The XBRL may simply be a means of transporting the information contained in the XBRL instance and described by the XBRL taxonomy, an interim step in the chain of using the information. All the information may exist within some application, but it exists only as XBRL for the time needed to perform some specific task. You can think of the XBRL instance, or more likely multiple XBRL instances, as a repository containing all the XBRL taxonomies and XBRL instances you need to fulfill your needs. That information repository can physically exist as the following:

✔ **Individual physical file:** The XBRL you have to work with may simply be an individual physical file. You access that file and do what you need. For example, a consumer of the information contained within the XBRL instance may need to use only one file for the purposes of performing some sort of analysis.

✔ **Set of physical files:** A repository is more likely a set of physical files. You somehow have to pull that set of physical XBRL instances and related taxonomies that you want to work with together. How will you do that? Your collection of files may be URLs on the Web — say, the financial statements of a set of companies you want to track in order to benchmark. You could use RSS or some other means to pull these separate physical files together into a set.

✔ **Existing relational database:** By this term, we mean that your repository of information is some existing relational database into which you place information extracted from an XBRL instance. Existing business systems use a lot of relational databases.

✔ **XML database:** Another type of database that can hold XBRL is an XML database. These databases aren't as popular as relational databases, but you don't have to shred the information, XBRL can easily fit into an XML database.

✔ **Standard XBRL relational database schema:** Another way to store XBRL is to create a standard relational database schema that is optimized to store all your XBRL. This database schema can hold any legal form of XBRL anyone can create.

✔ **Application profile-specific standard XBRL relational database schema:** Focusing on one XBRL application profile makes storing XBRL in a relational database much easier. If you use application profiles to remove possible options that it outlaws, you can end up with significantly less complex database schemas that are easier to use. The downside to this approach is that your database won't hold every possible form of XBRL; it will hold only your specific application profile.

For example, the U.S. SEC collects information from thousands of organizations. In one year, it receives millions of filings. Storing these filings as files on a computer hard drive may not scale for the SEC.

Further, users want to run queries against this data set of millions of files, extracting the information they need. Imagine running a query against a set of files trying to find the answer to a simple question you may have, such as "What is the net income of every company in the airline industry for 2009?" It's a simple enough question, but consider how this query is processed:

1. **You need to figure out the set of files you need to work with.**

   Of the millions of files, you need to somehow get only the files that contain the information you need.

2. **You need to go into each of the files and grab the piece of information you need.**

3. **You obtain your set of information back from the query in some format.**

   This process is made even more complicated when you change the query a little. Rather than querying all airlines for one year, consider querying one airline across a period of ten years. In this case, assuming that the taxonomy has been updated each year, the taxonomy used to create the XBRL instances has changed ten times.

On the other hand, the U.S. FDIC receives XBRL filings, shreds the information, puts the information into a relational database, and then stores an archive copy of the XBRL instance. You can query the relational database for this information.

Validate for quality and interoperability

Validation is the process of making sure that you created all your XBRL taxonomies and XBRL instances correctly. Another way to think of validation is to think of it as *error detection*.

Many different types of errors can occur, and so error detection or validation comes in many different flavors. The good news is that computer applications handle the vast majority of this error detection. Computers can't handle everything, however. For example, if you use the wrong concept to tag a number, a computer, in most cases, can't detect that error (but in other cases, it can).

Validation occurs at several points for reasons ranging from interoperability to automation enablement to cost effectiveness. To give you a better feel for validation, here are the different types of validation essential to any effective business information exchange:

✔ **XML validation:** Without a valid document in XML, validation is a non-starter. Business users should be able to take this level of validation for granted and never have to deal with it. All XBRL processors do XML validation under the hood.

✔ **XML Schema validation:** An XML document can be valid or well-formed XML, but it may not be structured correctly. That structure is what XML Schema validation provides. An XML parser generally performs XML Schema validation. The parser makes sure that the elements comply with the content model of an XML schema. It also ensures that the data types are correct. Most XML languages provide validation only to the extent of an XML schema. XBRL has a number of XML schemas that indicate how the XML syntax used by XBRL must be constructed, but XBRL goes far beyond XML Schema validation.

✔ **XBRL syntax validation:** Like XML and XML Schema, the XBRL syntax needs to be correct so that any XBRL processor can correctly interpret the XBRL taxonomy and/or XBRL instance (not just the XBRL processor used to create them). XML processors catch some types of errors; XML Schema validation detects other types of errors. The XBRL Specification conformance suite has, however, more than 400 additional tests that are requirements on XBRL syntax, but XML or XML Schema validation can't detect the errors. XBRL processors detect these types of syntax errors. Again, similar to XML validation and XML Schema validation, business users should be able to take this level of validation for granted and never have to deal with this level of validation. This classification also includes validation related to any XBRL modules utilized.

✔ **Best practices validation:** XBRL International issues a number of best practices. These best practices supplement XBRL syntax validation. For example, FRIS establishes a best practice that a fact may not be included twice within an instance document because it makes no sense to do so (exactly the same concept and context). This FRIS best practice prevents this problem from being introduced within a system.

✔ **Information model validation:** An information model is basically how your XBRL taxonomy is structured; XBRL taxonomies aren't random. Information model validation ensures that the information model is properly constructed. If extension is involved, it also ensures that extension XBRL taxonomies follow the information models of the base XBRL taxonomy they're extending.

For example, if a calculation is expressed in a certain manner in an XBRL taxonomy, this type of validation ensures that all calculations are expressed in a similar manner and that someone extending that calculation likewise followed that model. XBRL taxonomies aren't random; they follow some pattern. Information model validation enforces these modeling patterns.

✔ **Validation of other system constraints:** The system in which XBRL operates may impose other syntactic or semantic rules on how XBRL needs to be created to operate within that system. XBRL itself doesn't express all the necessary rules to make XBRL work effectively within a system. Best practices validation supplements the XBRL validation, but they're still not enough. Specific constraints or choices made by a system implementing XBRL still need to supplement XBRL validation and best practices. The U.S. SEC Public Validation Criteria (www.sec.gov/spotlight/xbrl/publicvalidationcriteria.htm) is an example of this validation category. This category of validation covers enforcement of any architecture constraints a system places on the XBRL used within a specific system, such as that the entity identifier scheme used by the SEC, which is enforced by the U.S. SEC Public Validation Criteria.

✔ **Creation-based business rules validation:** Business rules validation is the most interesting type of validation to a business user. It helps ensure that the information expressed within an XBRL instance or set of XBRL instances complies with the semantics expressed within an XBRL taxonomy. Business users sometimes call this *data integrity*. Business rules validation generally fall into two broad categories:

- *Computations,* all those numeric relationships within an instance. For example, "Does the balance sheet actually balance?"

- *Report-ability rules,* ensuring that everything that is supposed to be reported is actually reported. These rules are things like, "If this is reported, then this and this needs to be reported also."

✔ **Analysis-based business rules validation:** A consumer of an XBRL instance may have additional validation criteria imposed on an XBRL instance creator. For example, a specific current ratio threshold for a reporting entity is a rule placed, say, on a borrower by a lender. Analysts attach these rules to their XBRL taxonomy.

Feeling a little overwhelmed and perhaps a little concerned that you'll never be able to get your XBRL taxonomies and XBRL instances to be valid? Fear not! Software will take care of this validation for you. Besides, you already enforce a lot of these rules in your everyday workflow, but humans enforce the rules carefully and diligently by doing a lot of work. XBRL moves a lot of the human validation to computer processes. It doesn't take care of *all* the validation and error detection, but it does plenty enough to improve the quality of business reports and reduce the cost of creating the information.

All these different types of validation are important to different participants of an information exchange. Holes in validation result in human intervention to correct issues, which means increased costs and increased time to effectively use the information being exchanged. Good rules and good validation are critical to effectively automating information exchanges.

Maintain your XBRL solution

Things change. The XBRL taxonomy you either provide in your system or use in your system will change, and you need to communicate those changes. You need to remap systems for new taxonomies and their changes. The good thing is that XBRL has a solution called XBRL Versioning. (See our discussion of XBRL Versioning in Chapter 16.)

Collaborating with XBRL Consultants

You're probably going to be working with consultants who help you with aspects of your project relating to XBRL. You no doubt know how to work with consultants already. You need to pay particular attention to finding the consultant who brings the XBRL expertise that you need.

One XBRL consultant is probably not going to be able to bring everything you need to a project. In fact, finding one person who can is rare.

Look for these skills when hiring XBRL consultants:

- ✔ **Data modeler:** Building a taxonomy requires data modeling expertise and also specifically XBRL taxonomy-creation expertise. Not all data modelers have XBRL expertise. Teaching someone who understands data modeling how to understand XBRL is likely far easier than teaching someone who understands XBRL, data modeling.

- ✔ **Specific XBRL processor:** Developers may understand how to write code, but just because they can write code doesn't mean that they understand the best way to develop or use an XBRL processor. Likewise, just because they understand one XBRL processor doesn't mean that they understand a different XBRL processor.

- ✔ **XBRL architecture:** Just because someone is a fantastic software architect doesn't mean that they understand anything about how to select a proper architecture for an XBRL system. Teaching a good software architect about XBRL is easier than teaching someone who thoroughly understands XBRL about good software architecture.

- ✔ **Domain expertise:** Just because you understand a specific domain doesn't mean that you understand XBRL. And yet again, teaching a domain expert XBRL is vastly easier than teaching an XBRL expert about a specific domain.

At this point in XBRL's evolution, caution is in order. The number of XBRL consultants popping up these days is incredible! The demand for XBRL is increasing, and everyone is trying to make a buck. Don't allow them to waste your time or money or unintentionally risk your project.

Not even the best consultants know everything about everything. Good consultants understand their strengths and weaknesses and are comfortable telling you about their weaknesses. If a consultant pretends to know everything, be wary!

Before you hire a consultant, you need to know something about his knowledge and background. Ask a technical consultant the following questions to make sure that he can be effective and helpful on an XBRL project:

- ✔ **Do you understand XBRL?** Duh! And as good as we hope this book is, if the only exposure your consultant has to XBRL is via this book, you probably need to get a new consultant! *You* can read this book without a consultant's help. If you ask a consultant questions based on what you've learned from this book and he doesn't seem to understand what you're talking about, it's a bad sign.

✔ **Do you understand how to use XBRL processors?** A common mistake is to not use an XBRL processor or to literally end up building your own XBRL processor piece by piece until you realize that you really should have purchased one. XBRL processors provide a significant amount of leverage for working with XBRL. You need to make use of one. If your consultant is using SQL or XSLT alone without an XBRL processor, she's racking up a lot of hours unnecessarily.

✔ **Do you understand the advantages of an information modeling layer?** Understanding what an information modeling layer is and how you can use it to make a lot of things easier is important for your consultant to understand. If your consultant doesn't know what an information modeling layer is, cha-ching! You'll pay. You won't be able to create a consistent XBRL taxonomy, and you won't be able test your XBRL taxonomy adequately.

✔ **Do you understand XBRL Dimensions?** If your consultant claims to understand XBRL but doesn't understand XBRL Dimensions, she doesn't really understand XBRL. Look for a different consultant immediately.

✔ **Do you understand XBRL Formula?** As with XBRL Dimensions, if you don't understand XBRL Formulas, you really don't understand XBRL. Get another consultant.

✔ **Do you understand XML, XPath, XLink, XForms, and Xcetra?** Nowadays, you can find people who understand XML, but that wasn't always the case. A good understanding of XML is necessary to understand XBRL. However, beware: Understanding XML isn't enough to understand XBRL. XLink is a bit of a different animal, and not many people in the XML community really understand it well. So, be careful. XBRL makes a lot of use of XLink.

✔ **Do you understand XSLT?** XSLT is one of the most useful technologies when it comes to working with XML and is part of the XSL (Extensible Stylesheet Language) family, which includes XSLT (XSL Transformations), XSL-FO (XSL Formatting Objects), and XQuery. All these standards are helpful in rendering XBRL.

✔ **Do you understand data modeling?** Data modeling is a unique skill set that not everyone has. If you're building a taxonomy, data-modeling expertise is critical.

✔ **Do you understand architecture considerations?** You know, a framer can build a house without understanding architecture. When he gets done, it may not be a great house, or even a good one, but he can build one. You definitely want someone on your team who has years of experience at figuring out technical architectures.

Managing an XBRL Project

The biggest secret to managing an XBRL project is that XBRL projects are mostly like other projects. There are more similarities than differences. If you employ good practices on other projects, those practices will work for projects that have an XBRL component:

- ✔ Be sure to get good (and the right kind of) XBRL expertise. Just because someone is good at one aspect of XBRL doesn't mean they're good at all things XBRL. The best XBRL consultants understand this. (For more on this topic, see the previous section.)

- ✔ The more XBRL instance testing you do, the better the XBRL taxonomy will be. It's that easy. It's not just about the volume of XBRL instances for testing; it's building the correct XBRL instances. Be sure to check out the section on testing we provide earlier in this chapter.

- ✔ If you find that you're reinventing a lot of things, one of two things must be true: Either you have some specific requirements that are unique to your system, or you're making a big mistake. Be sure to check out the earlier section relating to application profiles to see whether you can leverage what others have created instead of unnecessarily reinventing the wheel.

- ✔ A taxonomy is a data model. If you're building a taxonomy, you need a good data modeler who has learned XBRL. Teaching a good data modeler about XBRL takes significantly less time than turning someone who understands XBRL into a good data modeler.

Identifying a Successful XBRL Project

Here are signs that your XBRL project is probably ticking like a Swiss watch:

- ✔ **Problems exist, but you have a list of them.** Problems always exist. Having a list of problems is actually a good thing. Perhaps an overly long list may have its issues, but having no list is a signal that something else may be going on. (See the symptoms of an XBRL project in trouble in the next section.)

- ✔ **Technical people are making the technical decisions.** Technical people should be making technical decisions.

- ✔ **Business people are making the business decisions.** Business people should make business decisions.

✔ **Good communication exists between technical and business people.** A good sign of communication is conflict. Technical people and business people come from two different worlds. With XBRL projects in particular, technical and business people interact a lot. Good, healthy conflict is a sign of communication. Clearly, the conflicts shouldn't persist but move to resolution, but conflicts are a part of effective communication.

✔ **Your prototype or proof of concept proves your system will work as expected.** The best way to keep your batting average high is to stack the cards in your favor. A good way to do so is by using prototypes effectively. Prototypes are a great communication tool to help you see whether requirements are understood by all parties correctly, to test ideas to see whether the ideas work, and so on.

✔ **Your processes are detecting bugs and issues that get resolved.** Bugs and other issues are part of the process, but you don't want them to get out of control or remain undetected. Mistakes are made on every project. Having a lot of bugs isn't an excuse to support bad practices; that isn't the point. Bugs, issues, and other problems are a part of life.

Monitoring an XBRL Project in Trouble

Here are signs that your XBRL project is perhaps in trouble and something may need your attention:

✔ **Your project has no problems.** Yeah, right! A good sign of problems is thinking that you have no problems. Every project has its issues. If you think your project has no problems, it basically means that people don't know how to recognize problems or that they see the problems but don't want others to know about them. A good dose of "management by walking around" and talking to people helps you see where problems may be hiding.

✔ **No proof exists that your system will work.** If you don't test your system and you can't prove that everything will work, some things probably won't work. Prove to yourself that everything works, and things will work.

✔ **No test cases exist.** If you have no test cases, chances are you're not doing any testing. Testing provides the proof that things work.

✔ **No tests are failing.** Test cases, if they exist, initially fail. As the project proceeds, things will be fixed, and tests will stop failing. If nothing ever fails a test, it means that something is definitely wrong. It may be the case that you have the wrong tests.

✔ **No prototype or proof of concept exists.** Prototypes exist in order to test an idea to see whether that idea will work. If you're repeating something that someone else has created, you have less of a need for a prototype. If you're doing something for the first time, you absolutely want to have a prototype. When you're building a taxonomy, it should include prototype XBRL instances that users of the system will create. No prototype XBRL instances for a taxonomy means that your taxonomy may not work as you want or expect.

✔ **No system requirements exists.** No system requirements means that anything is acceptable, right? Well, probably not. Requirements are critical to getting what you want out of any system — even a system that makes use of XBRL.

✔ **No architecture document exists.** No architecture document means no ability to test whether you're following your architecture. Or, maybe you haven't prescribed an architecture. That may cause inconsistent XBRL taxonomies and XBRL instances and is a pretty good bet that you won't like the results achieved out of your XBRL implementation.

✔ **Technical people are making business decisions.** Letting technical people make business decisions is a bad idea. Generally, they make business decisions only when they have to because the business people aren't making the decisions they need to make for some reason or another. Get to the bottom of why business people aren't making the business decisions.

✔ **Business people are making technical decisions.** Likewise, you don't want business people making technical decisions. In those cases, you may have an imbalance of power where business people are overriding or meddling in areas they shouldn't.

✔ **Business and technical people aren't communicating.** It's bad news if technical people and business people aren't communicating. If no disagreements occur or compromises are reached, you likely have some sort of communication problem.

Chapter 13

Complying with the SEC Mandate

*T*his chapter focuses on key aspects of the SEC mandate to use the XBRL format for SEC filings, what exactly the mandate calls for, who will be impacted by it, and options for complying. In addition, we look into the future in terms of what the 21st-century disclosure system will look like and how you and your company will be impacted.

To avoid having to type the long links in this chapter, go to www.dummies. com/go/xbrl. This takes you to a landing page where you can click the link you need.

Why the SEC Mandated XBRL

The SEC began collecting financial information from public companies in the early 1930s before copy machines, fax machines, and computers had been invented. People traveled to Washington, D.C., to public reference rooms to gather information they wanted to use for analysis or other purpose and then called key stakeholders about the event from SEC-provided payphones. In those days, you had to have pocket full of quarters if you went digging into SEC filings.

In 1984, the SEC spent $30 million to start the Electronic Data Gathering Analysis and Retrieval (EDGAR) system. This system made public financial information available electronically. Companies were phased into this new system over a three-year period. In 1993, the Clinton administration announced that EDGAR would be made available over the Internet — it was considered one of the first concrete examples of what the information superhighway could mean to the public.

The EDGAR database is really just like a big electronic filing cabinet. The data was there buried in the physical electronic documents, but EDGAR enabled these specially formatted files to be instantly accessed from anywhere on the planet using the Web. But it was still hard to get information out of the documents using anything other than labor-intensive, human error-prone processes. Companies, such as EDGAR Online, Inc., were spending untold millions of dollars trying to figure out how to parse the documents, map information, and provide reusable comparable data. Although these attempts were successful to some degree, they weren't truly successful.

The SEC had known about XBRL pretty much since the inception of the open-source standard. The SEC watched the XBRL International consortium grow and mature into a globally accepted metadata standard and watched projects, such as the FDIC's implementation of XBRL, succeed. But it wasn't until 2005 that Christopher Cox, then chairman of the SEC, contacted XBRL International and asked whether he could do anything to help XBRL. Cox knew XBRL wasn't ready for the tremendous volume of reports filed with the SEC, but he wanted to help make XBRL ready. He had a vision.

Cox called his vision *interactive data,* which is basically a more palatable name for XBRL. He wanted to change EDGAR from an electronic filing cabinet into an easily queryable electronic database of public company financial information. Cox became an advocate for XBRL. Eventually, the SEC provided funding to build the XBRL taxonomies needed to realize Cox's objective and then spent about $50 million to modernize the existing EDGAR systems to use the XBRL global open-source standard.

This new system was called Next-Generation EDGAR, which you can read about it at www.sec.gov/news/press/2008/2008-179.htm). Next-Generation EDGAR was to be a totally new architecture compliance reporting platform. Humans would no longer need to spend countless hours of drudgery getting information from SEC filings; instead, computers would be able to simply query the data and return the information sought. For example, rather than having a human manually extract information from multiple EDGAR documents, a computer application could automatically and accurately get that information for you, populating an analysis application, a Web application, or a spreadsheet that you created with just a click of your mouse.

Next-Generation EDGAR is part of the SEC's broader 21st Century Disclosure Initiative. You can get more information from the SEC Web site at www.sec.gov/disclosureinitiative.

In 2009, after almost a year's worth of public roundtables, comment, hearings, and such, the Obama administration, in one of its first acts, signed into law a mandate for all public companies to file interactive data with the SEC, phased in over a period of three years. Chairman Cox and his team at the SEC had set the stage to make the vision a reality.

The SEC mandate is really a number of mandates and other areas where the SEC is making use of XBRL. The first area where the SEC made information available in an XBRL format was its executive pay finder, which uses XBRL to make executive compensation information available for the largest 500 U.S. public companies. The SEC also used tagged data internally in a stock options backdating probe. In response to turmoil in the credit markets, the SEC announced a series of credit-rating reforms, which require rating agencies to make certain information available in XBRL format. The SEC is requiring mutual funds to make their risk/return summaries available in XBRL. And finally, the big one: the SEC is requiring public company financial information to be made available using XBRL.

The Ramifications of the SEC Mandate

Under the SEC mandate, public companies regulated by the SEC must provide XBRL versions of their financial information in addition to the current filing formats (such as HTML and ASCII). The mandate will be phased in over three years, with largest companies starting in June 2009 (about 500 companies), the next largest group the following year (about 1,800 companies), and the remainder following in the third year (about 12,000 companies). (The mandate has other detailed rules that you can read at `www.sec.gov/rules/final/2009/33-9002.pdf`.)

The mandate has some ramifications that aren't necessarily part of the actual ruling, but we believe are going to happen anyway. Here are examples:

✔ **Old filing formats will eventually go away.** The SEC has already stated publically that it intends to stop using the old filing formats (HTML and SGML). No timeline has been disclosed, as far as we know.

✔ **Both investors and the SEC itself will eventually be able to do a far better job at analyzing companies.** The entire analysis cost/benefit model will change. Further, this ease will change who gets analyzed. Most people don't realize it, but analysts track only about 20 percent of public companies because preparing the data for analysis using current SEC data formats is too costly. Also, a new type of analyst will appear — you! XBRL will help you keep an eye on public companies like never before. The term for this oversight is called *crowd sourcing,* which means letting the masses provide input.

✔ **Private companies will use XBRL.** Although the SEC regulates only public companies, it's only a matter of time before private companies will wind up using XBRL as well. For example, private companies required to file financial information with financial institutions in support of loans will likely be forced to make use of XBRL.

✔ **Not-for-profit organizations will use XBRL.** Not-for-profit entities who receive grants from the federal government, are foundations, have loans, or have other funding sources are highly likely to be pushed toward XBRL. Also, in the near future, a Next-Generation EDGAR-type system for not-for-profits may make this information conveniently available for analysis.

✔ **State and local governmental entities will use XBRL.** Approximately 88,000 state and local governments within the United States alone all report financial information to the Census Bureau — on paper! Other countries have similar situations. We expect them to also eventually move to XBRL. And again, you'll likely see a convenient Next-Generation EDGAR-type system that would make using the information in the financial filings of these entities easier.

✔ **Other regulators will follow the SEC lead.** The U.S. SEC wasn't the first regulator to make use of XBRL for regulatory financial filings — the Australian Prudential Regulation Authority (APRA) was. However, it's one of the largest and most publically visible. Other regulators will likely follow this trend toward electronic financial filings using XBRL.

XBRL filings by the SEC are nowhere close to being the end. These filings are really the beginning of a much bigger trend. XBRL will be used for all sorts of purposes over the coming years. The SEC did add a lot more momentum to the XBRL movement.

Meeting the SEC Mandate

We don't cover exactly how to comply with the SEC mandate in any level of detail because those who have to comply with the SEC mandate know who they are and have hordes of advisers and consultants helping them. But for those curious about the SEC mandate, here's an overview of the steps generally needed in order to meet the SEC mandate:

1. **Figure out when you'll need to start filing in the XBRL format with the SEC.**

   Your public accounting firm and/or your EDGAR filing service (if you have one) likely has that information or can help you figure it out. Whoever helps you with your current filing can, at a minimum, steer you in the right direction to meeting that SEC mandate. The SEC maintains a Web page at www.sec.gov/info/edgar.shtml of general information for EDGAR filers that includes information about XBRL filings.

2. **Figure out what approach you want to take.**

   You can break down this step into an initial short-term approach and then a long-term approach. The short-term and long-term approaches may be the same. Chapter 11 highlights the various approaches that you can use to meet the mandate to file XBRL with the SEC.

3. **Start earlier than you have to.**

   Yes, that's right. You definitely don't want to learn how to file and make everything work during your first required filing period using XBRL.

   Even if you don't actually submit the filing to the SEC, you'll want to do a minimum of one practice run to work the kinks out. We recommend doing two practice runs so that you can deal with rolling forward values from one report to the next; you can't get that practice using only one filing. Further, you may even want to do specific practice runs with your quarterly filings and another for your annual filings, which are significantly larger.

   After you work out all the kinks, doing your first filing should be a cinch.

4. **For your first filing, you can block tag the disclosures contained within your financial filings.**

   Block tag means you can tag things as big groups of information as opposed to tagging the individual details of all your disclosures. In the second year, you're no longer able to use the block-tagging approach. As such, you'll want to repeat your practice run one or two periods before your first full tagging of your financial information.

SEC-Specific Software and Services

Here's a sample of the specific services or software that you can use for filing with EDGAR:

- ✔ **Bowne:** Bowne (www.bowne.com/xbrl), one of the larger financial printers, has expanded its product offerings to also provide services for meeting SEC XBRL mandate.

- ✔ **Clarity Systems:** Clarity Systems (www.claritysystems.com) offers an integrated business-reporting software solution that you can use to create both SEC filings and generate XBRL for submission with the SEC.

- ✔ **EDGARfilings:** Also a financial printer, EDGARfilings (www.edgarfilings.com) provides its customers with software that allows them to prepare EDGAR submissions and the newly mandated XBRL.

- ✔ **Merrill Corp.:** Merrill Corp. (www.merrillcorp.com) is also one of the larger financial printers, and it has expanded its product offerings to include services for meeting the SEC XBRL mandate.

- ✔ **UBmatrix:** UBmatrix First Step Program (www.ubmatrix.com/products/sec.htm) provides you with the services, software, and training you need to create your XBRL for filing with the SEC.

The XBRL US Web page (`http://xbrl.us/Learn/Pages/ ToolsAndServices.aspx`) lists all the U.S. XBRL member's software and service providers who can help you file with the SEC.

The Cost of Meeting the SEC Mandate

The first question on the minds of those who have to comply with the SEC mandate is, "What will it cost us?" The final ruling document issued by the SEC (page 133 of the final ruling; see `www.sec.gov/rules/ final/2009/33-9002.pdf`) contained cost estimates, shown in Table 13-1.

Table 13-1	Estimated Costs of Compliance with SEC XBRL Mandate			
	First Submission with Block Text Footnotes and Schedules	*Subsequent Submission with Block Text Footnotes and Schedules*	*First Submission with Detailed Footnotes and Schedules*	*Subsequent Submission with Detailed Footnotes and Schedules*
Preparation face financials	$31,370	$4,310	$4,310	$4,310
Preparation footnotes	$1,750	$1,750	$17,500	$8,750
Preparation schedules	$250	$250	$1,750	$875
Software and filing agent services	$6,140	$6,140	$6,140	$6,140
Web site posting	$1,000	$1,000	$1,000	$1,000
Total cost	$40,510	$13,450	$30,700	$21,075
Upper bound	$82,220	$21,340	$60,150	$37,940

Table 13-1 shows data summarized from responses received from a questionnaire the SEC sent to a number of companies that participated within the voluntary filing program the SEC used to test XBRL. (Note that *face financials* refers to the primary financial statements, including the balance sheet, income statement, cash flow statement, and statement of changes in equity.) Key points to note include

✔ The time and therefore cost required for creating the XBRL formatted information is highest in the first year when you set everything up for the first time. The second filings will likely cost significantly less.

✔ You'll incur the majority of effort, and therefore the majority of the cost, matching your financial information to the XBRL taxonomy, which you'll use when you create the extension taxonomy you might need.

✔ We think the total cost estimates look a little low, but the costs should be lower than the upper-bound line shown.

✔ A significant portion of cost will be reconciling the XBRL formatted information to the other submitted formats (HTML or ASCII). When you don't have to reconcile the two formats (meaning you're only submitting XBRL), costs will be less. We anticipate filers will eventually push for filing only in XBRL.

Over the long term, public companies filing with the SEC will most likely experience a cost savings, not a cost increase, from filing with XBRL.

The Benefits Hidden in the Mandate

XBRL is for far more than reporting to regulators like the SEC. When you start preparing your filing with the SEC, think about ways you can apply XBRL internally.

One company, United Technologies Corporation (UTC), participated in the SEC's voluntary filing program used to test XBRL. UTC also got to try out XBRL and learn from the experience. UTC ended up seeing a positive ROI and eventually started using XBRL for other things that had nothing to do with SEC reporting. Many other companies will also discover other uses for XBRL. UTC employees documented their discoveries at www.journalofaccountancy. com/Issues/2007/Jun/RoiOnXbrl.htm.

Minimizing Your Effort and Maximizing Your Success

Some tips can help you successfully comply with the SEC:

✔ **Practice, practice, practice.** Filing a period (or preferably two) prior to your real filing will help you get everything in order. You don't need problems popping up at the last minute. Also, this practice provides an opportunity to train your personnel. Further, an SEC-provided previewer (https://ideapreview.sec.gov/previewer) lets you privately preview your interactive data submissions before you file them. This preview helps you understand how your XBRL filings will look to those using your filings.

✔ **Use an XBRL-enabled disclosure checklist.** You know that paper disclosure checklist that you use to create your filing, or maybe the one your public accounting firm uses? Find a version of that automated with XBRL Formula to double-check as many items as you can. You'll probably see that you can check 80 percent of those items using automated processes, which is a significant benefit of using XBRL. This checklist can help you see other ways that XBRL can be useful.

✔ **Use templates.** Have you ever used the American Institute of Certified Public Accountants publication *Accounting Trends and Techniques*? Try to find XBRL taxonomy templates you can use — no need to create your own from scratch. Finding these templates may be hard the first couple of years, but as more companies file, the best templates will be found on the SEC's Next-Generation EDGAR system. It will house all those XBRL filings created by other companies, which you can copy and reuse! Plus, someone will likely create applications that help you find companies in your specific industry.

✔ **Be sure to understand XBRL Formula.** Read the section about XBRL Formula in Chapter 16.

Part IV
Working with XBRL Taxonomies and Instances

The 5th Wave   By Rich Tennant

In the end, it was Edward Scissorhands' cousin, Jonathan Hammerhead, who brought the group to a consensus on an Extensible Business Reporting Language.

In this part . . .

This part points you to software for working with XBRL, and we even walk you through the task step by step to help get you started. We dig into the details of the XBRL modules to see what you have to work with there and drill into XBRL taxonomies and XBRL instances in more detail, covering what you need to know. We wrap up this part by making some predictions based on existing facts and some assumptions we make; you can use this information for predicting and therefore planning your future.

Chapter 14

Finding Tools and Services to Make XBRL Work

XBRL is brought to life within software (see Chapters 1 and 3). In this chapter, we dig deeper into the area of software and services to help you get the most out of what XBRL offers. We cover both locally installed software, which is how most of what we did in the past was accomplished, and software you use as a service (SaaS), which is a newer model that software creators are using to deliver functionality to their customers. We tell you how to find this software, and we provide information to help you select the software that's right for you.

Having the right tool for the right job can make a complex task simple. Likewise, having the wrong software tool or using a good tool for the wrong purpose can make something that is quite simple much more complex.

To avoid having to type the long links, go to www.dummies.com/go/xbrl. This takes you to a landing page where you can click the link you need.

The XBRL Software Landscape

We divide the software and services arena into several categories to make it easier to both communicate what software exists and help you understand what you may be looking for (and why) so that you can pinpoint the right solution, given all the alternatives. And, surprisingly, a lot of XBRL software alternatives are out there, which shows how much interest there is in XBRL.

But while the volume of software is a good indicator of the uptake of XBRL within the market, it points to another situation, which is survival of the fittest. The XBRL software market hasn't been through the evolutionary process that determines clear winners in the market, nor have the losers been vetted yet. For example, why does the world need ten-plus different XBRL processors? It probably doesn't, but none have been winnowed out yet.

We break down the XBRL software landscape into the following categories to make explaining it easier:

- ✔ Existing business systems contrasted with XBRL-specific systems
- ✔ Commercial XBRL software, free XBRL software, and open-source XBRL software
- ✔ Locally installed XBRL software versus XBRL software you use as a service
- ✔ Business-user XBRL software versus technical-user XBRL software
- ✔ Middleware versus end-user software
- ✔ Categories of XBRL software

Keep the preceding list in mind as you try to decide what the best XBRL software is for you. In some situations, certain categories are a better or worse fit for your needs. Be aware of your options so that you can make better decisions.

Existing business systems and XBRL-specific applications

XBRL-related software falls into two broad categories:

- ✔ **XBRL-specific software:** These applications enable you to work with XBRL and include XBRL validators, XBRL taxonomy-creation tools, and XBRL instance-creation tools.
- ✔ **Existing software applications that support specific functionality and XBRL features:** This category includes all the existing applications in the world that you may need to input or export XBRL to or from. For example, if you have an ERP system, you may want to get information out of or into that system using the XBRL format. As such, your software vendor likely needs to modify the business system to support XBRL.

What doesn't work is creating islands of XBRL that work with XBRL specialty software but that don't work with the other business systems you use every day. What's the point? You want all your different business systems, whether internal or external, to be able to effectively exchange information so that you can automate processes.

Although XBRL has existed for ten years, it wasn't mainstream for most of that time. When new ideas appear, it takes time for infrastructure to follow because no one is really sure whether the idea will succeed or fail. No one wants to invest in building infrastructure around brand-new ideas that may fail. Although regulators drove the early use of XBRL, broader use of XBRL is really only starting. Things like the U.S. SEC mandate of XBRL has drawn interest and exposure for the technology, and more software vendors are supporting XBRL. Unfortunately, it will take time before the software you need to really take advantage of XBRL exists.

Eventually, more and more of the applications that you use today will support XBRL. For example, your off-the-shelf accounting systems, your internally developed systems, your business-intelligence-reporting system, and all that software that makes your business run will one day support XBRL. The first wave of software will be standalone XBRL software and middleware that will help you implement XBRL functionality within your existing software applications. But eventually, more software applications will, at a minimum, allow you to get XBRL into and out of the application.

Software will be impacted even more profoundly in the future. XBRL will literally impact how software is written. Functionality to work with XBRL will be deeply embedded within software, and XBRL will assist in the initial recording of transactions. How do we know? Well, partly because one South African software application, which helps those accounting for pension fund information submitted to regulators, is already doing this task. XBRL is deeply integrated within the software application, leveraging what XBRL provides, which allows for the software application to work in new ways. (For more information, see `www.xbrl.org/Business/Regulators/SA%20XBRL%20Case%20Study%20-%20Success%20Story.pdf`.)

Commercial, free, and open-source software

People are generally confused about the differences between commercial software, free-to-use commercial software, and open-source software. However, the distinctions are important as you determine which software is the best for you.

To compare and contrast the differences, we look at key factors: who provides the software, how much they charge you to use it, the license under which it's made available, and whether you have access to the *source code* (the underlying computer program that makes the application do what it does, which lets you therefore change the application):

✔ **Commercial software:** By commercial software, we mean the likes of Microsoft Office, Adobe Photoshop, or SAP. You typically install this software on your computer or use it as a service. You pay a fee for this software, and you're typically not provided access to the source code. Generally, this software comes with a license that indicates that you can use it, under what terms, and that you can't let anyone else use the software.

✔ **Free-to-use software:** Free-to-use software is similar to commercial software except that the software creator charges no fee for you its use. The creator sometimes let you distribute his free software with software you may create. Depending on the situation, you may be able to distribute that free software within a product you create for free, or you may need to pay a fee if you redistribute the software. End-users generally don't care about redistributing software, but software vendors care a lot about it.

✔ **Open-source software:** Open-source software means that along with the software application, the source code is made available. If you like, you can edit that source code and make the software work differently. Open-source software is available under several different licenses. Generally, open-source software is free to use, but sometimes involves a fee. The license terms determine whether you can freely redistribute that software to others. The ability to make changes to software to get it to work in the way you want it to work is important to some users. Also, when you have access to the source code, you're less reliant on the software creators for future maintenance.

Open-source software is gaining significant popularity for a many reasons. Realize, though, that the license does matter. Keep in mind the old saying that, "There is no such thing as a free lunch." For example, many open-source software vendors make their software available for free, but then make their money providing support and other services. A good example of open-source software is Red Hat Linux (www.redhat.com).

Software as a product and SaaS

Another trend in software is to use software as a service (SaaS), which is when you don't really have software at all, but rather use a service that someone else maintains. That service connects to a software program that the provider maintains. Here is the difference between the two options:

✔ **Software as a product:** Software as a product is what most everyone is familiar with. You go to a store or Web site, you get a DVD or download a file, and then you install it on your computer. Microsoft Office and Adobe Photoshop are examples of software as a product.

✔ **Software as a service:** SaaS is an approach where vendors or software creators make software available as a service over a network, such as the Web, rather than installing an application locally on your computer. SaaS is growing in popularity. No real deployment effort is involved; you don't install anything other than a standard browser on your computer.

Whereas software as a product is the primary means users make use of software, SaaS is gaining popularity. Some estimate that SaaS makes up perhaps 30 percent of the market currently and is growing. The primary benefits of SaaS include things like ease of administration, ease of deployment, and lower total costs of using a software application. Another benefit of SaaS is that application programming interfaces (APIs) tend to be far more open and well-documented.

SaaS falls into a few categories:

✔ **End-user applications:** A third-party software provider operates these user applications. You generally use the third-party software to arrive at some desired result. An example is an accounting system that you use as a service instead of installing the software application locally on your computer.

✔ **Web services:** Also operated by a third party, these services are more like API-level interfaces that programmers use to write applications. You use their software to arrive at a result, but the result is something that another computer process or workflow would typically use. For example, within your workflow, you may use an API that performs XBRL validation as a service.

✔ **Outsourced service:** In this service, a third party performs a role for you using whatever means is necessary. This third-party literally does everything, delivering an agreed-upon end result. This type is the ultimate in SaaS . . . software and everything else as a service!

If you want to find out more about SaaS, check out *Cloud Computing For Dummies*, by Judith Hurwitz, Robin Bloor, Marcia Kaufman, and Fern Halper (Wiley).

Business versus technical user software

Software users fall into three general categories:

✔ **Business users:** Business users tend to be far less technical and really don't care about the technology for technology's sake; they just want to get their job done, preferably without learning about the underlying technology.

✔ **Technical users:** A technical user's role is to deal with the technology level of things commonly in the support of some business user. Not only do technical users need to deal with the technology, but they *like* to deal with technology. Technology people spend a lot of time trying to figure out ways to make technology easier for business users. However, what a technical user and a business user each defines as easy to use are generally two different things!

✔ **Semi-technical business user:** These types of users are business people who take the time to understand things like how to write Microsoft Excel macros. They're not professional programmers, but they're quite capable of writing code to get their jobs done, and they prefer writing code over doing tasks manually.

We make this distinction for a specific reason. While a lot of XBRL software is out there, most of it is appropriate for the technical user of XBRL, not for general business users. At this point in XBRL's life cycle, it makes sense because technical tools that the technical users will use to make the life of business users easier have to be built before the business user tools can be built.

Middleware versus end-user software

Middleware software is something that connects two things or provides a specific piece of functionality. End-users never see middleware; they just experience the results. Middleware provides things like a translation layer between two software applications. Middleware is somewhat like glue or plumbing because it connects things.

XBRL is also about connecting things. And as you may expect, because XBRL is the thing that can be put through a pipe and middleware is like plumbing, the two may be related. You'd be right!

The connection that middleware provides isn't like the export or import functionality software applications provide. Those functions aren't really middleware.

XBRL-related software features

The types of XBRL-related features and functionality that software provides (be it XBRL-specific software or your business systems, or local software or SaaS) generally fall into these categories:

✔ **XBRL processors:** A principle piece of XBRL software is the XBRL processor (or XBRL processing engine, as some people call it). Pretty much every other software tool that uses XBRL likely has an XBRL processor within it, serving that software application. XBRL processors do the heavy lifting related to XBRL, such as reading, writing, controlling, handling, or otherwise processing your XBRL, including validating to make sure that everything turns out okay. You can think of XBRL processors as somewhat similar to an XML parser, but truly they're much, much more. Middleware software vendors (or any software vendor choosing to enable its software for XBRL) create XBRL processors. Actually seeing an XBRL processor is hard because they're an API that understands XBRL, absorbing the complexity of the XBRL specifications, and then delivers results to other software applications.

✔ **Viewing:** You need a way to look at information expressed within an XBRL instance — for example, to use the information or to see whether that information is correctly created. You'll also want to look at XBRL taxonomies in order to understand them, even if you never create one. You can use viewer-type software applications to view these items. XBRL instance viewers help you read those XBRL instances. XBRL taxonomy viewers, well, they help you have a look at taxonomies. Keep in mind that if you're looking at an XBRL instance, you also need to look at the underlying XBRL taxonomy; without a taxonomy, the XBRL instance won't make much sense.

✔ **Creation and editing:** Although viewing is helpful, business users also need to be able to create XBRL instances and XBRL taxonomies. That's where instance- and taxonomy-creation and editing software comes in. Again, if you're creating or editing an XBRL instance, you need to view the XBRL taxonomy, at a minimum. You also may need to edit the XBRL taxonomy if you're allowed to add concepts, relations, and so on. Further, you may need additional functionality, such as the ability to create business rules that you want to put into your XBRL taxonomy.

✔ **Analysis:** Anyone else you give your information to may be doing some analysis and will likely want to view that XBRL instance information. To do so, they need to view the XBRL taxonomy upon which the XBRL instance is based. To do comparisons across different periods or across different providers of information, they need combined XBRL instances. What you may not expect is that they may also want to create XBRL taxonomies. They'd create an XBRL taxonomy to change the view of the information contained in the XBRL instances they receive, or they may want to add information, such as ratios, additional computed values, and so on, to an XBRL instance and the related XBRL taxonomy. As such, those performing analysis would use XBRL instance and XBRL taxonomy-creation functionality.

✔ **Other software:** Some examples of other functionality you may need include performing different levels and types of XBRL validation, caching XBRL taxonomies for local/offline use with an XBRL instance, storing all that XBRL within some sort of database, versioning XBRL taxonomies and XBRL instances, mapping XBRL to other information formats, mapping other formats to XBRL, or even mapping one XBRL taxonomy to another XBRL taxonomy. Clever XBRL search applications may even be in your future. And then there are all those technical utility applications for doing different one-off tasks.

Why You Want an XBRL Processor

The XBRL processor or XBRL processing engine is a key piece of software, and you need one to do anything serious with XBRL. You don't have to go buy one because most applications that work with XBRL come with one.

Although you can do some things without an XBRL processor, XBRL was built anticipating that you'd use an XBRL processor, not just an XML parser, to work with XBRL instances and XBRL taxonomies. An XBRL processor understands the semantics of XBRL, not just the syntax of XML. XML parsers don't understand XBRL semantics.

Here are some functions that an XBRL processor performs:

✔ **Discovery:** An XBRL processor performs the process of *discovery* of XBRL taxonomy pieces. The XBRL processor then puts the pieces together into a DTS (see Chapters 3 and 4). XBRL processors excel at this complex task; in fact, they have to — the XBRL Specification requires it.

✔ **Validation:** The XBRL processor can do many types of validation because of its unique understanding of the XBRL specification. An XML processor alone would have a hard time validating computations and other business rules that an XBRL processor can do easily. XBRL processors have rules engines built into them to process all these computations and other business rules and to help you make sure that everything is error-free and otherwise valid.

✔ **Resolving relations:** After the pieces are together into the DTS by the process of discovery, the XBRL processor takes all the relations networks and puts them together correctly, considering the rules of discovery, the arcs defining relations, and the arcs prohibiting relations, and generates the appropriate network of relations, which you then use. All XBRL processors perform this resolution process and get the same result because XBRL is a standard, and a lot of work goes into ensuring that they do get the same result.

✔ **Deciphering:** An XBRL processor knows how to do things like get information relating to a fact within an XBRL instance from the XBRL taxonomy that defines the concept to which that fact relates. Trying to do these types of things with an XML parser is certainly possible. All you'd have to do is implement the functionality that already exists within an XBRL processor.

XBRL processors have XML parsers built into them. Every application that does anything even remotely worthwhile or sophisticated with XBRL is going to need an XBRL processor supporting that functionality. That processor should be fully compliant to the XBRL 2.1 Specification. If it's not, it really can't call itself an XBRL processor, and it won't be able to handle all forms of XBRL thrown at it.

XBRL Software Products and Services

In this section, we dig into the software that makes XBRL do useful things for you. We cover both technical-user software and business-user software. We cover software made available as a product and software made available as a service. We cover commercial products, free software, and open-source software. We include end-user software and middleware. We don't cover all the existing software applications that make up your current business systems, such as your accounting system, and whether they support XBRL here; we cover only XBRL-specific software.

We also provide the following resources where you can get additional information about software and service products:

- ✔ **XBRL software (Bank of Spain XBRL Wiki):** This listing of commercial software products applications is available at www.xbrlwiki.info/ index.php?title=XBRL_Industry_Solutions.

- ✔ **XBRL processors (Bank of Spain XBRL Wiki):** This listing (www.xbrl wiki.info/index.php?title=Open_Source_and_XBRL) focuses on XBRL processors, providing both commercial and open-source XBRL processors.

- ✔ **XBRL products and services (XBRL International):** This list of products and services (http://xbrl.org/frontend.aspx?clk=SLK&val=96) is provided by XBRL International members and appears in alphabetic order by vendor. This list does contain a narrative providing a bit of information about each product or service.

- ✔ **XBRL tools (XBRL International):** This list (http://xbrl.org/Tools) of vendors who are members of XBRL International has links to the vendor's Web site and is categorized by type of product.

- ✔ **XBRL products and services** (XBRL U.S.): This long list of products and services (www.xbrl.us/vendors/Pages/default-expand.aspx) provides a bit of an explanation about each product or service. Many products and services are specific to XBRL filings with the U.S. SEC.

We could write an entire book covering all the products out there, but we don't have room. So, instead, we list products, include a bit of information, and provide you with a link to more information. We also tell you whether the software is commercial, free, or open source; software as a product or SaaS; and for the business user or the technical user. (We don't cover U.S. SEC specific software here; see Chapter 13, which is dedicated to meeting the SEC mandate.)

Exploring XBRL processors

Ah, the mighty XBRL processor! Tables 14-1 and 14-2 separate these XBRL processors into fully compliant commercial and open-source categories for your convenience. For XBRL processors, we indicate whether they're available in Java and Microsoft.Net.

Table 14-1	Commercial XBRL Processors		
Processor	*Web Site*	*Free or Fee*	*Versions*
Altova MissionKit	`www.altova.com/ solutions/xbrl- tools.html`	Free	Microsoft. Net
Batavia XBRL Java Library	`www.batavia-xbrl.com`	Fee	Java
CoreFiling True North	`www.corefiling.com/ products/truenorth. html`	Fee	Java, Microsoft. Net, Web service
CoyoteReporting XBRL Runtime Engine and XBRL Cloud	`www.xbrlcloud.com`	Fee	Java, Web service
Fujitsu Interstage XWand	`www.fujitsu.com/ global/services/ software/interstage/ xwand`	Fee	Java
Hitachi XiRUTE Library	`www.hitachiconsulting. com/xbrl/products.cfm`	Fee	Microsoft. Net
Reporting Standard XBRL API	`www.reporting standard.com/XBRL_ API.xhtml`	Fee	Java
UBmatrix Processing Engine	`www.ubmatrix.com/ products/processing_ engine.htm`	Fee	Java, Microsoft. Net

Table 14-2 provides a list of the open-source XBRL processors. Some of these processors are free; some require you to pay a fee if for commercial use. All make the source code available. License models vary.

Table 14-2	Open-Source XBRL Processors	
Processor	**Web Site**	**Description**
ABRA	www.xbrlopen.org	The Adaptive Business Reporting Automat (ABRA) publishes an open-source Java XBRL processor under the Apache license model.
Batavia	http://sourceforge.net/projects/batavia-xbrl	The Batavia XBRL Java library exposes an API for XBRL under a AGPL license.
Gepsio	http://gepsio.codeplex.com	The Gepsio API is a .NET-based document object model for XBRL taxonomies and instances.
Reporting Standard	www.reportingstandard.com/XBRL_API.xhtml	Under certain conditions, the source code of the XBRL API will be made available.
XBRLAPI	www.xbrlapi.org	XBRLAPI provides an open-source Java implementation of an XBRL processor under the GPL license. Offers only read-only functionality at this point.
XBRL Core	http://sourceforge.net/projects/xbrlcore	XBRL Core is a set of Java classes for creating, accessing, editing, and validating XBRL instances and taxonomies.

SourceForge has most of these processors. One way to evaluate these XBRL processors is look at the number of downloads from SourceForge to determine which ones are most frequently downloaded and therefore most popular. You can go to http://sourceforge.net/search/?type_of_search=soft&words=XBRL to run a search on XBRL and to turn up all the XBRL processors available.

Viewing XBRL information

Viewer software allows you to view XBRL taxonomies or XBRL instances. Figure 14-1 shows an XBRL instance viewer you can use to check out XBRL instances filed with the U.S. SEC (see http://viewerprototype1.com/viewer).

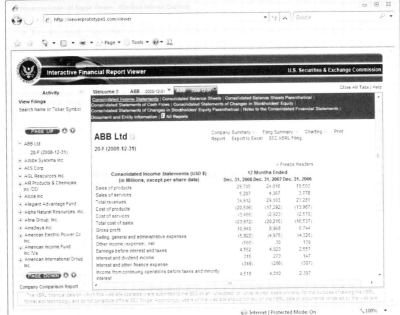

Figure 14-1:
An XBRL
instance
viewer
application.

Neither of these viewers let you edit anything: They're just for viewing.

Taxonomy viewers

XBRL taxonomy viewers are used for, well, viewing the contents of an XBRL taxonomy. Here is a list of XBRL taxonomy viewers:

- **ABRA XBRL Search:** www.abra-search.com/ABRASearch.html
- **CoreFiling Yeti Explore:** www.corefiling.com/products/yeti/index.html
- **Fujitsu Taxonomy Viewer:** www.fujitsu.com/global/services/software/interstage/xbrltools/
- **Semansys Taxonomy Viewer:** www.semansys.com/TaxonomyViewer/index.html
- **UBmatrix Taxonomy Designer:** www.ubmatrix.com/products/taxonomy_designer.htm
- **Snappy Reports XBRL Taxonomy Designer:** www.snappyreports.com/xbrl_taxonomy_designer.shtml
- **MetaSphere Taxonomy Guides:** www.taxonomyguides.com/

XBRL instance viewers

You can use XBRL instance viewers to look at the contents of an XBRL instance. Here's a list of XBRL instance viewers:

- ✔ **CoreFiling Touchstone:** www.corefiling.com/products/touchstone.html

- ✔ **Fujitsu Instance Dashboard:** www.fujitsu.com/global/services/software/interstage/xbrltools/xbrldashboard.html

- ✔ **Fujitsu Instance Viewer Plugin for Microsoft Internet Explorer:** www.fujitsu.com/global/services/software/interstage/xbrltools/xbrlviewerplugin.html

- ✔ **Hitachi Business Reporting Suite:** www.hitachiconsulting.com/xbrl/products.cfm

- ✔ **ReportingStandards XBRL Report Viewer:** www.reportingstandard.com/XBRL_Instance_Viewer.xhtml

- ✔ **Rivet Dragon View:** www.rivetsoftware.com/Products/Dragon_View/Default.aspx

- ✔ **Semansys XBRL Reporter:** www.semansys.com/xbrl_reporter.html

- ✔ **UBmatrix Taxonomy Designer:** www.ubmatrix.com/products/taxonomy_designer.htm

- ✔ **Xtensible Data iA Viewer:** www.xtensibledata.com/portal/products/ia0

Creating and editing XBRL

Creation tools let you not only view XBRL taxonomies and XBRL instances, but create or edit them as well. Editing includes extending someone else's XBRL taxonomy. Figure 14-2 shows the UBmatrix tool for creating XBRL taxonomies as an example of what a creation tool might look like.

XBRL taxonomy creators

You can use XBRL taxonomy creators to create a taxonomy from scratch or to extend an existing taxonomy with new concepts, resources, or relations. Here's a list of XBRL taxonomy creators:

- ✔ **Altova XML Spy:** www.altova.com/products/xmlspy/xmlspy.html

- ✔ **CoreFiling SpiderMonkey:** www.corefiling.com/products/spidermonkey.html

- ✔ **Fujitsu Taxonomy Editor:** www.fujitsu.com/global/services/software/interstage/xbrltools/xbrltaxedit.html

✔ **Reporting Standard XBRL Taxonomy Builder:** www.reporting standard.com/XBRL_Taxonomy_Builder.xhtml

✔ **Semansys XBRL Composer:** www.semansys.com/composer_wins_global_contest.html

✔ **UBmatrix Taxonomy Designer:** www.ubmatrix.com/products/taxonomy_designer.htm

✔ **Snappy Reports XBRL Taxonomy Designer:** www.snappyreports.com/xbrl_taxonomy_designer.shtml

XBRL instance creators

You can use XBRL instance creators to create XBRL instances, as you might expect. XBRL instance creators sometimes provide you with the ability to edit XBRL taxonomies. Here's a list of XBRL instance creators:

✔ **Altova XML Spy:** www.altova.com/products/xmlspy/xmlspy.html

✔ **Allocation Solutions DataXchanger:** www.allocationsolutions.com/products.html

✔ **CoreFiling ReportDirect:** www.corefiling.com/products/report directdatasheet.pdf

✔ **CoyoteReporting XBRL Report Runner:** www.coyotereporting.com/products.html

✔ **Fujitsu Instance Creator:** www.fujitsu.com/global/services/software/interstage/xbrltools/xbrlinscreate.html

✔ **Hitachi XBRL Business Reporting Suite:** www.hitachiconsulting.com/xbrl/products.cfm

✔ **Just Systems xfy:** http://na.justsystems.com/content-xfy-and-xbrl

✔ **NeoClarus iFile:** www.neoclarus.com

✔ **Reporting Standard XBRL Report Editor:** www.reportingstandard.com/XBRL_Report_Editor.xhtml

✔ **Rivet Dragon Tag:** www.rivetsoftware.com/Products/Dragon_Tag/Default.aspx

✔ **Semansys XBRL Reporter:** www.semansys.com/xbrl_reporter.html

✔ **Snappy Reports Heartbeat Reports:** www.snappyreports.com/xbrl_products_regulatory.shtml

✔ **UBmatrix Report Builder RBME:** www.ubmatrix.com/products/report_builder.htm

✔ **XBRLit:** www.xbrlit.com

✔ **Xtensible Data iF:** www.xtensibledata.com/portal/products/if

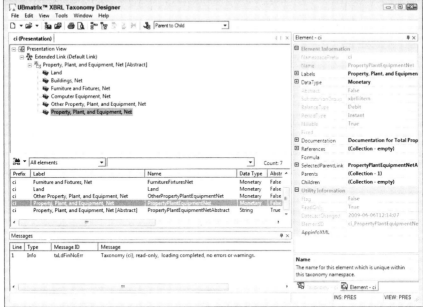

Figure 14-2:
An XBRL
taxonomy
creation
application.

Analyzing XBRL information

XBRL analysis software generally enables you to view one or more XBRL instances for the purposes of analyzing the data contained within those XBRL instances. You'll most likely want to look at the related XBRL taxonomy information when you perform this analysis. Here are examples of analysis software:

- **Altova MapForce:** www.altova.com/products/mapforce/xbrl_mapping.html

- **Edgar-Online I-Metrix Professional:** www.edgar-online.com/OnlineProducts/IMetrixProfessional.aspx

- **Fujitsu Instance Dashboard:** www.fujitsu.com/global/services/software/interstage/xbrltools/xbrldashboard.html

- **Microsoft FRx:** www.microsoft.com/frx/using/XBRL.mspx

- **Quantrix Modeler:** www.quantrix.com/QuantrixandXBRL.pdf

- **Rivet Crossfire Analyst:** www.rivetsoftware.com/Products/Crossfire/Default.aspx

- **SavaNet Analyst:** www.savanet.com/AboutAnalyst.aspx

Other XBRL-related tools and services

A plethora of other products will likely emerge as a consequence of XBRL's broad use. For example, clearly seeing changes that occurred between two versions of a taxonomy is beneficial to those creating XBRL instances, analysts, and taxonomy users as well. We mention the different tasks you'll likely need software to help you with when working with XBRL. That said, it's worth mentioning a few other software product categories:

- ✔ **Versioning:** As XBRL taxonomies change, you need to be able to see changes to the taxonomies. These taxonomy changes will impact XBRL instances where one instance is created using one taxonomy and another instance is created using a newer version of the same taxonomy.

- ✔ **Data storage:** All this XBRL data needs to be stored somewhere. Up to a point, storing XBRL instances as files on a hard drive works fine. For example, consider the U.S. SEC's use case. About 15,000 companies, and they're doing how many filings per year? Say that the SEC receives about 7 million documents a year. How well will a query of information in individual files perform when you want to do a comparison?

- ✔ **Business rules editor:** Business rules are great, but someone needs to create those rules. Taxonomy creators may include that functionality, but you may not need a full-fledged taxonomy editor to create business rules using XBRL Formula.

- ✔ **Standalone validators:** Many software applications have validators built in, but on some occasions, you may need only a standalone validator.

- ✔ **Rendering tools:** Humans need to read XBRL instance information, no doubt about that. You can take many approaches to rendering information, and many tools will do everything from basic renderings of information all the way to glossy reports of the information contained within an XBRL instance.

- ✔ **Mapping tools:** Users will undoubtedly need to map metadata of one source to another source, and XBRL may be on one side or both sides of the operation.

- ✔ **Search tools:** Perhaps a special category of tool, but XBRL search will be quite useful, especially if you have to scan 7 million documents or search the entire Internet for XBRL information. (We're sorry to say that we don't know of any XBRL search tools at the current time, but we feel that they're likely to be developed in the future.)

- ✔ **Enterprise XBRL Server Systems:** These systems are complete XBRL solutions.

Mapping software

Mapping software allows you to map XBRL information to some other source or destination or to map some other source or destination to XBRL. For example, a Microsoft Excel spreadsheet may be either a source for XBRL instance information or a destination for XBRL instance information that you're using for analysis. Anything can be a source or a destination really. Mapping is how you get the XBRL into or out of the source/destination.

Here are some of the mapping software products available:

- ✔ **Altova MapForce:** www.altova.com/products/mapforce/data_ mapping.html

- ✔ **Fujitsu Mapping Tool:** www.fujitsu.com/global/services/ software/interstage/xbrltools/xbrlmapping.html

- ✔ **Reporting Standard XBRL Mapper:** www.reportingstandard.com/ XBRL_Mapper.xhtml

- ✔ **Allocation Solutions DataXchanger:** www.allocationsolutions.com/

- ✔ **Snappy Reports Tagging and Mapping:** www.snappyreports.com/ xbrl_tagging_mapping.shtml

Standalone validation tools

Taxonomy and instance creators and viewers often have built-in validation capabilities. But sometimes you may need XBRL validation tools separate from creation or viewer tools (see Chapter 15). Many people can and will write macros to generate XBRL in this manner. But recreating an XBRL validation with a macro is way beyond most people's skill levels and an unnecessary duplication of functionality. Simply use a standalone validator.

Here's a list of standalone XBRL taxonomy and XBRL instance validation tools:

- ✔ **Altova XML Spy:** www.altova.com/xbrl.html

- ✔ **CoyoteReporting XBRL Cloud:** www.xbrlcloud.com

- ✔ **DecisionSoft TrueNorth:** www.corefiling.com/products/true north.html

- ✔ **Fujitsu Validator:** www.fujitsu.com/global/services/software/ interstage/xbrltools/xbrlval21.html

- ✔ **UBmatrix Taxonomy Designer:** www.ubmatrix.com/products/ taxonomy_designer.htm

XBRL databases

These tools manage, store, and query XBRL taxonomy and XBRL instance information:

- ✔ **Reporting Standard XBRL Database:** `www.reportingstandard.com/XBRL_Database.xhtml`

- ✔ **UBmatrix Database Adaptor:** `www.ubmatrix.com/products/database_adaptor.htm`

Enterprise solutions

Several solutions for building enterprise scale applications make use of XBRL, and you can use this software in conjunction with your existing business systems, adding XBRL functionality to those existing systems. Here's a list of enterprise solutions:

- ✔ **CoyoteReporting XBRL Cloud:** `www.xbrlcloud.com`

- ✔ **CoreFiling True North Enterprise:** `www.corefiling.com/products/truenorth.html`

- ✔ **Fujitsu Interstage XWand:** `www.fujitsu.com/global/services/software/interstage/xwand`

- ✔ **Hitachi Business Reporting Processor:** `www.hitachiconsulting.com/xbrl/products.cfm`

- ✔ **Snappy Reports Enterprise Network:** `www.snappyreports.com/xbrl_enterprise_network.shtml`

- ✔ **Reporting Standard XBRL Enabled Portal:** `www.xbrl4.org/regulators`

- ✔ **UBmatrix Enterprise Application Suite:** `www.ubmatrix.com/products/enterprise_application_suite.htm`

Discovering Software Applications That Support XBRL

These software applications include XBRL support. We can't list all of them, but these applications are worth mentioning so that you can get an idea of the types of business solutions that will eventually support XBRL:

- ✔ **Clarity Systems Clarity FSR:** `www.claritysystems.com/Product/FSR.aspx`

- **Microsoft FRx:** www.microsoft.com/frx/using/XBRL.mspx

- **Oracle-Hyperion Financial Reporting Manager:** www.oracle.com

- **SAP Enterprise Performance Management:** www.sap.com/solutions/ sapbusinessobjects/large/enterprise-performance- management/index.epx

- **Wolters Kluwer Accounting Software:** www.ubmatrix.com/ downloads/Wolters_Kluwer_Business_Brief.pdf

Finding XBRL Professional Services

Need a hired gun? Various organizations these days provide XBRL consulting services. Many of these professional services are provided by software vendors who have built XBRL software infrastructure. These software vendors leverage their products, provide consulting services, find out more about what people are doing with XBRL, and improve their products. Here are some of the major XBRL hired guns:

- **Business Reporting Advisory Group:** www.br-ag.eu

- **CoreFiling:** www.corefiling.com/services/index.html

- **Deloitte:** www.deloitte.org/dtt/section_node/0,1042, sid%253D195357,00.html

- **Ernst & Young:** www.ey.com/xbrl

- **Fujitsu:** www.fujitsu.com/global/services/software/ interstage

- **Hitachi:** www.hitachiconsulting.com/xbrl/products.cfm

- **IRIS:** www.irisindia.net/xbrl/index.php

- **KPMG:** www.kpmg.com/Global/WhatWeDo/Audit/Pages/ services.aspx

- **NTT Data:** www.nttdata.co.jp/en/media/2009/012200.html

- **PricewaterhouseCoopers:** www.pwc.com/extweb/service.nsf/doc id/8e1b9090174497ba85256bf10038d5d7

- **UBmatrix:** www.ubmatrix.com/products/targeted_solutions.htm

- **XBRLit:** www.XBRLit.com

Many of these professional services providers partner with other professional services firms to provide specific types of targeted solutions.

Discriminating Between XBRL Tools

When looking for XBRL software, keep the following points in mind as you try to determine the differences between the software applications:

- **Build or buy — know where to draw the line.** It's perfectly appropriate at times to generate XBRL from whatever means and then validate the XBRL you created with a standalone validator. For example, Microsoft Excel macros are a great tool for generating XBRL. A typical software program to generate XBRL is generally less than 500 lines of code (see Chapter 15). However, that number doesn't include code to validate the XBRL. No problem: Just use a standalone validator or use a validation Web service within your spreadsheet application. You can easily make many applications generate XBRL one way or another. Build the easy-to-create components; buy the more complex and specialized pieces. Evaluate tools based on the value they add to your complete solution.

- **Look for fully conformant XBRL processors.** The XBRL Specification has a definition of a fully conformant XBRL processor. This is what you want: Be sure to ask your software vendor whether it provides a fully conformant processor. Not all software supports all aspects of XBRL.

- **Look for support for XBRL modules.** Be sure the software you're considering supports the XBRL modules you need. (See Chapter 16 for an explanation of the different XBRL modules.) In particular, you'll most likely want support for XBRL Dimensions and XBRL Formula in most software. But you may need even more.

- **Ask specifically which XBRL conformance suites the software passes.** XBRL International provides several conformance suites that help ensure software interoperability. Ask your software vendor which of the XBRL International conformance suites they pass. XBRL 2.1 Specification, XBRL Dimensions, XBRL Formula, FRTA, and FRIS each have a conformance suite. (See Chapter 3 for more information.)

- **Make the software vendor prove that it can meet your needs.** Use sample XBRL taxonomies and XBRL instances (see Chapters 2 and 17) as use cases to see whether the software applications will actually do what you need them to do. See with your own eyes whether software really works. This up-front investment can save you a lot of frustration down the road.

- **Keep looking around.** Remember that XBRL is still maturing. As time goes on, more software becomes available. The more the business community experiments with XBRL, the better the software will get. Keep checking those lists we provide in the section "Exploring the Different Categories of XBRL Software Products and Services," earlier in this chapter.

✔ **Seek integrated software.** Keep the notion of integrated software in your mind as you look at XBRL software. By integrated software, we mean that all the functionality you need for performing a specific task is within one software application so that you don't have to switch between multiple applications. For example, when you create an XBRL instance and you can't extend your XBRL taxonomy within the XBRL instance-creation tool, you'll understand what we mean. Also, how integrated is the software, or how well can the software be integrated into your existing systems? How well does the software provide all the workflow components you need within that software product? Having islands of XBRL information in different applications that you have to flip between to do your work is something you want to avoid.

✔ **Build a prototype.** Probably the best advice we can provide is to start a prototype or proof of concept project, which will help you actually use software. Most software these days is available for a trial period. Get several different software products and try them out if you have the time. Start small and then get larger.

✔ **Compare notes with others.** Talk to others who are using the software you're considering. This step may take time, but it will save pain and suffering later. A great place to talk to people is at an XBRL conference. More and more people are using XBRL these days; seek them out and pick their brains.

✔ **Look for support.** When you evaluate software, you definitely want to evaluate the support you'll be receiving as part of the software license agreement. Support for XBRL software is no different than support for the other software products that you have; the same support evaluation criteria applies here to XBRL software.

Finding the Right Products and Services

Caution is in order when looking for XBRL software these days. Like a cowboy in the American wild, wild, west, you need to be a careful. The explosive growth of XBRL means an explosive growth of those trying to capitalize on the XBRL opportunity. Not all XBRL software is equal.

The lists of software vendors in this chapter contain a lot of good software. Those vendors are good places to start your efforts to find the software that will potentially meet your needs. This chapter also has great ideas that help you figure out whether software is right for you. With those two pieces of information, all you need to do is the legwork that's necessary to reach the right conclusions.

If you don't want to go through this effort, find a consultant who will do the legwork for you. Or, because more and more people want XBRL software, you'll likely soon be able to find some articles doing comparisons to help you figure this out. We're not aware of any such comparisons that exist as of this writing, but it's a good bet that they'll begin to appear.

Chapter 15

Creating and Using XBRL

*T*his chapter focuses exclusively on working with XBRL. We guide you through the process of viewing, creating, validating, extending, and otherwise interacting with XBRL. We work with both XBRL taxonomies and XBRL instances. This chapter won't turn you into an XBRL expert, but it does provide the first practical steps as you enter the waters of XBRL.

To avoid having to type the long links in this chapter, go to www.dummies.com/go/xbrl. This takes you to a landing page where you can click the link you need.

Getting Started on Your XBRL Journey

To work with XBRL, you need software. You can actually use any text editor, but text editors don't understand XBRL as well as an XBRL processor does.

For our journey, we have to pick specific software applications to use. We chose software that meets the following criteria:

▶ **It's free to try.** That way, you can download it and walk through the tasks we lead you through.

▶ **It can perform the task.** Clearly, the software needs to perform the task we want to perform.

▶ **It handles key basic tasks.** Our goal is to expose you to the basics, such as creating an XBRL taxonomy and XBRL instance.

You don't have to use the software we use in this chapter: You're free to choose a different software application. We've made the step-by-step instructions as general as possible. After all, we're not trying to teach you about all the details of using a specific software application: Our goal is to teach you about XBRL.

We start by exploring a few XBRL taxonomies and XBRL instances, which helps you get a general feel for XBRL. Then, our step-by-step exercises eventually walk you through the process of creating a basic "Hello World!" example XBRL taxonomy and XBRL instance. We wanted to show you how easy this task really is, even without an XBRL processor. We show you one commonly used approach to outputting XBRL, which is to create a simple application using macros within a spreadsheet. (We use Microsoft Excel.) We even provide the code examples that you can use as a basis for building your own XBRL generation application. We then build on that basic example and show you more parts of XBRL that help you achieve certain specific objectives. This layered approach helps you understand why XBRL includes each of these components and how to use that component. We use XBRL software applications and the important XBRL processors they contain.

We use the same basic example throughout the exercises, helping to provide continuity between the examples. We want to keep keying to a minimum. The examples include completed versions, so if something doesn't quite work out, you can still see the end result. If you get lost, don't worry; just start over or go back to one of the interim starting points that we provide you with.

After working through the examples, you should have a good solid understanding of how XBRL works and how to use some of the basic features of software to work with XBRL. During our journey, you'll perform common tasks related to XBRL.

The computer we used to create these exercises was running Microsoft Windows Vista, Microsoft Internet Explorer 7.0, and Microsoft Excel 2007. You may need to make slight adjustments for other software versions or other operating systems. Some software may have changed since we created these examples, so you may need to make slight adjustments accordingly. We assume that you know the basics of using these software applications.

Viewing an XBRL Taxonomy

Stick your big toe in the water by taking a look at an XBRL taxonomy with XBRL taxonomy viewing software. We use CoreFiling's Yeti Explorer to look at an XBRL taxonomy because it's a free application for viewing specific taxonomies, and you don't have to install software — it simply works through your browser. Here are the steps for viewing an XBRL taxonomy within this software application:

1. **Type this URL within the address box of your browser:** `http://big` `foot.corefiling.com/yeti/resources/yeti-gwt/Yeti.jsp`.

   The Open Taxonomy dialog box, shown in Figure 15-1, appears, listing XBRL taxonomies.

2. **From the list, expand the taxonomy labeled US GAAP (2008-03-31) by clicking its icon; select Commercial and Industrial from the list that appears.**

   You have to scroll down to find this taxonomy.

3. **Click the Open button.**

   Welcome to your first XBRL taxonomy! You can click around and explore the taxonomy. (Chapter 17 walks you through the process of exploring a taxonomy.)

4. **Type `http://tinyurl.com/cqad9k` into your browser's address box.**

   You see the concept Income Taxes Receivable within the taxonomy.

5. **As an alternate to Step 4, you could start with the Network 104000 – Statement – Statement of Financial Position, Classified and drill into the tree structure of Figure 15-2 until you find the concept Income Taxes Receivable.**

   Notice the tree of concepts that participate within the relations of the network on the left side of Figure 15-2. On the right, you see three tabs (Details, Relationships, and Tree Locations) that allow you to navigate between the detailed information of the selected concept, the relations the concept participates in, and the tree locations in which the concept exists. You can explore those tabs for various concepts and relations.

6. **To search for a specific concept by name, type the concept name, such as Cash, in the text box below the tab labeled Search in Figure 15-2 and click the Search button.**

   A list of concepts appears below the Search button — in this taxonomy, about 15 concepts have Cash as part of the label.

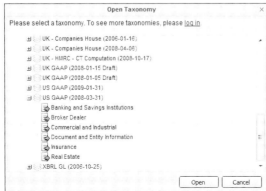

Figure 15-1:
The Open
Taxonomy
dialog box.

Figure 15-2:
An XBRL
taxonomy
viewer
application.

If you want, you can continue exploring that XBRL taxonomy or any other XBRL taxonomy provided with that viewer. (We count about 100 taxonomies in the list.) Chapter 17 provides additional insights on how to view an XBRL taxonomies and even points you to some smaller XBRL taxonomies that are easier to grasp as you learn more about taxonomies.

Viewing an XBRL Instance

Anxious to take a look at an XBRL instance? Yeah, we knew you were. We use the Interactive Financial Report Viewer, the U.S. SEC's prototype XBRL instance-viewing tool.

To view an XBRL instance, follow these steps:

1. Type `http://viewerprototype1.com/viewer` **into your browser.**

   You see a page titled Test Drive Interactive Data. On the left side is a list of companies. We use 3M Co, the first one, for our exploratory journey.

2. **Click 3M Co, which expands the tree and displays a list of financial statement filings 3M made to the SEC, and then select the first report, Quarterly Report (2008-09-30).**

   You see the consolidated income statement for the period selected within a tab, which is shown in Figure 15-3. Notice that the tab has other financial statements that you can open in the blue bar.

   Just below the blue bar are links to additional information about the company, filing summary information, charts, a way to print the report, and a way to export the entire statement into Microsoft Excel.

3. **Click the Export to Excel link just below the blue bar.**

   The SEC filing information for the filing you're looking at is provided to you in the form of an Excel spreadsheet.

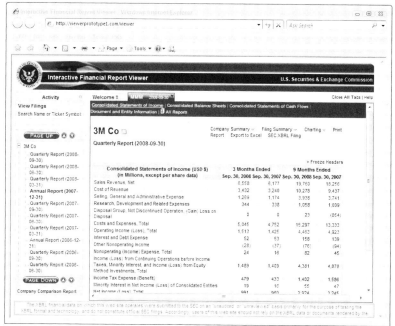

Figure 15-3:
The SEC
XBRL
instance
viewer
application.

Using XBRL looks a lot like other financial statements and reports, doesn't it? One thing to take notice of is that when you export the information to Excel in Step 3, you really didn't even see XBRL during the entire process of using it or performing that export. Software does all the work using the XBRL in the process.

Creating an XBRL Taxonomy and Instance

In this exercise, you create a basic XBRL taxonomy. You then use the concepts in that XBRL taxonomy to create an XBRL instance by using a Microsoft Excel spreadsheet that contains simple macros that generate the XBRL taxonomy and XBRL instance.

Figure 15-4 shows the information that the XBRL taxonomy and XBRL instance will be expressing within this exercise. This exercise is a simple breakdown of Property, Plant and Equipment.

Figure 15-4:
A breakdown of Property, Plant and Equipment, Net.

Example Company As of December 31, (Thousands of Dollars)		
	2007	2006
Breakdown of Property, Plant and Equipment, Net:		
Land	5,347	1,147
Buildings, Net	244,508	366,375
Furniture and Fixtures, Net	34,457	34,457
Computer Equipment, Net	4,169	5,313
Other Property, Plant and Equipment, Net	6,702	6,149
Property, Plant and Equipment, Net, Total	295,183	413,441

A quick look at Figure 15-4 shows you the following:

✔ The information is for Example Company and is as of December 31, 2007 and 2006.

✔ The information is expressed in thousands of dollars; we use U.S. dollars for our example.

✔ We have 12 pieces of data, the 12 numbers — 6 for 2007 and another 6 for 2006.

✔ The columns of information have totals. The data breaks down Property, Plant and Equipment, Net into its components: Land, Buildings, Furniture and Fixtures, Computer Equipment, and Other Property, Plant and Equipment. The total, Property, Plant and Equipment, Net is shown at the bottom.

We now create the XBRL taxonomy you need to communicate this business information and the XBRL instance that actually communicates the information based on that XBRL taxonomy. In this example, we generate XBRL from a Microsoft Excel spreadsheet that we created for you. We even keyed in all the data, but you can change that data, if you like. First, we walk through all the steps and then explain the bigger picture.

1. **Go to** `http://xbrl.squarespace.com/storage/xbrlfordummies/ helloworldexample/HelloWorldExample-2009-05-23.zip` **and download the Excel spreadsheet that you'll use to generate the XBRL taxonomy and XBRL instance.**

2. **After you download the ZIP file in Step 1, create a subdirectory on your computer somewhere, put the ZIP file in that subdirectory, and extract the contents of the ZIP file into that subdirectory.**

   The completed XBRL taxonomy (`HelloWorld.xsd`) and XBRL instance (`HelloWorld.xml`) that you generate are contained in that ZIP file. You can extract and rename them if you want; you'll overwrite them during the exercise.

3. **Open the Excel spreadsheet and go to the spreadsheet tab Hello World Taxonomy.**

   The spreadsheet looks like Figure 15-5. We prepared everything for you.

4. **Click the Create Taxonomy button.**

   The Excel macro creates a file named `HelloWorld.xsd` that is a valid XBRL taxonomy and puts the file in the same directory as the Excel workbook.

5. **Open that file in your browser or in a text editor to look at what you generated.**

6. **Create the XBRL instance and select the workbook tab Hello World Instance.**

   The spreadsheet looks like Figure 15-6.

7. **Click the Create XBRL Instance button.**

   The Excel macro creates a file named `HelloWorld.xml` and places it in the same subdirectory as your Excel workbook.

8. **Open that file in your browser or in a text editor to look at what you generated.**

   That's it: You're done! You created your first XBRL taxonomy and XBRL instance.

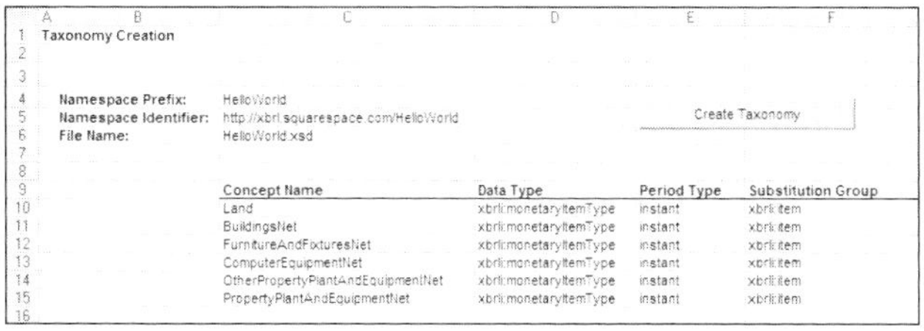

Figure 15-5: A spreadsheet for creating an XBRL taxonomy.

Figure 15-6:
The
spreadsheet
for creating
an XBRL
instance.

	A	B	C	D	E
1					
2	Example Company				
3	As of December 31,				Create XBRL Instance
4	(Thousands of Dollars)				
5					
6			2007	2006	
7					Validate Spreadsheet Data
8	Breakdown of Property, Plant and Equipment, Net:				
9	Land		5,347	1,147	Generate Mapping Information
10	Buildings, Net		244,508	366,375	
11	Furniture and Fixtures, Net		34,457	34,457	Clear Mapping Information
12	Computer Equipment, Net		4,169	5,313	
13	Other Property, Plant and Equipment, Net		6,702	6,149	Initialize Data
14	Property, Plant and Equipment, Net, Total		295,183	413,441	Get Data from Instance
15					
16					

The URL to the completed version of this XBRL taxonomy at this stage is
`http://xbrl.squarespace.com/storage/xbrlfordummies/hello`
`worldexample/HelloWorld.xsd`. The URL to the XBRL instance at this
stage is `http://xbrl.squarespace.com/storage/xbrlfordummies/`
`helloworldexample/HelloWorld.xml`.

The preceding steps describe a common use of XBRL: You generated an
XBRL taxonomy and an XBRL instance from information contained within
an Excel spreadsheet. Many of you have Excel spreadsheets, and you use
them to exchange information with others. The spreadsheet contains several
macros (written in Visual Basic for Applications) that generate the XBRL taxonomy and the XBRL instance.

If you look in the subdirectory where you saved the spreadsheet you downloaded, you see two XBRL files. The macro created those two files. The code in
the macro is written in a way that's easy to understand. The code is basic and
doesn't even make use of an XML parser or XBRL processor to generate the
XBRL — it simply writes out a text stream into a file. The code to generate the
XBRL instance is less than 250 lines. Yes, folks, generating XBRL is that simple.

You can use the macro code from this spreadsheet to help you understand
how to create your own macros for outputting XBRL.

We want to dig into a few aspects of XBRL that are critical to understand in
order to build XBRL taxonomies and XBRL instances correctly. First of all,
you need to figure out what goes into the XBRL taxonomy and what goes into
the XBRL instance. Here are the basics:

 ✔ Taxonomies define concepts. In this case, the concepts are the line
   items of the business report of our example.

 ✔ Concepts are reported in two periods, 2007 and 2006. Next year, concepts most likely are reported for 2008. This information is really determined at the time the XBRL instance is created, so you don't want to
   define the periods in the XBRL taxonomy. You also don't want to define
   specific concepts for specific periods, such as Land for 2007 and Land
   for 2006. You could, but then you'd have to add concepts to your XBRL
   taxonomy for each new year. Rather, create concepts for the line items
   and contexts for the periods.

✔ In our case, the entity preparing this information was Example Company. If you want other entities to be able to use this XBRL taxonomy, you don't want the specific entity in the XBRL taxonomy either. That information should go into the XBRL instance. You'd use the entity element, which is part of a context.

✔ The fact that the report is in thousands of dollars means that although you see the presented value 5,347 for Land for 2007 in the spreadsheet, the real value is 5,347,000. The creator of this spreadsheet report chose to create the report in thousands of dollars. Different report creators choose to present this information in different units, some in thousands, some in millions, and some maybe even in billions.

The point is that you need to decide how to model the XBRL taxonomy and XBRL instance. There are good and bad practices. These data modeling issues may be a new concern for many business users. Software applications generally help you figure this sort of thing out. But because we're coding this ourselves in this example rather than relying on software, we have to make these sorts of decisions ourselves. Chapters 17 and 18 talk about these types of details related to creating XBRL taxonomies and XBRL instances.

Although the previous discussion provides a basic understanding of how to get from the Excel spreadsheet to the XBRL taxonomy and XBRL instance, we omit quite a few details. However, if you like, you can go to the VBA in the Excel file and walk through it. You can use the Excel spreadsheet to reverse-engineer how everything works and get insight into the details. Chapter 4 can help you understand the contents of the different output files we're generating.

Using those other buttons

Refer to Figure 15-6, paying particular attention to the workbook's last five buttons. These buttons can provide you with a good sense of the work you need to perform when you create an actual XBRL instance.

✔ **Validate Spreadsheet Data:** Click this button to run a program that tells you whether the components of Property, Plant and Equipment add up to the total for the two periods shown. This validation is coded into the application to make a point: You can't exchange the validation rules you coded into your application with other software applications (other than Excel) because the other application doesn't understand your application's expression of these rules. The rules aren't in a standard transferable format: They're unique to the application in which those rules are processed.

What if you expressed those rules in the form of XBRL Formula and could exchange the rules? Yup, that is the point of XBRL Formula. First, you don't have to write the validator because XBRL provides one, and second, you can exchange those rules with others that use the information you created, helping them both to better understand the information and check whether it actually follows those rules.

✔ **Generate Mapping Information:** Click this button, and you see that some Excel comments are now in your spreadsheet. Hover your mouse pointer over cells with the comments, and information appears about the mapping to cells that are used to generate facts within your XBRL instance. These comments help you review your work to be sure that the mappings are correct. The actual mapping info is in the spreadsheet tab Mappings.

✔ **Clear Mapping Information:** This button simply clears the comments that contain the mapping information (see previous bullet).

✔ **Initialize Data:** This button zeros out all your values. The importance of this button becomes clear when you click the next button.

✔ **Get Data from Instance:** Generating information, zeroing it out, and then getting it back from the XBRL instance may seem odd, but this button does it to make a specific point. (Remember, the demo is to help you learn about XBRL.) The point is that not only can you generate information, but you can also extract that information from the XBRL instance you created. Extracting information would make more sense if you were pulling in XBRL instance data from some other XBRL instance created by someone whose data you actually wanted to use. For this demo, just realize what is going on. You can publish information; you can use the information. That is the value of XBRL in action! Pretty cool, don't you think?

Determining your additional needs

We hope the simple example in the preceding section helps you understand the basics of XBRL taxonomies and XBRL instances. We provided a populated spreadsheet because we didn't want to test your typing skills; after all, we assume that you can type already. If you want, you can change any of the concept names, values, or any other information in the spreadsheet. You just have to be sure that you key everything in correctly because you're not using an XBRL processor to help you get things right.

We want to point a few things out to help you understand the value of some XBRL components that we didn't use in our example. You have to admit that our "Hello World" example, described in the section "Creating a 'Hello World' XBRL taxonomy and instance," is fairly straightforward and easy; however, the functionality of what the XBRL can do for you is also limited. This exercise shows you some limitations of using only XML to achieve what you want to achieve. It also shows you what XBRL brings to the party.

You can send that XBRL instance with its supporting XBRL taxonomy to others, but you're not using the following XBRL characteristics yet when you create the information you're exchanging. (Refer to Chapter 4 to help understand the terms being discussed.)

✔ **Documentation of concepts:** We create a number of concepts in our XBRL taxonomy, but what is the meaning of the concepts? The meaning needs to be clear not just to you but to those with whom you exchange the XBRL taxonomy as well. XBRL has the ability to document the concepts you create within the XBRL taxonomy. Alternatively, you can point to documentation using XBRL references to concept definitions external to the taxonomy.

✔ **Polarity of fact values:** You probably took for granted that the numbers in the example should be entered as positive numbers. But how do you know for sure? In our example, it's rather clear, but what if you have thousands of concepts, some debits and some credits? XBRL has a means to help make its polarity clear, whether it should be entered as a positive or negative value: It's called the *balance attribute* of a concept.

✔ **Human-readable labels:** Although the element names in our exercise aren't that difficult to read, the element names aren't how we normally want to look at things. Rather than using FurnitureAndFixturesNet, business users would prefer something like Furniture and Fixtures, Net, which is more readable by humans. In addition, what if you need to provide your XBRL taxonomy to someone who speaks a different language? XBRL allows you to create labels in any number of languages. Each user can pick his own language to the extent labels are provided in that language for an XBRL taxonomy.

✔ **Calculations:** Our example has two calculations: The details of Property, Plant and Equipment add up to the total. But we didn't express that relationship in our XBRL taxonomy. Therefore, computer software won't be able to validate this rule. We can't send the rule with the XBRL taxonomy because the rule doesn't exist in the XBRL taxonomy, unless, of course, we write proprietary validation rules in our application (as we did). Alternatively, we could use XBRL Formula or XBRL calculation relations to provide these business rules for these calculations.

✔ **Organization of taxonomy:** Our XBRL taxonomy has six concepts. But what if it had 6,000 concepts? You'd want to organize that XBRL taxonomy so that the taxonomy users could easily find the concepts they needed. XBRL provides several ways to organize your XBRL taxonomy for different purposes. One way is to use the presentation relations.

So, the simple "Hello World" exercise shows you two things. First, it shows some limitations of traditional XML alone. Now, we're not saying that you couldn't create additional functionality using traditional XML. You can. But, you'd have to expend resources, effort, and money duplicating what XBRL already provides. As XBRL already has these additional components, why would you do that? Further, if you did build these additional features on top of XML, the solution would be proprietary. XBRL offers a standard approach to adding the characteristics that business users need.

Creating Resources for XBRL Taxonomy Concepts

In the previous section, we create a basic XBRL taxonomy and then tell you about all those things that we did *not* create in our "Hello World" basic example XBRL taxonomy. Now we add something you'll probably want: labels for the concepts created in the "Hello World" XBRL taxonomy. (Resources add information to an XBRL taxonomy concept — see Chapter 4.)

We use SpiderMonkey, an XBRL taxonomy-creation application provided by the software vendor CoreFiling, to add these labels. CoreFiling offers a free single-user version of SpiderMonkey at `www.corefiling.com/products/spidermonkey.html`. Click the Download SpiderMonkey link on the top right side of the page and fill in the marketing information requested, and, a day or so later, you'll receive a link you can click to download the software. (It's not immediate.)

We use the XBRL taxonomy you generated in the "Hello World" exercise you created. Alternatively, you can use the file `HelloWorld.xsd` in the ZIP file you downloaded for that exercise. In this exercise, we load the "Hello World" taxonomy and simply add English labels for each of the existing concepts. When we start, your XBRL taxonomy looks like Figure 15-7.

To add label resources to your XBRL taxonomy:

1. **From the menu ribbon in SpiderMonkey, open `HelloWorld.xsd`.**

   To do so, choose File➪Open, navigate to where you saved the file, select it, and then click the Open button.

2. **Click the plus button next to Isolated Concepts.**

   What you see should look like Figure 15-7. The first thing to notice is that your XBRL taxonomy created in Excel opens up in the SpiderMonkey XBRL taxonomy-creation application. This interoperability may not seem like much, but it's truly part of XBRL's core value.

   If the version you created doesn't open correctly, try the version from the ZIP file.

3. **Just to be safe, validate the XBRL taxonomy by choosing File➪Validate.**

   A new tab called Problems opens on the bottom of your application and contains the message No Validation Errors or Warnings. (Click the X on the tab if you want to close the Problems tab.)

4. **Select the concept BuildingsNet and double-click the concept.**

   A set of tabs appears on the right-hand side of the application.

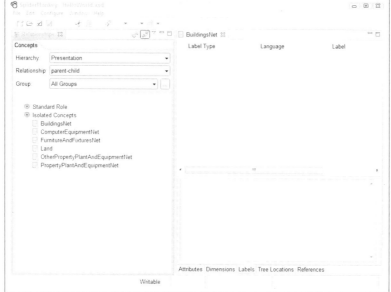

Figure 15-7:
The starting
point for
creating
an XBRL
taxonomy
in Spider-
Monkey.

5. **Select the Labels tab (which is to the right of where you selected the concept.)**

6. **In the Labels tab (with the concept BuildingsNet selected), select and enter the following:**

   a. For Label Type, select Standard Label from the combo box.

   b. For Language, select English (United States) from that combo box.

   c. For Label, type in Buildings, Net.

7. **Select the concept ComputerEquipmentNet.**

   The tree view on the left now shows the label you entered.

8. **Select each concept, repeating Step 6 and adding labels for Computer Equipment, Net, Furniture and Fixtures, Net, Land, Other Property, Plant and Equipment, Net, and Property, Plant and Equipment, Net.**

9. **Save your taxonomy by choosing File⇨Save.**

Your XBRL taxonomy should now look like Figure 15-8.

The labels make the XBRL taxonomy look a little nicer to the human eye. Also, you can see how handy it is have a way to add labels for other languages. Labels make for better functionality than always having to look at those ugly element names.

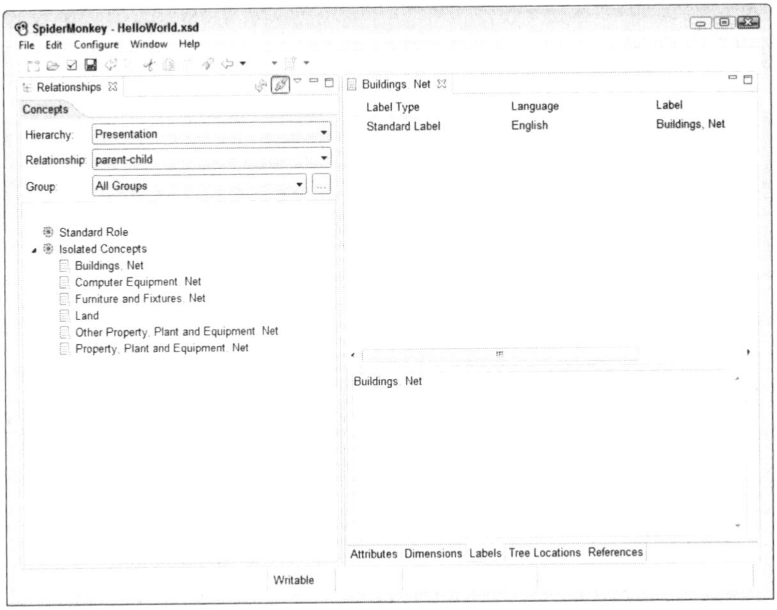

Figure 15-8:
The XBRL
taxonomy
after you
add labels.

Creating Relations Between XBRL Taxonomy Concepts

Creating relations is more or less similar to adding resources. In this section, we add two types of relations:

✔ Presentation relations organize the XBRL taxonomy in a particular order.

✔ Calculation relations express the calculations that exist and help verify that the XBRL instance is created correctly.

After you add labels to your taxonomy (see preceding section), do the following:

1. **In the tree view, select the node labeled Standard Role.**

   Standard Role is the network where we build these relations. All the existing concepts are under the node Isolated Concepts because the XBRL taxonomy doesn't have any relations yet.

2. **To create a concept, right-click over Standard Role, choose Create Child, and then choose Item.**

   A New Item as Child dialog box appears. The Namespace combo box already contains the correct value.

3. **In the Label text box, type Breakdown of Property, Plant and Equipment, Net.**

   Notice how the Element Name is entered for you.

4. **Finish the other portions of the form by entering the following information:**

   a. For Item Type, select string from the combo box.

   b. For Period Type, select instant from the combo box.

   c. Select the Abstract check box.

   d. Select the Nillable check box.

5. **Click the Finish button.**

   The concept is added in the Standard Role; if you accidently added it under Isolated Concepts, see the next step.

6. **(Optional) If your concept doesn't appear under Standard Role, drag the concept from the Isolated Concepts to the Standard Role node; if your concept appears in the correct spot, skip to Step 7.**

7. **Next, drag each of the other concepts and add them as children of the concept that you just created in the order shown in Figure 15-9.**

   Done! Your application should look like Figure 15-9.

Now, isn't Figure 15-9, which has the concepts organized in the order that you want, easier to read than the flat list of concepts that you couldn't order? This organization is indispensible in a situation where you're working with an XBRL taxonomy that contains several hundred concepts.

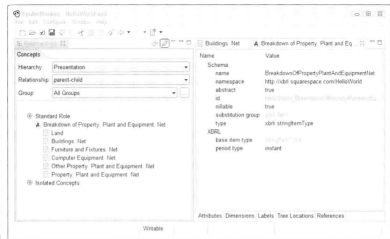

Figure 15-9:
The XBRL taxonomy after creating presentation relations.

You can also express the calculation relationships that exist between the total and the subcomponents of Property, Plant and Equipment, Net:

1. **Select the Hierarchy combo box at the upper left of the Relationship Tree and change the value from Presentation to Calculation.**

   The calculation relationship tree view looks like where you started before you created the presentation relations in the previous set of steps. You create the calculation relations in basically the same way that you create the presentation relations except that you don't need to create a concept to do it.

2. **Drag the concept Property, Plant and Equipment, Net to the Standard Role.**

3. **Drag the concept Land as a child of that first concept.**

4. **Repeat Steps 2 and 3 for all the concepts until your result looks like Figure 15-10.**

   Notice that a Weight of 1 is added for each concept except the first. The value is the weight value of the concept contributed to the total: 1 is the value added or subtracted (if it's a –1). The total doesn't have a weight itself because it's not added to anything. Finally, note that the one concept used in the presentation relations — Breakdown of Property, Plant and Equipment, Net — isn't needed, which is why it stays down in the Isolated Concepts node.

   You should really do one more thing to tidy up your XBRL taxonomy. To make understanding the value you want used within the XBRL instance easier, indicate that each of the numeric concepts is a debit as opposed to a credit.

5. **Select the Attributes tab and, where it says balance, select debit for each of the six numeric concepts involved in the calculation.**

6. **Validate the taxonomy by choosing File⇨Validate.**

   You should get a message indicating that you have no errors.

7. **Save the XBRL taxonomy by choosing File⇨Save.**

Your XBRL taxonomy now contains the labels added earlier and also presentation and calculation relations, which makes the taxonomy a little easier to look at and work with. The calculations also help you make sure that the numbers properly add up in your XBRL instance.

The URL to the completed version of this XBRL taxonomy at this stage is `http://xbrl.squarespace.com/storage/xbrlfordummies/hello worldexample2/HelloWorld2.xsd`.

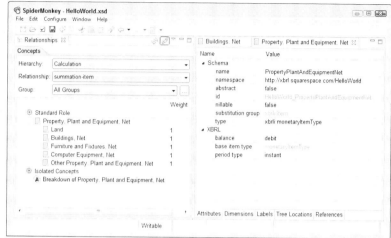

Figure 15-10:
The XBRL
taxonomy
after
creating
calculation
relations.

Extending Someone Else's Taxonomy

Suppose that you were running an airline and you wanted to use the XBRL taxonomy from the previous two sections — the one with the labels resources, presentation relations, and calculation relations. (If you didn't create this taxonomy, don't worry; we point you to a file you can use.) Your airline has airplanes, and airplanes aren't a concept in that XBRL taxonomy. But you *do* use the other concepts in that XBRL taxonomy, so it's still a good starting point. Well, no problem. You can't modify that XBRL taxonomy, but you can extend it.

Here's how you do it: You modify the taxonomy, but you do it virtually by creating another XBRL taxonomy that gets added to the DTS that adds what you need.

How? Good question. First, you need a new concept for airplanes. You also need a new label for that concept. You need to add a relation that adds the concept to the presentation relations of the other taxonomy in the correct spot. Finally, you need to add the calculation relation.

To add all these pieces to your XBRL taxonomy using SpiderMonkey:

1. **Create a taxonomy in SpiderMonkey by choosing File⇨New Taxonomy.**

   A dialog box asks you what type of taxonomy you want to create.

2. **Click New Extension Taxonomy and then click the Next button.**

   Another dialog box asks you for the name of the XBRL taxonomy.

3. **Type** My.xsd **in the text box and click Next.**

   Another dialog box appears asking you for the location of the base taxonomy to use for the extension.

4. **Enter the taxonomy location by selecting the Enter Taxonomy Location radio button.**

   To use the version of the XBRL taxonomy we provide you on the Web, type `http://xbrl.squarespace.com/storage/xbrlfordummies/helloworldexample2/HelloWorld2.xsd` into the text box.

5. **Click Next.**

   Another dialog box asks where you'll physically store the extension taxonomy you're creating on your local computer.

6. **Click the Browse button and, using the view that appears, choose the subdirectory where you'd like to store the extension taxonomy and then click Next.**

   Another dialog box that relates to Serialization Settings appears.

7. **Change the Primary Language to English (with no dialect, the first English in the list of many settings for that language) and then click Next.**

8. **Another dialog box appears, where you have to enter two things:**

   a. Taxonomy schema namespace: `http://www.example.com/My`

   b. Namespace prefix: **My**

9. **Click the Finish button.**

   Your extension taxonomy is created and stored on your computer where you specified.

10. **Expand the Standard Role tree and double-click the Land concept.**

    Within the application, what you see should now look like Figure 15-11.

    Your extension XBRL taxonomy looks identical to the `HelloWorld2.xsd` XBRL taxonomy from the previous section because you referenced that XBRL taxonomy as a base, and you haven't made any changes yet.

    Now you need to add the concept Airplanes.

11. **In presentation view, select the concept Computer Equipment, Net, right-click and choose Create Child, and then choose Item from the menu that appears.**

    You see the Create New Element dialog box again.

12. **Enter the following information:**

    a. Label: Airplanes (this field also auto-generates the Element Name)

    b. Item Type: Monetary

    c. Period Type: Instant

    d. Abstract: Not checked

    e. Nillable: Checked

13. **Click Finish.**

    You've now added your own concept without modifying the base XBRL taxonomy you're extending.

    You don't want to forget to modify the calculations to adjust them for the new Airplanes concept you added.

14. **For the Hierarchy, select Calculation and drag the Airplanes concept just after Computer Equipment, Net to make it a sibling of that concept in the calculation relations.**

    You also need to update that balance attribute value on the Attributes tab. Airplanes is also a debit.

15. **Click the Airplanes concept, select the Attributes tab, select the balance attribute, and select debit from the drop-down list.**

    Your extension taxonomy calculation relations should look like Figure 15-12.

16. **Validate your extension XBRL taxonomy by choose File⇨Validate.**

17. **Save your extension XBRL taxonomy by choosing File⇨Save.**

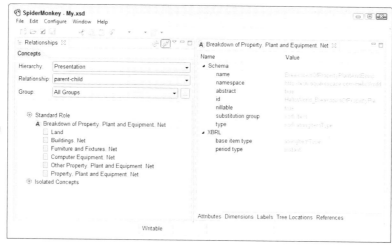

Figure 15-11:
The extension taxonomy starting point.

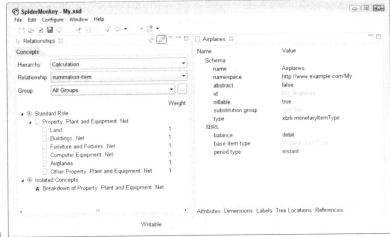

Figure 15-12:
The
extension
taxonomy
calculation
relations
after
adding the
Airplanes
concept.

We'd like to point out a few things in Figure 15-12. Look on the right where it says Schema and namespace. Notice that the concept you added has the value you entered for your namespace. If you look at all the other concepts, they have the namespace value from the base XBRL taxonomy. Click some of the other concepts to see for yourself that they're from a different namespace of the `HelloWorld2.xsd` taxonomy that you extended.

You can see a completed version of the `My.xsd` extension XBRL taxonomy at `www.xbrlsite.com/Examples/Extension/My.xsd`. The extension XBRL taxonomy is located on a totally different Web site than the base XBRL taxonomy from the previous section. These two XBRL taxonomies work together to provide the needed set of XBRL taxonomies that include the Airplanes concept and the other components of Property, Plant and Equipment, Net. The base XBRL taxonomy is physically unmodified.

Creating an XBRL Instance that Uses Extension

You can create an XBRL instance using the extension XBRL taxonomy created in the previous section. You create this XBRL instance by modifying the first Excel spreadsheet that you used to create our "Hello World" XBRL taxonomy. You have all the XBRL taxonomies you need to create this XBRL instance. We encourage you to create this XBRL instance using the Excel spreadsheet and then repeat this process using your XBRL instance-creation software of choice. The new business report that you create in this section looks like Figure 15-13.

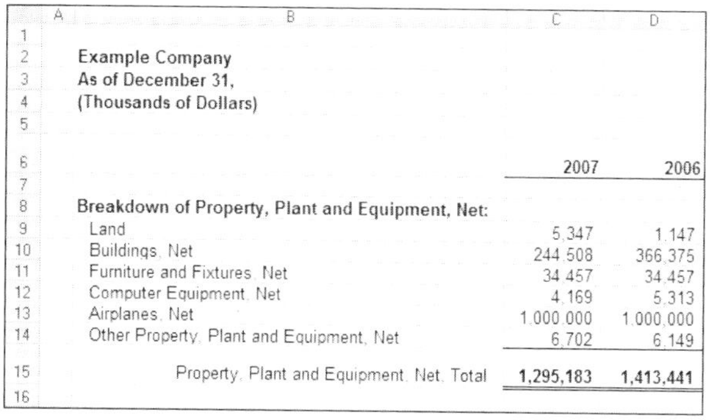

Figure 15-13:
The new
business
report
includes the
Airplanes
concept.

	A	B	C	D
1				
2		Example Company		
3		As of December 31,		
4		(Thousands of Dollars)		
5				
6			2007	2006
7				
8		Breakdown of Property, Plant and Equipment, Net:		
9		Land	5,347	1,147
10		Buildings, Net	244,508	366,375
11		Furniture and Fixtures, Net	34,457	34,457
12		Computer Equipment, Net	4,169	5,313
13		Airplanes, Net	1,000,000	1,000,000
14		Other Property, Plant and Equipment, Net	6,702	6,149
15		Property, Plant and Equipment, Net, Total	1,295,183	1,413,441
16				

Notice that you now have a line item for Airplanes. The values are $1,000,000 for both 2007 and 2006; the totals have changed to reflect the new line item.

We need to modify our "Hello World" Excel spreadsheet to work with our new extension XBRL taxonomy, adding the line item for Airplanes. This process gives you a good idea of how extensions work. It also shows you how you can easily modify your application and provides you a better idea of how the Excel macro-based application works.

You need to do the following steps in order to express this new business report:

1. **On your local computer, create a new subdirectory named Airplanes.**

2. **Open your `HelloWorld.xls` Excel spreadsheet that you used in the first exercise.**

   You can create a copy of that spreadsheet by saving it in a different location.

3. **Save this spreadsheet as `Airplanes.xls`, thereby creating a new spreadsheet in the subdirectory you created in Step 1.**

4. **Go to the spreadsheet named `Hello World Instance` and insert a new row into your Excel spreadsheet between Computer Equipment, Net and Other Property, Plant and Equipment, Net.**

5. **In that new row, add the following:**

   a. In column B, add the label for the line item Airplanes.

   b. In column C, add the value **1000000** for the period 2007.

   c. In column D, add the value **1000000** for the period 2006.

6. **In row 15, adjust the Excel formula to reflect the row you added or simply adjust the numbers to reflect the new total you see in Figure 15-15.**

Your spreadsheet should look like Figure 15-15 when you're finished. You need to adjust the mappings to reflect the new row and the fact that two existing rows have moved.

7. **In the Mappings spreadsheet tab, add Airplanes to the mappings by either copying or adding two new rows.**

8. **For each column in the two new rows, add the following data:**

   a. Spreadsheet: Use Hello World Instance for both rows.

   b. Cell: Use C13 for the first row and D13 for the second row.

   c. Concept: **My:Airplanes** for both rows. Notice that the namespace prefix is pointing to your extension XBRL taxonomy.

   d. Context: I-2007 for the first row, I-2006 for the second.

   e. Units: U-Monetary for both rows.

   f. Decimals: INF for both rows.

   g. Scale: 1000 for both rows.

Now, you added the row for Airplanes on the `Hello World Instance` spreadsheet, so you need to adjust the physical location that the mapping information looks at to reflect that new location.

9. **Fix** `HelloWorld:OtherPropertyPlantAndEquipment` **and** `HelloWorld:PropertyPlantAndEquipment` **to point to the correct cells.**

Basically, add one to the cell number reference increasing that number by one for the one row you added. Figure 15-14 shows you what the last several rows of the `Mappings` spreadsheet should look like now.

You want to use your XBRL extension taxonomy for your new XBRL instance because it contains the concept Airplanes.

Figure 15-14: Mappings after adjustments for adding Airplanes.

Spreadsheet	Cell	XBRL Concept	Context	Units	Decimals	Scale
Hello World Instance	C9	HelloWorld:Land	I-2007	U-Monetary	INF	1000
Hello World Instance	D9	HelloWorld:Land	I-2006	U-Monetary	INF	1000
Hello World Instance	C10	HelloWorld:BuildingsNet	I-2007	U-Monetary	INF	1000
Hello World Instance	D10	HelloWorld:BuildingsNet	I-2006	U-Monetary	INF	1000
Hello World Instance	C11	HelloWorld:FurnitureAndFixturesNet	I-2007	U-Monetary	INF	1000
Hello World Instance	D11	HelloWorld:FurnitureAndFixturesNet	I-2006	U-Monetary	INF	1000
Hello World Instance	C12	HelloWorld:ComputerEquipmentNet	I-2007	U-Monetary	INF	1000
Hello World Instance	D12	HelloWorld:ComputerEquipmentNet	I-2006	U-Monetary	INF	1000
Hello World Instance	C14	HelloWorld:OtherPropertyPlantAndEquipmentNet	I-2007	U-Monetary	INF	1000
Hello World Instance	D14	HelloWorld:OtherPropertyPlantAndEquipmentNet	I-2006	U-Monetary	INF	1000
Hello World Instance	C15	HelloWorld:PropertyPlantAndEquipmentNet	I-2007	U-Monetary	INF	1000
Hello World Instance	D15	HelloWorld:PropertyPlantAndEquipmentNet	I-2006	U-Monetary	INF	1000
Hello World Instance	C13	My:Airplanes	I-2007	U-Monetary	INF	1000
Hello World Instance	D13	My:Airplanes	I-2006	U-Monetary	INF	1000

10. To change your taxonomy, go to the Taxonomy spreadsheet tab.

You need to refer to the `My.xsd` extension XBRL taxonomy. That taxonomy pulls in the base XBRL taxonomy `HelloWorld2.xsd`.

You don't want to directly refer to the `HelloWorld2.xsd` schema location because it's being referred to indirectly by our extension.

11. Change the `Write Schema Ref` value to No.

You still want to put the `HelloWorld.xsd` namespace identifier and prefix into the XBRL instance.

12. Add a new row to the Taxonomy spreadsheet, which is how you refer to the extension taxonomy, with the following in that row:

a. Namespace Prefix of taxonomy: Enter **My** into the cell.

b. Namespace identifier of taxonomy: Enter **http://www.example.com/My** into the cell.

c. Location and name of file: Enter **http://www.xbrlsite.com/examples/extension/My.xsd** to use the copy we put on the Web for you to use.

d. Write Schema Ref: Enter **Yes** because we do want to write a reference to this schema within the XBRL instance.

e. Write Schema Location: Enter **No** because we won't be using schema locations.

What you have should look like Figure 15-15. You need to output a different filename, though.

13. Go to the Setup spreadsheet tab and change the filename to `Airplanes.xml`.

When you're done, the spreadsheet should look like Figure 15-16.

Figure 15-15:
The taxonomy spreadsheet after adjustments.

Namespace Prefix of taxonomy	Namespace identifier of taxonomy	Location and name of file	Write Schema Ref	Write Schema Location
HelloWorld	http://xbrl.squarespace.com/HelloWorld	HelloWorld.xsd	No	No
My	http://www.example.com/My	http://www.xbrlsite.com/examples/extension/My.xsd	Yes	No

14. **To check your work, go back to the `Hello World Instance` spread-sheet tab and click the Generate Mapping Information button.**

    Notice the red triangles in the upper-right corner of the cells; they indicate Excel comments that were created. You can hover over the cells and check your work by seeing whether the concepts you see in the comment matches what you expect the line item of your report.

15. **When you think everything is ready, click the Create XBRL Instance button to output your XBRL instance.**

    It puts the XBRL instance file named `Airplanes.xml` into the same sub-directory as the Excel spreadsheet.

16. **Validate your XBRL instance using your favorite validator.**

    We used UBmatrix Taxonomy Designer to validate our XBRL instance because it has a nice calculation validation report. Your output should look something like our validation report shown in Figure 15-17, which shows that everything is valid and the numbers add up.

CoreFiling SpiderMonkey doesn't validate XBRL instances, only XBRL tax-onomies. To validate your XBRL instance, you need to get an XBRL instance validator. CoreFiling has an XBRL validator called TrueNorth, which offers a 30-day free trial. You can get that software at `www.corefiling.com/products/truenorth.html`. Just follow the instructions, install the soft-ware, and then come back and follow these steps to validate your instance:

1. **Open the TrueNorth validator.**

2. **Choose File⇨Open and point to your instance document.**

    A message says that everything is okay. It's not exciting, we know, but that's good because it means you got everything correct. Good job!

Notice a couple of things from the validation report:

✔ The calculations add up correctly, which the validation report confirms. You achieve validation by using those calculation relations you created.

✔ You're not looking at funky-looking element names; rather, you can use the nicer looking labels that you created when you added the label resources.

✔ See lines 9 and 18 in the validation report, which has your concept, Airplanes, defined in your namespace `My`. You didn't physically modify the base taxonomy `HelloWorld2.xsd` to create an extension, but instead imported that XBRL taxonomy as a base and then modified the relations in your extension XBRL taxonomy. The combined DTS reflects both XBRL taxonomies.

Figure 15-17: The calculation validation report showing calculations are valid.

Line	Label	W	B	D-P	Value	Source	Message
1	*Default Link* [http://www.xbrl.org/2003/role/link]						
2	Context *I-2006*[at 2006-12-31 for Example Company]						
3	**U-Monetary**						
4	**HelloWorld:Property, Plant and Equipment, Net**			D	INF	1,413,441,000	both	OK
5	HelloWorld:Land		1	D	INF	1,147,000	inst	
6	HelloWorld:Buildings, Net		1	D	INF	366,375,000	inst	
7	HelloWorld:Furniture and Fixtures, Net		1	D	INF	34,457,000	inst	
8	HelloWorld:Computer Equipment, Net		1	D	INF	5,313,000	inst	
9	My:Airplanes		1	D	INF	6,149,000	inst	
10	HelloWorld:Other Property, Plant and Equipment, Net		1	D	INF	1,000,000,000	inst	
11	Context *I-2007*[at 2007-12-31 for Example Company]						
12	**U-Monetary**						
13	**HelloWorld:Property, Plant and Equipment, Net**			D	INF	1,295,183,000	both	OK
14	HelloWorld:Land		1	D	INF	5,347,000	inst	
15	HelloWorld:Buildings, Net		1	D	INF	244,508,000	inst	
16	HelloWorld:Furniture and Fixtures, Net		1	D	INF	34,457,000	inst	
17	HelloWorld:Computer Equipment, Net		1	D	INF	4,169,000	inst	
18	My:Airplanes		1	D	INF	6,702,000	inst	
19	HelloWorld:Other Property, Plant and Equipment, Net		1	D	INF	1,000,000,000	inst	

Reflecting on Your Creations

In this chapter, you create a base XBRL taxonomy, an extension XBRL taxonomy, and an XBRL instance. You create XBRL taxonomies by writing macros within a spreadsheet or by using specialized XBRL software. You create XBRL using one application and then validate it using another application. The basic step-by-step examples that you walk through illustrate most of what you'll ever do with XBRL. Your real-life XBRL taxonomies and XBRL instances probably have more concepts and facts in them than do these examples, but the general idea is exactly the same as what we describe in this chapter's steps.

To really entrench this knowledge of creating XBRL taxonomies and XBRL instances, we encourage you to repeat each exercise using the XBRL software of your choice.

If you haven't walk through creating this example or, for some reason, creating it didn't work out for you, you can find the completed XBRL instance at `www.xbrlsite.com/Examples/Airplanes/Airplanes.xml`. You can get the Excel spreadsheet that correctly generates this XBRL instance at `www.xbrl site.com/Examples/Airplanes/Airplanes-2009-05-23.zip`.

Performing Analysis Using XBRL

For a walkthrough of using the analysis capabilities of XBRL, we utilize one of our favorite software vendors, the U.S. SEC, and its online Test Drive Interactive Data application. In the section "Viewing an XBRL Instance," we look at one filing for a company. The following steps compare two different filings for the same company, showing you how you can leverage XBRL for analysis.

1. **Point your browser to** `http://viewerprototype1.com/viewer`.

   The Test Drive Interactive Data page appears.

2. **To compare filings, click the Company Comparison Report button.**

   It's the second button on the left-hand side of the screen. Look below the View Filings button.

   For this exercise, we use United Technologies because it has a lot of filings. The SEC company comparison is separated into three steps, which you can see in red.

3. **Find the Search Name or Ticker Symbol text box, type UTX into the box, and then select United Technologies.**

   The input form helps you limit the list to United Technologies.

4. **From the Select Filing (Period) drop-down list box that appears, select the last item on the list, Quarterly report, 2005-03-31.**

5. **From the Select Filing Report drop-down list box that appears, select Statement of Cash Flows.**

6. **Type UTX into the Search Name or Ticker Symbol text box and select United Technologies.**

7. **In the Select Filing (Period) drop-down list box that appears, select the second to the last item on the list, Quarterly report, 2005-06-30.**

8. **From the Select Filing Report drop-down list box that appears, select Statement of Cash Flows.**

9. **Click the Display Report button.**

You see the statements of cash flow for United Technologies for the two selected periods. This is so easy, and you really don't see any XBRL: XBRL is hiding in the background, allowing the computer to do all the work. XBRL makes it possible to grab information from two different physical reports and put that information together on this Web page.

Now, this comparison isn't really that sophisticated, and we admit that we picked a clean comparison. But what is going on is quite a good demo of what XBRL enables. Try to compare two different statements using the EDGAR system. That process involves opening two different documents, finding the statement you want, and then somehow putting the information side by side, usually by cutting and pasting. Imagine doing this comparison for more than two periods (say, five periods) or doing it across several different companies.

You can find another good example of using XBRL for comparisons at
`http://xbrl.rienks.biz/examples`.

Chapter 16

Differentiating XBRL Modules

XBRL is really a family of specifications. In this chapter, we meet that family in detail. Although this chapter doesn't make you an expert in any of these XBRL modules, it helps you realize what the modules are and what you can use them for.

Although not technically a module, we cover the XBRL Global Ledger taxonomy in this chapter, too. We show you what it is and how it may be useful to you.

XBRL Is a Set of Specifications

XBRL isn't just one specification; rather, it's one base specification and several additional modules that each add specific functionality to the base XBRL specification. You can use the additional modules if you need the functionality that they provide, or you can ignore them if you don't need the functionality. The modules are physically separate packages of functionality that you can call on when you need to.

Part of the reason these additional modules were created was that real-world use of XBRL showed that the additional functionality was needed. Rather than have each XBRL implementation create the required functionality separately within that implementation, the members of the consortium decided, in certain cases, to work together to create something that all implementations could use as deemed appropriate. The result is the additional modules that expand XBRL's functionality.

PWDs, CRs, and RECs

In the XBRL world, a specification can achieve various levels. The first level is that of a public working draft (PWD). A *public working draft* is a version that is released to the public for feedback and comments. Public working drafts can change, sometimes dramatically.

The next level is that of a candidate recommendation (CR). A *candidate recommendation* is a document that has been widely reviewed and is published to gain implementation experience prior to being published as a recommendation. A candidate recommendation is less likely to change, but can if implementation experience shows that a change is necessary.

The final level is that of recommendation (REC). Progressing through the public working draft stage and candidate recommendation stage vets the materials, and eventually they become a *recommendation*. At the recommendation stage, two or more members of XBRL International have created interoperable implementations of the recommendation specification. A conformance suite, which exercises all aspects of the specification, is used to ensure software vendor interoperability.

The granddaddy of all these modules is the XBRL 2.1 specification. The modules don't work with older versions of XBRL (2.0, 2.0a, or 1.0). Further, each module is compliant with the XBRL 2.1 specification. The modules were created using the extensibility features of XBRL 2.1. As such, the XBRL modules won't break compliant XBRL processors.

 XBRL International provides a technical working group roadmap that outlines timelines of its future plans for XBRL and for the additional modules. The URL for the roadmap is www.xbrl.org/XSB/XBRL-International-Technical-WGs-Roadmap-2008-11-26.htm. (To avoid having to type these long links, go to www.dummies.com/go/xbrl. This takes you to a landing page where you can click the link you need.)

The base XBRL 2.1 was published in December 2003 and has remained unchanged since that time. There are no known plans for changes to the base XBRL 2.1 specification communicated in XBRL's roadmap, which goes to the end of 2010.

The XBRL Family of Specifications

The patriarch of the XBRL family of specifications is the XBRL 2.1 specification that is the base for each module. Here are the modules in the XBRL family of specification:

✔ **XBRL Dimensions Specification:** Allows XBRL taxonomy authors to define and restrict dimensional information that XBRL instance authors may use in the segment and scenario elements of a context element of XBRL instances. Fundamentally, XBRL Dimensions enables XBRL taxonomies and XBRL instances to be created that leverage the multidimensional model.

✔ **XBRL Formula:** Allows XBRL taxonomy authors to create business rules that you can then use to validate XBRL instances. XBRL Formula also enables users to programmatically generate XBRL instances based on a set of rules.

✔ **XBRL Rendering Specifications:** Provides standard mechanisms for rendering information contained within XBRL instances so that a human can use it. Humans still want, or have, to work with information contained in XBRL instances, and this specification gives them various ways to get at the documents' information.

✔ **XBRL Versioning:** Lets you communicate changes made to XBRL taxonomies (changes to the concepts, resources, and relations contained within a taxonomy). These specifications help both taxonomy publishers (who need to communicate changes) and taxonomy users (who need to understand the changes). This versioning control helps you with the process of, say, remapping your business systems for changes to an XBRL taxonomy.

✔ **Generic Linkbase Specification:** Allows for the creation of new types of resource or relations networks. The sky is literally the limit! The ability to create new types of resource and relations networks allows for expressing and connecting new types of metadata to an XBRL taxonomy in a similar manner to other XBRL linkbases.

We drill into each of these family members later in this chapter. A second cousin is XBRL Global Ledger. It's not really a module, but it's included on the XBRL roadmap. XBRL Global Ledger is more like an application profile, a way of making use of XBRL, which is provided by XBRL International.

Leveraging the Multidimensional Model Using XBRL Dimensions

In order to understand what XBRL Dimensions is and why it's important, you need to be familiar with the multidimensional model. Most business people make use of the multidimensional model, but they may not realize it or understand that they are. Because this understanding is important, we take time to explain about multidimensional analysis and the multidimensional model. (See `www.xbrl.org/Specification/XDT-REC-2006-09-18.htm` for a copy of the XBRL Dimensions specification.)

Using the model for analysis

Most people understand what a database is. A *database* is just a way of storing data used by business systems. Pretty much all databases these days are relational databases. Databases are an organization of tables that contain fields and rows of data. Figure 16-1 shows you a basic database table.

State Name	Abbreviation	Capital	State Since
Alabama	AL	Montgomery	1818
Alaska	AK	Juneau	1959
Arizona	AZ	Phoenix	1912
Arkansas	AR	Little Rock	1836
California	CA	Sacramento	1850
Colorado	CO	Denver	1876
Connecticut	CT	Hartford	1788
Delaware	DE	Dover	1787
Florida	FL	Tallahassee	1845

Figure 16-1: A basic database table.

Figure 16-1 shows a table that contains information about U.S. states: the two letter abbreviation, the name of the state, its capital, and when it became a state.

Organizations use relational databases heavily. For example, accounting systems operate on top of relational databases. Relational databases are commonly called Online Transaction Processing (OLTP) systems.

Relational databases contain a lot of information because so many databases exist. Many software vendors provide relational databases, so they come in many different proprietary flavors. People like to analyze the useful information contained within these OLTP systems, taking advantage of what they can learn from all that data. But relational databases are optimized for transaction processing, not analysis. If you've ever tried to wade through a sea of database tables to put together a query for a report, you know what we mean.

Data warehouses, sometimes called *data marts,* were created to put all this data from all these different flavors of databases together to make the data easier to use. (If you want to find out more about data warehouses, we recommend *Data Warehousing For Dummies* [Wiley], by Alan R. Simon.)

Data warehouses take vast volumes of information for multiple databases and put all that data together into one big data warehouse, which is then used to analyze this information. The analysis is called online analytical processing (OLAP). OLAP systems are optimized for analysis, whereas OLTP systems are optimized for transaction processing.

OLAP systems use something known as a multidimensional model for expressing data. The multidimensional model makes accessing the data fast and flexible. One enabled feature of these OLAP systems is the ability to create queries on the fly because of the speed and flexibility of the multi-dimensional model. Business intelligence (BI) systems sit on top of data warehouses, making all this data available for use to business users.

But the multidimensional model is more than the ability to slice and dice information. The multidimensional model is inherently flexible, allowing for flexible access to information rather than the more rigid formats of relational models. Business-intelligence software shows the value of the multidimensional model.

Getting a grip on the model

XBRL Dimensions is a standard approach to modeling XBRL information that is easy to get into and out of the multidimensional model. You need at least a basic understanding of the multidimensional model in order to understand XBRL Dimensions. The multidimensional model basically breaks data into two components: the values themselves, called *measures,* and the dimensions of those values.

A simple example can help you come to grips with the multidimensional model. Figures 16-2 and 16-3 show sales information the way you might see it on a report printed on a piece of paper or one of those electronic pieces of paper, such as an HTML page or a PDF page.

The analysis in Figures 16-2 and 16-3 shows two breakdowns of the same information. Figure 16-2 shows a breakdown by product group and then by region; Figure 16-3 shows a breakdown by region and then by product. Note that the Grand Total of both breakdowns of the analysis is exactly the same. The breakdowns are the same information presented in two different ways.

Only one value (or measure), Sales, is shown in the analysis. That value has three dimensions: region, product, and period. More dimensions, such as the company reporting the information and the currency in which the information is reported, actually exist, but those dimensions are the same for all values in both breakdowns, so they seem somewhat invisible to you.

The analysis in Figures 16-2 and 16-3 is presented to you here on paper; that physical presentation is static and hard to change. You can present this analysis in another way, the pivot table, which allows a user to dynamically pivot the data across it's dimensions. Many business people are familiar with the pivot table. Figure 16-4 shows a Microsoft Excel pivot table that expresses the same information from Figures 16-2 and 16-3.

Breakdown by Product, by Region (thousands of Euros)

Product	Region		2003	2002	2001
Pharmacueticals	Asia		2,864	2,471	2,009
	Europe		5,317	4,732	4,233
	US and Canada		5,568	5,527	4,576
	Other Regions		1,147	1,715	1,690
		Sub Total	14,896	14,446	12,507
Generics	Asia		807	634	503
	Europe		1,616	1,383	1,359
	US and Canada		1,508	1,660	1,378
	Other Regions		489	890	918
		Sub Total	4,420	4,567	4,158
Consumer Health	Asia		1,457	1,263	1,025
	Europe		2,834	2,592	2,462
	US and Canada		2,765	3,074	2,570
	Other Regions		767	1,340	1,365
		Sub Total	7,823	8,270	7,421
Other	Asia		895	1,398	1,315
	Europe		1,790	2,746	2,826
	US and Canada		1,673	3,225	3,038
	Other Regions		540	1,154	1,200
		Sub Total	4,899	8,523	8,379
		Grand Total	32,038	35,805	32,465

Figure 16-2:
Breakdown by product, then by region.

Breakdown by Region, by Product (thousands of Euros)

Product	Region		2003	2002	2001
US and Canada	Consumer Health		2,765	3,074	2,570
	Generics		1,508	1,660	1,378
	Pharmaceuticals		5,568	5,527	4,576
	Other Products		1,673	3,225	3,038
		Sub Total	11,515	13,486	11,562
Europe	Consumer Health		2,834	2,592	2,462
	Generics		1,616	1,383	1,359
	Pharmaceuticals		5,317	4,732	4,233
	Other Products		1,790	2,746	2,826
		Sub Total	11,557	11,453	10,879
Asia	Consumer Health		1,457	1,263	1,025
	Generics		807	634	503
	Pharmaceuticals		2,864	2,471	2,009
	Other Products		895	1,398	1,315
		Sub Total	6,023	5,766	4,852
Other Regions	Consumer Health		767	1,340	1,365
	Generics		489	890	918
	Pharmaceuticals		1,147	1,715	1,690
	Other Products		540	1,154	1,200
		Sub Total	2,943	5,101	5,173
		Grand Total	32,038	35,805	32,465

Figure 16-3:
Breakdown by region, then by product.

Figure 16-4: Pivot table breakdown by product and then by region.

The pivot table looks slightly different than the paper-based analysis shown in Figures 16-2 and 16-3 due to its formatting. If you note the grand totals, you can see that the information is the same, only presented slightly differently. You have, again, a breakdown of sales by product and then by region for the periods 2001, 2002, and 2003. The nice thing about pivot tables is that you can easily pivot the data using the drop-down list boxes to show it by region and then by product, as shown in Figure 16-5.

Figure 16-5: Pivot table breakdown by region and then by product.

Although using static paper in a book makes getting the full experience of a pivot table difficult, part of a pivot table's value is that you can pivot data across different dimensions, presenting the data in different ways to meet the different needs of information users.

For both the Excel pivot table and for the paper report, Figure 16-6 shows what the data used to generate this information actually looks like.

	A	B	C	D	E	F	G	H
1	Sales Analysis (With Breakdown)							
2								
3	Entity	Units	Concept		Product	Region	Period	Value
4	Sample Company	Euros	Sales		Consumer Health	Asia	2001	1,025
5	Sample Company	Euros	Sales		Consumer Health	Europe	2001	2,462
6	Sample Company	Euros	Sales		Consumer Health	Other Regions	2001	1,365
7	Sample Company	Euros	Sales		Consumer Health	US and Canada	2001	2,570
8	Sample Company	Euros	Sales		Generics	Asia	2001	503
9	Sample Company	Euros	Sales		Generics	Europe	2001	1,359
10	Sample Company	Euros	Sales		Generics	Other Regions	2001	918
11	Sample Company	Euros	Sales		Generics	US and Canada	2001	1,378
12	Sample Company	Euros	Sales		Other Segments	Asia	2001	1,315
13	Sample Company	Euros	Sales		Other Segments	Europe	2001	2,826
14	Sample Company	Euros	Sales		Other Segments	Other Regions	2001	1,200
15	Sample Company	Euros	Sales		Other Segments	US and Canada	2001	3,038
16	Sample Company	Euros	Sales		Pharmaceuticals	Asia	2001	2,009
17	Sample Company	Euros	Sales		Pharmaceuticals	Europe	2001	4,233
18	Sample Company	Euros	Sales		Pharmaceuticals	Other Regions	2001	1,690
19	Sample Company	Euros	Sales		Pharmaceuticals	US and Canada	2001	4,576
20	Sample Company	Euros	Sales		Consumer Health	Asia	2002	1,263
21	Sample Company	Euros	Sales		Consumer Health	Europe	2002	2,592
	Sample Company	Euros	Sales				2002	1,340

Figure 16-6: The actual information that supplies both pivot tables.

When people like U.S. SEC ex-Chairman Christopher Cox talk about *interactive data*, they're talking about the ability to do things like pivot data in this manner — that's part of the interactive nature that XBRL helps create. XBRL separates the data itself and the presentation of the data, freeing users of the information to present the information as they see fit.

Most people don't really think about it, but pretty much all information is multidimensional. Paper is okay for working with one, two, and maybe even three or four dimensions. But as the number of dimensions increases, the more complicated it is for the information to be effectively expressed on a two-dimensional piece of paper.

Computers don't have such limitations. Pivot tables, and other tools for expressing information, can leverage all sorts of capabilities provided by computer applications to communicate information. This lack of limitations is why the multidimensional model is so powerful — it provides you with flexibility. No longer does information need to be locked into the single presentation format that the information creator used to express the information; instead, users of information, if it's expressed in this flexible manner of the multidimensional model, are free to reformat the information as they see fit.

A cube is a common way of looking at multidimensional information. The cube in Figure 16-7 provides a good metaphor for understanding the multidimensional model.

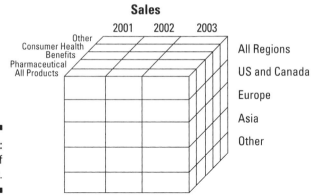

Sales

Figure 16-7:
A cube of
data.

Figure 16-7 uses this common abstraction, which we use to explain multi-dimensional concepts. You may recall from school the three axes (dimensions) shown in this cube: the X axis (from left to right), the Y axis (from top to bottom), and the Z axis (front to back). In the cube in Figure 16-7, the X axis covers the periods 2001, 2002, and 2003; the Y axis covers the regions All Regions, US and Canada, Europe, and so on; and the Z axis lists products, such as All Products, Pharmaceuticals, Generics, Consumer Health and Other.

A cube simply allows you to visually comprehend the relationship between the information; it's only an abstraction to help explain the model. If you were to introduce more axes, you'd need more dimensions, which would be hard to express in a graphic like this. As such, sometimes dimensions are locked or held constant to make data fit into an understandable cube form. In this case, the entity and units are being held constant; these locked views are commonly referred to as *slices* of the information. You can break the larger cube into cells. Each cell is an intersection between a period, a region, and a product for the concept Sales. The shaded cell in Figure 16-7 represents sales for the period 2002, the product pharmaceuticals, for all regions.

Grasping the basics of XBRL Dimensions

XBRL Dimensions provides a number of features for those using XBRL:

✔ **Model multidimensional information:** XBRL Dimensions provides the ability to model information within an XBRL taxonomy using the multidimensional model. XBRL Dimensions allows users to model hypercubes (a.k.a. cubes, or data cubes), the dimensions (axes) of those cubes, domains of the dimensions, and members of the domain. You can also model the primary items (a.k.a. concepts) that exist within a hypercube. XBRL Dimensions supports hierarchies within this dimensional information.

✔ **Express contextual information about a business fact within an XBRL instance:** XBRL Dimensions allows for the expression of information about a business fact being reported within an XBRL instance. This information, which amounts to metadata, is articulated within a context element entity or <scenario> element.

✔ **Articulate constraints on contextual information:** XBRL Dimensions provides the ability to articulate constraints with which an XBRL instance creator must comply. The XBRL taxonomy tells you what the and <scenario> portion of contexts can and can't contain— it controls what's allowed.

✔ **Validate contextual information against constraints:** XBRL Dimensions provides the ability to validate an XBRL instance against established constraints expressed within an XBRL taxonomy.

✔ **Extending contextual information:** XBRL Dimensions provides a formal, consistent, specified approach to extend dimensional information. Just like you can add concepts of an XBRL taxonomy, so, too, can you extend the contextual information such as adding hypercubes, dimensions, domains, members, or primary items.

XBRL Dimensions uses specific terminology. Here's the key terminology related to XBRL Dimensions:

✔ **Hypercubes:** In XBRL, a *hypercube* is similar to a multidimensional model cube. Hypercubes bring together a set of dimensions and primary items (which is really a dimension).

✔ **Dimension:** In XBRL, a *dimension* is equivalent to a multidimensional model dimension.

✔ **Domain:** In XBRL, a dimension has a *domain*, which you can think of as the total dimension, an aggregation of all the members, should that be appropriate. Dimensions don't need to have totals, but they can, though, if you need to express them.

✔ **Member:** In XBRL, a *member* is similar to an multidimensional member.

✔ **Primary item:** In XBRL, the term *primary item* is used to mean member as defined by the multidimensional model.

✔ **All/Not all:** XBRL Dimensions uses Boolean algebra and the *All* and *Not All relations* to create any set of allowable members a user might need within a dimension. With a combination of All and Not All, you can express pretty much anything that needs to be expressed. This allows XBRL taxonomy creators to articulate that certain specific cells should never be used or have values within an XBRL instance.

✔ **Explicit member:** An *explicit member* is a member defined within an XBRL taxonomy and is literally explicitly defined.

✔ **Typed member:** A *typed member,* or implicit member, is implicit. These are defined within an XML Schema rather than within an XBRL taxonomy. Typed members provide for additional flexibility in creating members.

✔ **Default Dimension:** A primary item can participate in more than one hypercube, each of which has a different set of dimensions. *Default dimensions* take this into consideration, enabling the expression of the correct dimensional information for each hypercube in which a primary item participates.

Typed members have some issues that you should be aware of if you intend to use them. Simple typed members are generally okay, although you can't express hierarchies with simple typed members. Avoid complex typed members, if possible, for several reasons. First, complex typed members can have literally any XML content model, making an interface required for creating them quite complex. Second, complex typed members can't express hierarchies — they're flat, meaning that you can't express relations between typed members like you can explicit members. Third, XBRL Formula doesn't work nearly as well with complex typed members as they do with explicit members or simple typed members.

Default dimensions have some issues you should be aware of if you intend to use them. Most issues relate to uncommon and complex uses of default dimensions. One particular issue occurs when you use XBRL Formula validation. Again, beware! If you're careful and conscious of what you're doing, you can use default dimensions safely. If you don't want the trouble, stay away from default dimensions or hire a good consultant.

Expressing Business Rules Using XBRL Formula

XBRL Formula enables the expression of business rules within an XBRL taxonomy, exchange of those business rules within a standard format, and validation of XBRL instances against expressed business rules. What makes business rules so interesting, however, is the fact that now with XBRL, all that information is in a structured format and therefore you can express business rules and get computers to enforce those rules. When information is unstructured, humans have to enforce these rules using manual effort.

Getting a grip on business rules

The ability to express business rules is probably the single most powerful feature of XBRL, other than the fundamental ability to express business information in a standard structured format.

You can define business rules in many ways; there really isn't one standard definition. Rather than trying to create just one definition here, we provide you with several definitions of business rules:

- ✔ A formal statement that defines or constrains some aspect of a business that is intended to assert business structure, or to control or otherwise influence the behavior of the business

- ✔ A way of expressing the business meaning (semantics) of a set of information

- ✔ A formal and implementable expression of some business user requirement

- ✔ The practices, processes, and policies by which an organization conducts its business

For more information about business rules, see the Business Rules Group at www.businessrulesgroup.org/first_paper/br01c0.htm.

Business rules exist in the form of relationships between pieces of business information. Some examples can help you better understand exactly what they are:

- ✔ **Assertions,** such as the balance sheet balances or Assets = Liabilities + Equity

- ✔ **Computations,** such as Total Property, Plant and Equipment = Land + Buildings + Fixtures + IT Equipment + Other

- ✔ **Process-oriented rules,** such as "If Property, Plant, and Equipment exists, then a Property, Plant and Equipment policies and disclosures must exist."

- ✔ **Regulations,** such as "The following is the set of ten things that must be reported if you have Property, Plant and Equipment on your balance sheet: deprecation method by class, useful life by class, amount under capital leases by class . . ." and so on

- ✔ **Instructions** or documentation, such as "Cash flow types must be either operating, financing, or investing."

The components of XBRL Formula

XBRL Formula is part of the XBRL family, but it's actually a family in and of itself. XBRL Formula is a set of modular specification that works together — it's not just one specification. These specifications are separate for the same types of reasons the XBRL family of specifications is modular — so that you can use what you need and ignore the rest.

Here are the members of the XBRL Formula set of specifications:

- **Functions:** A collection of common functions used to obtain information out of an XBRL instance in support of XBRL Formula or other purposes.

- **Formula:** Allows for the expression of formulas (a.k.a. business rules). You can even express formula results in the form of an XBRL instance, enabling the chaining of different XBRL instances and XBRL Formula into a work flow.

- **Variables:** Allow for the definition of variables that a formula then uses.

- **Filters:** Establish filters for working with subsets of fact values of different types from one or more XBRL instances. Various types of filters correspond to useful filters when working with XBRL instances.

- **Consistency assertions:** Check a computed item to an existing source item. Allow for the evaluation of whether the source and the computed item are consistent. These assertions allow for the verification of the accuracy of XBRL instance information.

- **Value assertions:** Check as a computation. Allow for the creation of values that you can subsequently use for further processing, which may include creation of new information within an XBRL instance.

- **Existence assertions:** Check for the existence of a source item. Allow for verification of existing information and further processing.

- **Validation:** Verifies value assertions, consistency assertions, and existence assertions. Extends the functionality of the three different types of assertions.

- **Generic labels:** Provide for the labeling of any XBRL element, attribute, or value. Labeling is useful in providing human-readable information or documentation for a formula, but you can also use it for other purposes.

- **Generic references:** Provide for the references of any XBRL element, attribute, or value. Generic references are useful in providing human-readable information or documentation for a formula, but you can use them for other purposes, too.

All these specifications work together to support the expression of information in the form of business rules that document relationships. You can use this information to communicate such relationships from the producers to the consumers of this business information. These business rules help enable effective information exchange by ensuring validity of the information being exchanged.

Separating business rules from applications

Knowing what business rules are is important because they're extraordinarily useful for business information exchange. But what is even more important is how business rules were created and used in the past, and how they'll be created and used in the future.

You may remember when someone building a computer application had to also build a place to store the application's data. Well, those days are over with the advent of the standard relational database management system (RDBMS) and structured query language (SQL) for accessing information within a database. Basically, the database is now separate from the application, so you can buy a standard SQL database and use that database to store data, rather than every software vendor building its own data storage scheme. This separation between the database and the application occurred in the 1980s.

The separation of business rules from the actual application likewise provides efficiencies:

- Rather than paying programmers to update rules, business users can update the rules themselves, saving both time and money.

- Rather than having programmers create validation for each thing they want to validate (called *one-to-one programmatic validation*), you can use a business-rules engine to do validation (many-to-many rules-based validation). Further, these rules engines can hide much of the complexity of expressing rules from the business users.

- Because the business rules are separated from the application or database, creators of information sets can use the business rules established to constrain that information set. Creators can then exchange those business rules with users of the information set, which helps analysts understand the information. Both creators and analysts use the same set of business rules, which makes things clearer to both creators and consumers of the information.

Automating workflow

After the business rules are separated from applications, applications can exchange them. Expressing these business rules in a standard way has additional advantages. Because you can exchange the rules with others, for example, you can

- Use the rules to explain the information you're collecting
- Determine which information needs to be collected from those creating XBRL instances
- Validate the XBRL instance information prior to it being submitted
- Automatically determine which information collection forms should be used by which type or quality of entity submitting information

These business rules promote an understanding of business policies and procedures, facilitate consistent decision-making, and force order to rules and policies because they're clearly expressed. And it's all done with increased flexibility because of the separation of the processing logic from the rules and the resulting ability of the business users to control the processing logic easily without understanding programming.

Creating Human-Readable XBRL Information Using XBRL Rendering

Although automated processes can consume the information contained in XBRL instances, humans many times need to consume this information, too. Although computer processes read the information, they don't need nicely formatted presentation formats to do their reading. Computers prefer easy-to-digest angle brackets — all that markup stuff humans find challenging to come to grips with. Humans, on the other hand, do need nice, easy-to-read formats to consume this information.

The XBRL Rendering specifications help provide the ability to render XBRL instance information so that humans can consume that information. You can obtain additional information relating to rendering specifications from XBRL International at `www.xbrl.org/Specifications`.

Getting a grip on rendering

Rendering XBRL isn't really that much of a challenge. You can use many mechanisms for rendering XML-type information into formats consumable by humans. XSLT, as an example, can transform one type of XML into another type of XML or other formats, such as HTML, PDF, DocBook, or even Microsoft Word and Excel formats, which are also XML in their 2007 versions. XBRL is easy to render because each fact value is easily identified within an XBRL instance.

However, you generally need to take an extra step to render XBRL information. In Chapter 2, we discuss a content model that the creators of XBRL decided not to use — the one that most other XML languages use to help render their XML into more human-readable formats. Well, we need to get that information back. XBRL generally doesn't use the XML content model; this information on relations is stored in linkbases. (Refer to Chapter 4 for more information on linkbases.) Having to get this rendering information from linkbases isn't a problem because XBRL processors can help you. But, there are some challenges:

- ✔ **One-to-one renderings:** If each creator of an XBRL instance had to create his own way to render that XBRL instance, it would be bad for two reasons. First, creating one-to-one renderings is time-consuming and therefore costly. Second, if you want to compare information across XBRL instances and each XBRL instance is rendered differently, comparison across XBRL instances can be quite challenging.

- ✔ **One-to-many renderings:** What we really want is one-to-many renderings. *One-to-many* means that one template is created that expresses how to render the fact values of an XBRL instance created with a certain taxonomy or set of taxonomies. If extensions aren't allowed, this task is actually relatively trivial. However, if extensions are allowed, it makes rendering more challenging. You can easily create one-to-one renderings, but if you can't share them between software tools, they really don't provide what you need.

- ✔ **Standard for one-to-many renderings:** The issue that rendering specifications need to solve is the ability to create a one-to-many set of formatting information that allows for renderings in a variety of formats, such as HTML, PDF, Word, Excel, and so on, that software applications can share, a standard.

The components of XBRL rendering

The human rendering of XBRL instance information has several different aspects covered by the different components that comprise the set of XBRL Rendering specifications:

- **Inline rendering (HTML version):** For formatting XBRL-based information within an HTML document for human consumption, but also for consumption by automated processes

- **Inline rendering (other formats):** For the formatting of XBRL-based information within other types of documents (other than HTML) that allows for human or automated consumption

- **Rendering linkbase:** For connecting rendering information to an XBRL taxonomy (for example, providing HTML information that explains how information expressed within an XBRL instance for that specific XBRL taxonomy should be rendered); different rendering formats are supported

Maintaining XBRL Taxonomies and XBRL Instances Using XBRL Versioning

Things change. This adage holds true for things expressed in XBRL, be it an XBRL taxonomy or an XBRL instance. XBRL Versioning enables the communication of these types of changes in a global standard way to both humans and to computer processes. XBRL Versioning helps publishers of XBRL taxonomies communicate changes to their taxonomies and also helps users of those taxonomies understand how a taxonomy they use has changed. Therefore, taxonomy users can determine what adjustments, such as mappings to the XBRL taxonomy, the users need to make to their systems.

Communicating these changes is important because it enables the possibility of writing computer software applications to update systems for many, but not all, of these types of changes, which saves you time and money. XBRL Versioning may not be sexy, but it's helpful. (For more information relating to XBRL Versioning, see www.xbrl.org/SpecCRs.)

Getting a grip on versioning

Versioning relates to changes in XBRL taxonomies and XBRL instance. For example, consider the following possible types of changes:

- ✓ **Changes between taxonomy versions:** XBRL U.S. has stated that it will change the US GAAP taxonomies each year. When a new taxonomy is released, you need to understand the changes made to the taxonomy.

- ✓ **Changes to your mappings:** Coordinating the concepts you use within your internal business systems with the concepts used within an XBRL taxonomy is referred to as *mapping*. During the mapping process, you create a way to link your internal systems to, in this case, an XBRL taxonomy. Say that you've set up your systems to work with a specific XBRL taxonomy. However, a newer version of that XBRL taxonomy has added concepts, removed existing concepts, and made changes to relations and resource networks within the taxonomy. You need to update your systems to reflect these changes.

- ✓ **Analysis and comparisons:** Suppose that an entity releases information in one year based on one XBRL taxonomy and in the next year uses a new version of the XBRL taxonomy. Then imagine that you need to do a comparison between the two XBRL instances that use two different versions of the same XBRL taxonomy. Consider what a comparison may look like over a five-year period, which is common period used for financial-reporting types of analysis.

You get the idea that changes can cause issues. Take a look at the specific types of things that may change within an XBRL taxonomy or XBRL instance:

- ✓ **DTS or taxonomy-level changes:** Changes to a DTS may include the addition of new concepts to the taxonomy schema or the removal of concepts. The addition or removal of networks may occur.

- ✓ **Concept-level changes:** A concept may have changes to its name or changes to any of the various attributes of that concept.

- ✓ **Relation changes:** The addition or removal of relations or changes to existing relations may occur.

- ✓ **Resource changes:** The addition or removal of resources or changes to existing resource information may occur.

- ✓ **Instance changes:** Between two XBRL instances, things can change. For example, changes to an XBRL taxonomy concept changes the name of the fact value used within an XBRL instance (which comes from the XBRL taxonomy).

The components of XBRL Versioning

Like other XBRL modules within the XBRL family, the XBRL Versioning specifications are a set of specifications that work together to provide the needed functionally. In XBRL Versioning's case, here are the components:

- ✔ **Versioning Specification Part 1 – Content:** Describes the types of changes to concept definitions and resources that can exist between all the files that make up a DTS. In most situations, changes between DTSs would be between two consecutive versions of the same set of XBRL taxonomies. Basically, versioning content explains the things that have changed.

- ✔ **Versioning Specification Part 2 – Syntax:** Prescribes a syntax for creating reports of changes described in Part 1. This syntax enables the creation of computer applications to read these changes and automate many processes relating to updating systems for such changes. For example, you can now create automatically updated mapping tables that communicate taxonomy changes.

- ✔ **XBRL Infoset:** Helps versioning work correctly. It formally describes the content of a DTS without regard to the syntax used to express this syntax. This specification allows for consistent serialization of XBRL DTS information so that changes can be accurately identified. Technical people need this specification to make versioning work correctly, but business people don't generally need to understand it. For more information on XBRL Infoset, see www.xbrl.org/Specification/ Infoset/PWD-2009-02-04/infoset-PWD-2009-02-04.html.

Creating Custom Resources and Relations Using Generic Linkbases

The Generic Linkbase is a specification for creating custom resource type or relations type networks within linkbases (see Chapter 4). You can use these resources and relations to extend the power of XBRL. For example, XBRL International used the Generic Linkbase Specification to create the XBRL Formula specification.

Getting a grip on Generic Linkbases

The need that the Generic Linkbase Specification serves is twofold. First, it allows XBRL International to not have to write a new linkbase specification every time it creates a new XBRL module that requires linkbases, such as XBRL Formula. Second, it allows others to create XBRL-compliant linkbases for any number of other purposes. Using the Generic Linkbase Specification as a foundation to build on provides leverage, allowing things built in a similar manner to be more quickly implemented in software applications with less work.

For example, the Generic Linkbase Specification was used to create the XBRL Formula linkbases. While an XBRL processor may not understand the specifics of a linkbase you've created, it does provide for a large amount of leverage. This standard way of connecting other nonstandard information to your XBRL information makes tasks you perform significantly easier.

The Generic Linkbase Specification serves another purpose. Linkbases can provide human-readable documentation, references, or other resources to any XBRL element, attribute, or value. For example, they can provide a label that describes a context contained within an XBRL instance in any number of languages using a Generic Linkbase. You can then use this information, say, within a software application to provide a better user experience, allowing users to not have to deal with technical stuff.

XBRL Generic Linkbases components

Unlike many of the other XBRL modules, the Generic Linkbase Specification is one simple specification. It has only one part. However, a few things can help you understand and make use of Generic Linkbases:

- ✔ **Generic Linkbase Specification:** Find the specification itself at www. xbrl.org/SpecCRs.

- ✔ **XBRL Formula Specification:** The XBRL Formula Specification uses the Generic Linkbase Specification. A great way to learn about using this type of functionally is to explore how the XBRL Formula specification used it. You can basically use XBRL Formula to reverse-engineer how to create your own linkbase for some another purpose.

- ✔ **Link Role Registry:** The Link Role Registry (LRR) allows you to define and use specific extended link, arc, and resource roles for various purposes and use definitions others have created. If you're into the Generic Linkbase specification, see www.xbrl.org/LRR.

The XBRL Global Ledger Taxonomy

The XBRL Global Ledger taxonomy (XBRL GL) is really in a class by itself. Not really a module, but more than a taxonomy, XBRL GL serves a specific need. Integration of two business systems may be anywhere between a simple copy-and-paste task all the way up to a complex series of ETL (Extract, Transform, Load) tasks. XBRL GL exists to make these information exchanges easier for accounting-type business systems.

Getting a grip on XBRL GL

XBRL GL is a modular set of taxonomies, specification-type guidelines, and best-practices documents. XBRL GL documents and prescribes XBRL GL Instance Standards and a GL Taxonomy Technical Architecture. Its purpose is to provide a standard (canonical) format for representing and exchanging information commonly found in accounting and business systems. Using XBRL GL, organizations can eliminate many of the difficulties and complexities traditionally encountered when exchanging common types of business information. Users of XBRL GL benefit in terms of reduced costs, increased timeliness of information, improved information quality, and improved data usability and reusability.

XBRL Global Ledger is an XBRL taxonomy created by the members of XBRL International. The best way to describe XBRL GL is to explain what you can use it for:

- Standard integration format for software vendors to create journal entries for import or export to or from a general ledger system

- Integrating branch office feeder systems with consolidated systems in the central office for accounting consolidations, budgeting and forecasting, or other reporting functions

- Exchange of information used for accounting write-up work, compilations, review, or audits between a client and CPA

- Creation of internal or external audit schedules for maintaining an audit trail

- Moving data from one accounting system to another accounting system during a change in accounting systems

- Enabling drill down from summarized financial reporting or accounting information into its detail; or aggregation from the detail to the summaries

- Summarizing financial information that will be used in higher level accounting reports or statements.

The focus of XBRL GL is on common types of business information commonly found in the business systems that operate in most organizations. Examples of these systems include the general ledger, chart of accounts, accounts receivable subsystems, accounts payable subsystems, payroll subsystems, fixed asset subsystems, inventory subsystems, job costing subsystems, and so on. You get it: accounting systems, or ERP systems, as we call them these days.

You can use XBRL to create what XBRL GL provides: Proof is that XBRL GL exists, and it's 100-percent XBRL. You can even create your own XML language for doing what XBRL GL does. You can do such integrations in several different ways. These integrations aren't sexy or exciting, but they're needed by literally every organization that has more than one business system. XBRL GL is the way, the canonical approach, that's being accepted around the world (or at least probably will be) for representing information exchanged between business systems.

Could information be transferred between business systems prior to XBRL GL existing? Of course, it could. Everyone would simply come up with his way and create countless import and export applications to get accounting information from one place and put it someplace else. Why was everyone creating it his own way? Well, because the canonical way did not exist. Now it does. Hallelujah, brother! Accountants everywhere are singing and dancing in the streets.

Accountants, taxes, and XBRL GL

Only two things in life are certain: death and taxes. Tax collectors around the world have shown a lot of interest in XBRL GL. Government tax administrators around the world have been using proprietary formats for exchanging information — or even worse, manually exchanging information on paper. But the tax guys are becoming more efficient thanks to XBRL GL.

Around the world, tax administrators are collaborating to create more standard formats, rather than proprietary formats, to exchange tax-related information. This collaboration is important because, for example, the U.S tax-collecting agency, the Internal Revenue Service (IRS), has tax treaties with more than 100 other countries for exchanging tax information for various administrative reasons.

These tax administrators have generally agreed to use XBRL as a standard format for exchanging information with taxpayers and as a standard tax audit file format. These tax guys and their e-filings and e-audits are pretty progressive. Maybe this tax and accounting stuff isn't that thrilling, but administering these things is pretty important.

Chapter 17

Digging Deeper into XBRL Taxonomies

*I*n this chapter, we cover additional important details of an XBRL taxonomy. We also look at important big-picture considerations. We explain how an XBRL taxonomy is more than a dictionary. We walk you through approaches to looking at an XBRL taxonomy and what to look for in a taxonomy. We point you to sample and example XBRL taxonomies, as well as production taxonomies, that help you understand XBRL taxonomies better. We also highlight the characteristics of a good XBRL taxonomy.

Consolidating Your Knowledge

An XBRL taxonomy is a body of knowledge for some business domain expressed in a standardized electronic format. The XBRL taxonomy contains the experience, insights, rules, conventions, and other knowledge of professionals who operate within that domain. This knowledge is in a form that both humans and computer software applications can read. Because computers can read this domain knowledge, you can make computers do things they've never been able to do thanks to these standardized bodies of domain knowledge that exist in a global standard format that a computer can now understand.

None of these things that computers can do for you with XBRL are magic. What looks like magic is a result of good and proper use of a technology for what it was intended to do. However, if you don't understand these technological tools or how to use them, you can end up with a dissatisfying outcome.

Fundamentally, XBRL taxonomies are data models, and you should treat them as such. Just as you can have good and bad database schemas (which are also data models), you can have good and bad XBRL taxonomies. XBRL taxonomies impact XBRL instances. You can't create a good XBRL instance from a bad XBRL taxonomy.

One challenging aspect of using XBRL is what you're asking XBRL to do for you. Getting two different computerized business systems to effectively communicate with each other, exchanging business information between them, is difficult, even for technical people. Today, millions of people use millions of computers all connected by one network, the Web. The challenges can't be understated, and the fact that it works so well is utterly astonishing. We salute the technical people who pulled it together.

XBRL's goal is to allow businesspeople to exchange information in an automated process: Think of this process as an information-supply chain, without involving a technical person. Why no technical person? Well, technical people can do this information exchange stuff with one hand tied behind their back already; they do it every day. But not everyone has technical wizards at their beck and call, and involving a programmer or the IT department makes the process longer and more expensive.

The personal computer and one of its killer applications, the electronic spreadsheet, has been a blessing for business users. But not all IT departments view spreadsheets as a blessing because of the issues they cause (see Chapter 6). But what if business users can get the flexibility they want, and IT departments can also get the control they need in order to keep everything working like a Swiss watch? Properly used, that is what XBRL can provide.

The XBRL taxonomy is the key to achieving this balance of flexibility and control. The key to using XBRL to create a truly effective automated exchange of business information within an information-supply chain is to build an appropriate XBRL taxonomy. XBRL taxonomies are essentially models of the information being communicated, and those models are similar to database schemas. To create a well-articulated XBRL taxonomy information model, business users need to learn about modeling business information. To aid business users in this process, technical people need to understand what business users consider important so that they can build the tools business users need to achieve their goals. Business users shouldn't need to rely on technical experts to create their information models. Self-sufficient business users are the only way to achieve a true automated business-user-to-business-user exchange of business information.

Distinguishing Between Important Aspects of XBRL Taxonomies

XBRL has some sharp edges, and, if you're not careful, you can cut yourself. Understanding certain characteristics of XBRL and of the business system in which you'll use your XBRL taxonomy helps you figure out how to engineer your XBRL taxonomy. Not all business systems that make use of XBRL taxonomies are the same, nor are the XBRL taxonomies themselves. This section helps you make the distinction between these important aspects that influence how your XBRL taxonomy works so that you can create the correct XBRL taxonomy for your system.

An XBRL taxonomy can be more than a dictionary

An XBRL taxonomy is somewhat like a dictionary. This simple analogy is helpful to people during their introduction to XBRL. But actually, a taxonomy can be much more than a dictionary. It can be more like what is called an ontology, or it may fall somewhere in between a dictionary and an ontology. A taxonomy is a body of knowledge for some business domain, so the more information you can provide within an XBRL taxonomy, the more powerful it is, and the more you can do with it.

Most people are familiar with the term dictionary and less familiar with the terms taxonomy and ontology. All these terms are types of classification systems that have different characteristics. The following list helps you understand the important differences between XBRL taxonomies.

- ✔ **Dictionary:** A dictionary is basically a list of words and definitions arranged in alphabetical order so that you can find the word you're looking for. A dictionary doesn't have a hierarchy. It's simply a flat list of words. Some XBRL taxonomies can be just that — lists of concepts from some domain and nothing more.

- ✔ **Classification:** A *classification* is a grouping of something based on some criteria. Grouping things together usually serves some purpose. Think of your music collection. Each song in your music collection is a lot like a dictionary. The ability to group your songs by album, genre, or the number of stars you've assigned is helpful in finding the music you want. Classifications tend to be lists that you can sort, but they tend to not have a hierarchy. You can look at a classification as a somewhat shallow hierarchy.

✔ **Taxonomy:** Taxonomies are classifications that have rich, potentially deep hierarchies. Think of your music collection again. A play list that you create is an example of a simple taxonomy. Your play list can have multiple levels, you can search, sort, and filter within those levels, and the levels are usually related in some way — for example, music you may want to listen to if you're making dinner with your significant other, or the music you might listen to if you're working out. A taxonomy is a rich classification system, but you can also think of it as a simple ontology. A taxonomy's hierarchy tends to be less formal and more implicit than explicit, but it also incorporates the characteristics of a dictionary and a classification system.

✔ **Ontology:** An ontology is a set of well-defined concepts that tends to be more formal and explicit in describing a specific domain. Ontologies are generally defined using class and subclass relations similar to, say, classes and subclasses in object-oriented programming or for, say, members of the animal kingdom. Classes and subclasses have defined properties and relations. An ontology's goal is to provide a formal, referenceable set of concepts that you can use in communications within a domain. So, an ontology is also expressed as a hierarchy, but the hierarchy is more explicit and much richer in meaning than a taxonomy.

XBRL taxonomies fall anywhere in the spectrum described in the previous list. You can find reasons to create dictionaries and reasons to create ontologies. The majority of XBRL taxonomies that you see today are, well, basically like taxonomies as we describe them in this list. They're classification systems, they do have a hierarchy, but the hierarchy generally isn't expressed richly enough for them to be considered an ontology. The concepts in today's XBRL taxonomies do have properties, but they're somewhat limited. This limited use of XBRL's capabilities is due to the rush to get taxonomies created; software limitations; limited experience with XBRL, and therefore limited understanding by many of how to use XBRL's power to express metadata; lack of understanding of the value of such metadata; and other such factors. More of XBRL's capabilities will be utilized in the future.

In the future, many XBRL taxonomies will be much more like ontologies, providing a robust, rich set of useful metadata for business domains that you can leverage in many ways. Not all taxonomies need to be ontologies. Two candidates for significant additional metadata are the US GAAP and IFRS XBRL taxonomies.

The XBRL taxonomy is the entire DTS

You shouldn't look at XBRL taxonomies in isolation but instead consider the entire DTS. There really is no difference between what some people call a "base XBRL taxonomy" and an "extension XBRL taxonomy" (see Chapter 4) In fact, a taxonomy can be both a base and an extension at the same time.

The idea that something is a base or an extension is really relative to something else. For example, consider your parents. Your parents are also someone's children.

Good XBRL taxonomies are modular components, like Legos, which you piece together to maximize comparability, minimize maintenance, and otherwise meet the needs of taxonomy users. All the components of the set that makes up the DTS work together. If the chain of XBRL taxonomies has one weak link, you can end up with a flawed information model.

Not all business systems that make use of XBRL taxonomies will allow extension of the DTS; those making use of XBRL within some system or solution make this business decision. You can't state within a taxonomy, "Hey, it's okay to extend me." The system or solution in which the taxonomy operates determines whether extension is allowed. However, even if a taxonomy works within a system or solution that doesn't allow extension, you can actually extend it. Systems that don't allow extension must communicate the message that extensions aren't allowed in one way or another, usually within the documentation of that specific business system.

XBRL taxonomies categories

For the sake of convenience, when we look into XBRL taxonomies in this chapter, we put them into four categories:

- **Financial-reporting taxonomies:** You use financial-reporting taxonomies for general financial reporting. Public or listed companies generally use these taxonomies to report their financial statements, such as their balance sheet, income statement, and related disclosures. Examples are the US GAAP, IFRS, and EDINET XBRL taxonomies. These taxonomies tend to be general use, but a regulator can also use them. Many different user groups use these taxonomies for many things.

- **Regulatory taxonomies:** Regulatory taxonomies are specific to a regulator. The regulator, those who file with the regulator, and those who make use of information provided by the regulator are the ones who typically use these taxonomies.

- **XBRL Global Ledger taxonomies:** XBRL Global Ledger taxonomies are in a class by themselves. This taxonomy provides a canonical approach to exchanging business information between business systems that deal with accounting type business information. (Chapter 16 discusses this taxonomy.)

- **All other taxonomies:** This category covers all other taxonomies not defined in one of the prior categories.

Systems that use XBRL taxonomies

Business systems exist to meet some business need. Business systems have certain specific characteristics. Understanding these characteristics can help you choose the type of XBRL taxonomy that you'll need for your business system, maximizing the utility that XBRL can provide to that system. Building an XBRL taxonomy inappropriately for a given system is like putting a square peg in a round hole. Matching the XBRL taxonomy characteristics and the business system is critical.

Closed and open systems

One way of looking at a business system is to look at how open or how closed that system is in terms of participation within that system. These definitions help you understand what we mean:

- ✔ **Closed systems:** *Closed systems* have strong boundaries. The participants within the system are usually known and can generally communicate easily and effectively with one another. Most regulators have closed systems; in fact, most systems are closed systems. An example of a closed system is the U.S. FDIC. The FDIC collects a specifically defined information set from a specific and known set of constituents: financial institutions regulated by the FDIC. All filers with the FDIC have their own identifying number, and they know what they have to submit and when. The FDIC and the institutions they regulate share a direct channel of communication.

- ✔ **Open systems:** *Open systems* have boundaries that are more vague than closed systems. Generally, you don't even know exactly who participates within the system. An example of an open system is e-mail. Another example is if all publicly traded or listed companies took it upon themselves to put their XBRL financial information on their Web sites. Investors and financial analysts use financial information directly from the reporting entities' Web sites. You have no clear channel of communication because you can't tell who the system participants are.

Making a closed system work is easier than using an open system because closed systems are easier to control, but you can make both types work. Both need rules to govern how the system operates. For example, rules need to clarify where the physical files are located that contain business information, how you find them, how users are notified of new business information, any constraints on XBRL taxonomy extension, and so on. XBRL doesn't provide all these rules out of the box because XBRL isn't a complete system; it's a tool.

Static and dynamic system information models

System information models are typically either static or dynamic:

- ✔ **Static:** Allows no extension to XBRL taxonomies. Basically, you can think of the information collected as a form. The form may change between periods, but someone submitting information to the system can't modify the information model, extending that model with additional information. A good example is tax forms. Tax forms change annually, but the corporations completing their tax filing for a particular year aren't allowed to change the form they're filing.

- ✔ **Dynamic:** Allows extension to XBRL taxonomies. The information collected is fluid, and those submitting information can change it. A good example is financial reporting as practiced in the United States. Filers to the U.S. SEC can extend the US GAAP taxonomy.

Static systems are easy to make work with XBRL. In fact, in many cases, you may not even need all of XBRLs features for such systems. XBRL can still provide value if the information requires business rules to validate the information or other key features that XBRL provides.

 Dynamic systems are exponentially more challenging to implement than static systems. But dynamic systems are exactly the business use case XBRL was designed to handle. It's your responsibility to constrain the system. If you want system users to be able to extend the XBRL taxonomy only in certain places, you need to define those extension points, communicate that information to system users, and enforce those extension rules within your system. XBRL doesn't do these tasks out of the box.

Simple and complex system transactions

We want to be clear about what we mean by *transaction*. We aren't talking about things like the carefully orchestrated messages passed between, say, two Web service interfaces.

A business information exchange is fundamentally a transaction, a message. Most people don't think of things such as business reports in this way, but in reality, that's really what they are. XBRL taxonomies define the information models of these transactions if XBRL is used within a system. The size and complexity of a business-information-exchange transaction, and therefore the XBRL taxonomy, can vary:

- ✔ **Simple transaction:** A transaction can be simple in that the information set is small and static, meaning that the user submitting information can't change it. For example, consider a simple transaction that has, say, ten data points that are set up, users can't change them, and the same information is collected year after year. This scenario is a simple transaction.

  ✔ **Complex transaction:** Think of a complex transaction as a larger set
    of information, maybe hundreds of data points, that is exchanged. The
    information submitter has the ability to change the information set,
    which may fluctuate from one data collection period to another.

Many times, XBRL is overkill for simple transactions. You may have reasons to
use XBRL, but you may also have good reasons to avoid the potentially heavy
infrastructure load that XBRL brings to bear in order to solve simple business-
information-exchange use cases. One use case where XBRL can help with
simple transactions is when you have a high volume of different sets of simple
transactions, and you need business users to add simple transactions in the
future.

XBRL excels at handling complex transactions, particularly if the systems
are dynamic, allowing for user adjustments to the information model or for
changes to the information model over time.

Further, many types of transactions, either simple or complex, have
information models that need to be communicated with a low or even zero
tolerance for error. XBRL brings a business-rules engine that provides an
ability to express robust meaning far beyond the capabilities of XML to
validate only syntax. If you need a high degree of semantic precision, XBRL
taxonomies can, and should, contain the expression of these business
semantics to rigorously enforce the true nature of the information model,
eliminating all chances of miscommunications, misunderstandings, and
errors.

High or low level of information reuse

You can categorize business information and the systems that manage that
information in terms of the level of information reuse as follows:

  ✔ **Low level of information reuse:** You can use information in only
    one form. This level may be because one information point is highly
    dependent on another information point, and using the information
    separately would make no sense.

  ✔ **High level of information reuse:** Alternatively, you can use information
    in a wide variety of forms and presentation formats.

Many times, the facts contained within an XBRL instance don't depend on
other items for interpreting their meaning. Information that is critical to
interpreting the facts is organized in such a manner that that information is
always available to the fact value. For example, consider the concepts Net
Income or Number of Employees for a particular company, for a particular
period of time, and for a specific scenario, such as actual or budgeted, and
also consider how many times an organization may use those types of
concepts in all the information it communicates.

A properly constructed XBRL taxonomy can make reusing such information child's play, whereas an improperly constructed XBRL taxonomy can inadvertently add the same challenging characteristics, such as the XML content model, that XBRL worked so hard to allow you to remove from your information model's architecture.

Another way to think about information reuse is the term that is commonly used to describe XBRL: interactive data. How an XBRL taxonomy is created can increase or decrease this potential for interactivity. If you need the interactivity, you need to understand how to create your XBRL taxonomy to maximize the possibility of information reuse.

XBRL taxonomies don't understand each other

Just because two different sets of domain knowledge are expressed as XBRL taxonomies doesn't mean that the two XBRL taxonomies will work together or otherwise understand each other. Each XBRL taxonomy is literally a different information model or schema. You can map one XBRL taxonomy to another XBRL taxonomy, and you may definitely have reasons for doing so. But you need to make two different XBRL taxonomies work together; XBRL contains no special magic glue.

Managing Your XBRL Taxonomy

You can implement XBRL using different approaches and techniques (see Chapter 12). Employing the following practical techniques contribute to the creation of a high-quality XBRL taxonomy:

- ✔ Application profile
- ✔ Information model
- ✔ Logical model

The only way to get your software to work correctly is to test it. A *conformance suite* is a set of positive and negative tests that help you prove that everything is working as it needs to. Conformance suites can enforce an application profile, an information model, and a logical model. It automates much of the testing that is impossible to manually perform. A conformance suite attempts to cover the entire spectrum of possibilities; it's disciplined and formal. Individual and unorganized testing may leave gaps that let errors creep into your business systems.

Looking at XBRL Taxonomies

XBRL taxonomies are XML files, and you don't want to read the contents of the taxonomy in that form unless, of course, you're a computer. Even technical people have a hard time understanding the concepts, relations, and resources in a XBRL taxonomy by reading taxonomy schemas and linkbases, relying on the angle brackets to interpret the information the taxonomy expresses. Even with a technical tool that reads XML but doesn't understand XBRL, reading an XBRL taxonomy can be challenging for small taxonomies and impossible for larger taxonomies.

On the other hand, the angle brackets within the technically oriented taxonomy schemas and linkbases express the true meaning of the XBRL taxonomy. That meaning doesn't come through to a reader of, say, a printout of an XBRL taxonomy. So, what is the best approach to understanding the information expressed within an XBRL taxonomy? Good question! The short answer is that there is no one best way for looking at an XBRL taxonomy to understand what it means. There are good ways to achieve specific types of understanding.

The physical taxonomy files

One option to looking at an XBRL taxonomy is to look at the physical files that make up the taxonomy (see Figure 17-1). You can find this listing of the physical files at `http://xbrl.iasb.org/taxonomy/2009-04-01`.

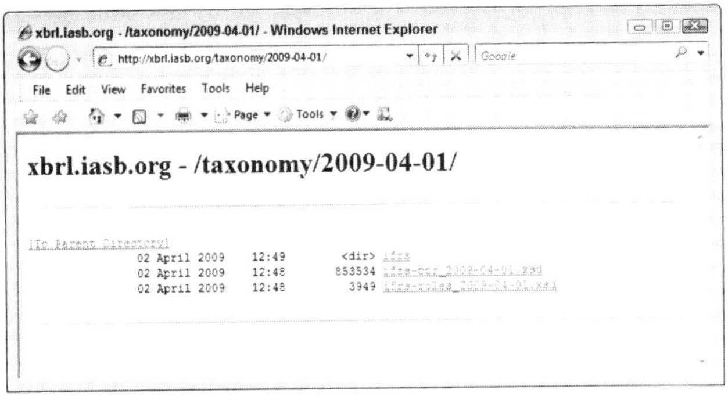

Figure 17-1:
Looking at an XBRL taxonomy's physical files.

Figure 17-1 shows the top-level directory of the IFRS taxonomy set of physical files. You can see the files, open the files, and look at the angle brackets to your heart's desire. But who would want to look at the files? Well, software developers need to in order to understand the taxonomy components from which the user of a software application may select. (For example, the software developers who developed this next way to look at an XBRL taxonomy had to look at the taxonomy's physical files.)

Taxonomy viewer

Take the set of files from Figure 17-1, feed it to a software application that understands XBRL taxonomies, such as an XBRL taxonomy viewer, and you get what you see in Figure 17-2 and at `http://tinyurl.com/8b3kz4`.

Notice what happens when you place the URL into your Web browser address bar. Not only does it load the XBRL taxonomy, but it also takes you to a specific concept in the taxonomy, within a specific type of network, and within a specific network of that type. Literally, you can link one application to another application using a URL.

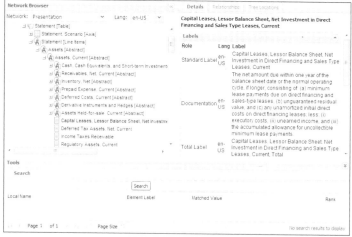

Figure 17-2: Looking at an XBRL taxonomy using a taxonomy viewing application.

The viewer application may not be the official files, but it's a rendering of the official files, which is the next best thing. The value of using an XBRL taxonomy viewer is that the taxonomy is interactive. You can change views and show different types of information, and you can even search and filter taxonomy components, getting the precise view you may desire.

Taxonomy printouts

Another approach to looking at an XBRL taxonomy is to look at a printout of the taxonomy. Figure 17-3 shows a paper-based printout of an XBRL taxonomy. Applications can generate printouts, or you can use several approaches to creating PDF taxonomy printouts. Printouts can be easy to read and useful, and you can generate them in a wide variety of layouts.

Printouts do have a number of downsides. For example, trying to print the entire US GAAP taxonomy yields thousands of pages of paper! In this age of green-friendly thinking, you may not want to kill all those trees. Trying to read all the detailed nuances of the taxonomy can be challenging because many may not appear on the printout simply because they won't fit on the page. Along these same lines, these paper and electronic paper type printouts aren't interactive, and you can't reconfigure the view as you can in software applications. Searching and filtering can also be tough for this reason. All that said, paper and PDF renderings are useful in certain situations.

Figure 17-3: Looking at an XBRL taxonomy by using a printout.

Presentation Report						
ID	Bal	Per	Nil	Type	NS	Label
240	D		I	T Monetary	us-gaap	Assets, Total
241		D		(String)	us-gaap	Liabilities and Stockholders' Equity [Abstract]
242		D		(String)	us-gaap	Liabilities [Abstract]
243		D		(String)	us-gaap	Liabilities, Current [Abstract]
244		D		(String)	us-gaap	Accounts Payable and Accrued Liabilities [Abstract]
245	C		I	T Monetary	us-gaap	Accounts Payable
246	C		I	T Monetary	us-gaap	Accrued Liabilities
247	C		I	T Monetary	us-gaap	Employee-related Liabilities
248		D		(String)	us-gaap	Taxes Payable [Abstract]
249	C		I	T Monetary	us-gaap	Accrued Income Taxes Payable
250	C		I	T Monetary	us-gaap	Sales and Excise Tax Payable
251	C		I	T Monetary	us-gaap	Accrual for Taxes Other than Income Taxes
252	C		I	T Monetary	us-gaap	Taxes Payable, Total
253	C		I	T Monetary	us-gaap	Interest and Dividends Payable
254	C		I	T Monetary	us-gaap	Accounts Payable and Accrued Liabilities, Total
255		D		(String)	us-gaap	Debt, Current [Abstract]
256		D		(String)	us-gaap	Short-term Borrowings [Abstract]
257	C		I	T Monetary	us-gaap	Bank Overdrafts
258	C		I	T Monetary	us-gaap	Commercial Paper, Current
259	C		I	T Monetary	us-gaap	Bridge Loan
260	C		I	T Monetary	us-gaap	Construction Loan

Alternative rendering formats

A popular format that is somewhere between a software application and paper is taking a look at XBRL taxonomy information within a Microsoft Excel spreadsheet. Figure 17-4 shows an example of such a rendering of an XBRL taxonomy.

Everyone knows how popular spreadsheets like Excel are for pretty much everything. Figure 17-4 shows some of what you can do to customize an XBRL taxonomy printout using Excel macros. Also, you can use the spreadsheet application's searching and filtering features to get exactly the view of the XBRL taxonomy that you desire. Basically, the only limits you have are your abilities to program and to come up with creative ways to make the information more readable for your specific needs. Using macros to satisfy your specific needs is possible because computer applications can read the XBRL and pretty much do whatever you want, unconstrained by some specific fixed format.

Taking this approach to reading an XBRL taxonomy has one fairly big downside: the possibility of mistakes. You have to carefully read the XBRL and put all the pieces together correctly. Using an XBRL processor makes this task much easier.

Figure 17-4:
Looking at
an XBRL
taxonomy
information
within a
Microsoft
Excel
spreadsheet.

US GAAP Taxonomy, CI Entrypoint, Presentation

	Line	Balance	Period Type	Type (Data Type)	Label	References
	1				Network (104000 - Statement - Statement of Financial Position, Classified)	
	2		Duration	(String)	Statement of Financial Position [Abstract]	
	3		Duration	(Hypercube)	Statement [Table]	SEC Regulation S-X (SX) 210.03 (Presentation)
	4		Duration	(Dimension)	Statement, Scenario [Axis]	AICPA Audit and Accounting Guide (AAG) AAG-BRD 4.6 2006-05-01 (Presentation)
	5		Duration	Domain or Member	Scenario, Unspecified [Domain]	AICPA Audit and Accounting Guide (AAG) AAG-BRD 4.6 2006-05-01 (Presentation)
	6		Duration	(String)	Statement [Line Items]	SEC Regulation S-X (SX) 210.02.29, 30, 31.5 (Presentation); SEC Regulation S-X (SX) 210.04.3 (Presentation)
	7		Duration	(String)	Assets [Abstract]	
	8		Duration	(String)	Assets, Current [Abstract]	
	9		Duration	(String)	Cash, Cash Equivalents, and Short-term Investments [Abstract]	
	10		Duration	(String)	Cash and Cash Equivalents, at Carrying Value [Abstract]	
	11	Debit	Instant	Monetary	Cash	FASB Statement of Financial Accounting Standard (FAS) 95.7.fn1 (Presentation); SEC Regulation S-X (SX) 210.02.1.5 (Presentation)
	12	Debit	Instant	Monetary	Cash Equivalents, at Carrying Value	FASB Statement of Financial Accounting Standard (FAS) 95.8, 9 (Presentation); SEC Regulation S-X (SX) 210.02.1.5 (Presentation)
	13	Debit	Instant	Monetary	Cash and Cash Equivalents, at Carrying Value, Total	FASB Statement of Financial Accounting Standard (FAS) 95.7, 26 (Presentation); FASB Statement of Financial Accounting Standard (FAS) 95.7.fn1 (Presentation); FASB Statement of Financial Accounting Standard (FAS) 95.8, 9 (Presentation); SEC Regulation S-X (SX) 210.02.1.5 (Presentation)

Other useful alternative options for formatting include generating ways
to read taxonomies using WPF/XAML (Microsoft's Windows Presentation
Foundation) or Adobe's FLEX.

Make friends with a programmer if you have a good idea of how you want to
see your XBRL taxonomy. Many of these types of alternative renderings are
surprisingly easy to create with only a little programming knowledge.

Taxonomy official documentation

The physical taxonomy files don't contain enough information to help you
completely understand all that you need to know in order to use an XBRL
taxonomy. Information that an XBRL taxonomy can't express is generally
contained in documentation provided with the taxonomy. Official documentation
and other guidance are provided for most taxonomies (see Figure 17-5). This
official documentation can be helpful in getting started with an XBRL taxonomy.
On the other hand, this type of guidance can also be about as useful as most
software application's user manuals.

As an example of official documentation, you can find the official guidance for
the US GAAP XBRL taxonomy at http://xbrl.us/taxonomies/Pages/
US-GAAP2009.aspx in Figure 17-5. All sorts of things, in terms of both technical
and user documentation, are available at this site.

Taxonomy user guidance

These days, many XBRL taxonomies create guidance for how to actually use
a taxonomy. The US GAAP taxonomy created what it calls a preparer's guide
(http://xbrl.us/Documents/PreparersGuide.pdf).

Figure 17-5:
The official
Web page
of the US
GAAP
taxonomy.

The IFRS XBRL taxonomy's official documentation (`www.iasb.org/XBRL/ IFRS+Taxonomy/Support+materials.htm`) is a good example of the extent some taxonomies are going to. The IFRS is literally providing a book.

For SEC filers, the EDGAR filer manual has user guidance at `http://xbrl. us/Documents/PreparersGuide.pdf`. See Chapter 6 of that EDGAR filer manual for XBRL guidance provided by the SEC.

Third-party taxonomy guidance

Third parties provide guidance for XBRL taxonomies in many forms. Search the Web by using phrases such as "XBRL taxonomy best practices," "modeling business information using XBRL," and "engineering XBRL taxonomies."

What to Look for in an XBRL Taxonomy

The previous section covers the approaches to looking at an XBRL taxonomy. But what exactly are you looking for? What you're looking for is typically determined by what you want to do with the taxonomy. Some people may want to create an XBRL instance. Others may want to understand an XBRL instance created by someone else. Others may need to create an extension taxonomy or provide additional metadata of some kind. Those are just a few of the reasons. All use cases for understanding a taxonomy are typically covered within the use case of creating an XBRL instance.

We take that perspective and explain the key things you should be looking for. We use the US GAAP taxonomy to provide examples:

- ✔ **Find the right piece(s) to build your DTS when you have alternatives.**
When you have alternatives or options, you need to find the correct pieces of the XBRL taxonomy to use. Many taxonomies cover all alternatives, providing options for each. You'd never use all the alternative options provided by the XBRL taxonomy. You do need to find the alternative applicable or preferred by you. Each alternative adds to the volume of the taxonomy that you have to deal with. You typically won't use all possible alternatives, but you might like to know what alternatives exist. For example, the US GAAP taxonomy provides information relating to the different industries that might report using that taxonomy. About five main industries exist within the taxonomy; you'll typically use only one. Even within one industry, you have options. For example, a company creating a financial statement would create a cash flow statement using either the direct or indirect method, never both at the same time. So, to piece taxonomy together, you need to grab the correct components and the correct alternatives. You need to glean this information about taxonomy components and alternatives from taxonomy documentation and from the taxonomy itself.

- ✔ **Find the appropriate concepts.** Many taxonomies have thousands of concepts — for example, the US GAAP taxonomy has about 15,000 concepts. You need to sort, search, filter, and use other means to locate the exact concept you want to work with. Finding the right concept isn't just reading a label, and, in fact, you may not know exactly what the label may be. Information in the taxonomy documentation and references for each concept helps you find concepts and understand whether you have the correct concept or whether some other concept is more appropriate. Looking at concepts relative to other concepts is helpful in finding the ones you're looking for.

  One good place to find the appropriate concepts is in the presentation relations. Another good area is the calculation relations, if you know you have some computation that a concept may participate in. Looking at the business rules of the taxonomy is yet another way to be sure that you have the correct concept in the taxonomy. Also look at the concept's attributes, such as its data type, balance, or period type.

- ✔ **Find the appropriate networks.** Concepts exist within networks. For example, Inventory Policy is most likely within the Accounting Policies network within the network of presentation relations. Other cases, such as the following situations, aren't so simple or straightforward:

  - Alternative presentation and calculation relations that are consistent with one another, such as the alternative income statements provided by the US GAAP taxonomy, can exist.

  - Alternative presentation and calculation relations that aren't consistent due to the need or choice to express these relations in separate networks can exist, as is the case in many disclosures within the US GAAP taxonomy. This inconsistency can occur because of how XBRL works or how a taxonomy creator decided to model their taxonomy.

You may need to explore to find what you're looking for. Business users of a taxonomy shouldn't find this search difficult because they generally have a thorough understanding of the data they're working with. Making your way around a taxonomy to find it is another story. Be persistent and use the features available within a taxonomy-viewer application.

✔ **Find the appropriate relations and resources.** Just because you found a concept doesn't necessarily mean that you've found *all* the relations in which that concept participates that you may be interested in. However, finding the right concept is generally the first step to finding the relations. But it works the other way around, too. Relations can help you find concepts. If you know the general area within a taxonomy where something may exist, look for a concept that can also exist in that relation. Using this approach can help you find the concept you're looking for, even if you're unclear what that concept is called. However, if you've located the concept, you can generally find relations or resources information easily if you're using taxonomy viewer software.

✔ **Determining whether something you need is missing.** You may not find what you're looking for for two reasons. It does exist, but you just can't find it, or it doesn't exist in the taxonomy at all. One of the gravest errors that you can make when using a taxonomy that allows extensions is to recreate an existing concept. This mistake causes all sorts of problems when you create your XBRL instance and for those analyzing that XBRL instance. You need to perform an exhaustive search of the XBRL taxonomy for something before you stop looking. Be patient, be persistent, and use good software applications to help you in your search.

XBRL Taxonomy Samples and Examples

A good place to start when working with XBRL taxonomies isn't the complex gargantuan XBRL taxonomies that you may have to use because some evil regulator mandated that you use it. Instead, start small and then, as your understanding grows, you'll gain insight on how to understand these significantly larger and more complex XBRL taxonomies.

When you explore taxonomies, you must explore XBRL instances at the same time. The whole point of creating a taxonomy is to properly express the information you need to express. How can you possibly know whether you built your taxonomy correctly if you're not looking at the resulting XBRL instance that's created by a user of your XBRL taxonomy? You need to look at XBRL taxonomies and XBRL instances together as you learn about the information models that exist in the taxonomies.

The following good samples and examples may help you understand XBRL taxonomies and the related XBRL instances. You can apply this knowledge to understanding larger taxonomies that you'll likely be working with:

- ✔ **USFRTF Patterns Guide:** Prior to the creation of the US GAAP taxonomy, the team creating that taxonomy put together a number of small XBRL taxonomies and XBRL instances to help identify what might exist within the US GAAP taxonomy and how these pieces might be modeled. You can see the XBRL taxonomies and XBRL instances at `www.xbrl.org/us/USFRTF/USFRTF-PatternsFiles-PWD-2007-04-17.zip`, along with an explanatory document at `www.xbrl.org/us/USFRTF/USFRTF-PatternsGuide-PWD-2007-04-17.doc`.

- ✔ **XBRLS Business Use Cases:** This set of small XBRL taxonomies and XBRL instances focuses on specific business use cases and uses a documented application profile, information modeling layer, logical model, and automated tests to construct the XBRL taxonomies. See the examples at `http://xbrl.squarespace.com/storage/xbrls/XBRLS-BusinessUseCases-2008-04-18.zip` and the documentation at `http://xbrl.squarespace.com/storage/xbrls/XBRLS-BusinessUseCases-2008-04-25.pdf`.

- ✔ **XBRLS comprehensive example:** The two previous examples are great, but if you look at them in isolation, you can miss many of the nuances of a larger XBRL taxonomy. The different pieces of the taxonomy must work together correctly. The comprehensive example basically takes each one of the XBRLS business use case examples and puts them together into one XBRL taxonomy. It then provides one XBRL instance that shows everything working together. Go to `www.xbrlsite.com/examples/comprehensiveexample/2008-04-18` to see this example and related documentation.

To avoid having to type these long links, go to www.dummies.com/go/xbrl. This takes you to a landing page where you can click the link you need.

Exploring Real Production Financial Reporting Taxonomies

We want to explain a little about the details of a few XBRL taxonomies to give you a sense what these look like and what they do. We chose the category of financial-reporting taxonomies because they're generally well-constructed XBRL taxonomies, business people generally understand financial reporting, and because financial-reporting XBRL taxonomies are publically available. We provide brief overviews of the US GAAP, IFRS, and EDINET taxonomies.

The US GAAP XBRL taxonomy

The US GAAP taxonomy expresses financial-reporting concepts that public companies use to create financial reports typically filed with the U.S. SEC and shareholders. The financial information filed with the SEC has gone into the EDGAR system in the past; XBRL filings will go into the SEC's new Next-Generation EDGAR system (see Chapter 13).

However, because US GAAP relates to all companies in the United States, you can use the taxonomy for any type of financial reporting under US GAAP (for example, private companies can provide financial information to financial institutions that give them commercial loans). The taxonomy covers FASB financial-reporting standards, the U.S. SEC, industry-specific reporting practices, common practices, and other reporting practices that are collectively referred to as US GAAP.

The on-ramp for the US GAAP taxonomy is this Web page on the XBRL US Web site: `http://xbrl.us/taxonomies/Pages/US-GAAP2009.aspx`. On this page, you can find links to other information that helps to describe the XBRL taxonomy and how to use it. You can find the actual XBRL taxonomy files at `http://taxonomies.xbrl.us/us-gaap/2009/index.html`.

A better way of looking at the UGT is to use a taxonomy-viewer application, which you can find at `http://viewer.xbrl.us/yeti/resources/yeti-gwt/Yeti.jsp`. When you load this URL into the address bar of your browser, you see the Open Taxonomy dialog box, shown in Figure 17-6.

Figure 17-6:
Looking
at the US
GAAP
taxonomy.

The US GAAP taxonomy is organized to be modular; it has about 500 different files. However, you'd never use all these pieces. The UGT is broken down into the following industries or activities that drive how companies report or tend to report:

✔ Commercial and Industrial Companies (CI)

✔ Banking and Savings Institutions (BASI)

✔ Brokers and Dealers in Securities (BD)

✔ Insurance (INS)

✔ Real Estate (RE)

Each industry or activity is organized in the form of an *entry point*. An entry point is the set of taxonomy pieces that you'd use if you were, say, preparing a report for a specific company in a specific industry or activity. For example, an airline wouldn't need the insurance or real-estate entry point; it would need only the commercial and industrial companies' entry point, because this entry point will lead to the set of concepts and relations that are directly relevant to airlines.

There's a lot to know about the taxonomy and how to use it. Here are helpful pieces of information and tips for starting your journey of understanding the US GAAP taxonomy:

✔ Five entry points pull together information by the financial-reporting industry. Probably 90 percent of you will make use of the CI entry point of the US GAAP taxonomy. If you're in one of the other specialized industries, you'd use one of those entry points.

✔ The spot that holds the most information about the taxonomy is this Web URL hosted by XBRL US: `http://xbrl.us/taxonomies/Pages/US-GAAP2009.aspx`.

✔ The easiest and best publically available view of the taxonomy that we're aware of is at `http://viewer.xbrl.us/yeti/resources/yeti-gwt/Yeti.jsp`.

✔ XBRL US offers classes to help those preparing financial statements to use the taxonomy. For information about these classes, contact XBRL US (`http://xbrl.us/Pages/feedback.aspx`).

✔ The taxonomy expresses approximately 15,000 concepts and 20,000 relations and has a total of about 140 networks.

✔ Each industry entry point has between 50 and 75 presentation networks that organize the concepts into logical groupings. These networks fall into two categories: statements and disclosures.

✔ The taxonomy doesn't express all computations, so be careful. You may need to add computations using XBRL Formula in order to ensure the integrity of your information.

✔ XBRL US publishes a preparer's guide that helps explain how to use the taxonomy: `http://xbrl.us/Documents/PreparersGuide.pdf`.

✔ The EDGAR Filer Manual has information about how to submit XBRL information to the SEC at http://sec.gov/info/edgar/edgarfm-vol2-v11.pdf.

The IFRS XBRL taxonomy

IFRS is being adopted around the globe for financial reporting. As you might expect, IFRS has an XBRL taxonomy. The International Accounting Standards Committee Foundation (IASCF) is in charge of XBRL activities relating to IFRS, including creating and maintaining the IFRS XBRL taxonomy. Unlike US GAAP, IFRS doesn't cover specific industry disclosures. Because the IFRSs don't cover specific industry common practice disclosures, the IFRS taxonomy likewise doesn't cover these industry common practices. Hence, you can regard the IFRS taxonomy as a general-purpose reporting taxonomy with concepts representing disclosure requirements specifically addressed within IFRS.

Here's a summary of the IFRS XBRL taxonomy's most helpful pieces:

✔ The primary location of information about the taxonomy is www.iasb.org/XBRL/IFRS+Taxonomy/IFRS+Taxonomy+2009.htm.

✔ The best human-readable version of the taxonomy that we can find is at www.abra-search.com/ABRASearch.html?locale=en&taxonomy=ifrs_2009-04-01.

✔ The actual physical taxonomy files are available at http://xbrl.iasb.org/taxonomy/2009-04-01.

✔ A human-readable version of the taxonomy is at www.iasb.org/XBRL/IFRS+Taxonomy/IFRS+Taxonomy+2009.htm.

✔ The taxonomy expresses approximately 2,700 concepts, about 4,000 relations, and approximately 110 presentation networks.

✔ The taxonomy really has only one entry point. These networks have three categories: statements, notes, and dimensional information.

✔ The IFRS taxonomy is available in multiple languages (about 11 languages, meaning 11 XBRL label resources). See www.iasb.org/Translations/Available+translations.htm.

✔ The IFRS Taxonomy Module Manager at www.xbrl-ifrs.org/ITMM helps you build user specific entry points into the IFRS taxonomy.

✔ An IFRS XBRL taxonomy user guide is available at www.iasb.org/XBRL/IFRS+Taxonomy/Support+materials.htm.

The EDINET XBRL taxonomy

The Japan Financial Services Agency (JFSA) created and maintains the
EDINET taxonomy that expresses financial reporting concepts under
Japanese GAAP. Japanese public companies typically use the taxonomy
to create financial reports that are filed with the JFSA and made publically
available within their EDINET system, which is similar to the SEC EDGAR and
Next-Generation EDGAR systems. Also, the companies use the taxonomy to
create financial reports that are filed with the Tokyo Stock Exchange and
the National Tax Agency of Japan. The latest version of the taxonomy is the
EDINET Taxonomy 2009.

Here are the EDINET XBRL taxonomy's most helpful pieces of information:

- You can find the taxonomy in both Japanese and English at `www.fsa.go.jp/search/20090309/editaxonomy20090309.zip`.

- The summary information of the taxonomy is available at `www.fsa.go.jp/search/20090309/tsummary_en20090309.zip`.

- A human-readable version of the taxonomy appears at `www.fsa.go.jp/search/20090309/alist20090309.xls`.

- The taxonomy expresses approximately 4,800 concepts.

- The taxonomy, in its current form, covers only the primary financial
  statements, but notes of financial statements and other information will
  be covered in the near future.

- The taxonomy is broken down into the 24 industries or activities that
  have regulatory industry-specific accounting rules or reporting forms.

- Although the EDINET Web site (`http://info.edinet-fsa.go.jp`) is
  in Japanese, you can click the XBRL link at the bottom of the page to go
  to `https://info.edinet-fsa.go.jp/E01EW/BLMainController.jsp`, where you can find recently-issued XBRL data for more than 5,000
  public companies and 3,000 investment funds.

International Taxonomy Architecture Effort (ITA)

The financial-reporting community is leading the way with what it's trying to
achieve with XBRL. The three major XBRL taxonomies that exist are the
US GAAP, the IFRS, and the EDINET XBRL taxonomies. However, all three
taxonomies were developed independently. As such, the architectures of the
XBRL taxonomies are different.

In the early days of XBRL, some forward thinkers in the XBRL community were pushing for one XBRL taxonomy for financial reporting that everyone around the world would use. Theoretically, this unified taxonomy made a lot of sense. From a practical perspective, it didn't. At that point, not many countries had adopted IFRS. Furthermore, no one really agreed on how to create an XBRL taxonomy. Those issues, combined with many other reasons, means that today we have basically three XBRL taxonomies for financial reporting. These three different XBRL taxonomies with three different architectures exists in part because all three of these sets of financial reporting standards exist and are in use today.

Much learning about how to best build XBRL taxonomies has taken place since those early days of XBRL. The International Taxonomy Architecture (ITA) is a joint effort to create a common architecture for financial reporting XBRL taxonomies. Members include the U.S. SEC (US GAAP taxonomy), IASCF (IFRS taxonomy), JFSA (EDINET taxonomy), and the European Commission. The IASCF began this process in October 2007. You can find the ITA comparison (Comparison Framework for EDINET, IFRS, and US GAAP XBRL Taxonomies) at www.xbrl.org/TCF-PWD-2009-03-31.html.

Theoretically, the possibility exists for the creation of one set of financial reporting standards that would be used globally (IFRS) and one means of expressing that information in an electronic format (XBRL), which could result in an unprecedented ability to compare financial information from around the world. Whether the financial-reporting community has the resolve to pull off this feat is yet to be seen, but it's trying.

Even if the goal of one XBRL taxonomy that all companies would use for financial reporting never happens, you can discover things from this project:

- Different XBRL users can implement XBRL in different ways. That's why this group even has to go through the process of creating the ITA. The current three different architectures won't necessarily work together. For XBRL taxonomies to work together, they have to be made to do so — just being in XBRL is not enough.

- Even if the financial-reporting supply chain can't agree on one set of financial-reporting standards to use globally and even if there isn't a complete agreement of an XBRL architecture, the ability to create comparable financial information is still a possibility thanks to mapping! Mapping one set of financial information to another is a little more complicated than a simple mapping; you'd actually need to reconcile one set of standards to another, somewhat like you can reconcile your book numbers to your tax numbers. But it's possible. Book and tax numbers are reconciled all the time. XBRL does make this goal much easier.

- Finally, this group is spending a lot of time and effort trying to agree on a good architecture for financial reporting. Understanding what that architecture is can provide clues as to what architecture you may want to use when working with XBRL.

Looking at Other XBRL Taxonomies

The best way to understand XBRL taxonomies is to look at lots of them. Figure 17-7 shows an XBRL taxonomy viewer (see www.abra-search.com/ ABRASearch.html?locale=en&taxonomy=p_all) that lets you look at many different XBRL taxonomies all in one spot. The XBRL taxonomy viewer shown in Figure 17-7 has about 100 different XBRL taxonomies you can explore to get ideas on how to build XBRL taxonomies, should you need to do so.

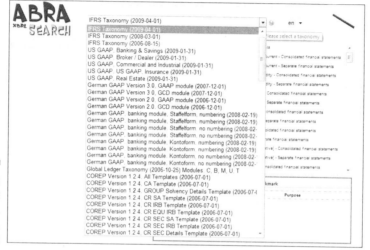

Figure 17-7:
Looking at other XBRL taxonomies.

Identifying a Good XBRL Taxonomy

An XBRL taxonomy is a data model. Like any other data model, there are good data models and not-so-good data models. We want to summarize the characteristics of what generally makes an XBRL taxonomy work well. These days, the best results are generally arrived at by having good balanced collaboration between the domain experts and the technical experts responsible for creating the XBRL taxonomy. Many of these characteristics are applicable to all taxonomies; other characteristics are dependent upon the characteristics of the business systems in which the XBRL taxonomy will be used. Here are some of the characteristics of a good taxonomy:

✔ **It models data.** A good data model, well, models data. Many creators of XBRL taxonomies focus too much on how concepts and relations look in the taxonomy (the presentation) rather than how well they work. Both are important. Further, the best way to be sure that your taxonomy works is not to look at its presentation, but instead to test the data model within an XBRL instances to be sure that they can be correctly created.

✔ **It's modular.** Don't force users to use what they don't need. Make it easy for them to use what they need but not what they don't need or don't want. One part of achieving this goal is to make the taxonomy modular. Create lots of modules so that taxonomy users can easily ignore what they don't need.

✔ **It has lots of small networks.** In the spirit of modularity, another thing that helps users take what they need and ditch the rest is to create many small networks rather than a few large networks. Basically, this approach is about making the networks modular so that users can grab what they need and ignore what they don't. Many times, modularity involves physically separating networks using separate files; other times, it means that the same physical file can contain multiple but separate networks. The specific situation dictates the appropriate approach.

Lots of small pieces are better than a few big pieces because having the computer put pieces together is easier than requiring the computer to take things apart. If you use small networks, you can use the network to identify the piece you want to work with — that information (the network itself) exists within the XBRL taxonomy. But if you want to take one large network and break it into individual pieces, there is no place within the taxonomy to break up that one large network of relations. Maintenance can also be much easier on a small network. This strategy to use lots of small pieces is similar to why computer programs are typically made up of many smaller and reusable subroutines instead of one big program.

✔ **It contains no duplication.** Good data models express things once. If the same thing is expressed more than once, the two pieces need to be kept synchronized, which can be a hassle. Think, small, modular pieces.

✔ **It's consistent.** An XBRL taxonomy's structures should be consistent unless you have a specific reason. Usually, inconsistent modeling happens because you're unaware of the inconsistency of your approach. If you're not thinking about consistency, you can pretty much guarantee that you're being inconsistent. An information-modeling layer can help you create a consistent XBRL taxonomy.

✔ **It uses consistent style.** Just like style guides exist for writing manuscripts or essays, taxonomies should use some sort of style guide to keep, for example, labels consistently styled in regard to spelling, abbreviations, capitalization, and so on. A *style guide* is simply something that helps achieve this goal. One specific example of what a style guide can do is to help you spell words consistently ("Long Term" or "Long-Term" or "Long-term" or "Long term," and so on). A good example is the US GAAP taxonomy style guide at www.xbrl.org/us/usfrtf/XBRL-StyleGuide-RECOMMENDATION-2007-03-08.doc. This style guide can give you a good understanding of what a style guide is and why it's important.

✔ **It follows best practices.** Things like the FRTA have lots of good practices that help create a high-quality XBRL taxonomy. FRTA is definitely a best practice for financial-reporting type taxonomies, but it's even useful for nonfinancial-reporting taxonomies.

✔ **It includes documentation of the taxonomy.** It's impossible to explain all that is needed about how to use an XBRL taxonomy within the XBRL taxonomy itself. Enter good documentation. Further, writing the document forces you to put yourself in the users' shoes and view the taxonomy from their perspective. Providing sample XBRL instances should be part of your taxonomy documentation.

✔ **It has clearly articulated extension guidelines.** Extensions, if allowed, shouldn't be able to break the taxonomies that they're extending. The first rule of extensions is that they need to follow all the other rules on this list. An extension is just another taxonomy within the DTS. One of the tricky things about extensions is to decide when to create an entirely new network of relations and when to augment an existing network of relations for the changes you need to make. Properly balancing reuse and creation is both an art and a science that takes experience to get the right end result. Further, taxonomy documentation should provide explicit guidance as to how to use extensibility. Finally, sample XBRL instances provided with the XBRL taxonomy should include specific samples of how to use extensibility.

✔ **It expresses all computations.** When you define concepts within your taxonomy, be sure to define all the computation-type relations that exist for those concepts. You can express many computations using XBRL calculations, but you can't express many other types, so use XBRL Formula to provide business rules. Either way, articulate all computations within the taxonomy because not doing so simply invites computation errors.

✔ **It includes a maintenance plan.** If the a taxonomy doesn't have a maintenance plan, rest assured that its maintenance hasn't been planned for. When you create a taxonomy, you're responsible for maintaining that taxonomy, and you need a plan for maintaining it. The time to create that plan isn't when you need to start maintaining it, but rather when you first create the taxonomy. You'll make decisions differently after you think through the maintenance process. Part of the maintenance plan should be a versioning plan that includes how you'll communicate taxonomy changes to its users.

✔ **It's been proven to work correctly.** Be sure that your taxonomy works as expected by proving to yourself that it works correctly. Test, test, and then test some more. The larger and more diverse the taxonomy users are, the more important thorough testing is, and the bigger the downside of an unforeseen bug existing within your production taxonomy. Not proving to yourself that the taxonomy works is a recipe for problems. If you can't prove that it works, you haven't done enough testing. (Chapter 12 has information on testing taxonomies.)

✔ **It's elegant.** A good taxonomy looks elegant. If the taxonomy doesn't look elegant, look deeper. There are usually reasons why. Start with this list to help you figure out why you don't see what you expect to see.

Chapter 18

Understanding the XBRL Instance

*I*n this chapter, we drill into additional important details of the XBRL instance. We also look at important big-picture considerations, consolidating your knowledge of XBRL instances. We explain the relationship between an XBRL instance and its XBRL taxonomies. We walk you through a thought experiment, which helps you see how XBRL instances work. We examine various approaches to looking at the business information contained within an XBRL instance. We point you to sample and example XBRL instances and their related XBRL taxonomies, which you can use to expand your understanding of them. We also point you to real production XBRL instances. We end this chapter by highlighting the characteristics of a good XBRL instance.

To avoid having to type the long links in this chapter, go to www.dummies.com/go/xbrl. This takes you to a landing page where you can click the link you need.

Consolidating Your Knowledge of the XBRL Instance

XBRL taxonomies express a body of knowledge of a business domain in a standardized electronic format (see Chapter 17). Those XBRL taxonomies contain the insights, rules, conventions, and other insights and understandings of professionals that have expertise within a particular domain. These collections of professional expertise become the basis for expressing information within an XBRL instance, which you can think of as a new type of business report. XBRL instances are, however, really about the broader category of business information exchange, of which the business report is a part.

Although looking at XBRL instances as business reports helps turn something that is abstract and challenging to understand into something tangible and easier to understand, don't let the term *business report* limit your perception of what XBRL instances are and do. After all, XBRL is about exchanging all sorts of business information, not just reports.

These new business reports are intended to provide characteristics that improve upon their legacy paper versions and the electronic versions, which are little more than digital paper. (Electronic spreadsheets have their good points but also disadvantages.)

One key characteristic of an XBRL instance is an ability to automate some business process. If a business process is automated — and not all business processes should be automated — then the conclusions reached by such an automated process should be no different than the conclusions reached by the previous manual process.

Another key characteristic of an XBRL instance is flexibility, often times called *interactivity.* XBRL separates the information from the presentation of the information allowing for increased flexibility when it comes to presenting business information.

You can think of an XBRL instance in many ways. Here's a summary of the important things that an XBRL instance is:

- **Standard structured publishing format:** An XBRL instance is a standard physical format for publishing business information. Some people like to think of it as a standard database of sorts because you can query the XBRL instance and extract information you need from it. Another way to look at it is as a standard publishing medium. The key word, though, is *standard,* which is the magic in the XBRL sauce.

- **Standard transfer protocol:** You have to be able to physically get the information from the person who creates it to the person or persons who will be consuming the information. XBRL instances also perform this role. A *transfer protocol* is a physical means, a medium, for getting information from one point to another.

- **Enabler for standard query approach:** Because the published format of XBRL instances is a standard, you can create a standard query approach and query across multiple XBRL instances. A standard query approach is critical because many consumers of XBRL instance information want to compare information from multiple XBRL instances.

- **Independently usable facts:** An XBRL instance is also a bag of facts. Applications can effectively grab the values of facts within an XBRL instance and use those fact values. Users can use one fact, or they can use multiple facts because the facts exist in a form that enables one fact to be used independently without regard to other facts within the XBRL instance. Sometimes, certain information makes no sense unless it's used with other information, but where you can use information independently, XBRL provides the mechanism for doing so.

An often overlooked fact is that you can combine XBRL instances and use them together — for example, when comparing information, such as a five-year time series. Or, you may want to combine information for one period for several companies in a specific industry to do a comparison.

Distinguishing the Important Aspects of an XBRL Instance

XBRL taxonomies have a significant impact on how XBRL instances are created; after all, they do define the information model that an XBRL instance uses. But an XBRL instance also defines certain information. We make you aware of this flexibility in this section. We also look at several approaches to creating XBRL instances, as well as the categories of XBRL instances.

We then do something that helps you appreciate the subtleties of XBRL instances. We use one of Albert Einstein's tools, a thought experiment, to help you understand a few important things about XBRL instances.

The relationship between the XBRL instance and the XBRL taxonomy

A question that people often ask when working with XBRL is, "What goes in the XBRL taxonomy, and what goes in the XBRL instance?" Although most of the time the answer to this question is clear, in some cases, it's not quite so obvious. You have flexibility in determining the architecture of your XBRL taxonomy. Certain approaches to architecting your XBRL taxonomy can provide necessary functionality within your XBRL instance. However, that same approach can cause more problems than it solves if not architected correctly, or if the architecture is good but the required functionality was misinterpreted. We want you to be aware of this flexibility — it can help you, or it can cause you problems.

We can't go into every detail of the question of where you should define what amounts to metadata, but we do want to provide you with a taste of what we're talking about by providing examples:

✔ **Concepts:** An XBRL taxonomy is typically the best place to define concepts. The creators of XBRL instances define concepts once in an XBRL taxonomy and then use them many times within their XBRL instances. For example, Sales may be a concept you define within an XBRL taxonomy. Comparability is maximized if a concept is defined within an XBRL taxonomy. However, there are approaches to defining concepts within an XBRL instance. This makes it so that you can add concepts without creating a taxonomy extension. However, a ramification of this approach is usually reduced comparability.

✔ **Periods:** An XBRL instance is normally the best place to express period information. For example, consider the concept Sales. You can create the concept `Sales2009` and `Sales2010` in an XBRL taxonomy. But in subsequent years, you'd have to add concepts for future sales amounts, such as `Sales2011`. Design of the XBRL instance allows for period information within a context to be associated with fact values. However, you can define period-specific concepts within an XBRL taxonomy.

Building a usable, maintainable, well-designed XBRL instance and XBRL taxonomy takes some thought and understanding of data modeling; it's not something that you should do haphazardly. These rules always have exceptions. Good judgment, knowledge of data modeling, understanding how the components of XBRL work, and thorough testing can help you get to your desired result. You can only know the impact of all these decisions by seeing how XBRL instances created against your XBRL taxonomy actually function as a combined unit.

An XBRL taxonomy drives the XBRL instance. You never should look at an XBRL taxonomy and an XBRL instance separately. They're an inseparable pair, each impacting the other. (Chapters 4 and 17 tell you a great deal about how to build an XBRL taxonomy.)

For example, the relations networks defined within an XBRL taxonomy serve somewhat as a filtering mechanism for pulling specific facts from an XBRL instance. You can have different types of filters: presentation, calculation, definition, or others you might create. Those creating XBRL instances can create and provide these networks that serve as filters, but those consuming the information in the XBRL instance can also create their own networks to serve as filters in the form of an XBRL taxonomy. Each relations network provides one view into the bag of fact values that an XBRL instance makes available, allowing you to focus on those specific facts. For example, a balance sheet presentation network allows for the identification of all facts that exist in that balance sheet. Working in conjunction with other information, such as the period portion of a context, you can render the XBRL instance information using the network filter and the period context information.

If you don't like the XBRL taxonomies you get from an XBRL instance creator, create your own! Generally, people think that the creator of an XBRL instance creates or provides the only XBRL taxonomy that can be used with an XBRL instance. This isn't the case. XBRL instance users can provide their own metadata for use in organizing an XBRL instances. For example, if you don't like the organization of a certain network or if you don't like the labels the creator of the XBRL instance provided, no problem. Create your own, add it to the DTS, and enjoy the interactivity of XBRL!

Approaches to creating XBRL instances

You can take many different approaches when creating an XBRL instance. We distill these approaches down to three general approaches:

- ✔ **Generate from some system:** Under this approach, you export information from within an existing business system to XBRL in some manner. Usually, you use a mapping to help convert information from the existing system to the desired XBRL instance. Many times, these systems store their data within a relational database.

- ✔ **Map to existing document:** Under this approach, you map information from an existing document (such as a spreadsheet or word-processing document) to XBRL and then use the document and mapping to generate an XBRL instance. An example is mapping the financial information from an existing word-processing document to generate an XBRL instance. (In Chapter 11, we call it the bolt-on approach.)

- ✔ **Enter information into XBRL instance-creation tool:** Under this approach, you enter information directly into an XBRL instance-creation tool, which then generates an XBRL instance. This approach is a lot like filling out a form; it's just that the form output is a standard publishing format, XBRL.

Which approach you use to create an XBRL instance depends on your specific situation. Furthermore, you might use one approach in the short term and a different long-term approach. Software vendors, budgets for modifying existing systems, and other such constraints have an impact on the alternative you use. (Refer to Chapter 11 for additional information.)

Categorizing XBRL instances

As with XBRL taxonomies, for the sake of convenience and to help you get a sense for XBRL instances, we categorize XBRL instances into three groups:

✔ **Financial-reporting instances:** This group includes financial statements created using XBRL. For example, an SEC filing falls into this category.

✔ **XBRL Global Ledger instances:** These types of XBRL instances can provide information that you'd aggregate into financial-reporting-type XBRL instances. Or, you can see these types of XBRL instances as the detailed information you'd drill down into from a more summarized financial-reporting-type XBRL instance. The key point is the connection between the more summarized financial-reporting-type and the more detailed XBRL Global Ledger-type XBRL instances.

✔ **All other instances:** This category basically represents everything else and crosses many different domains. We don't go into this group in detail because it's a bottomless pit, but examples include employee expense reports, tax returns, sales reports, sales commission calculations, many of the spreadsheets you create and exchange with others, CSV listings you create, and business-intelligence reports you use and want to share with others external to your organization. Like we said, it's a bottomless pit of opportunity!

A thought experiment

Albert Einstein was famous for the thought experiments he used to explain complex situations using simple stories. We have a thought experiment for you. The purpose of the thought experiment is to help you better understand how XBRL instances actually work. The first thing the experiment shows you is the important pieces impacting the usability of XBRL instances. The second important aspect the thought experiment shows is that the way business users implement XBRL determines the results received from that XBRL-based information.

The ultimate goal you're trying to achieve with XBRL is to automate some process. You many times reap significant benefits from realizing this goal. We're not saying that all business processes are automatable or that all processes should be automated. What processes to automate and where to include humans is up to those creating business processes. Errors, inconsistencies, ambiguities, and other such factors sometimes keep processes that can and should be automated from being automated, requiring human intervention to execute the process. This is not because you *want* to involve humans; it's because you *have* to involve humans due to errors, inconsistencies, ambiguities, and other factors.

Think of the Web. Imagine that every company in the world created quarterly and annual financial information and put that information in an XBRL instance on its Web site. Forget about whether you *could* get every company to make this information available or even if they *should* make it available.

(It's a thought experiment, so just play along.) Imagine that you wanted to analyze all that information for some purpose — say, to find a good investment. Here are the challenges you'd run into:

✔ **Finding the XBRL instances:** You need to find those XBRL instances. How do you do that? You have two possibilities:

- *Push* means that in some way, perhaps via an RSS feed that pushes this information to you, you're made aware of each of the XBRL instances.

- *Pull,* for example, is when you discover the XBRL instances via a search engine and then pull the information to where you can use it.

But somehow you need to discover the complete set of XBRL instances you need for your analysis. For our experiment, say that a search engine finds all the right XBRL instances, and *only* the right XBRL instances, and makes them available to you. So, you have all the information.

✔ **Having comparable concepts and relations:** You have all the XBRL instances, delivered somehow by your search engine. If each XBRL instance uses a different XBRL taxonomy, comparisons between XBRL instances are more challenging. You can still compare information by mapping each company's XBRL taxonomy to an XBRL taxonomy you create as a master comparison taxonomy. You'd have to create this mapping for every XBRL instance in this case.

An alternative is that every company agrees to use the same XBRL taxonomy. Say they did that; in fact, say every company used the IFRS XBRL taxonomy for financial reporting. But now say that companies are allowed to extend the base IFRS XBRL taxonomy. Thus, in effect, now each company is using a unique XBRL taxonomy, and you're back to having different concepts and relations again. However, for this experiment, say that extension isn't allowed, so you have perfect comparability.

✔ **Putting all the instances together:** You have a complete set of XBRL instances, and you have only one XBRL taxonomy with no extensions allowed, so you have perfect comparability at the XBRL taxonomy level. You now put all the XBRL instances together into one massive, combined XBRL instance containing all information for all companies in the world. Easy enough: After all, XBRL's purpose is to achieve this sort of result.

✔ **Resolving entity conflicts:** You pull all the XBRL information together into one XBRL instance. Do you have conflicting contexts? Theoretically, no. Each company reports only its information, not the information of others. Each context should be of the reporting company; therefore, each company provides its own entity identifier within its context. Again, say that every company had one unique identifier, and that every company can be uniquely identified and identified only once (meaning no duplication). So, we can have no entity conflicts.

✔ **Dealing with period conflicts:** What if companies had different fiscal year-ends? We all use the same calendar, right? Well, you may run into the situation where different companies use different fiscal year-ends, not ending on the same calendar date. A fiscal year is some financial period (say July 1 through June 30); it may not be a calendar year. But for this thought experiment, say that every company has the exact same fiscal year-end, which is December 31.

✔ **Handling unit conflicts:** Different countries use different currencies; therefore all this information is reported in all sorts of different units, from U.S. dollars, to UK pounds, the euro, Japanese yen, or Chinese renminbi, or something else. But say that you can convert to some standard currency — say, the euro for this comparison. For the sake of this experiment, assume that this conversion was done in real time and accurately. As such, you have no unit conflicts.

✔ **Agreeing on standard metadata:** For this perfect world thought experiment, say that you've standardized industry sector identifiers (identifying companies as being a bank, an airline, in retail, and so on), geographic areas (used to differentiate operations in Europe, Asia, and so on), standardized entity information for identifying parent companies as opposed to a subsidiary, and any other thing that can cause a comparability issue. Your metadata is perfect. As such, you can identify parent companies and which industry sector a company is in, you can differentiate between budgeted and actual information with XBRL instances, and so on. You use XBRL Dimensions to construct this dimensional information, which is totally standardized across all companies reporting information. (Remember, it's a thought experiment. Einstein pretended he was riding on a light beam, for Pete's sake!) So, all this metadata is standardized enabling comparability.

✔ **Coming up with an analysis interface:** You have a huge set of information, all in XBRL, for all the companies in the world. All the companies are uniquely identified. All the companies use exactly the same XBRL taxonomy to report their information, and no extensions are allowed. Everyone uses the same fiscal period for reporting their information. All the numeric values use one standard currency. All parent companies are clearly identified, and all actual information is differentiated from any budgeted information. Basically, everything is perfect: You've achieved information nirvana. You have an easy-to-use business-user interface that's even better than the popular Apple iPhone in terms of usability. It's the perfect business-user application.

So what is your point, you ask? One point is that reality can be messy. Reality isn't perfect. All the issues pointed out in the list do exist. Another point is that many things are possible technically but maybe not politically. Technically, you can do everything we mention as we walk through the issues to resolve each issue in some way with XBRL. In fact, that is typically quite easy. The harder part is actually doing it — for example, agreeing on a standard format like XBRL, standardizing how entities are uniquely identified, standardizing on industry sectors and geographic areas, and so on.

Some agreements are already being reached in the area of financial reporting. XBRL itself is a step in that direction. IFRS is another step. But financial reporting is only one business domain.

This experiment points out the major moving parts of working with XBRL instances. We use financial reporting only as an example in our thought experiment. Each different business domain will decide how to employ the technology of XBRL within their domain.

Looking at XBRL Instances

As with XBRL taxonomies, XBRL instances are XML files, and you don't want to read them in that form unless you're a computerized business system; in that case, XML *will* be your preferred format. Another thing to consider when making use of an XBRL instance is that you'll definitely want to also be able to examine the XBRL taxonomies (the entire DTS) upon which the XBRL instance is based. Again, as with XBRL taxonomies, XML tools that read XML but don't understand XBRL won't satisfy your needs.

In this section, we list various approaches to making use of the information within an XBRL instance.

The physical XBRL instance files

One option for looking at an XBRL instance is to look at the physical XML files that make up the XBRL instance. Figure 18-1 shows the XBRL instance of the "Hello World" example (see Chapter 15), which you can find at `http://xbrl.squarespace.com/storage/xbrlfordummies/helloworldexample/HelloWorld.xml`.

Figure 18-1 isn't the only physical file needed to understand the XBRL instance. You can see the reference to the XBRL taxonomy HelloWorld.xsd. That taxonomy schema further references linkbases, and all these pieces of the DTS work together to help you use the XBRL instance information. In most cases, you need an XBRL processor to put all these pieces together for you. So, we're only showing you one of many files that you'll need.

Fundamentally, every approach to using XBRL instance information actually uses the XML files that express the XBRL information. Software applications read these files and reorganize this information in some way. To explain this concept better, in the next section, we wrap a software application around the XML files and take a look at XBRL.

```
<?xml version="1.0" encoding="utf-8"?>
<!-- HelloWorld Example -->
<!-- Date file created: 31/01/2008 9:23:05 PM -->
<xbrl xmlns="http://www.xbrl.org/2003/instance" xmlns:xbrl="http://www.xbrl.org/2003/instance"
   xmlns:link="http://www.xbrl.org/2003/linkbase" xmlns:xlink="http://www.w3.org/1999/xlink"
   xmlns:xsi="http://www.w3.org/2001/XMLSchema-instance" xmlns:iso4217="http://www.xbrl.org/2003/iso4217"
   xmlns:HelloWorld="http://xbrl.squarespace.com/HelloWorld" xsi:schemaLocation="">
   <link:schemaRef xlink:type="simple" xlink:href="HelloWorld.xsd" />
   <!-- Contexts -->
   <context id="I-2007">
      <entity>
         <identifier scheme="http://www.ExampleCompany.com">Example Company</identifier>
      </entity>
      <period>
         <instant>2007-12-31</instant>
      </period>
   </context>
   <context id="I-2006">
      <entity>
         <identifier scheme="http://www.ExampleCompany.com">Example Company</identifier>
      </entity>
      <period>
         <instant>2006-12-31</instant>
      </period>
   </context>
   <!-- Units -->
   <unit id="U-Monetary">
      <measure>iso4217:USD</measure>
   </unit>
   <!-- Fact values -->
   <HelloWorld:Land contextRef="I-2007" unitRef="U-Monetary" decimals="INF">5347000</HelloWorld:Land>
   <HelloWorld:Land contextRef="I-2006" unitRef="U-Monetary" decimals="INF">1147000</HelloWorld:Land>
   <HelloWorld:BuildingsNet contextRef="I-2007" unitRef="U-Monetary" decimals="INF">244508000</HelloWorld:BuildingsNet>
   <HelloWorld:BuildingsNet contextRef="I-2006" unitRef="U-Monetary" decimals="INF">366375000</HelloWorld:BuildingsNet>
   <HelloWorld:FurnitureAndFixturesNet contextRef="I-2007" unitRef="U-Monetary"
      decimals="INF">34457000</HelloWorld:FurnitureAndFixturesNet>
   <HelloWorld:FurnitureAndFixturesNet contextRef="I-2006" unitRef="U-Monetary"
```

Figure 18-1:
Looking at the tags within a physical XBRL file.

Instance viewer

Figure 18-2 takes the exact same XBRL instance file shown in Figure 18-1, feeds it into a basic XBRL instance-viewer application (UBmatrix Taxonomy Designer), and renders the information that the XBRL instance contains. (See Chapter 14 for more info on instance viewers.)

The first thing you can see is what was meant by the term interactive data. If you notice the menu options, you can see that the application allows the user to reorder the XBRL instance facts into various orders. In Figure 18-2, we see them sorted first by entity, then by period, and then the actual fact. You can see other sort orders that the application offers.

In addition to the ability to reconfigure the fact values, XBRL viewer applications generally provide for the ability to validate XBRL instance information to be sure that the XBRL syntax is correct and that the information within the XBRL instance conforms to specified business rules. You can also include new ways of looking at the information by adding XBRL taxonomy pieces to what the XBRL instance viewer has so that you have more metadata to work with. For example, suppose that you read Chinese. If you find a set of label resources that someone has created expressing labels for concepts in Chinese, or if you create such a label resource, you simply add that label resource to the DTS, and the XBRL instance viewer can show you the information within the XBRL instance using the Chinese labels. XBRL instance-viewer applications know how to do this and many other things that are useful to users.

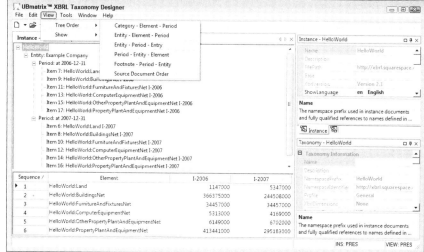

Figure 18-2:
Looking at
an XBRL
instance
using an
instance
viewing
application.

Rendering of XBRL instance information

What if you just wanted to look at the information within the XBRL instance
on paper? No worries. Figure 18-3 shows what it would look like.

Figure 18-3:
An XBRL
instance
styled for
human con-
sumption
using an
XSLT style
sheet that
generates
a PDF.

Example Company
As of December 31,
(Thousands of Dollars)

	2007	2006
Breakdown of Property, Plant and Equipment, Net:		
Land	5,347	1,147
Buildings, Net	244,508	366,375
Furniture and Fixtures, Net	34,457	34,457
Computer Equipment, Net	4,169	5,313
Other Property, Plant and Equipment, Net	6,702	6,149
Property, Plant and Equipment, Net, Total	**295,183**	**413,441**

What you see in Figure 18-3 is the "Hello World" example with a rendering
application applied to the XBRL instance: an XSLT style sheet. (Go to
`http://xbrl.squarespace.com/storage/xbrlfordummies/hello`
`worldexample/HelloWorld-ToFO.xsl` to see the style sheet we used.)

Figure 18-3 should look pretty familiar; it's pretty much what you get today. We show you the XSLT as one approach to rendering XBRL. The approach is rather basic, and you do have to create those style sheets somehow. But many software applications walk you through the process of creating such renderings in several different output formats (see Chapter 14). Many software development tools, such as Windows Presentation Foundation, Adobe Flex, microformats, and AJAX widgets (see Chapter 7), can also help you render XBRL. The point is that because XBRL is interactive, you're not locked into any one format. The sky is literally the limit!

XBRL instance creator

When you create XBRL, you want to view the information within the XBRL instance (and don't forget the related XBRL taxonomies) as you create your XBRL instance. Figure 18-4 is the basic application for creating an XBRL instance.

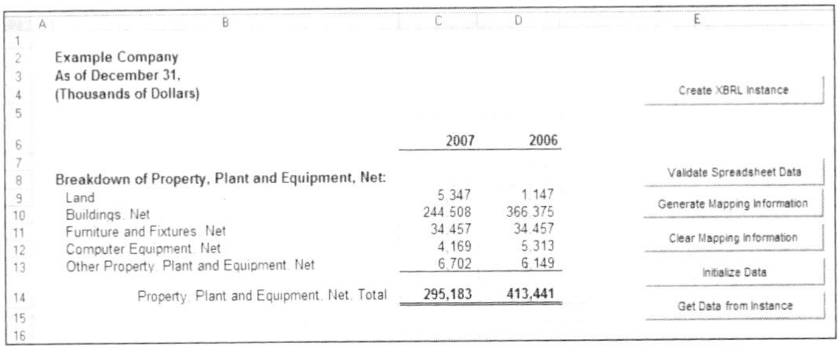

Figure 18-4:
An XBRL
instance
using an
instance
creator
application.

Chapter 15 walks you through using the XBRL instance-creation application shown in Figure 18-4. You can also see where to download this application from that chapter. Our point is that XBRL instance-creation tools are also tools for looking at and using XBRL instance information and the related DTS that supports that instance.

Instance rendered with OLAP cube or pivot table

None of the previous approaches to viewing the XBRL instance information are particularly interactive, except for the XBRL instance-viewer application. One drawback of the nicely formatted information within a document, such as a word-processing document, is that changing the format becomes challenging. These applications basically lock information into one format for the user of the information, typically determined by the information preparer.

But you can use other options, such as business-intelligence (BI) software. BI applications make use of the multidimensional model and allow for reconfigurable views of business information. Another term for this is OLAP, or Microsoft Excel pivot tables. Figure 18-5 shows a simple Excel pivot table for the "Hello World" information set.

Figure 18-5:
An XBRL instance using a Microsoft Excel pivot table.

	A	B	C
1	Entity	http://www.ExampleCompany.com#Example Company	
2			
3	Sum of FactValue		
4		[As of] 2006-12-31	[As of] 2007-12-31
5	Buildings, Net	366,375,000	244,508,000
6	Computer Equipment, Net	5,313,000	4,169,000
7	Furniture and Fixtures, Net	34,457,000	34,457,000
8	Land	1,147,000	5,347,000
9	Other Property, Plant, and Equipment, Net	6,149,000	6,702,000
10	Property, Plant, and Equipment, Net	413,441,000	295,183,000
11			

Although Figure 18-5 is a simple example, if you've ever played around with Excel pivot tables, you know how flexible, yet readable, they can be. OLAP cubes are similar to pivot tables, except they're typically even more powerful and provide more formatting options.

If you haven't yet read Chapter 16's discussion of XBRL Dimensions and the multidimensional model, it's worth doing so now.

Feeding XBRL instance information into an Excel pivot table or a BI application in order to make use of the information in the XBRL instance is easy. Applications simply take the XBRL formatted information and reformat the XBRL syntax into some syntax the BI application understands, the information is imported, and the BI application takes everything from that point using existing functionality. The more about XBRL the BI application understands, the less you have to do outside the actual BI application to make use of XBRL.

Software vendors are better understanding the connection between BI platforms and XBRL. As more BI applications support XBRL, the easier this process of using XBRL within these applications will become. But these BI applications do have limitations.

Interactive information hypercube viewer

Although BI software is quite a powerful rendering solution for lots of different types of business information, it does have two potentially limiting factors: OLAP tends to prefer numbers over textual information, and it likes to aggregate those numbers. The same is true with Excel pivot tables.

However, a lot of business information, such as the descriptions of accounting policies relating to those numbers, is textual in nature. Some of this textual information, such as financial-disclosure narratives, can be complex. Further, textual information isn't aggregated, and other numeric information doesn't need the aggregation abilities of OLAP cubes or pivot tables. Yet, the fact that OLAP cubes and Excel pivot tables not only expect to perform aggregation, but, in fact, are optimized to perform such aggregations can get in the way of what business users actually want to use the OLAP cubes for. You can find ways around these issues, but you may need a new approach to looking at OLAP cubes: Remove the OLAP part and keep everything else.

We'd like to introduce the notion of the (drum roll, please) *interactive information hypercube*. Now, no software vendor has put all these pieces together yet, but several software vendors (see Chapter 14) have implemented pieces, so we're confident that something like the interactive information hypercube, which put all the correct pieces together, will one day exist. We believe that the interactive information hypercube will play a major role in business reporting in the future for three reasons:

- ✔ **A lot of information should be interactive.** You simply can't reconfigure information presented within a fixed document format. For information to be interactive, flexibility is needed, and hypercubes provide that flexibility.

- ✔ **Information is more than numbers and aggregation.** OLAP cubes were built to handle numbers and aggregation of those numbers. They're not sufficient for XBRL as they are today because they don't support textual information and narratives, and they're optimized to aggregate information.

- ✔ **Multidimensional is about flexibility.** The multidimensional model is what would make the idea of an interactive information hypercube work. It provides the flexibility and the metadata that drives that flexibility. Business information is multidimensional.

Figure 18-6 shows an prototype of an interactive information cube. Figure 18-6 takes the earlier "Hello World" example and modifies it to use XBRL Dimensions (see Chapter 16) via the information model used by XBRLS, an application profile of XBRL (see Chapter 12). Then, using information model metadata, the contextual information from the XBRL instance, and other XBRL taxonomy information, an interactive information hypercube is generated. This human-readable rendering of the information contained within the XBRL instance is reconfigurable. The creators of the XBRLS application profile created the prototype in order to help determine what that information model of XBRLS needed to look like to obtain interactivity. For more information, see `http://xbrl.squarespace.com/xbrls`.

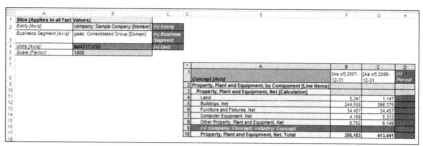

Figure 18-6:
Looking
at an
interactive
information
cube.

Knowing What to Look for in an XBRL Instance

The previous section covers approaches to looking at information contained within an XBRL instance. But what exactly are you looking for within an XBRL instance? What you're looking for has a great deal to do with what you'll be doing with the XBRL instance information. Some people may want to review an XBRL instance that they've just created. Others may want to look at an XBRL instance someone else created. Yet others may take several XBRL instances and analyze the information across multiple periods for one entity (a time series) or for a number of different entities (cross-entity comparison).

The processes you can use these instances in can be totally automated, or humans can be involved between different stages within a process. When working with these XBRL instances, you'll need to consider the XBRL taxonomies upon which the XBRL instances are based. You may even want to reconfigure the XBRL instance information by modifying the XBRL taxonomy.

A business user should be able to use an XBRL instance and reach the same conclusions as someone using the same information expressed in some legacy reporting format, such as paper, HTML, or PDF. The information really hasn't changed; only the efficiency, and perhaps the effectiveness, of how you can use that information are different. The information's format really shouldn't impact the information itself. Humans and computers should reach the same conclusions, whether information is being pumped through some automated process without human involvement enabled by XBRL or whether the process is implemented using humans at each step.

You can use computer software to automate the decision-making process, but the conclusions should be the same ones reached by their human counterparts using older, human-intensive processes. The efficiencies — and perhaps the effectiveness — of reaching the conclusions may have changed, but the actual conclusion shouldn't change just because you're using a new format.

So how do you achieve this objective? Here's what you need to consider as you look within your XBRL instance, using your view of choice:

- ✔ **Appropriateness of XBRL taxonomy:** The XBRL taxonomy, or rather the set of XBRL taxonomies in the DTS, should be appropriate for the needs of the XBRL instance user (see Chapter 17). But because the XBRL taxonomy plays such a crucial role in understanding the XBRL instance, you can see why its appropriateness is important.

- ✔ **Information integrity:** Just like its legacy counterparts, information expressed within XBRL instances needs to add up correctly. If you can't rely on the integrity of the information contained within an XBRL instance, you certainly can't send it through some automated process.

- ✔ **Ability to find the information you want:** The fundamental piece of an XBRL instance is the information the XBRL instance contains. That information is expressed as the values of facts, or fact values. Those facts are related to concepts within some XBRL taxonomy: contexts, units, and perhaps footnotes provided within the XBRL instance. You'll want to find the fact values you need within the XBRL instance, so you need to be able to search, sort, filter, find, and otherwise discover the information within the XBRL instance. A key to this task is organization of the information that describes the fact from within the XBRL taxonomy. This XBRL taxonomy information includes the definition of a concept and helpful information, such as human-readable labels and other resources. For example, if you want to know about Sales, you have to find that concept and be sure that you're working with the right concept, wading through potentially thousands of other concepts.

- ✔ **Relation of information to other information:** Looking at individual fact values is sometimes okay, but generally, the fact values you're working with are associated with other fact values you need to use. The order of these fact values makes a difference; they often flow to a set of business information. For example, a financial statement has a flow to it: balance sheet, income statement, cash flow statement, statement of changes in equity, policies, and disclosures. Understanding one piece of information outside this flow can be challenging or even impossible. Because flow is important, information is organized in the form of statements in the first place. Imagine trying to read a balance sheet that was an unorganized list of fact values. Information needs to be used with other related information.

- ✔ **Fact values within a context:** Users of information contained within an XBRL instance need to understand the context of the fact values they're making use of. The business user must be able to somehow understand and differentiate the contexts of XBRL instance information, whether by visual presentation or another method of understanding the context. For example, putting different periods into different columns, as today's reports do, is one approach to working with different contexts.

✔ **Additional needs for numeric fact values:** The units required for numeric type fact values are just another type of context information; users need to understand the units being used. Information needs to be scaled as the user desires. *Scale* relates to whether the numeric information is expressed in thousands, millions, or maybe billions. XBRL instances don't have scale information. All information within an XBRL instance is expressed as their actual values. Scaling is likewise true of the polarity of the information. *Polarity* means whether the information needs to be added or subtracted relative to other information. Also, is that polarity expressed as a positive or negative in the human-readable rendering being used?

✔ **Information flow fits your needs:** The flow of information contained within an XBRL instance is important in many cases. Consider a financial statement as an example. Perhaps the order of the different statements or disclosures is important, or maybe a human needs to read two separate paragraphs of textual information in a certain order.

✔ **Interactivity of the information:** We talk about XBRL making information interactive, but are you getting the interactivity that you desire? XBRL taxonomies drive much of this interactivity. If the creators of the XBRL instance don't provide what you need in terms of interactivity within their XBRL taxonomy, you may need to provide it.

XBRL Instance Samples and Examples

As with XBRL taxonomies, the complex gargantuan XBRL instances that are filed with regulators for some hard-to-comprehend domain aren't the best place to start. Instead, start small and then use those first small steps to grow your well-grounded foundation. Then, when you get to the bigger XBRL instances, instead of feeling overwhelmed, you can apply this sound base of understanding to working with them. You can definitely apply the examples to these larger XBRL instances.

Just as when you explore XBRL taxonomies, you should explore the XBRL instance; the reverse is likewise true. When you're looking at samples and examples, looking only at an XBRL instance is a mistake. The XBRL taxonomy is the information model for the XBRL instance: You definitely need to understand that model. (Chapter 17 points you to good samples and examples of XBRL taxonomies and related XBRL instances.)

If you look at one XBRL instance in isolation, you'll miss a lot about what you're trying to achieve with an XBRL instance. We point you to a unique additional sample — a small repository containing a number of XBRL instances. This repository example allows you to examine issues related to the use of multiple XBRL instances. This repository has five XBRL instances all created using one taxonomy. Testing comparability across multiple XBRL instances is the reason for the creation of this example. This example also covers issues relating to locating XBRL instances so that you can use them together. You can get the XBRL taxonomies, XBRL instances, and documentation via the RSS feed located at `http://xbrl.squarespace.com/storage/samplerepositorymini/rss-RepositoryMini.xml`.

Exploring Real Production Financial-Reporting-Type XBRL Instances

The filings of public companies to the U.S. SEC are one good set of publically available XBRL instances. All these XBRL instances are publically available and free to use at `www.sec.gov/idea/searchidea/webusers.htm`. They do tend to be large, relatively complicated XBRL instances because of the use of sophisticated extensions, and the domain of public company financial reporting is complex and may not be familiar to everyone. However, these XBRL instances are a great resource for learning about XBRL. The more you put into understanding these XBRL instances, some of which are bound to be good and some likely not so good, the more you get out of the process.

For an RSS feed of the last 100 XBRL filings to the SEC's Next-Generation EDGAR system, see `http://www.sec.gov/Archives/edgar/usgaap.rss.xml`.

By starting with the smaller examples and samples mentioned in the previous section, you can get more out of tackling these larger, more sophisticated, commercial-strength XBRL instances.

Chapter 15 shows you how to view an XBRL instance using the U.S. SEC XBRL instance-viewing application. You can find these instances at `http://viewerprototype1.com/viewer`. Figure 18-7 shows you what one of these XBRL instances looks like when rendered by the SEC's systems.

Figure 18-7 looks a lot like a typical financial statement you may have run across prior to XBRL. That's the idea. But, because of the XBRL publishing format, you're not locked into only one format.

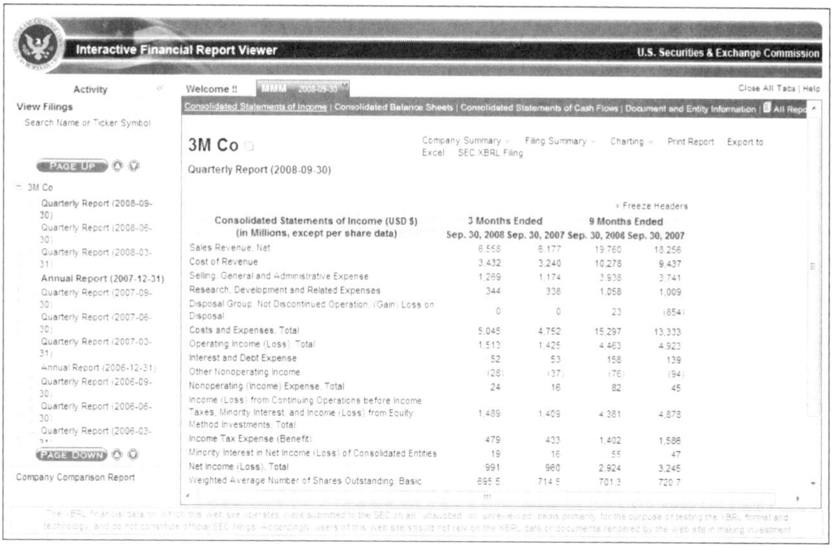

Figure 18-7:
An XBRL
instance for
a financial
report filed
with the
U.S. SEC.

Identifying a Good XBRL Instance

An XBRL instance is a standard publishing format and a transport medium. The ultimate judgment of whether an XBRL instance is good or not is whether it meets your needs. XBRL instances have general characteristics that contribute to them either working well or being less suited for typical tasks. This list helps you evaluate an XBRL instance's characteristics, whether it's the ones you create for others or the ones others have created that you're using:

✓ **Communicates information:** Fundamentally, XBRL instances communicate information. The baseline from which an XBRL instance will be judged is how that same information is being communicated today. A business user should reach the same conclusions using the business information, whether he's using business reports of today or an XBRL instance. Using the information may be more efficient and the information may be more reconfigurable, but the same conclusions should result from the same information. If an XBRL instance doesn't achieve this baseline benchmark, it's not a good XBRL instance.

✔ **Enables comparison of information:** XBRL's role isn't to determine what should be compared, but if information is deemed comparable and it still can't be compared, the XBRL instance isn't performing its function. The issues may be with the XBRL taxonomy, with the contextual information being articulated, or some other reason. No technical reason exists for something that can be comparable to not be comparable. Poor metadata management is generally the culprit if information isn't comparable.

✔ **Possesses data integrity and accuracy:** All the i's should be dotted, and the t's should be crossed. In accounting lingo, everything should tick and tie, as well as foot and cross cast. You achieve this goal by expressing every possible relationship or business rule within the metadata of the XBRL taxonomy that supports the XBRL instance. If an error exists, one of two things must be true: It's either not possible to express a business rule, or it's possible, but the XBRL taxonomy creator neglected to do so. Expressing these relations in an XBRL taxonomy is the first step. The second step is validating the XBRL instance against those rules. Computers, not humans, should be enforcing business rules when possible.

✔ **Operates like a good database:** XBRL taxonomies are data models, and they need to be a good one (see Chapter 17). An XBRL instance is a lot like a database. A good XBRL instance is like a good database. Techniques for creating good databases are well understood from years of using relational databases, so we don't go into them here: Those who know databases understand these techniques.

✔ **Carries no excess baggage:** Unused components of an XBRL taxonomy shouldn't be connected to an XBRL instance. Many times, XBRL taxonomies express more than one option for relations. The creator of the XBRL instance may use only one of those options. If so, don't connect both networks to the XBRL instance. For example, in financial reporting, a company will either be a corporation or a partnership, not both. In the US GAAP taxonomy, presentation and calculation networks exist for both types of entities. Connecting both a corporation and a partnership's networks to an XBRL instance makes little sense. Doing so adds no value to the user of the information, so don't connect the excess networks. XBRL instances should connect only the networks that they use and need. Less is more. Don't burden XBRL instance users with useless networks and resources.

✔ **Has taxonomies that work:** One important key to a good XBRL instance is a good XBRL taxonomy. This advice includes extension taxonomies. One characteristics is that the XBRL taxonomy has been proven to work correctly, and the secret to proving that is proper testing. (Be sure to read about the characteristics of a good taxonomy in Chapter 17.)

✔ **Has extensions that are consistent with the base and that work:** Any XBRL taxonomy that extends a base XBRL taxonomy should work in a manner consistent with that base XBRL taxonomy. You should look at all XBRL taxonomies from the point of view of the entire DTS, not individually in isolation. Again, testing is key to achieving this characteristic.

✔ **Is internally consistent:** The XBRL instance should be internally consistent. For example, if in the entity identifier, the scheme in one place is http://www.sec.gov/cik, in another it's http://sec.gov/cik, and in yet another it's http://www.sec.gov/CIK, a computer application doesn't understand that you're talking about the same entity, even though you used the consistent identifier of, say, 123456, because the schemes don't match. (Look carefully; each one is different.) Both the number and the scheme must match, not just the number. This mistake, although obvious, is a common one made in the U.S. SEC's early XBRL voluntary filings. Our example is only one place where inconsistencies can exist; there are many other places.

✔ **Is consistent across instances:** As with the previous characteristic, XBRL instances should also be consistent across instances. To use the same example as in the previous bullet, if a company used the entity identifier scheme of http://www.sec.gov/cik in one XBRL instance, http://sec.gov/cik in another XBRL instance, and http://www.sec.gov/CIK in a third XBRL instance, even though they provide the identifier 123456 consistently in all three XBRL instances, a computer won't recognize the combined identifier and scheme as the same entity. Remember, computers are really dumb!

✔ **Is interactive:** If the XBRL instance you're creating or using isn't interactive, the reason is typically poor taxonomy design, poor instance creation, or a combination of both. Using the XBRL instance is where the rubber meets the road. If a user of the XBRL instance can successfully do what he needs without breaking things, the XBRL instance is good one. Usability is the ultimate test for an XBRL instance.

✔ **Automates processes:** Take this one step further and consider multiple XBRL instances being used within some business information-supply chain; a good test of XBRL instances is the successful automation of some process that was previously a manual process. If you can achieve this automation, you can't argue with that result: You've done everything right! But if you can't effectively automate that manual process, you can't characterize the XBRL instance as a good one.

✔ **Follows best practices:** As with XBRL taxonomies, following best practices, such as FRIS, can help you create a high-quality XBRL instance. For example, FRIS prohibits the pathological case where duplicate fact values (same concept, same context, two values that can be either the same or different) exist within an XBRL instance. Good XBRL instances follow FRIS and other best practices.

✔ **Is elegant:** As with XBRL taxonomies, good XBRL instances give you a sense of elegance when you use them. If they don't seem elegant, look deeper — there's usually a specific reason for it. This list is a good starting point for helping you figure out the reason the instance isn't as elegant as you think it should be.

Chapter 19

Predicting What XBRL Will Become

In This Chapter

▶ Peering into XBRL's future

▶ Looking at specific ways to use XBRL

▶ Envisioning XBRL killer applications

▶ Considering what can go wrong (so you can avoid it)

▶ Predicting changes to XBRL

X BRL has existed since 2000, yet it's still a maturing global supply chain standard for business information exchange. As we experiment with using XBRL to solve business-information-exchange problems, we learn more about XBRL and how to effectively use it. We know where we are today, but where will we be tomorrow? In this chapter, we go out on a limb and make predictions about the future of XBRL, its usage, and even potential problems. We even make predictions about probable changes to XBRL itself, based on ten years of experience from building and working with the XBRL standard.

The Future World with XBRL

Many technologies have come and gone. XBRL doesn't look like it'll be a passing fad; rather, it will probably be a key characteristic of the business systems of organizations large and small around the globe in the future. Eventually, XBRL will reach the point where it's fulfilling its intended destiny, but it's not there yet. XBRL solves problems that need to be solved in order to exchange business information. XBRL has been proven to work, and strong evidence, from its use by regulators and the organizations they regulate, indicates that XBRL will be with us for some time in some form or another. But what form? If XBRL isn't around solving your business-information-exchange problems, something certainly will be. You need relief from the information overload that you're experiencing now.

Islands of yet another information format will serve little purpose and not take you beyond where you are today. Today, businesses can exchange business information with, or without, XBRL. However, XBRL does have its advantages. Yet, the problems that XBRL has solved thus far are generally the problems of big regulators, and highly skilled technical people alongside business users with domain expertise are implementing the technology.

But technical people solving problems for regulators isn't the vision XBRL aspires to achieve. The objective of XBRL is the automated exchange of business information from one business user to another business user with no direct assistance from the IT department. Technology folks will offer plenty of assistance, but it should be in the form of software applications that let business users achieve their goals. Business users should be operating their own information-supply chains (see Chapter 7).

Is this goal achievable? The people at XBRL International believe that it is, and we do, too. It's certainly a goal worth trying to achieve. Only time will tell if it's possible.

Facts and Assumptions

Big regulators are successfully making use of XBRL today. But take a look at XBRL from the vantage point of where many of you are — in the enterprise. Your enterprise may be big or small. (Chapter 5 breaks "you" down into a number of different categories.)

We use provable facts, and we make assumptions, based on evidence, to look into the future for areas where opportunities exist or where missteps can occur. We use these facts and assumptions to make our case for the future, providing you with useful information you can use to plan your course of action. You can use our facts and assumptions as a basis for creating your own assessment, if you want.

Known and generally indisputable facts

Here's a summary of what we believe are some generally indisputable facts about our future as it relates to XBRL:

- ✔ You exchange information.
- ✔ Garbage in, garbage out.
- ✔ Computers are dumb and need certain specific things, such as formally defined formats and no ambiguity, to exchange business information effectively using automated processes.

✔ XBRL does work. Big regulators, such as the U.S. FDIC and regulators throughout Europe and Asia, have shown that XBRL works.

✔ Automated business information exchange is a broad category. Different parties who exchange business information have different needs.

✔ Your company or organization commonly has more than one business software application.

✔ Your business exchanges business information with more than one party, but you don't exchange information with everyone.

✔ The quantity of information that businesses exchange will only continue to grow.

Assumptions about XBRL's future

What assumptions can we make about XBRL's future? We call these assumptions rather than facts because you can dispute them. We do, however, provide justification for each assumption:

✔ XBRL is a global standard and will remain a global standard. The pace of adoption by regulators and those they regulate is strong evidence that the market will likely continue to embrace XBRL.

✔ XBRL won't always work perfectly. This assumption is easy to justify — nothing ever works perfectly.

✔ You like options, but you're willing to give up certain options if you gain simplicity, effectiveness, or efficiencies. But, you can give up options only to the degree that your use cases are being met. You can't compromise on certain things.

✔ XBRL will change. Everything changes. Exactly how XBRL may change isn't clear, but it's a sure bet that it will continue to evolve.

✔ Not every business information-supply chain will have the resolve to become what it could possibly become. Politics, human nature, and other things will cause some, perhaps many, business information-supply chains to not realize what they could realize. On the other hand, other business information-supply chains will achieve their potential. The determining factor is the business domain itself, not XBRL.

✔ The global market will come up with new, interesting, unexpected, and exciting uses for XBRL. That assumption is easy to make — that's why free markets are so great!

XBRL Means New Types of Software

A lot of software vendors will add XBRL as an import and/or export feature within their existing business software products. Other software vendors will create new XBRL-specific products. Taking another approach, other software vendors will fundamentally change the type of software they build, how they build that software, and how that software works within business processes that those software applications serve.

Software vendors will build this new software — some new and some that already exist. Some new startup companies will move boldly and quickly; other established, and perhaps larger, software vendors will move slowly, methodically, but deliberately. Look at the list of XBRL International members as a clue to who is moving and who is not. This list isn't the only clue: You don't have to be a member to implement XBRL, and not all members are implementing XBRL.

You can think of XBRL's impact on software in another way as well. Rather than thinking of XBRL as a means of exchanging business information, think of what business software can do because of XBRL and because we can automatically exchange business information leveraging this standard approach. Also, think of the standardized metadata expressed in XBRL, such as the US GAAP and IFRS financial-reporting taxonomies. What new types of business software can you build as a result? What new types of software will need to be built to make use of XBRL effectively?

XBRL as part of an enterprise service bus or XML pipeline

People disagree as to what exactly an *enterprise service bus* (ESB) is, but few disagree as to what it's trying to achieve — information flow.

Information flow, as we use the term in this case, is the effective automation of business processes. The desired theoretical coefficient of friction of such a system would be zero, but just like in physics, some sort of friction will generally always exist; you can only minimize friction.

Think of an ESB as middleware. You can look at an ESB or XML pipeline as software that sits between business systems and enables the exchange of information between those systems. The business systems can be internal or external to your organization.

If you start thinking about XBRL within your organization, it won't take long to realize that if, say, a number of your business systems make use of XBRL, either one of two things have to be true: Each software application provides the required XBRL infrastructure, or all those applications share one common XBRL infrastructure. If organizations share their XBRL infrastructure, you'll have fewer interoperability issues between the multiple implementations of XBRL within the different business systems.

More and more organizations are using XML to exchange all sorts of information within their organization and with outside parties. It's highly likely that XBRL will need to be a part of these XML pipelines of information. (Chapter 2 covers what XBRL brings to the table.)

Integrated functionality

A lot of XBRL software today is standalone as opposed to integrated. By standalone, we mean that you must use multiple software applications, instead of just one application, to complete a task. For example, you can find many standalone XBRL taxonomy-creation tools, but few accounting systems have the integrated features to create an XBRL taxonomy for two reasons. The first software applications to support XBRL were newly created applications rather than existing software applications modified to support XBRL. This reason makes sense. Software vendors are reluctant to implement every new "next great technology" right away. Before they modify their systems to support technologies like XBRL, the market needs to accept the technologies to some degree. For XBRL, that acceptance is now here. More and more software applications are beginning to support XBRL within those business systems.

The second reason products tend to be separated appears to be the need to focus. For example, many software products are either XBRL taxonomy-creation applications or XBRL instance applications. But when you start building an XBRL instance and then realize that you need to extend the XBRL taxonomy you're using, you have to exit your XBRL instance-creation application and move to your XBRL taxonomy-creation tool. In that situation, you'll quickly understand why XBRL instance-creation applications need to have integrated XBRL taxonomy-creation functionality.

Improved search and discovery of business information

One thing that XBRL provides is a structured publishing format for information. That structured publishing format improves search capabilities and gives you the ability to more easily discover the information you need.

XBRL will be part of the Semantic Web (see Chapter 6). You'll likely learn a great deal about the Semantic Web from the U.S. SEC's Next-Generation EDGAR system (see Chapter 13), which makes use of XBRL. By the time you read this book, that system will be up and running, and you'll be able to see what the Semantic Web is all about.

The Semantic Web in general, and XBRL more specifically, will greatly improve your ability to search for and discover information you might need. The Semantic Web will likely change the job you do and how you do it — for example, by allowing you to spend more time analyzing and less time looking for information and rekeying information.

Growing use of application profiles

Today, each XBRL taxonomy is created using a somewhat different architecture. The general-purpose nature of XBRL makes it too complex for business users to use in this general form. Each different XBRL taxonomy implementation picks different pieces, parts, and approaches of XBRL to use in expressing the XBRL taxonomy. All are 100-percent XBRL-compliant, but each is different. These differences cause two things:

✔ Interoperability between each XBRL taxonomy is harder to achieve. We're not saying that each XBRL taxonomy really needs to be interoperable: They don't. But if you *do* need to make them interoperate, just the fact that two taxonomies are both based on XBRL isn't enough to achieve the interoperability.

✔ Each implementer of XBRL has to figure out pretty much the same things for each implementation, repeating the same effort over, and over, and over.

Application profiles are a common approach to solving this sort of problem, and they have a side benefit to boot: They make XBRL easier to use. We believe that several application profiles will be created, and they will be the implementation patterns for XBRL. No one will use just general XBRL. No one really uses general XBRL today; each XBRL taxonomy uses different pieces and parts within their XBRL taxonomy architecture. In effect, each XBRL taxonomy is, today, its own unique application profile. (To better understand application profiles, see Chapter 12, where we cover them in detail.)

Groups are already working together to create application profiles for XBRL implementations. XBRL Global Ledger is basically an application profile. The US GAAP taxonomy is an application profile; it even calls itself such within its architecture documentation. A number of governments around the world are starting to talk about SBR as an application profile or an approach for governments to implement XBRL in a consistent manner. XBRLS (see Chapter 12) is an application profile.

However, most application profiles aren't documented formally enough to be as useful as they can be. None of them work out of the box. No software applications leverage the application profiles to make using XBRL easier. But soon they will. After business users realize the practical nature of using application profiles to make their life easier, they'll gladly give up a small amount of flexibility in order to gain significant reductions in implementation complexity.

Specific Uses for XBRL

Don't think of XBRL as only a way of exchanging business information. Instead, think of what software applications will now be capable of doing because of XBRL. We've put together what can best be called a wish list of such applications. This list contains applications that don't exist today, but we wish did. These specific financial-reporting examples can help you see ways that you can leverage XBRL's existence for other business-reporting needs.

- ✔ **Automated disclosure checklist:** Today, preparers of financial disclosures use disclosure checklists when they create financial statements to make sure that they don't forget something. This disclosure checklist is a lot like a pilot's checklist for taking off or landing an airplane. For an audited financial statement, these disclosure checklists can run around 100 printed pages. You can automate many, but not all, of these checks, letting a computer application check that the financial statement has been created properly.

  The disclosure checklist is basically a set of business rules. Disclosure checklist business rules are for creating a financial statement. You can create similar rules for other types of business reports. Because XBRL expresses the information within the business report in a structured manner, you can make a computer tick and tie things in the report to ensure that everything adds up and to check for other requirements that the report must meet. Computers are good at checking things like, "If this exists, you need to disclose these three things also." These automated checklists will revolutionize business reporting. In fact, another way to look at creating financial reports is that the software application you're using won't let you do the wrong thing; it will *only* let you create the report correctly. Now, a computer will never be able to check certain things, and humans will still focus on those sorts of things. But, a computer can handle lots and lots of mundane tasks currently performed by people.

- ✔ **Financial-reporting disclosure templates:** Most accountants who create public company financials are familiar with AICPA's *Accounting Trends and Techniques.* The publication is a summary of best practices of financial reporting and disclosure, a comparison of the reporting practices of about 600 organizations, which the AICPA has been publishing annually for many years. This summary of reporting best practices contains basically high-quality disclosure templates. The publication is put together with a lot of manual effort. But the new method of examining the disclosure practices of public companies will be easier than ever with XBRL, thanks to the SEC's Next-Generation EDGAR public filing database. Accountants and attorneys already use public filings with the SEC EDGAR system to help them figure out the best approaches to articulating disclosure information. With the Next-Generation EDGAR system, you'll be able to query the system and find specific disclosures by looking for specific reported concepts, filtering, sorting, slicing, and dicing until you get what you need. The SEC's new system will be a comprehensive database of practices from which you can glean best practices, making disclosures easier and improving disclosure practices. You can access this best practices in disclosures without all that manual effort required to put together the 600-company summary. Thanks to XBRL, you can make computers do this work for you.

✔ **Post entries to an XBRL instance:** Imagine an XBRL instance with its supporting XBRL taxonomy providing a business rule for every computation within that XBRL instance. Imagine what would amount to posting a transaction to that XBRL instance and the business rules of the XBRL taxonomy updating subtotals, totals, related computations, and so on as you make the adjustment in a transaction you're posting. Imagine being able to post that or any other entry to an XBRL instance and all the values that are impacted by that adjustment being updated to their adjusted values using the business rules that express the relations. Sound like magic? Not really. Have you ever used Microsoft Excel's goalseek functionality? Posting an entry to an XBRL instance works in a similar way. Anyone who has ever created a complex report and then had someone request a last-minute adjustment to that report, requiring them to recalculate all the numbers impacted by that adjustment, will certainly appreciate this feature. Further, imagine being able to create an XBRL instance in this manner: transaction by transaction with business rules keeping the information in balance throughout the entire process.

✔ **Interactive information hypercube viewer:** Imagine an implementation of an interactive information hypercube (see Chapter 18) where you can exchange a business report with anyone else, and they could interact with that information. Every computer desktop would eventually support interactive information hypercube viewers. What would be different is that the interactive information hypercube viewer would behave something like a Microsoft Excel pivot table, allowing the user of the information to adjust the report flawlessly (not like copy/paste). You'll be able to add XBRL instances to the viewer, creating a comparison between multiple XBRL instances for multiple periods or multiple companies.

Remember, interactive information is leveraging all the functionality of your computer, not a PDF that leverages all the functionality of paper.

✔ **Leverage taxonomy information:** Charlie, by his own admission, is a pretty average accountant. But using an XBRL taxonomy makes him a significantly better accountant. Here's why. Financial-reporting experts created the information contained within the XBRL taxonomy. If you gave ten accountants a blank slate and had them create, say, the US GAAP taxonomy, many couldn't do it, the results would certainly be inconsistent, and not all of them would be right. You can leverage a significant amount of information within XBRL taxonomies.

These XBRL taxonomies are a new way of articulating information that has never existed in this form. If you look at an XBRL taxonomy, such as the US GAAP XBRL taxonomy or the IFRS XBRL taxonomy, you'll begin to realize what we're saying. Furthermore, an accountant who understands the information contained in the XBRL taxonomy and who also understands how to write Excel macros will be able to achieve interesting and useful approaches to putting that XBRL taxonomy information to use. Things are different because the taxonomy information is in a computer-readable format that has never been available, particularly in a global standard format. These new interesting and useful approaches will become increasingly valuable as more and more metadata gets added to XBRL taxonomies.

Another interesting financial-reporting use of XBRL taxonomies will be the conversion of the United States from US GAAP to IFRS. We expect that XBRL taxonomies for the US GAAP and IFRS will play a major role in this conversion process. We know that at least one Big 4 public accounting firm has a _mapping,_ or association, between US GAAP and IFRS. What having this mapping means is that the company has created computer-readable associations between the pieces of US GAAP and IFRS. You can use these mappings for all sorts of different things.

What Can Go Wrong

XBRL isn't perfect, nor is any consensus-based standard. Making XBRL do the things we want it to do isn't without its challenges. Here are some of these potential challenges and reasons why they'll likely occur:

✔ **Too many XBRL taxonomies:** Just like the case where financial reporting is done with three different XBRL taxonomies (US GAAP, IFRS, EDINET), each of which uses a different XBRL architecture, this situation can occur within other business domains, too. Many times, coordinating different efforts is too hard, there's an unwillingness to do so, or people are unaware that they're duplicating what someone else is already doing. Further, business interests may be perceived to, or actually do, conflict. Having too many XBRL taxonomies isn't the end of the world. Mappings can usually resolve this situation, but many times, mappings are time consuming to create and maintain. The market will eventually dictate what it needs. Politics becomes a factor as certain groups try to control XBRL taxonomies. Eventually, things will end up where they do, and the situation won't be perfect.

✔ **Poor-quality taxonomies:** You can construct XBRL taxonomies in many ways, sometimes resulting in less-than-optimal functionality within the system in which they'll be used. Many times, what suffers is comparability of information and analysis. Bad XBRL taxonomies are a lot like bad database schemas.

✔ **Poor software interoperability:** Many things contribute to poor software interoperability, including shortcuts by developers, short-sightedness, and ambiguity within the XBRL specification. The biggest loser here may be the business user as what could be one global standard (which would benefit the majority of business users) gets fractured into proprietary fiefdoms. Business users have a big interest in what XBRL becomes and should exercise their right to vote by demanding what they need from XBRL.

✔ **Lack of motivation to maintain XBRL:** For XBRL to work, someone needs to maintain the XBRL specifications. The specification is the basis of the promise of what XBRL can offer. There has to be resolve to make XBRL work, keep it working, and change it to meet the changing needs of its constituents. Maintaining XBRL takes time and costs money. XBRL is just a technology created by a group who cooperated in the past. Problems need to be resolved as they come up. These issues may or may not get resolved. Users can drift more and more toward proprietary solutions, defeating the purpose of XBRL. But if the XBRL standard can't meet their needs, business users really have no choice but to go with what works for them.

✔ **Inappropriate expectations:** XBRL won't do everything for all people. It has its place. Using it for the wrong reason or in the wrong way doesn't produce an effective result; it's like trying to put a square peg into a round hole.

✔ **No mass-market adoption:** EDI and SGML are two examples of standards that never really achieved mass adoption. The simpler and more internationally usable XML, a subset (application profile) of SGML, did achieve critical mass and mass adoption. Many predict mass-market adoption of XBRL will occur, but nothing is certain.

Changes to XBRL and Usage of XBRL

We really go out on a limb here and predict possible future changes to XBRL and how XBRL is used. These predictions aren't groundless, but rather based on ten years of watching XBRL evolve, discussions within XBRL International members, and involvement with XBRL implementations. Here are some predictions we can make and our reasoning behind the predictions:

- **Definition relations will be used more.** Definition relations are one of the most underutilized but powerful features of XBRL. Definition relations have a great deal of potential that currently isn't exploited by most XBRL taxonomies. XBRL taxonomies will grow, in many cases, to be more like ontologies with the use of definition relations. (See Chapter 14 for more information.)

- **Calculation relations may vanish.** There is no real need for both XBRL Formula and XBRL calculation relations. Both are syntaxes for achieving an end. XBRL Formula is significantly more powerful than XBRL calculation relations. Calculation relations can provide nowhere near what XBRL Formula can provide. As such, we believe XBRL calculation relations may become obsolete.

- **Precision attribute may be deprecated.** The precision attribute that is used within facts in XBRL instances will likely be deprecated. The decimals attribute and the precision attribute serve the same purpose. The FRIS suggests using decimals. The XBRL specification provides an algorithm for converting from decimals to precision, but not from precision to decimals. You don't really need both. We believe precision will be deprecated. Stick with using decimals on facts in XBRL instances.

- **Contexts will move to a multidimensional model.** If you look at the contents of a context element within an XBRL instance (see Chapter 4 for more information), you'll notice that four things are packed together: entity information, entity segments, periods, and scenarios. Each of these pieces of a context is really a dimension of a fact value. This approach to articulating dimensional information has its drawbacks. First, you can't establish a hierarchy of the context information. Second, packing four different things into the context element (as opposed to separating each) leads to duplication. Third, you don't really need some of these dimensions. For example, XBRL Global Ledger doesn't make use of the period portion of a context. Further periods may have different hierarchies; for example, consider the difference between calendar periods and fiscal periods. If you were to go back and look at XBRL 1.0, you'd see that all this contextual information was, in essence, separated into individual components. The bottom line is that it seems obvious that all context information should work similar to XBRL Dimensions; why not simply use XBRL Dimensions for all contextual information rather than have two approaches to articulating dimensional information?

✔ **RDF/OWL used to express XBRL.** They may not be created by, but we feel it's highly likely that someone is going to create a way to use RDF and OWL to represent information that XBRL currently represents. Today, XBRL is viewed as a syntax. We propose that the most important characteristic of XBRL isn't the syntax, but rather its semantics. XBRL has no logical model, but it needs one. RDF and OWL are logical choices for expressing such a logical model of business reporting. Some other syntax, even perhaps RDF and OWL, may conceivably replace the XBRL syntax. We believe that there will eventually be a lossless approach to moving between the XBRL syntax and the RDF/OWL syntax of expressing the semantics of business information.

✔ **Standard XBRL logical model will be created.** The creation of a logical model for XBRL goes hand in hand with the previous prediction. Although agreement exists for XBRL's syntax, agreement doesn't exist for XBRL's semantics. A physical model for XBRL exists, but not a logical model. Whether it's created by XBRL International or an ad hoc standard created by the market, someone will create a logical model for business information exchange. Alternatively, you can create several logical models. The benefits of a logical model are too great for this not to occur. The question is really will it be a global standard or multiple proprietary solutions and therefore different as each vendor implements their own logical model.

✔ **Standard XBRL API will be created.** Discussions relating to creating an API for XBRL have taken place within XBRL International on several occasions. We believe that the creation of API for XBRL will eventually occur, either by XBRL International or as an ad hoc standard API created by the market.

Part V
The Part of Tens

"Oh, Anthony loves working with XBRL. He customized all our documents with a sound file so they all close out with a 'Bada Bing!'"

In this part . . .

In grand *For Dummies* tradition, this part provides you with useful reminders and tips to help you from getting bogged down with the details of XBRL. We give you a list of ways you can flatten the XBRL learning curve, avoiding common mistakes that waste your time. Our next list is the key technical concepts that must be understood by anyone to truly grasp XBRL; we explain these technical concepts in a way business readers can understand them. And we end our journey with a list of commonly confused XBRL odds and ends, explaining them in case you need these more technical details.

Chapter 20

Ten (or So) Ways to Flatten the XBRL Learning Curve

In This Chapter

▷ Gathering information from others

▷ Expanding your knowledge by doing

*I*f you've read other parts of this book, and you know what the XBRL elephant looks like, you can break down that big elephant into smaller pieces that you can eat one piece at a time. (If you can't identify that elephant in a lineup, see Part I.) Some people out there will tell you about shortcuts to understanding and working with XBRL. Don't listen to them — there are no shortcuts. Work is required.

What you don't need to be doing is working in the wrong areas; heck, you have plenty of work to do in the right areas! The key to learning what you need is to understand enough about XBRL to know when someone is leading you down the correct path. To achieve this goal, you have to know what *you* want and need to accomplish. That is why understanding XBRL's big picture first is so critical: It helps you understand what you can, and cannot, get from XBRL.

This chapter helps you flatten the XBRL learning curve. It won't make learning XBRL effortless, particularly in the current phase of XBRL's maturity. But it can help minimize wheel spinning, find starting points, and, combined with the other chapters in this book, get on a path to where you want to arrive: solving real business problems. This chapter is important for a simple reason: It will save you time and money.

Gaining an Important Perspective on Learning

You can learn by making your own mistakes or from the mistakes others make. Another term for learning from your own mistakes is creativity. Being creative is a good thing. However, many people make the mistake of confusing creativity with control. We point out this misconception because we don't want you to fall into this trap.

True creativity is incredibly expensive most of the time. Creativity involves trying many things, seeing what works and what doesn't, and moving toward your goal. Sometimes you're lucky and stumble on something that works sooner rather than later. But the laws of probability are at play here. On average, creating something new takes a lot of time and effort.

There can be a better way. Pablo Picasso said, "Good artists copy. Great artists steal." But don't misinterpret what we're saying. You have to stay within the law — don't be calling us if you go to jail for violating someone's license agreement or copyright. In that case, call your attorney. (We hope you have a good one.)

Learning from an approach taken by a public taxonomy, such as the US GAAP Taxonomy, by reading its architecture document (see http://xbrl.us/Documents/SECOFM-USGAAPT-Architecture-20080428.pdf) and using those ideas is a good practice. (To avoid having to type these long links, go to www.dummies.com/go/xbrl. This takes you to a landing page where you can click the link you need.) Copying that same document and holding it out as your work is definitely not a good idea — and it's plagiarism.

Step one to implementing XBRL is understanding what has already been done, figuring out what works well, and seeing whether you can apply a similar solution to your set of circumstances. If you can, don't reinvent the wheel. An amazing amount of sharing goes on because of the Web; take advantage of it.

Use your skills, experiences, and other background to build the better mousetrap!

The trick is to understand when you're reinventing the wheel and when you're building a better mousetrap. The "If it's not invented here, it's no good" attitude can be expensive. Not considering the truly specific needs you have in your situation, though, can also be expensive. Balance is the key.

Building a Prototype or Proof of Concept

One of the best ways to truly understand XBRL is to build a prototype or proof of concept. We provide enough of a starting point in this book to help you realize many of the things XBRL may be able to do for you. We point out many tasks others use XBRL for and where you may be able to apply XBRL in your organization. We even walk you through some tasks step by step. You can take all these things and come up with a prototype or proof-of-concept solution to a specific business problem you have.

Many software vendors make trial versions of their software available for free for a limited time period. Take advantage of that offer: You don't have to re-create existing functionality in your prototype or proof of concept; just create the pieces that don't exist for your specific needs. And definitely start small. Trying to build too big of a prototype or proof of concept won't generally get you where you need to be. You may be surprised how much this process of prototyping a solution helps you understand and grasp the realities of working with XBRL.

Another way of building a prototype can be significantly easier than building your own prototype, under the right circumstances — reverse-engineer someone else's prototype, which may be available publically. The prototype you reverse-engineer doesn't even need to be exactly the prototype you'd create, but if it's close enough, you can use this process of working backward to jump-start your learning process. That starting point can allow your prototype or proof of concept project to move along faster.

You don't have to go through this process alone! Plenty of experts, such as consultants and software vendors, can help you. Of course, you'll likely need at least a small budget for your prototype or proof of concept project, but a hired gun, when used correctly, can really put you on the express bus to XBRL understanding.

Taking Advantage of the Expertise of Hired Guns

Consultants. Maybe you don't like using consultants, but the truth is that in today's world, most projects can't live without them. If used correctly, consultants can be extremely valuable resources. If used incorrectly, you may as well be throwing your money down the drain.

An old joke helps make this point: A man was having trouble with his car, so he took it to a mechanic. He asked the mechanic how much it would cost to fix the car, and the mechanic said he couldn't really say without looking at the car. The man agreed, and the mechanic opened the hood, looked around for about a minute, twisted a fitting on the engine, and solved the problem. The owner of the car told the mechanic that it was a miracle, and he wanted the mechanic to bill him for what it was worth to fix the problem. The mechanic gave the owner a bill for $250. The car owner was aghast and said to the mechanic, "$250? It took you only a minute to twist a fitting." The mechanic replied, "Yes, it took me about 2 seconds to twist the fitting actually, it took me 58 seconds to look at what was going on, and it took me 30 years of experience to understand which fitting I needed to twist and in what direction." The owner paid the bill.

Sometimes fiddling around trying to figure out what XBRL fitting to twist can cost significantly more than forking out some of your hard-earned money to have an experienced guide walk you through the process. Consultants can be a good investment if used in the correct manner.

We don't recommend paying a consultant to do all the work; having them do all the work, without you gaining any XBRL knowledge, doesn't help you learn. Use the consulting fees you pay as an investment in training for you and your organization. This approach isn't appropriate in all situations, but for certain types of projects, even just a day with a consultant with the right expertise can be invaluable.

Two key words here are "right experience." Chapter 12 has a list of things to help you identify whether the consultant you're considering forking out dough to hire truly has the right stuff, so to speak.

Working with Software Vendors

In many cases, software vendors are a good source of XBRL expertise. Be sure to read the previous section about using hired guns and realize that many software vendors have a professional-service aspect to their organization that works with their customers to implement solutions, learn about customer problems, and then cycle what they learn back in to software products and features for their particular company. Seek out these professional services consultants.

Although most software vendors offer trial software products to their customers, learning how to use a software product effectively can still be quite challenging. It's particularly an issue if you're shopping around for software and trying to pick the best one.

Don't get roped into letting software vendors give you only their prepared demos that they've orchestrated to perfection. Let them give their demos but then ask good questions, such as the ones we list in Chapter 14. Your job is to be a knowledgeable customer. Do your homework and be prepared!

Another thing to do is ask around. Talk with others who have used the software vendors you're considering or their competitors. A great place to do research is at XBRL conferences. XBRL International typically holds two conferences per year, and most XBRL vendors have a booth in them or at least attend. Attending conferences can be an expensive initial investment, but if you're really jumping into XBRL in a big way, the investment is worth it and generally results in a reduction of total cost. See the XBRL International Web site (http://xbrl.org) for conference locations and dates.

Taking a Class

We have only a limited number of pages to communicate the key aspects of XBRL in this book, which is why we call it a starting point. Sometimes, group interaction helps you understand certain areas of XBRL. More and more classes are being offered on XBRL these days. These classes come in all sorts of formats, including one- or two-hour webinars, one- or two-day events, training offered at conferences, and even weeklong boot camps that offer total immersion into the world of XBRL.

Every class is different, and the proper class and format for you depends on your needs. Consider this list of possible XBRL training needs:

- You can't learn much about XBRL in an hour, a day, or even two days, for that matter. Particularly at this level of XBRL's maturity, figuring out the right match in what is offered and what you need can be challenging. Focus is key. We know that you don't have weeks to take out of your daily lives to learn about XBRL or any other topic. Learn in bite-size chunks.

- As XBRL matures, software will get better, more books will be written, more examples and sample implementations will exist, and more consultants will know about XBRL. All these changes can help reduce what you need to understand about XBRL in order to make it do what you need. Just realize where XBRL is in its life cycle and adjust your expectations accordingly.

- If you want to learn about XBRL in depth, don't necessarily do it all at once. Sometimes in-depth saturation training can provide a significant jumpstart. On the other hand, taking a class, applying your skills, learning from applying your skills, and then taking another class after you've gotten your hands dirty a bit can be a good approach. Mixing classroom training and real-world understanding from on-the-job training or supported study is a good approach, especially in the area of something like XBRL taxonomy creation.

✔ A particular problem for business users these days is that training can be too technical due to the state of XBRL software applications and business people who are capable of delivering training. A business person in a technical-oriented class can be frustrating. Realize that as software improves and as more business-oriented people understand XBRL, classes will become less technical. Many times, the participants in classes are a mixture of business-oriented and technical-oriented participants. Meeting the needs of both groups at the same time can be hard.

Asking Questions on Mailing Lists

A great way to learn is to get on mailing lists. Yahoo! (`http://groups.yahoo.com/search?query=XBRL`) hosts more than 100 XBRL-related mailing lists. Two particularly good mailing lists are

✔ **XBRL-public mailing list** (`http://finance.groups.yahoo.com/group/xbrl-public`): This list is for general XBRL information. Ask any question you want. It has about 1,500 members, and anyone can become a member. Don't really like asking questions? No worries. This list has been active for more than nine years, so it has a significant archive of information you can dig into.

✔ **XBRL-dev mailing list** (`http://tech.groups.yahoo.com/group/xbrl-dev`): This list is where XBRL geeks, many of them software vendors, hang out. These technical people tend to be open, helpful, friendly, and patient and enjoy sharing information. This list has about 500 members and has been active for about five years. It's technical, but you can really ask any question you want.

Although these two lists are probably the most active and general lists, many other XBRL mailing lists exist. For starters, Google Groups (`http://groups.google.com`) has another 18 XBRL-related lists.

Writing a White Paper

"What!?" you may ask? "You want me to write a white paper on XBRL, and I don't even know anything about XBRL! Are you crazy?" Actually, no, we're not crazy. A great way to learn about something is to write about it.

Believe it or not, no one was born being an XBRL expert. Everyone started somewhere. So, yeah, write a white paper. Here are some ideas that can help you with that endeavor:

- ✔ **Collaborate with someone who does know XBRL.** If you have an area of expertise but don't know XBRL, and you want to see how XBRL will impact that area, collaborate with an XBRL expert.

- ✔ **Copy what other domains have done.** We're not really talking about stealing. For example, the CFA Institute, an association of investment professionals, wrote a white paper to explain XBRL to its members (see `www.cfapubs.org/toc/ccb/2009/2009/3?cookieSet=1`). You can use ideas from that white paper to help you explain XBRL to your domain, your organization, or some other group.

- ✔ **Write a university research paper.** Students and professors, what a great opportunity to write about how the things we do will be transformed by XBRL!

Helping on a Public XBRL Taxonomy Project

Although time-consuming, a good way to learn is to get involved in a public XBRL taxonomy-creation project. Often, volunteer members of XBRL International staff these projects. Some volunteers have little or no experience with XBRL, but others can have significant XBRL expertise. Maybe you'll start by doing grunt work, but after you pay your dues, so to speak, being involved in this type of project can be a significant learning opportunity.

Don't sell yourself short or be scared because you don't feel you have enough knowledge about XBRL to bring to a project. Remember, your task is to learn about XBRL. What you do have is business-domain expertise. That business-domain knowledge is a critical aspect of every XBRL project, and if you have it, you're bringing a lot to the party. When the XBRL discussions start, stay tuned in. Keep something in the back of your mind. How long did it take for you to accumulate your knowledge of your business domain? We assure you that it would take significantly longer for someone with technical knowledge of XBRL to learn the business-domain knowledge that you possess than it would for you to learn about XBRL.

XBRL International (`www.xbrl.org`) is a good place to seek out public taxonomy projects. Another good place to look is the XBRL jurisdictions, which you can locate via XBRL International. Look around, and you'll find them.

Can't find a public XBRL taxonomy project? Start one! Sure, why not? You may create something useful for your area of domain expertise, or you may spark others to help you create an XBRL taxonomy for a specific business domain. Creating an XBRL taxonomy too much to bite off? Maybe create a set of label resources for a business domain within a specific language that you know. Or, create business rules or a definition linkbase turning a taxonomy into an ontology. You may be surprised at all the opportunities that exist!

Joining an XBRL International Working Group

Another way to get experience and learn is to join XBRL International and then get on one (or more) of the working groups. Again, don't forget about all the business domain expertise that you bring to the table (see preceding section). Don't be scared that you don't know enough about XBRL to contribute. The experience you get is the payment you receive: expertise in XBRL.

Much of the work of XBRL International is done by volunteers contributing to achieve some specific task within a working group. Some tasks are large; some tasks are small. Many XBRL jurisdictions likewise have working groups. A good place to start your search is at the XBRL International Web site (www. xbrl.org).

Chapter 21

(Nearly) Ten Keys to Understanding How XBRL Works

In This Chapter

▶ Explaining key technical ideas to business readers

▶ Grasping how XBRL actually does what it does

▶ Seeing what XBRL will do

*T*his chapter has one specific focus: explain key concepts in terms that you, a business reader, can relate to. You don't need to understand these concepts to use XBRL. However, for those who are curious or who like to understand *how* things work, this chapter is for you.

Syntax Is Fairly Unimportant, Except Where It's Critical

Syntax is fairly unimportant to business users, but of critical interest to technical people. The following examples of different syntax all say the same thing — namely, that John Doe's salary is $145,000:

✔ **Plain text:** John Doe's salary is $145,000

✔ **CSV (comma separated values):** John, Doe, 145000

✔ **HTML:** <p>John Doe's salary is $145,000</p>

✔ **XML:** <my:salary name="John Doe">145000</my:salary>

✔ **RTF (Rich text format):** {\rtlch\fcs1 John Doe's salary is $145,000}

Syntax really doesn't matter much to business people except for two important things:

- ✔ The entire world is moving to one agreed-upon syntax for exchanging information, which is XML.
- ✔ The syntax needs to be able to do what you need it to do. If it doesn't work for what you need, what good is it?

XML provides a couple of critical things:

- ✔ **Multilingual support:** A big problem with exchanging information is all the different characters that have to be expressed. XML was built in a manner to solve this problem.
- ✔ **The ability to express a hierarchy of information:** Compare and contrast XML to CSV. CSV is basically a flat list of things; you can't express a hierarchy. XML can express hierarchies; you can nest tags within other tags. Also, you can't define the information you're expressing (basically, the column headings) within the CSV information. XML solves this problem, too: It's self-describing. (In other words, you can describe the metadata.)

Syntax is critical to certain technical things, which is why XML is so great: It solves those technical problems. Business people just use it and don't have to worry about a lot of technical things getting in the way. You, as a business person, care way more about semantics than you do about syntax.

The Power of Semantics

Fundamentally, XBRL is a method of expressing semantics or meaning. XBRL expresses these semantics using the XML syntax because the XML syntax provides all the technical things that XBRL needs. Here are some examples of meaning that you can express within an XBRL taxonomy:

- ✔ A concept's name, such as CashAndCashEquivalents
- ✔ A concept's definition, such as "An asset which is in the form of currency or can easily be converted to physical currency."
- ✔ Whether a concept is a debit or a credit
- ✔ Whether a concept is "as of" (like Trade Receivables on a balance sheet) a point in time or "for a period" of time (like Net Income on an income statement)
- ✔ A concept's English label, such as Cash and cash equivalents

✔ A concept "contributes" to the value of the sum of the related concept AssetsCurrent

✔ The concept CashAndCashEquivalents on the balance sheet and cash flow statement

Meaning exists, whether computers and XBRL exist or not. However, because computers and XBRL exists, both humans and computers can understand the meaning expressed. This meaning, which business people deeply care about, is expressed in the form of metadata within an XBRL taxonomy.

Metadata Expresses Meaning

Metadata is data about data. Technical people love to debate about what is data versus metadata. Definitions of metadata abound; the term is over-loaded with meaning. Semantics is a form of metadata. Metadata is information that describes or classifies other information. Just think of metadata as data, but at somewhat of a different level. Consider an invoice. Data on the invoice may include

✔ The invoice number of I-10001

✔ The invoice date of July 1, 2005

✔ The invoice total amount of 9000

The metadata for the invoice may include

✔ Every invoice *must* have an invoice number, an invoice date, a customer number, at least one line item, and a total amount.

✔ The amount is expressed in U.S. dollars.

✔ The sum of the line item amounts of the invoice must equal the total invoice amount.

✔ All invoices that are 90 days past the invoice date are considered past due.

Business Rules Can Change Processes

Business rules are semantics. Business rules help keep information correct; they help manage what people commonly refer to as *data integrity,* or the relations between one piece of information and another piece of information. Maintaining data integrity is critical to exchanging information effectively.

Everyone has heard the saying, "Garbage in, garbage out." Business rules keep garbage out of your business systems.

For example:

- ✔ A business rule might express an assertion such as "Assets MUST equal total liabilities plus total equity."
- ✔ A business rule might express an If-Then type of condition, such as "If property, plant and equipment (PPE) exists on the balance sheet, then a PPE policy and a PPE disclosure MUST exist and they MUST contain. . . ."
- ✔ A business rule may provide a definition, express calculations, articulate process-oriented information, articulate regulations, or be instructional in nature.

Business rules are extremely helpful to business people. You have many business rules, whether you refer to them by that term or not, because you have lots of information, and that information has many relationships. If information is structured, a computer can do many things to help a business person make sure that information is correct.

Unstructured Information Is Impossible for a Computer to Use Effectively

Consider the following example of unstructured information:

```
Inventory

Inventory consists of produce purchased for resale and supplies and is stated at
the lower of cost or market using the first-in, first-out (FIFO) method. Inventory
as of December 31, 2006 and 2005 amounted to $45,594 and $34,456, respectively.
```

Although the information may be structured in terms of being, say, a paragraph within a financial statement, a computer application sees it as a blob of text. For example, a computer can't automatically go in and grab the value for inventory as of December 31, 2005, from this blob of text.

Okay, a computer *could* grab that information. A programmer could hard-code something that goes to a specific set of characters and returns that value. But if that paragraph was created even slightly differently than the example, the application would break and not be able to automatically and, more importantly, accurately grab that specific value. If you had ten people create similar blobs of text, retrieving that specific piece of information would get even more complicated to. This solution obviously isn't a good one.

To a degree, computers can grab specific useful information from within a larger chunk in a process referred to as parsing. If a computer can effectively parse information, other processes can effectively reuse that data. Computers use parsing because information is structured for presentation, not meaning, so a computer really has no idea what it's looking at.

A great example of parsing is the process of *screen scraping,* a computer process that tries to glean information from a Web page, but it's expensive, brittle, requires lots of programming, and isn't reliable.

Why Information Shouldn't Be Structured for Presentation

Have you ever used your Web browser to view the source of an HTML Web page? If you do, you'll see tags such as <html>, <p>, <b>, or <bold>, and so on. HTML provides structure to Web pages. Consider this simple example:

```
<html>
<p><bold>Inventory</bold></p>
<p>Inventory consists of produce purchased for resale and supplies and is stated
at the lower of cost or market using the first-in, first-out (FIFO) method.
Inventory as of December 31, 2006 and 2005 amounted to <bold>$45,594</bold> and
<bold>$34,456</bold>, respectively.</p>
</html>
```

You can see the following from this code:

✔ The information is structured.

✔ Some information is specifically identified.

✔ Instructions on how to present that information is provided.

Using the tags provided, the information is presented in the form of a Web page:

```
Inventory

Inventory consists of produce purchased for resale and supplies and is stated at
the lower of cost or market using the first-in, first-out (FIFO) method. Inventory
as of December 31, 2006 and 2005 amounted to $45,594 and $34,456, respectively.
```

Could a computer grab the inventory amount as of December 31, 2005, from this code? Sure, it could, and it could do it more easily than with the pure blob of text without the markup. But a human would have to figure out whether you need the first <bold> tag or the second one.

What if two different companies created their financial statements in this way? Could someone write a computer application to grab that information? Sure, but again, nothing helps make sure that both companies expressed the information consistently, so programmers must construct computer applications to deal with the inevitable inconsistencies. As such, companies can spend millions of dollars trying to parse information, but the parsing still isn't really that accurate. Parsing is brittle, and the smallest changes can cause problems, so only companies with big budgets can even afford to try to grab the information.

Structuring information for presentation just doesn't do the trick for getting at the information and enabling a computer to do something with the information in a reliable way.

HTML is a common way to structure information for presentation to a human in, say, a Web browser. But this information is less useful to a computer trying to do something else with that information, something other than that one presentation format that was provided. In fact, the information generally isn't understandable to a computer in terms of meaning, only in terms of how that information should be presented.

Information Structured for Meaning Is More Useful

Computers can uniquely identify each piece of information expressed using a syntax structured for meaning. Consider the following example of structured information, which is structured at a finer level of detail and for meaning:

```
<Inventory>
  <ConsistsOf>produce purchased for resale and supplies</ConsistsOf>
  <StatedAt>lower of cost or market</StatedAt>
  <ValuationMethod>FIFO</ValuationMethod>
  <Value2006>$45,594</Value2006>
  <Value2005>$34,456</Value2005>
</Inventory>
```

If you understand how an XML parser works, writing a rather simple query, such as getItem("/Inventory/Value2005"), that "walks the tree of information" and reliably gets to the exact tag with the value $34,456 is easy to do. The query is intuitive and works much like finding a file in a subdirectory on your computer.

Writing such a query is way easier than trying to ferret through the blob of text to find the value for 2005. Additionally, you can easily structure those pieces of information into the form of a paragraph of text, which looks exactly like what you see in a financial statement today:

```
Inventory

Inventory consists of produce purchased for resale and supplies and is stated at
the lower of cost or market using the first-in, first-out (FIFO) method. Inventory
as of December 31, 2006 and 2005 amounted to $45,594 and $34,456, respectively.
```

Generally, taking information structured in terms of meaning and further articulating how it should be presented is easy. Taking information that is structured for presentation and further determining its meaning, however, is less likely, much more costly, and less reliable. So, are we saying that you have to deal with those funky tags when you work with a business report? Not if you don't want to.

But using the text within the preceding two blobs is nearly impossible and prohibitively expensive, too, if everyone created their own "tags," and one company called what we all refer to as Inventory different things, such as Inventory, Inventories, El Inventory, la Inventory, and so on. Sure, you can get information from your structured financial statement, but when you try to compare two different financial statements, you'd need to go through a mapping process and tell the computer that Inventory and Inventories and El Inventory and la Inventory all mean the same thing.

What if a global standard definition for Inventory were created? Well, there already is. That is what IFRS is all about: one global set of meaning. And what if we expressed that IFRS term in the form of a dictionary that a computer can understand? Well, that is exactly what XBRL is all about.

A Global Standard for Information Structured for Meaning

With a syntax, semantics, metadata, business rules, and information structured for meaning, we have everything we need to automate the exchange of business information. Everyone could, individually, create their own syntax, their own semantics, and their own business rules; express their own meaning; and, within one organization, do all the things XBRL offers, except for one thing:

easily exchange information with others who use a different syntax, different semantics, and different business rules. Further, software would be more expensive because different software applications would be created for each different syntax.

If everyone took this approach to making business information available, it could still work. You'd simply need to map one approach to each other approach where you wanted to use information created using different approaches together. Although more expensive, this task would be possible. You'd do this mapping for everyone you want to exchange information with, basically doing what people do today: Creating many one-to-one mappings between different approaches to structuring information to make it reusable.

However, a better way is to create a global standard approach and get everyone to use that approach, which is exactly what XBRL is.

You can see that that the following syntax really looks quite similar to the structured syntax from the previous section — it's just that everyone agrees to use the same structured syntax.

```
<ifrs:InventoryComponents contextRef="D-2006">produce purchased for resale and
          supplies</ifrs:InventoryComponents>
<ifrs:InventoryCostBasis contextRef="D-2006">lower of cost or market</
          ifrs:InventoryCostBasis>
<ifrs:ValuationMethod contextRef="D-2006">FIFO</ifrs:ValuationMethod>
<ifrs:Inventory contextRef="D-2006" unitRef="USD" decimals="0">45594</
          ifrs:Inventory>
<ifrs:Inventory contextRef="D-2006" unitRef="USD" decimals="0">34456</
          ifrs:Inventory>
```

Chapter 22

Top Ten Technical Odds and Ends

Much as we want to, we can't cover *every* conceivable aspect of XBRL in a book this size. In this chapter, we help you understand ten or so things that would clutter and complicate a basic explanation of XBRL, but are useful to know.

Covering the Basics of XLink

XBRL makes heavy use of XLink, the XML Linking language. (You can read the XLink specification at `www.w3.org/TR/xlink`.) You can spend your entire professional career using XBRL and never have to understand anything about XLink. But XLink does provide useful features that may be helpful to you. The XLink specification and what exactly XLink provides can be challenging to grasp. For those who have never worked with XLink, particularly technical people who will need to understand it, an introduction to XLink can help you understand what XLink does and why it's important.

The hardest thing to understand about XLink is the physical components — lots of details go into making XLink's functionality work. We don't go into the details of how XLink physically works; you can get that from the XBRL and the XLink specifications. We do provide the highlights, however.

What XLink provides is actually quite simple: connections between resources. It also is a mechanism for defining resources that add information to an XBRL taxonomy or XBRL instance.

XLink provides a standard way of connecting resources. That standard way is XML. XBRL could have defined its own approach to creating needed connections between resources, but XBRL chose to leverage the standard XLink rather than create its own approach for communicating information about these connections.

You can use the following pieces of XLink to create connections between XBRL concepts (relations) or between an XBRL concept and additional information of some sort (resources):

- ✔ **Linkbases** are physical XML files that contain extended links.

- ✔ **Extended links** are contained within linkbases, and within an extended link are locators, arcs, and resources. Extended links have an `xlink:type` attribute value of `extended`.

- ✔ **Locators** point to things — in XBRL's case, usually concepts — in an XBRL taxonomy and resources within an extended link. However, locators can really point to anything, typically within some XML file. Locators have an `xlink:type` attribute value of `locator`.

- ✔ **Arcs** connect locators together. Arcs connect two locators forming a relation, or they can do things such as connect a concept to a resource, adding information about a concept. Arcs have an `xlink:type` attribute value of `arc`.

- ✔ **Resources** contain additional information. Resources have an `xlink:type` attribute value of `resource`.

Listing 22-1 shows you what the XML inside a linkbase looks like.

Listing 22-1:   Guts of a Linkbase

```
<linkbase
 xmlns="http://www.xbrl.org/2003/linkbase"
 xmlns:xsi="http://www.w3.org/2001/XMLSchema-instance"
 xmlns:xlink="http://www.w3.org/1999/xlink"
 xsi:schemaLocation="http://www.xbrl.org/2003/linkbase http://www.xbrl.org/2003/
              xbrl-linkbase-2003-12-31.xsd">
 <labelLink
  xlink:type="extended"
  xlink:role="http://www.xbrl.org/2003/role/link"
  xlink:title="Labels, All">
 <loc
  xlink:type="locator"
  xlink:href="Example.xsd#example_BuildingsNet"
  xlink:label="example_BuildingsNet" />
 <labelArc
  xlink:type="arc"
  xlink:arcrole="http://www.xbrl.org/2003/arcrole/concept-label"
  xlink:from="example_BuildingsNet"
  xlink:to="example_BuildingsNet_lbl" />
 <label
```

```
  xlink:type="resource"
  xlink:role="http://www.xbrl.org/2003/role/documentation"
  xlink:label="example_BuildingsNet_lbl"
  xml:lang="en">Documentation for Building</label>
 </labelLink>
</linkbase>
```

In Listing 22-1, you see a linkbase that contains a labelLink extended link composed of one locator, one arc, and one label resource. We don't go into more depth because it would mean explaining intimate technical details, which isn't our goal. We simply want to introduce linkbases should you choose to further explore them.

Knowing How XBRL Uses XLink Roles

The three different types of roles provided by XLink and used by XBRL are commonly confused. For XBRL purposes, XBRL taxonomy schemas define all these roles. XLink requires no such definitions, but XBRL does. Here are the three different types of roles:

- ✔ **Extended link roles:** Extended links can have a role attribute, the value of which is called an *extended link role*. XBRL uses extended link roles to define and differentiate networks of relations or resources.

- ✔ **Resource roles:** Resources can have a role attribute, the value of which is referred to as a *resource role*. Resource roles are used to categorize resources. For example, an English label, such as Cash and Cash Equivalents, would be defined in an XLink resource. That resource can have a role, such as http://www.xbrl.org/2003/role/terseLabel, that categorizes that label as a specific type of label, a terse label in our example.

- ✔ **Arc roles:** Arcs can have a role attribute, the value of which is referred to as an *arc role*. Arc roles are used to categorize arcs. For example, the relation between Cash and Current Assets would be created by using an XLink arc. That arc role can have a role, such as www.xbrl.org/2003/arcrole/summation-item on a calculation arc, categorizing that arc.

Comparing XLink Extended Links and XBRL Networks

Another common mistake is to confuse XLink extended links and XBRL networks. An XBRL network is something that XBRL defines. Extended links are something defined by XLink. XLink extended links are the means, the syntax, used to create an XBRL network.

The difference between the two is this: An XBRL network consists of one or more XLink extended links, all of which have the same XBRL type (presentation, calculation, definition, label, reference, or other type), and all of which have the same extended link role attribute value. You can have only one network of an XBRL type with the same extended link role attribute value within an XBRL DTS. Any number of physical XLink extended links can make up an XBRL network. Don't make the common mistake of referring to extended links when you're really referring to an XBRL network of a certain type.

Using Tuples to Express Compound Facts

Simple facts basically hold one value (see Chapter 4). *Compound facts* are made up of one or more simple facts or other compound facts and are expressed in XBRL in the form of what is known as a *tuple.* Tuples physically bind facts together to form compound facts. You create this binding within a taxonomy schema. Tuples are XML Schema complex types.

Here's an example to help you see what tuples do: Suppose that you want to express information about the salary and bonuses paid to a company director. Well, a company can have more than one director. For example, suppose that you have two directors, Clark Kent and Lois Lane. Clark had a salary of $20,000 and bonuses of $10,000. Lois had a salary of $40,000 and bonuses of $20,000. How do you communicate in an XBRL fact which salary and which bonuses go with which director?

Well, that is where tuples come in. Tuples bind the name of the director, that director's salary, and that director's bonuses together so that XBRL instances users know which salary and bonuses go with which director. But first you have to create the bindings within a taxonomy schema. Listing 22-2 shows the definition of a tuple within a taxonomy schema.

Listing 22-2: Definition of a Tuple within an Taxonomy Schema

```
<element name="DirectorName" type="xbrli:stringItemType"
          substitutionGroup="xbrli:item" xbrli:periodType="duration" />
  <element name="DirectorSalary" type="xbrli:monetaryItemType"
          substitutionGroup="xbrli:item" xbrli:periodType="duration" />
  <element name="DirectorBonuses" type="xbrli:monetaryItemType"
          substitutionGroup="xbrli:item" xbrli:periodType="duration" />

  <element name="Director" substitutionGroup="xbrli:tuple">
  <complexType>
   <complexContent>
   <restriction base="anyType">
    <sequence>
```

```
  <element ref="ci:DirectorName" />
  <element ref="ci:DirectorSalary" />
  <element ref="ci:DirectorBonuses" />
  </sequence>
 </restriction>
 </complexContent>
</complexType>
</element>
```

Notice the element Director with the value `xbrli:tuple` for the `substitu tionGroup`. That concept binds together the concepts `DirectorName`, `DirectorSalary` and `DirectorBonuses`, which you can see in the preceding taxonomy schema fragment.

The best way to understand the role tuples play is to look at fact values within an XBRL instance. We do so first without and then with tuples to show you the situation tuples address. Listing 22-3 shows a fragment of an XBRL instance without tuples.

Listing 22-3:   XBRL Instance Fragment without Tuples

```
<ci:DirectorName
 contextRef="D-2003">Clark Kent</ci:DirectorName>
<ci:DirectorSalary
 contextRef="D-2003"
 unitRef="U-Monetary"
 decimals="INF">20000</ci:DirectorSalary>
<ci:DirectorBonuses
 contextRef="D-2003"
 unitRef="U-Monetary"
 decimals="INF">10000</ci:DirectorBonuses>

<ci:DirectorName
 contextRef="D-2003">Lois Lane</ci:DirectorName>
<ci:DirectorSalary
 contextRef="D-2003"
 unitRef="U-Monetary"
 decimals="INF">40000</ci:DirectorSalary>
<ci:DirectorBonuses
 contextRef="D-2003"
 unitRef="U-Monetary"
 decimals="INF">20000</ci:DirectorBonuses>
```

In Listing 22-3, you can see the concepts `DirectorName` and `Director Salary` each two times. You're smart and may be able to figure out which facts go together. But a computer program has no way to understand that the first `DirectorName` and `DirectorSalary` go together. Likewise for the second. However, if you look at Listing 22-4, which shows the tuple Director, you can understand which sets go together.

Listing 22-4:   XBRL Instance Fragment with Tuples

```
<ci:Director>
 <ci:DirectorName
  contextRef="D-2003">Clark Kent</ci:DirectorName>
 <ci:DirectorSalary
  contextRef="D-2003"
  unitRef="U-Monetary"
  decimals="INF">20000</ci:DirectorSalary>
 <ci:DirectorBonuses
  contextRef="D-2003"
  unitRef="U-Monetary"
  decimals="INF">10000</ci:DirectorBonuses>
</ci:Director>

<ci:Director>
 <ci:DirectorName
  contextRef="D-2003">Lois Lane</ci:DirectorName>
 <ci:DirectorSalary
  contextRef="D-2003"
  unitRef="U-Monetary"
  decimals="INF">40000</ci:DirectorSalary>
 <ci:DirectorBonuses
  contextRef="D-2003"
  unitRef="U-Monetary"
  decimals="INF">20000</ci:DirectorBonuses>
</ci:Director>
```

In Listing 22-4, you can see the physical binding that tuples provide, nesting the facts that go together within the tuple Director.

Creating Segment and Scenario Contextual Information

An area of confusion for many XBRL users is the segment and scenario elements of the context element found in XBRL instances. (Chapters 4 and 16 cover the basics of using these pieces of an XBRL instance's context.) These two elements act in exactly the same way. Both are quite flexible, allowing literally XML as content other than elements of the XBRL 2.1 Specification namespace.

To express segment and scenario information today, you can use XBRL Dimensions or create your own XML schema, which defines concepts you can use.

The XBRL Dimensions approach for defining the XML that goes into the segment and scenario elements within a context is provided as a module of XBRL (see Chapter 16).

The other approach is to define your own XML schema. You can figure out the details from an example at www.xbrlsite.com/patterns/2005-07-07/BasicCalculation-instance.xml.

To avoid having to type these long links, go to www.dummies.com/go/xbrl. This takes you to a landing page where you can click the link you need.

We'd like you to understand these two key points:

✔ To get anything into the segment and scenario element, you need a user interface. If you can put literally any XML into those concepts, you need what basically amounts to an XML editor to enter that information. Basically, users have to create the XML, which they then somehow use in the segment and scenario elements.

✔ In order to get users to put the correct information into the segment and scenario concepts, you basically have to write a specification to define how a user would do so.

✔ Only after you define how your XML schema would be used can you then create a mechanism for constraining that information.

✔ Your XML schema won't be able to express hierarchies of relations between the elements you define that are understandable to XBRL.

Basically, what we're saying is that if you want to create your own XML schema for the contents of the segment or scenario context elements, you'd literally have to duplicate what XBRL Dimensions has already created.

Listing 22-5 shows an example of a context element that uses XML Schema defined segment and scenario element contents.

Listing 22-5:   An Example of a Context Element

```
<context id="I-2009">
  <entity>
   <identifier scheme="http://www.SampleCompany.com">SAMP</identifier>
   <segment>
     <seg:ReportingSegment><seg:Group /></seg:ReportingSegment>
   </segment>
  </entity>
  <period>
   <instant>2009-12-31</instant>
  </period>
  <scenario>
   <sce:Premise><sce:Actual /></sce:Premise >
   <sce:Verification><sce:Audited /></sce:Verification>
  </scenario>
</context>
```

XBRL Dimensions solves these and other issues you'd run into in defining an XML schema for segment and scenario element content.

XBRL Dimensions is probably the best alternative to use 99 percent of the time. Rarely will XBRL Dimensions not meet your needs. You can create your own approach, but with flexibility comes responsibility. If you choose not to use XBRL Dimensions, you have a lot of responsibility for making things work correctly.

Another aspect to the use of the segment and the scenario elements is trying to figure out exactly what goes into the segment element and what goes into the scenario element. The XBRL Specification is vague in this area, and people disagree as to what goes where. The fact is that it doesn't matter which of the two elements you use. For example, the US GAAP Taxonomy Architecture settled on always using the segment element to contain XBRL Dimensions information and never allowing scenario to be used at all. That decision solves the problem of figuring out which to use. Using only one of these elements, segment, or scenario eliminates taxonomy creators from having to figure out whether they should use segment or scenario.

The key point to take away is that providing content that segment or scenario context elements use can be somewhat complicated at this stage of XBRL's evolution. When in doubt, the best thing to do is use XBRL Dimensions. If that approach doesn't seem to work, get a really good XBRL consultant to help you figure out how to create a solution that will meet your needs.

Using XBRL Footnotes to Add Comments

XBRL instances can also contain what are basically comments but are referred to in XBRL as *footnotes*. The XBRL instance uses XBRL footnotes as comments or notations that refer to one or more fact values. These footnotes can contain what amounts to XHTML markup as the comment, which can make for a richly expressed comment.

XBRL footnotes are a resource-type linkbase contained within an XBRL instance. A footnoteLink extended link within a linkbase within the XBRL instance contains footnote resources. This linkbase operates just like any other resource-type linkbase with one slight difference: The locators point to the id attribute of a fact contained within your XBRL instance, rather than a concept within an XBRL taxonomy schema.

Listings 22-6 and 22-7 show an example of an XBRL footnote as it would exist within an XBRL instance. Listing 22-6 shows the facts. Notice the id attributes contained in each fact.

Listing 22-6: Facts with ID Attributes Used by Footnotes

```
<ci:Land id="Item-01" contextRef="I-2003" unitRef="U-Monetary"
          decimals="INF">5347000</ci:Land>
<ci:Building id="Item-02" contextRef="I-2003" unitRef="U-Monetary"
          decimals="INF">244508000</ci:Building>
<ci:FurnitureFixtures id="Item-03" contextRef="I-2003" unitRef="U-Monetary"
          decimals="INF">34457000</ci:FurnitureFixtures>
```

Listing 22-7 shows the resource-type linkbase that expresses the XBRL footnote.

Listing 22-7: Footnotes within an XBRL Instance

```
<link:footnoteLink xlink:type="extended" xlink:role="http://www.xbrl.org/2003/
          role/link" xmlns:link="http://www.xbrl.org/2003/linkbase">
  <link:loc xlink:type="locator" xlink:href="#Item-01" xlink:label="FactSet-01"
          />
  <link:loc xlink:type="locator" xlink:href="#Item-02" xlink:label="FactSet-01"
          />
  <link:loc xlink:type="locator" xlink:href="#Item-03" xlink:label="FactSet-01"
          />
  <link:footnoteArc xlink:type="arc" xlink:arcrole="http://www.xbrl.
          org/2003/arcrole/fact-footnote" xlink:from="FactSet-01"
          xlink:to="Footnote-01" />
  <link:footnote xlink:type="resource" xlink:role="http://www.xbrl.org/2003/
          role/footnote" xlink:label="Footnote-01" xml:lang="en">This is a
          footnote discussing Land, Buildings, and Furniture and fixtures
          for 2003.</link:footnote>
</link:footnoteLink>
```

XBRL users have suggested using XBRL footnotes for all sorts of things in many different ways. XBRL instance creation and viewing software supports these uses somewhat inconsistently at this stage of XBRL's evolution.

Although XBRL footnotes exist, use them with caution.

Using Resources to Add Information

Something commonly missed by XBRL users is the fact that you can define your own linkbase resources using XBRL. You can do so using several different approaches. Examining the reference linkbase offers some clues as to these different approaches as does the Generic Linkbase Specification (see Chapter 16), which provides even more power in the area of adding resources to an XBRL taxonomy.

The first question you may have is why you would even want to add information to an XBRL taxonomy. Well, the reason is that often XBRL taxonomy creators have lots of additional information (metadata) that they'd like to connect to an XBRL taxonomy, but XBRL doesn't seem to have a spot to hold that information. Well, actually, XBRL does have spots to hold that additional information.

As an example, take a look at how the `reference` element, which is a linkbase resource, works. Creating a reference will help reveal the pros and cons of some easy approaches and some more sophisticated approaches to adding information to any XBRL taxonomy.

You may want to refer to the section "Covering the Basics of XLink," earlier in this chapter, to understand what resources are. Also, Chapter 4 is helpful in understanding the coming discussion.

Listing 22-8 shows a simple reference resource, which a reference linkbase would contain.

Listing 22-8:   Reference Resource Element

```
<reference
   xlink:type="resource"
   xlink:role=http://www.xbrl.org/2003/role/reference
   xlink:label="xasb_SomeReference">
   <ref:Name>XASB</ref:Name>
   <ref:Number>95</ref:Number>
</reference>
```

We don't want to get into a lengthy discussion about the syntax of a reference element within a reference linkbase. We focus here on the *parts* of a reference. The bold `<ref:Name>` XML element in Listing 22-8 is a reference part. Reference parts are special XBRL elements that you can use within a reference element.

You know that an element is a reference part because its `substitionGroup` attribute has the value `link:part`. You define these parts within a taxonomy schema. For example, the link part in Listing 22-8 was defined in this taxonomy schema made available by XBRL International `www.xbrl.org/2004/ref-2004-08-10.xsd`.

If you open that URL and look at it, you can find that part element's definition. Be sure to notice the `substitutionGroup`, which is how these parts are differentiated from XBRL concepts and other taxonomy schema contents.

Here are the important things for you to understand about different approaches to defining additional information for your XBRL taxonomy:

- ✔ **You can create your own proprietary approach to adding information to your XBRL taxonomy.** However, an XBRL processor certainly wouldn't understand the approach you've created, so you have to write code in order to link your additional information to the XBRL taxonomy you're using. Writing code means getting programmers involved, which takes time and costs money. An example of this approach is to simply put this additional information within a relational database table and somehow connect the relational database table to the XBRL taxonomy.

- ✔ **You can add information by defining your own reference parts**. Okay, this approach is a bit of a hack, but we mention it for a specific reason. Reference parts are defined within a taxonomy schema that becomes part of your DTS. After defining a reference part, you can use those reference parts within the reference element. XBRL processors are required to read any reference part that you add; they'll understand these parts. Therefore, you can define any reference parts you desire, and an XBRL processor will be able to work with those reference parts and the information they contain, connecting them directly to concepts within your XBRL taxonomy. Reference parts don't have to necessarily relate to references. This is the hack. You can use reference parts to define what would amount to any data table, and you can use XBRL to connect information in that table to an XBRL taxonomy, and then an XBRL processor, without any modification, can use that table! That's the point. You get a spot to hold your additional information (XBRL will see it as a reference linkbase), but if you're using what you created, say, internally to your organization, who cares whether you put something else in the reference linkbase? You created a mechanism for adding information to your taxonomy without writing one single line of code or involving a programmer!

- ✔ **You can add information by defining your own resource-type linkbase using the generic linkbase specification.** XBRL allows you to actually add any type of information structure you can express in XML as a resource. All you do is define an XML schema for the information model that you want to maintain within your new resource. If you're familiar with XML Schema, you'll know how to do this task. But realize two important things if you use the generic linkbase approach. The first is simply the fact that you can express literally anything. The second is that just because you do so doesn't mean that an XBRL processor will understand the resource you defined, nor is it required to. That means having to involve a programmer and writing code. You'll write less code than implementing a proprietary approach to connecting to your proprietary information format because XBRL does provide a framework you can leverage.

Time after time, we see creators of XBRL taxonomies desiring to connect additional information to their XBRL taxonomy, but they tend to do it in proprietary ways, commonly using some sort of relational database. That approach is fine in many circumstances, but an easier way is to use XBRL itself to express this additional information. If you're building an internal system, using the reference linkbase hack we describe can help you achieve what you need — in many cases, without writing a single line of code! If you're a stickler for creating a solution for adding information to an XBRL taxonomy more by the book, XBRL can still help you to a large degree; the generic linkbase provides you with helpful functionality for adding information to your XBRL taxonomy. The downside with the generic linkbase approach is that, in many cases, you'll have to write some code to read that information.

Adding New Types of Relations

Adding new types of relations is easy using the definition linkbase. All you do is define your own arc role to express the type of relation, and you can go to town and express any sort of relation you may desire. If, for some reason, you need a lot more expressive power than the definition linkbase can provide, use the Generic Linkbase Specification.

A great example of using the definition linkbase to add relation information is the XBRL Dimensions Specification. Read that specification at `www.xbrl.org/Specification/XDT-REC-2006-09-18.htm` and look at the XML Schemas that XBRL Dimensions defined. It's an excellent example of extending the power of XBRL to express new types of relations. If you need to add relations, reverse-engineering XBRL Dimensions is a good guide to getting a quality result.

Expressing Blocks of Information

Representing a discrete fact value is simple using XBRL — for example, the discrete fact value of, say, 1234, for the concept Cash for a specific period. But what about more complex information structures, which are sometimes referred to as *blocks of text?* Listings 22-9 and 22-10 show two different types of blocks of text that are representative of what you may encounter.

Listing 22-9: Block of Text: A Table of Information

```
Name                               Director   Fair Value of
of Director    Salary     Bonus       Fees   Options Granted

-------------  ---------  ---------  ---------  ---------------
John James             0         0    60,000                 0
Buck Rogers      879,639 1,213,486         0           569,000
Clark Kent             0         0    24,200                 0
Lois Lane              0         0    57,000                 0

               ---------  ---------  ---------  ---------------
Total            879,639 1,213,486   141,200           569,000
               =========  =========  =========  ===============
```

Listing 22-10: Block of Text: A Paragraph of Information

```
Inventory consists of produce purchased for resale and supplies and is stated at
       the lower of cost or market using the first-in, first-out (FIFO)
       method.  Inventory as of December 31, 2006 and 2005 amounted to
       $45,594 and $34,456, respectively.
```

Listing 22-9 is what amounts to a table of information. Listing 22-10 is a paragraph of text, or what is sometimes referred to as prose. You can express both of these blocks of text as discrete values using XBRL, breaking the table or the paragraph into individual pieces and then creating taxonomy concepts to express each individual piece of information. XBRL Dimensions or tuples are helpful in turning tables and prose into discrete information pieces. But sometimes, for some reason, you don't want to break information into discrete pieces.

These tables or prose are commonly structured in some way. One more complex example is the structure of a table, such as the earlier Listing 22-9. This structure is commonly articulated using markup (angle brackets), such as XHTML, to express the table. But XBRL simple fact values don't allow markup to be part of the fact value. As such, you can't include XHTML, other forms of XML, or any other forms of markup within an XBRL simple fact value.

Should you need to express things like tables or prose as blocks of text type information, you can get around this constraint in the following ways:

✔ **Use escaped markup:** One approach is to change the physical angle brackets into something that doesn't include angle brackets, thus getting around the no-markup-allowed constraint. Using escape characters to express the markup achieves this goal. For example, we will use escaped XHTML to show how this approach works. You can turn the markup

<p>Hello world</p> into <p>Hello world </p>. What this approach allows you to do is literally put anything that XHTML allows inside an XBRL simple fact value, which is quite a bit because XHTML is quite rich in expressive power. Applications that use the XBRL fact value information can easily convert the escaped XHTML (or whatever format you use) to normal XHTML when presenting the information to a user. Many RSS feeds use this approach for embedding XHTML or just HTML, into the RSS feed. You can find plenty of algorithms for converting to/from escaped XHTML. And remember, you can use this approach to embed any other form of XML into an XBRL fact value.

✓ **Use plain text:** Another option is to use formatted plain text within the fact value. The problem with plain text is that maintaining the formatting can be challenging, and you really don't get that much expressive power. You use invisible tabs, spaces, carriage returns, and line-feed characters to achieve the formatting you desire. This approach can work in many situations, though.

✓ **Use JSON:** JavaScript Object Notation (JSON) is a data-exchange format that is easy for both humans and computers to work with. A nice characteristic is that it can represent anything that XML can represent. As such, you can express your block of information within JSON in the XBRL instance and then convert it to whatever format you want the user to see when you use the XBRL instance. (For more on JSON, see http://json.org.)

✓ **Use base 64:** XBRL has a type (data type) called xbrli:base64Binary ItemType. As with other XBRL types, it's a specialization of an XML Schema type, xs:base64Binary. The binary characters are represented as a limited set of ASCII characters, none of which are the pesky angle brackets that make XML processors think the value is markup. Using base 64 works a lot like the escaped markup approach described previously. You can use reliable algorithms and functions to convert to/from base 64.

Index

• *C* •

• F •

● *T* ●

Business/Accounting & Bookkeeping

Bookkeeping For Dummies
978-0-7645-9848-7

eBay Business
All-in-One For Dummies,
2nd Edition
978-0-470-38536-4

Job Interviews
For Dummies,
3rd Edition
978-0-470-17748-8

Resumes For Dummies,
5th Edition
978-0-470-08037-5

Stock Investing
For Dummies,
3rd Edition
978-0-470-40114-9

Successful Time
Management
For Dummies
978-0-470-29034-7

Computer Hardware

BlackBerry For Dummies,
3rd Edition
978-0-470-45762-7

Computers For Seniors
For Dummies
978-0-470-24055-7

iPhone For Dummies,
2nd Edition
978-0-470-42342-4

Laptops For Dummies,
3rd Edition
978-0-470-27759-1

Macs For Dummies,
10th Edition
978-0-470-27817-8

Cooking & Entertaining

Cooking Basics
For Dummies,
3rd Edition
978-0-7645-7206-7

Wine For Dummies,
4th Edition
978-0-470-04579-4

Diet & Nutrition

Dieting For Dummies,
2nd Edition
978-0-7645-4149-0

Nutrition For Dummies,
4th Edition
978-0-471-79868-2

Weight Training
For Dummies,
3rd Edition
978-0-471-76845-6

Digital Photography

Digital Photography
For Dummies,
6th Edition
978-0-470-25074-7

Photoshop Elements 7
For Dummies
978-0-470-39700-8

Gardening

Gardening Basics
For Dummies
978-0-470-03749-2

Organic Gardening
For Dummies,
2nd Edition
978-0-470-43067-5

Green/Sustainable

Green Building
& Remodeling
For Dummies
978-0-470-17559-0

Green Cleaning
For Dummies
978-0-470-39106-8

Green IT For Dummies
978-0-470-38688-0

Health

Diabetes For Dummies,
3rd Edition
978-0-470-27086-8

Food Allergies
For Dummies
978-0-470-09584-3

Living Gluten-Free
For Dummies
978-0-471-77383-2

Hobbies/General

Chess For Dummies,
2nd Edition
978-0-7645-8404-6

Drawing For Dummies
978-0-7645-5476-6

Knitting For Dummies,
2nd Edition
978-0-470-28747-7

Organizing For Dummies
978-0-7645-5300-4

SuDoku For Dummies
978-0-470-01892-7

Home Improvement

Energy Efficient Homes
For Dummies
978-0-470-37602-7

Home Theater
For Dummies,
3rd Edition
978-0-470-41189-6

Living the Country Lifestyle
All-in-One For Dummies
978-0-470-43061-3

Solar Power Your Home
For Dummies
978-0-470-17569-9

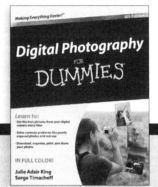